NARODNIKI WOMEN

Russian Women
Who Sacrificed Themselves
for the Dream of Freedom

The ATHENE Series

General Editors
Gloria Bowles
Renate Klein
Janice Raymond

Consulting Editor
Dale Spender

The Athene Series assumes that all those who are concerned with formulating explanations of the way the world works need to know and appreciate the significance of basic feminist principles.

The growth of feminist research has challenged almost all aspects of social organization in our culture. The Athene Series focuses on the construction of knowledge and the exclusion of women from the process—both as theorists and subjects of study—and offers innovative studies that challenge established theories and research.

On Athene—When Metis, goddess of wisdom who presided over all knowledge was pregnant with Athene, she was swallowed up by Zeus who then gave birth to Athene from his head. The original Athene is thus the parthenogenetic daughter of a strong mother and as the feminist myth goes, at the "third birth" of Athene she stops being Zeus' obedient mouthpiece and returns to her real source: the science and wisdom of womankind.

Pergamon Title of Related Interest

Mamonova RUSSIAN WOMEN'S STUDIES: Essays on Sexism in Soviet Culture

Related Journals
(Free sample copies available upon request)

ISSUES IN REPRODUCTIVE AND GENETIC
   ENGINEERING: Journal of International Feminist Analysis
WOMEN'S STUDIES INTERNATIONAL FORUM

NARODNIKI WOMEN

Russian Women Who Sacrificed Themselves for the Dream of Freedom

Margaret Maxwell

PERGAMON PRESS
Member of Maxwell Macmillan Pergamon Publishing Corporation
New York Oxford Beijing Frankfurt São Paulo Sydney Tokyo Toronto

Pergamon Press Offices:

U.S.A.	Pergamon Press, Inc., Maxwell House, Fairview Park, Elmsford, New York 10523, U.S.A.
U.K.	Pergamon Press plc, Headington Hill Hall, Oxford OX3 0BW, England
PEOPLE'S REPUBLIC OF CHINA	Pergamon Press, 0909 China World Tower, No. 1 Jian Guo Men Wai Avenue, Beijing 100004, People's Republic of China
FEDERAL REPUBLIC OF GERMANY	Pergamon Press GmbH, Hammerweg 6, D-6242 Kronberg, Federal Republic of Germany
BRAZIL	Pergamon Editora Ltda, Rua Eça de Queiros, 346, CEP 04011, Paraiso, São Paulo, Brazil
AUSTRALIA	Pergamon Press Australia Pty Ltd., P.O. Box 544, Potts Point, NSW 2011, Australia
JAPAN	Pergamon Press, 8th Floor, Matsuoka Central Building, 1-7-1 Nishishinjuku, Shinjuku-ku, Tokyo 160, Japan
CANADA	Pergamon Press Canada Ltd., Suite 271, 253 College Street, Toronto, Ontario M5T 1R5, Canada

Copyright © 1990 Pergamon Press, Inc.

All rights reserved. No part of this publication may be reproduced, stored in a retrieval system or transmitted in any form or by any means: electronic, electrostatic, magnetic tape, mechanical, photocopying, recording or otherwise, without permission in writing from the publishers.

First edition 1990

Library of Congress Cataloging in Publication Data

Maxwell, Margaret.
    Narodniki women : Russian women who sacrificed themselves for the
dream of freedom / by Margaret Maxwell. -- 1st ed.
        p.   cm. -- (The Athene series)
    Includes bibliographical references.
    ISBN 0-08-037462-X (alk. paper) : -- ISBN
0-08-037461-1 (pbk. : alk. paper) :
        1. Soviet Union--History--19th century. 2. Soviet Union-
-History--20th century. 3. Women revolutionists--Soviet Union-
-Biography. 4. Radicalism--Soviet Union--History. I. Title.
II. Series.
DK219.3.M39   1990
947.08--dc20   89-23073
                                                                                    CIP

Printed in the United States of America

∞™

The paper used in this publication meets the minimum requirements of American National Standard for Information Sciences -- Permanence of Paper for Printed Library Materials, ANSI Z39.48-1984

Contents

Foreword

The names of some of the women in this book, once considered heroines by the Russian people, are known in the Soviet Union, but what they did, what they thought, and what they fought for have been forgotten. It is one of the many gaps in Soviet historiography. They were long ago labeled *bourgeois*, *"Menshevik,"* or some other pejorative term, automatically making them "enemies of the Revolution" and therefore, up to now, not worth remembering—except possibly to use them as object lessons for their "errors." Vera Zasulich, whose Marxist writing, if it is ever collected, may equal in volume and possibly in significance that of George Plekhanov, who is called the father of Russian Marxism and who sought Zasulich's advice on almost every word he wrote, receives part of a column in the 1970 edition of the *Bol'shaia Sovetskaia Entsiklopediia*. Plekhanov gets seven full columns!

These women stoutly maintained they were not feminists. They saw themselves as equal partners of their male comrades, fighting for the same goals. But we see in Margaret Maxwell's presentation of their stories that their frustration at the humble roles assigned them in the patriarchal society of tsarist times has feminist undertones. Here is Vera Zasulich, an orphan girl about to be sent off by her rich relatives to be trained as a governess, a prospect she abhorred:

> If only I had been a boy, I could have done almost anything, [and then] the distant specter of revolution appeared, making me equal to a boy. I too could dream of action.

That "dream of action," that idea of being equal to a boy, that way of getting out from under the male-dominated family brought many a young woman into revolutionary circles in which there was generally a collegial relationship of equality between men and women. Then came the bitter disappoint-

ment when the revolution cast them out, as a new, male-dominated regime
took over. These events caused Maria Spiridonova, who in the early days
of the revolution was head of perhaps the largest political party in Russia,
to link the failure of the revolution to the paucity of women in leadership
positions in the revolutionary government. Katerina Breshkovskaya never
complained in her early career of being outranked by men. But after being
driven into exile in 1919, she wrote that, despite her experience and knowledge and that her "head was in good order," she had given up expecting
statesmen to pay attention to her words—because she was a woman.

Margaret Maxwell's book introduces us to the individual careers of pre-
revolutionary Russian women inspired by the democratic and humanitarian
ideals of many separate movements. She also shows how Western European
and American women in crisis situations became involved with them. Her
story invites speculation: What if women from feminist, *narodnik,* and the
various reformist circles had acted together, not just in times of crisis but
continuously? Could the Russian women who fought for freedom and their
ideals have then been so easily betrayed? Is not the necessity for women to
work together a lesson we can learn from this book? Is it not a call for solidarity? Is it not an important message for the international reader?

Narodniki Women explores a segment of history about which almost as
little is known in America as in Russia. The stories of these brave and indi-
vidualistic women, so well told in these pages, are important for all of us
engaged in women's studies and for the general reader to know.

Tatyana Mamonova

Introduction

Chekhov's plays have popularized the image of Russian gentry women at the end of the nineteenth century as gentle, charming dreamers. In *The Three Sisters,* Olga, Masha, and Irina sit around the tea table, endlessly ruminating about the exciting lives they would lead if only they could get to Moscow. People with this image of Russia's pre-revolutionary women may find it difficult to believe that women of the same background as the three sisters had for more than a generation been entering the ranks of Russia's revolutionaries. Included among them were country gentlewomen, school girls, teachers, clerks, doctors, even ballerinas like Pavlova and Karsavina. Many of them plotted and carried out daring attacks on the lives of tsarist officials from one end of the Russian Empire to the other. They often got to Moscow—with their fares paid by the state—for a stay in the Butyrki Prison, the dispersion point after 1900 for those sentenced to life imprisonment at hard labor in Siberia.

An American journalist, Leroy Scott, went to Russia in 1908 to interview young women activists. He published his observations in an article, "The Women of the Russian Revolution," in the December 26, 1908, issue of *The Outlook,* and concluded:

> When, in the happier future, the history of the Russian Revolution is written, one feature of this great struggle which will distinguish it from other movements of its kind will be the part played by women. Women's immemorial role in such a period has been to wait at home and suffer. The Russian woman has shared like and like with man; in leadership, in the dangerous clandestine education of the masses, in throwing the terrorist's bomb, in prison, in Siberian mines, on the scaffold.

How wrong he was! Russia's revolutionary women, the most active and numerous of whom were not Bolsheviks, are today all but forgotten. They

were members of the nineteenth-century *Narodnoye,* or Populist, Movement and of its twentieth-century heir, the Socialist Revolutionary party,
which carried on the *Narodniki* tradition of individuals sacrificing themselves for their ideal of freedom.

History belongs to the victors. The Populists and the Socialist Revolutionaries lost. The Bolsheviks won. And the Bolsheviks created their own version of the revolutionary women: the heroine of socialist labor; the woman
who, as the subordinate partner of man, worked to build Soviet society.

The Bolshevik revolutionary woman as she is made to appear in Soviet
publications is an abstraction, dutiful and dull. In contrast, each of the
women in this book is a fascinating individual, an intelligent, strong-willed
person with a record of leadership, decision making, and action. Those who
were not hanged, and survived Siberian exile and imprisonment under the
tsars, came back to be either spectators or to play active roles in revolutionary politics after 1917. One was, in fact, the leader of what was probably
the largest political party in revolutionary Russia, the Left Socialist Revolutionaries. But, committed to the ideal of political freedom, they soon
clashed with Bolshevik authoritarianism and found themselves again in
prison and exile.

It is from these women that the careers sketched in this book have been
drawn. They represent an extinct species, but the role they and their sisters
once played should not be forgotten. They stand as an inspiration and a
warning to women everywhere. Their careers illustrate that in the course of
events, social and economic conditions in a certain time and place may
quickly emerge in which women can take the initiative and function co-
equally with men in large-scale endeavors. Then, as quickly as they
emerged, conditions change and women suddenly find themselves shunted
aside and pushed into traditional subsidiary roles.

Not all the women in this book are *Narodniki,* nor are these few representatives all the *Narodniki* women. If the word *Narodniki* is strictly defined
and limited to a narrow time period, only those in the Going-to-the-People
Movement of the 1870s are *Narodniki,* but if the term is broadly interpreted
to mean those who devoted and often sacrificed their lives for the *Narod*—
the people—it has general applicability. As for numbers, the women included in this book are only a very few of the hundreds of women who
served as leaders, and the thousands who were members of the many student and intelligentsia circles, the popular movements, and by the end of
the nineteenth century, the illegal political parties of tsarist Russia.

This book is not an analysis of the social, economic, and political condition of Russia in the half century preceding the 1917 Revolution. Dozens
of books exploring all aspects of that subject are readily available. It is not
a history of the Russian revolutionary movement, a topic that over the decades has had ample coverage. This book is history as story. Its purpose is

to lift individual Russian revolutionary women out of the category of the usual one- or two-line references or complete omission in textbooks and monographs on Russian history from the 1870s through the 1917 Revolution.

On the assumption that such fragments do not tell a reader or a student of Russian history what he or she would really like, or ought, to know about these neglected figures in the Russian revolutionary movement, this book undertakes to tell the story of each woman included in its pages. So far as possible these stories are told in the women's own words, or those of their contemporaries, hence the frequent quotation of conversations, self-analysis and description of personal feelings. Several of the women were prolific writers. In addition to their revelations about themselves, they often provide colorful details which, put together as they are here, enable them to emerge as real human beings.

The academic paraphernalia of footnoting has been reduced to a minimum, but for each chapter there are bibliographical notes designed to guide the reader who would like to look further into the topic or a quoted detail to the source of the author's information. This procedure is based on the assumption that a bibliographical essay is more useful than voluminous, often pointless and always tedious footnotes.

Acknowledgments

The friends, relatives, and former colleagues who offered me encouragement over the more than a decade of research and writing that went into this book are too numerous to mention individually, but their support and belief in my endeavor have been invaluable. Without the riches of the New York Public Library's Slavic Division and the help of the knowledgeable librarians who staff it, I could not have written this book. Especially useful were the manuscripts and the photographs in the George Kennan Collection. Other sources of information include the Columbia University Library, the Wellesley College Library, and the document collection of the Hoover Institution on War, Revolution, and Peace at Stanford University. Mark Piel of the New York Society Library was tireless in his efforts in my behalf, especially in the matter of interlibrary loans. I owe a special debt of gratitude to Janice Raymond, whose faith in the work was responsible for Pergamon's decision to publish it in the Athene Series, and to Tatyana Mamonova for her encouragement in the early stages of putting the book together and her assistance in the tricky matter of transliterating Russian names and terms from the Cyrillic alphabet to the Roman.

A note on transliteration:

In general, the Library of Congress practice has been followed in the text of this book for the transliteration of the Cyrillic into the Roman alphabet, with certain exceptions: the Й kratkiy (the short Й at the end of a word) has usually been rendered as "y," except in certain names it is i: Nikolai. The letter Я is rendered as "ia" except in some names it is rendered "ya": Sanya, *Narodnaya Volya*. The soft sign in the middle or at the end of words is rendered as an apostrophe: Khar'kov.

The Russian spelling of the name Catherine is Ekaterina, pronounced Ye-katerina. To make the name more recognizable to a non-Russian audience, it has been rendered in this book as Katerina.

Esser has been used to express the initials of the Socialist Revolutionary party because it approximates the Russian pronunciation of SR.

Photo Credits

Part I

NINETEENTH-CENTURY WOMEN FIGHTERS FOR FREEDOM

1

Vera Zasulich:
The Victory of Conscience
Over Force

Uznitsa (The Girl Prisoner)
by IA. P. Polonski

What is she to me? Not wife, not lover
And not my own daughter.
So why does her cursed fate
Haunt me day and night?
As if calling me, in the anger of innocence,
Into the courtroom to defend her.
As if her suffering cast a spell
Over my poor heart.

Rolling grey clouds over St. Petersburg threatened snow. It was mid-April in the rest of the world, but still March in tsarist Russia where time lagged thirteen days—counted Old Style according to the Julian Calendar—and the grip of winter lingered in the northern capital.[1] Once the cold and lonely abode of bears and wolves, St. Petersburg in 1878 was imposing but still looked unfinished. Its broad streets and boulevards intersected vast, badly paved, empty squares, each with its monumental public building, church,

---

[1]The Julian Calendar, used in Russia until changed by the Bolsheviks in 1918, was thirteen days behind the N. S., or "New Style" Gregorian Calendar of Western Europe. The dates in this book are O. S. (Old Style) to 1918.

3

or barracks. Streets and avenues abruptly receded into grassy spaces, edged with the crude, wooden hovels of the poor.

It was March 31, 1878, and all St. Petersburg seemed to be hurrying toward the First District Circuit Court on Liteiny Prospekt. Fashionably dressed ladies in their stylish carriages, with smartly turned-out coachmen in colorful caftans behind fast trotters, sped along the Neva River Esplanade. Facing its wide expanse on the land side was the Tsar's Winter Palace, grand in its immensity, with its pastel walls and white rococo trim. On the other side flowed the Neva River where, midst blocks of ice on the recently frozen-over river, slow-moving barges loaded with hay looked like floating peasant huts.

As carriages turned up Gorokhovaya Street, the columns of the Admiralty with its quaint spire came into view. Directly in front of it stood the huge monolith topped with a golden angel, dedicated to Aleksandr I. Beyond, to the left, was the impressive Falconet statue of Peter the Great reigning in his horse at the very edge of a precipice as he stretches out his hand toward the Neva and tramples the enormous serpent of conspiracy under his horse's feet. Turning into the Nevsky Prospekt—the city's main avenue that ran in a straight line through all the radiating circle of streets and canals of St. Petersburg—the carriages drove through the commercial section of primitive-looking, colorful shops and open market stalls with imaginative signs depicting their wares, and turned into fashionable Liteiny Prospekt where the Court Building could be seen some distance away.

Young men and women had begun to gather in the streets around the Court before six o'clock in the morning. Long before the trial was scheduled to open, a huge crowd had assembled. People of all ages, from all ranks of society, wearing everything from rags to colorfully embroidered sheepskins and Parisian gowns, were pushing and shoving along Liteiny Prospekt and the adjoining streets and sidewalks: magistrates, soldiers, society ladies and gentlemen, merchants with wolfskin coats over their caftans, workers in the costumes of their trade, buxom, kerchiefed serving women, rustic peasants—all with looks of excitement on their faces.

No one without a ticket could expect to get through the inspection of a double line of gendarmes at the entrance to the Court House, but everyone in the streets hoped at least to get a glimpse of Vera Zasulich, the current popular heroine, "Verochka," Little Vera, who on January 25 had shot the hated governor of St. Petersburg, General Trepov, with an English Bulldog pistol. She was on this day being brought to trial for murder.

Why did she do it? Why did this upper-class girl (her deceased father had been an army officer) shoot Governor-General Trepov? Was her motive personal or political? It was known that her answer to the initial police questioning was that she shot him because he ordered the flogging of a prisoner in the St. Petersburg House of Preliminary Detention, a student named Bogoliubov.[2] The governor said he gave the order because the prisoner had shown disrespect by failing to remove his cap when he walked toward him in the prison yard. Preparations for the whipping, and the sound of the slow, steady strokes of the whip on the naked body of Bogoliubov as he was held down on the whipping block by prison guards, caused a near riot. As news of the incident circulated, people in all ranks of society, including the court ladies in the Tsaritsa's salon, expressed indignation. All said they were shocked to learn that the brutal practice, which everyone thought had been outlawed years before, was still being used in Russia's most enlightened city—St. Petersburg.

People talked. But they did nothing. Trepov (a great favorite of the Tsar since the early 1860s when, as chief of police in Warsaw, he had carried out bloody reprisals after an uprising in Poland) received no reprimand. Bogoliubov, a physical wreck, became mentally deranged and was sent off to a mental hospital in Kazan to die.

As members of the crowd before the Court House discussed the case, many said with certainty that Vera Zasulich shot Trepov in revenge because Bogoliubov was her lover. It has to be a "crime of passion," they said, because she was being tried in a civil court with a jury. Political crimes, everyone knew, were tried behind closed doors. There were others equally certain Zasulich had shot Trepov as an act of political protest, even though she was not a proclaimed member of any radical group. They were convinced Zasulich's trial would be a miscarriage of justice, as they believed all the other recent trials had been, and foresaw her condemned to death, prison, or exile with hard labor in Siberia. They expected a huge demonstration in the streets as soon as the verdict was announced, with the usual bloody confrontation by police and gendarmerie.

Those with tickets, including the fashionable ladies who had for weeks been sending their requests on delicately colored scented notepapers to the presiding judge, Anatoly Fyodorovich Koni, made their way to the entrance of the building. Congregated there were generals in full dress uniform with more orders on their chests than hairs on their heads, artillery officers, officers of the General Staff, and silk-hatted men wearing heavy, black, fitted greatcoats with beaver collars. One of the ladies remarked to no one in particular that it reminded her of the crush at the theatre a few weeks back when the "Divine Patti" sang.

---

[2]Bogoliubov (whose real name was Arkhip Stepanovich Yemelianov) was a student at the Veterinary Institute when he was arrested during the police break-up of a peaceful demonstration in the Kazan Cathedral Square on December 6, 1876. He had been sentenced to fifteen years at hard labor in Siberia, even though—according to some witnesses—he was a spectator, not a demonstrator.

More red upholstered chairs than the room could comfortably hold had been moved into the large, dimly lit, stuffy courtroom. As people filed in, medals of the orders of St. Ann, St. George, and St. Vladimir sparkled on gold-braided red and blue uniforms, adding glitter to the assembly of spectators who greeted each other quietly at first. But waving, blowing kisses, and calling out clever remarks, the crowd became more animated. Had it not been for the whitewashed walls and the great windows with small panes and no curtains, observers might have thought they were at a social function.

A buzz of conversation continued until shortly after ten o'clock when uniformed court officials and members of the jury, in frock coats and white ties, began to file in. Most of the twelve men in the jury box were distinguished-looking state counselors of various ranks, but there was one titled landowner, a principal of a religious school, an artist, and a student.

The black-robed jurists entered, led by Judge Koni who had been chosen by the officials of the court to be presiding judge in the case of the State versus Vera Zasulich. He had been called to the Winter Palace by Aleksandr II where the Tsar personally invested him with his office. The jurists sat at a long table facing the audience. Behind them in comfortable armchairs sat many of the highest officials in the Tsar's government, led by the Chancellor, Prince Aleksandr M. Gorchakov. Several secretaries of state were there, as was Field Marshall Count Barantzev in full dress uniform, his chest covered with gold, diamond-encrusted medals. Count Stroganoff represented the powerful Ministry of the Interior. In places reserved for the press sat several foreign journalists, including Sir Donald MacKenzie Wallace and the famous Russian writer, Fyodor Dostoevsky, who had himself been sentenced to death by a tsarist court, only to have his sentence revoked at the last minute, replaced by a term in the *katorga* (hard labor imprisonment).

All eyes turned to watch the prisoner brought in. Women raised their opera glasses to get a better look. They saw a comely young woman of medium height wearing a plain black prison gown. Her smooth dark hair was combed close to her head and two long braids fell down her back. The pale thin features of her face carried traces of spiritual suffering and physical deprivation, but her intelligent grey eyes shone with an inner warmth. She gave the impression of being a quiet person without the least affectation, but an observer could not doubt that under her modest exterior was an ardent soul and an inflexible will.

Two armed gendarmes led Vera to the prisoner's bench and continued to stand on either side of her with swords unsheathed. The lawyers took their seats at a long table to the side. The government prosecutor, an official in the Ministry of Justice, Konstantin Ivanovich Kessel, had taken the unenviable job of prosecuting this case after two others in the Ministry refused it. The defense lawyer was the forty-two-year-old Peter Akimov Aleksandrov, noted for his captivating oratory and his record of defending youthful

Vera Ivanovna Zasulich

reformers, who in Russia in the 1870s almost without exception ended up in prison facing criminal charges.

Presiding Judge Koni opened the session of the First Division of the St. Petersburg Circuit Court on March 31, 1878, at eleven o'clock sharp. He first advised the jurors of their obligations, duties, and rights, concluding: "Your liberty is complete, and you must arrive at your own personal decision in this case."

As Judge Koni gave this advice to the jury he remembered the invitation he had received from the Minister of Justice, Count Palen, a few days before, to come to his office. As the two men settled into comfortable armchairs and a lackey served tea, the minister suavely said to Koni, "You know the Tsar is very much interested in this case. He even went to the House of Preliminary Detention to look at the prisoner. Trepov is, as I am sure you know, a great favorite of his." Count Palen went on, "It is possible, is it not, dear Anatoly Fyodorovich, that as presiding judge you can guarantee a guilty verdict." Koni was startled, but after a painful pause he blurted out: "No. Never. I cannot." Palen appeared to be almost overcome with surprise. In the Russian autocracy, it was usual for an official to accept the Tsar's slightest wish as law. Koni continued, "When a case is tried before a jury, the decision on guilt or innocence is made by the jury." Then he added that if the ministry wanted a fixed verdict, the case should have been taken before a police court, a military court-martial, or even a senate judicial committee. "Too late, too late," moaned Palen. Information on the date of the trial, the name of the court, and the presiding judge in the Vera Zasulich case had already been posted and had been published in the newspapers.

Palen knew Vera Zasulich had shot Trepov for political reasons. He knew she had not done it to avenge a lover. He knew she should have been tried for a political crime behind closed doors. But he was aware of the silent resentment against the Ministry of Justice boiling beneath the smooth surface of St. Petersburg society. From the lowly man in the street to high officials in the government came whispering about the ministry's mishandling of punitive actions against hundreds of young people picked up for "political offenses" that were peaceful in nature. Rumors were circulating, and some hard evidence had come to light of inhuman treatment by the police, the army, and the jailors of these men and women, almost all of them sons and daughters of Russia's landowning and office-holding class. There was also criticism of the secret trials and the long sentences to hard labor in Siberia. Even women, in the recent Trial of the 193, had been sentenced to five or more years in the mines of Kara.

Comment in St. Petersburg society and officialdom on such matters rarely got beyond the walls of private homes and a few liberal clubs, but in the tsarist autocracy, that such discussions took place at all was considered dangerous. Even more frightening, a girl had dared to shoot a government official and, to the amazement of all officials of the autocracy—and the Tsar himself—had become an instant heroine. All over Russia, but especially in St. Petersburg, people at first whispered, then began to shout "Brave Vera" to show their approval of her attack on an old officer whose flagrantly corrupt practices, maladministration, and cruelty had earned him the hatred of the people while he had gone unreprimanded by the Tsar whose favorite he remained.

The autocracy was caught in a dilemma. For its higher purpose of absolute rule, quick, severe punishment of Zasulich was required; but to avoid what threatened to become open criticism of yet another secret trial, the Ministry of Justice decided to give her a public jury trial. And Koni made it clear he would do his duty as a judge to see that the jury was free to reach its own decision. No wonder Count Palen, sitting in his office opposite Koni, clasped his head in his hands and repeated over and over, "What's to be done? What's to be done?"

In the crowded courtroom, presiding Judge Koni asked the secretary of the court to read the indictment. He proceeded, giving a factual account of the crime, and ended with these words:

> Vera Zasulich is accused of being admitted January 24, 1878, to the reception room of the police governor of St. Petersburg with the premeditated resolve to attack him criminally. She is accused of having fired and hit him in the left side with a shot from a revolver of sufficiently high caliber to have wounded him gravely enough that his still being alive is due to the accident of circumstance and not to the will of the accused.

Judge Koni had seen General Trepov on several occasions around and about the city during the weeks before the trial, but the governor chose not to appear as a witness. The secretary of the court read a note from Trepov saying that for medical reasons he would be unable to appear. The note was accompanied by a medical certificate signed by his physician.

Two of Trepov's aides and a guard were among the twenty people, including a dozen women petitioners in the room at the time of the shooting, who testified. Each in turn recognized the young woman sitting on the prisoner's bench as the one who came into Trepov's reception room on January 24, and, as the first petitioner, presented the governor with a request for a certificate of good behavior (of the kind women needed in order to apply for positions as private teachers). They went on to testify that after the governor granted her request, as he turned away to approach the next petitioner, she shot him. Each said that after one shot, she dropped her gun on the floor, made no attempt to retrieve it to fire a second shot, and did not resist arrest.

Trepov's aides were not asked, nor did they volunteer information about the severe beating one of them gave Vera before and during their interrogation. Vera told her lawyer the aide seemed intent on gouging out her eyes and beating her to death but was pulled away by someone who said, "Stop. Consider the consequences."

After the testimony of Trepov's aides, Judge Koni addressed the prisoner:

> You have been accused of a premeditated attempt to murder Governor-General Trepov. These witnesses have testified you came to his residence January 24, posing as a petitioner, carrying a revolver, and that with that weapon you seriously injured him. Are you guilty of this crime?

She replied, "I admit that I fired one shot at him."

"Would you tell us why you committed this act? Was it your intent to kill Governor-General Trepov?"

"It was indifferent to me whether I killed or merely wounded Trepov. My motive was to punish the one who ordered a prisoner named Bogoliubov whipped with birch branches in the St. Petersburg House of Preliminary Detention on July 13, 1877. If he had not done that, I would not have shot him."

"How did you know about this [the whipping]?"

"Last summer I was living in the country with my sister, teaching her children. In July, as I read the St. Petersburg newspaper, *Novoe Vremia,* I came across a small item about the beating of a prisoner that had been done on the order of Trepov because the prisoner had failed to take off his cap, a gesture of respect required of prisoners."

"Did you know the prisoner?"

"He is completely unknown to me."

"What did you do then?"

"I came to St. Petersburg."

"Did you come to commit a crime?"

"No. I came to St. Petersburg on a family matter; I have relatives in the city. But when I got here I soon began to hear details about the whipping. I spoke to several who had been in the prison at the time and witnessed what happened."

At this point Zasulich's lawyer, Aleksandrov, asked that three prisoners who had been in the Preliminary Detention Prison in July 1877 be called as witnesses. The prosecution objected, but Aleksandrov cited the law permitting this and said it was essential for the jury to know about the whipping in order to understand Zasulich's motive.

Two wan, pale men and a young woman appeared. They had been brought in directly from one of Russia's grimmest prisons, the Peter Paul Fortress. They told in thin voices, trembling with tears and indignation, their stories of Trepov's cruelty.

When the prison witnesses' testimony ended, the presiding judge asked Vera Zasulich whether she had anything to say. She stated:

> When I got to St. Petersburg, I learned from several people that soldiers were sent to the prison and they threw many prisoners into the dungeons. I learned

also that Bogoliubov was not given the usual twenty-five blows of the birch, but was whipped until he could no longer move and was half-dead. I also heard about the conditions at the House of Preliminary Detention. Political prisoners were held there for years, before and after sentencing, and were treated so badly many went mad and several committed suicide.

I happen to know well the horror imprisonment can inspire—not to mention what happens to those who have been whipped, maltreated, and placed in dungeons. I also know well the hardness of heart, the barbarity of those who inflict such tortures, not as punishment, but as viciousness, as outpouring of personal vengeance committed in moments of fury. It seems to me such things should not pass unnoticed by the public.

When I saw the item in the newspaper that a prisoner had been whipped on Trepov's order, I thought: "The public has been informed. It will be moved by it." Not at all. People knew, and everyone kept silent. What did that mean? It meant that nothing hinders Trepov, or anyone else in authority, from committing again and again these same savage deeds, these same brutal violences. And I know how easy it is to find a pretext for doing it.

I searched for but I could not find any other means. Even now I do not see any other means. So I resolved—at the price of my own life—to show to society and to those in authority that no one can be sure of doing whatever he likes with impunity, that no one can be allowed to carry his contempt for human dignity to such lengths.

In a tremulous voice, Zasulich said, "To me it is a frightful thing to raise one's hand against a human being, but I found I had to do it." She became so choked with emotion she could not speak. Judge Koni advised her to stop and compose herself.

Among the spectators, suppressed sobs could be heard as many of the finely dressed men and women wiped away tears and lowered their eyes in shame. As one of the ladies in waiting to the Tsar's cousin, the Grand Duchess Katerina, later wrote, "I felt I was guilty." A journalist said, "I felt it was not she who was being judged, but me, all of us—society."[3]

"You say you are familiar with the experience of solitary confinement. Have you ever been a prisoner?"

Zasulich replied that she had been held as an accused person several years ago.

The judge asked, "What is your profession?"

Zasulich hesitated and said, haltingly, "I have been an exile." She halted

---

[3]Elizabeth Narishkin-Kurakin, *Under Three Tsars*, New York, 1931. Born into the ancient princely Kurakin Family, and united in marriage to another, the Naryshkins, Elizabeth was Lady-in-Waiting to the Grand Duchess Katerina, cousin of Aleksandr II. She reported hearing the Bogoliubov flogging discussed in the Tsaritsa's parlor. The journalist was G. K. Gradovski whose article "Delo Very Zasulich" appeared in *Golos* (The Voice), April 2, 1879, no. 92 (reprinted in *Itogi 1862–1907*, Kiev, 1908, pp. 429–36.

again, "I have been a teacher, but, it is difficult to say." She went on, "I sketched my biography for my lawyer who wishes to refer to it in his presentation." Aleksandrov, her attorney, rose to confirm that he expected to bring out essential biographical facts and there was no need to take the time to go into them at this point.

After a few more questions directed at Vera Zasulich, Judge Koni recognized several other witnesses, then turned the case over to the prosecuting attorney, Kessel. The prosecutor slowly got to his feet. As he began to speak, his voice was pitched so low he could hardly be heard. He was so nervous he had to take repeated sips of water and often looked as if he were about to faint. He put the case on purely criminal grounds and went over the evidence to show it amply proved that the accused had simply committed an act of premeditated attempted murder. As for her motives, he said:

I believe what she says about her conviction that she had to protest official cruelty. But what Trepov did or did not do is not the question at issue here.

Everyone has his or her own sentiments, sympathies, antipathies. But when these sentiments are transformed into acts that violate the law, with the intent to kill, justice demands punishment. . . . Did she have the right to impose justice herself? Could she act as prosecutor, defender, and judge? I do not believe, gentlemen of the jury, that you can excuse such conduct. If any official is guilty, he is answerable to the courts, has the right to the justice of the law, and cannot be exposed to the summary justice of an individual outside the law.

Vera Zasulich is guilty of murder. It is the inviolability of human life I defend in calling for a guilty verdict. I conclude with the prisoner's own words: "It is a frightful thing to raise one's hand against a human being." And I am persuaded that in the depth of her soul Zasulich herself knows that no eloquent discourse in the courtroom can erase the spots of blood that stain the hands of the murderer.

The reaction of the spectators to the prosecutor's words was glacial silence, and the jurors appeared unmoved.

Aleksandrov began his defense by addressing the jury, saying he agreed entirely with the prosecution concerning the established facts of the case.

Who dreams of denying that to take justice into your own hands is a crime? This is an incontestable verity. . . . But justice is not ordinarily served by examining only the crime itself. It is necessary to examine and weigh motives.

Aleksandrov said all evidence confirmed that the event of January 24 in Trepov's audience room was intimately connected with the event that had taken place in the Preliminary Detention Prison on July 13 of the previous year. But the connecting link between the two events was missing unless one examined Zasulich's past. Examination of her past, he went on, is instructive not only in trying to determine the degree of Vera Zasulich's culpability, but "it enables us to look at that soil which among us has in recent years produced so many crimes and criminals." He was obviously referring to the idealistic urge for reform by Russia's educated youth and their brutal treatment by the autocracy.

He gave biographical facts, saying she was born in the Province of Smolensk in 1852.[4] Her father, an army captain, had died when she was three, leaving her mother with inadequate support and five children. Zasulich was turned over to the family of a wealthy relative and spent her childhood on their estate near the village of Biakolovo.[5]

When she was fifteen the family sent her to a boarding school in Moscow. At the end of the two-year course of study she took the exam to qualify as a governess and passed it with high honors. The following summer she worked in Moscow as a clerk for a minor government official. In the fall she went with her mother to St. Petersburg where she got a job in a bookbinding shop. In her spare time she audited university lectures, a privilege recently made available to women. She concentrated on the new science of phonetics, being taught as a way to improve language instruction. Among other students she chanced to meet Anna Nechaeva and, through her, her brother Sergei.[6]

At this point in his presentation of Vera Zasulich's biography, Aleksandrov asked:

> Who was Nechaev? What was he planning? Vera Zasulich didn't know. He was simply another student. Everyone is now aware that Nechaev at a later date ran afoul of the law for his criminal and revolutionary acts for which five years ago he was tried and condemned. But who knew Nechaev then, in 1869, before he got involved in politics? No one. Certainly not the seventeen-year-old girl who on three or four occasions, at his request, delivered letters of whose contents she was ignorant to people he indicated.

Insignificant as this chance meeting of Nechaev was to Vera Zasulich, Aleksandrov noted, it raised a suspicion in the minds of the secret police that she was connected with Nechaev's revolutionary activities. She was ar-

---

[4]This date is erroneous. Lev Deich's obituary of her, "Pamiatka Ushedshikh . . .," *Golos Minuvshego,* May-December, 1919, nos. 5–12, pp. 199–200, gives her birth date as July 29, 1849. Aleksandrov, making her younger than she really was, strengthened his case. And many witnesses testified to Zasulich's girlish appearance at the trial, despite the fact she was twenty-eight-years old.

[5]An interesting fact is that the three Zasulich daughters who were farmed out and reared by foster families became revolutionaries; the son and daughter who remained with their mother did not. Vera's brother entered the army, and, like his father, was an officer.

[6]Sergei Nechaev, a low-born schoolteacher, became a disciple of the anarchist, Mikhail Bakunin. He soon embraced ideas far more radical than those of his mentor, but his dedication to the idea of immediate revolution had attracted almost no followers at the time Zasulich met him in 1869, when, as she later wrote, she found his ideas half-baked.

rested and held in a detention prison for one year. She was then taken to the Peter Paul Fortress and kept there in solitary confinement for another year. During all that time not a shred of evidence was found against her.

Then Aleksandrov asked his listeners to consider how Vera Zasulich passed these critical years of her life.

> In the midst of what games? Of what fêtes? Of what felicities? What gilded dreams caressed her imagination inside the somber walls of Litovski Prison and behind the deep casements of the Peter Paul Fortress? Inside prison walls, isolated from the world and society, she remained two long years without seeing her mother, her relatives, her friends. Only rarely did she receive news of those dear to her, and then only through a prison guard. Without work or occupation, without distraction except on rare occasions when a book got through the stringent prison censorship, her only activity was the few steps it took to traverse her tiny cell. What did she see beyond its grilled iron gate? Only the sinister face of the guard who brought her meager food. What did she hear? The grinding of the locks of the prison doors opening and closing, the clank of rifles during the routine changing of the guard. Then outside the narrow casement window, which let in scarcely any light, she could hear the cadenced steps of the guards, and at the quarter hour, day and night, the lugubrious sound of the clock of the Peter Paul Tower.

Aleksandrov stressed the fact that in place of the affection and friendship of the society of free men and women, this girl had only the consciousness that behind the prison walls to the right and left of her were fellow sufferers, victims of an equally miserable fate.

At last, after two years in prison, she was released. She was free! She could begin to live again! Within a few days a police officer came to the place she was staying with an order to take her back to prison. It was surely a mistake. She tried to explain she had been officially released because no incriminating evidence against her had been found. She was innocent.

Vera was taken back to prison—without a trial, or a hearing, simply on orders "from somewhere". One night she was put in a horse-drawn police carriage and taken to the town of Kresty, about three hundred miles west of Moscow, where she was turned over to the local police chief. He made out some papers, then told her she was not being imprisoned. She was simply to stay in the town on her own, but under police surveillance. She must report to the police bureau every Saturday. Then she was taken to the door and turned out into the street in a strange town. She had two rubles in her pocket and a box of French chocolates under her arm. She was in a state of bewilderment. As an ex-prisoner, under active police surveillance, her chances of finding work to support herself, or even to find a place to stay, were dim. But, for once, fortune smiled on Vera. A sympathetic family took her in.

After a few months in Kresty, Vera was sent to another city under the same conditions and restrictions. Then to another, and another. She became a wandering exile. Police harassment continued. Every house she lived in was subject to search; she was constantly called in for questioning.

At the end of the third year, the questioning tapered off. She was left unmolested for quite a long time in the city of Kazan. She decided one day just to walk away. Nothing happened. After that, for two years she lived a precarious existence, free but never knowing when the ominous knock on the door might come. In the summer of 1877 she was in the country, near Moscow, caring for her sister's children. It was there she saw the newspaper item about the whipping of a prisoner.

Then in telling detail Aleksandrov used the skill of his oratory to describe the whipping so vividly, as Vera, with her prison experience, was able to imagine it. The courtroom audience broke out in thunderous applause. Tears flowed freely. Even the jurors could not hold back their tears. Zasulich herself seemingly did not notice she was sobbing, but as Judge Koni tried to bring the court to order she straightened up and sat with her eyes riveted on the inspiring face of the orator. She was as if spellbound by his rendering of her thoughts and feelings.

Aleksandrov went on to picture Zasulich's reaction after coming to St. Petersburg and learning many shocking details of the Bogoliubov affair. A fateful question arose in all its disquieting urgency. Who will stand up for the insulted honor of a defenseless political prisoner? She expected intercession by the press. The press remained silent. She expected the public to cry out in indignation. Public opinion did not crawl out of the seclusion of private study rooms, intimate circles, and conversation among friends. She expected, finally, that lawyers and judges would speak out. From that source too, nothing was heard. She began to realize the futility of her expectations. But the anxiety of her soul gave her no peace. Again and again the picture of Bogoliubov and his torture rose before her. Then, suddenly, an idea flashed like lightning into her head.

> Everyone is silent. A shout is needed! I myself can do that! I have enough breath in my body for a loud shout. I will shout, and force people to listen.

"When I commit a crime," Zasulich thought, "the silenced question about the disgrace of Bogoliubov's punishment will be forced into the open. My crime will provoke a public trail, and Russia, in the person of her people's representatives [the jury] will be compelled to pronounce a verdict, and the verdict will not be on me alone. . . . And Europe will be looking on, that Europe which likes to call us a barbarian state in which the knout serves as the main attribute of government."

Since publicity was her aim, whether the shot directed at Trepov killed him did not matter. To take his life was not her goal. What she wanted was to appear at the judgment bench, because alongside her would be the case of Bogoliubov. When she stepped over the threshold of the governor's house to achieve this aim, she knew she was sacrificing everything . . . her liberty, the rest of her broken life, the little that had been given her by the stepmother of her fate.

As Aleksandrov put it:

> It is not to bargain over this or that extenuation of her guilt that she is here today, gentlemen of the jury. She was and she remains the selfless slave of her idea, in the name of which she raised the bloody hand. She came in order to submit to you all the burden of her aggrieved soul, to open before you the sorrowful page of her life, to relate honestly all that she has endured, thought, and felt, all that moved her to commit a crime, and she has exposed her aim and what she expected from it.

He said that for the first time a jury in Russia was being asked to judge a woman who had committed a crime to fight for an idea.

> If for the general welfare, if for the sake of public safety, she must be punished, then let your chastising justice take place. She may go out of here judged guilty, but she will not go out disgraced, and her wish will remain that there be no future repetition of the causes that will evoke acts like hers.

As Aleksandrov sat down, thunderous applause broke out. It quieted as Judge Koni addressed Vera Zasulich and said: "To you belongs the last word. What do you have to say?" She replied, "I have nothing to say."

Judge Koni then began his instructions to the jury. With scrupulous impartiality he went over the evidence and the testimony. He completed his remarks by telling the jury it had three questions to decide:

1. Is Vera Zasulich guilty of shooting General Trepov with a large caliber gun?
2. In firing this shot, was she guilty of an attempt to kill him?
3. If she did intend to kill him, did she with premeditation take all measures to achieve her aim? And, if he did not die, was it due to circumstances and not her will?

Then he said, "Gentlemen of the jury, in reaching your decision, examine coldly the arguments of the accusation and the defense."

The twelve men filed out to the jury room for deliberation. Judge Koni went to his chambers. He looked out the window and was amazed at the size of the crowds gathered on Liteiny Prospekt and Shpalernaya Street. He noticed many young people wearing wide hats, high boots, and plaid shawls, engaged in animated conversation, sharply gesticulating and obviously in a high emotional state of expectation awaiting news of the verdict. A court attendant said the police anticipated trouble when the expected guilty verdict came and were ready for it.

The jury deliberated for about ten minutes in their room, filled with clouds of tobacco smoke, then rang their bell to signify they had reached a verdict. Judge Koni walked into the courtroom. The jurymen followed, white-faced, close behind each other, and stood in their box. The foreman with a shaking hand gave Judge Koni a sheet of paper with the verdict written on it. He looked at it and, without changing his expression, handed it back to the foreman to read to the court.

There was deathly silence in the courtroom. Every spectator was holding his or her breath. One of them later confessed his heart almost stopped beating. Only the prisoner sat unmoved, with her eyes stubbornly riveted on some far point in the celing.

The foreman started to speak. He read the first question: "Is Vera Zasulich guilty of shooting General Trepov with a large caliber gun? No. Not Guil . . ."

As if touched off by an electric spark an explosion of sound burst forth, drowning out the rest of his sentence. Ear-splitting applause. Hysterical sobbing. Foot stomping. People crossing themselves. Crashing howls of "Hurrah!" "Bravo Aleksandrov!" "Well done!" "Vera! Verochka! Long live Vera!"

Never within the walls of that courtroom had there been such a wild demonstration of unrestrained joy. Koni was appalled to hear the men sitting in armchairs behind the bench, among them the highest officials in the realm, clapping and hallooing, with the Chancellor, Prince Gorchakov, in the lead. Koni turned to see the old, red-faced, bemedaled Field Marshal Barantzev yelling and clapping excitedly. He stopped when Koni gave him a look, but started again as soon as the judge turned his head. Did not these men realize this day's event had turned into a trial of the tsarist government?[7] In declaring Vera Zasulich innocent, the jury, with society's approval, had declared them guilty.

Upper-class and court-circle spectators in transports of joy, heedless of the implications of the trial, carried Aleksandrov out of the building on their shoulders. Over the din of courtroom noise, which Judge Koni decided it was useless to try to control, he spoke to Zasulich telling her she was free to go. She seemed to be the only one who gave no evidence of joy. Indeed, she appeared stunned. She had been sure that she would be hanged after the farce of a trial. Later she said she was numb, and a sadness came over her at the realization that if she had been judged guilty her life would have been out of her control. She had given up her freedom. Now, unexpectedly,

---

[7]One observer, Sir Donald MacKenzie Wallace, in chapter 33 of his book *Russia* (rev. ed., London, 1908), saw the trial not as a triumph of justice but a set-back to the development of a free and independent judicial system in Russia. Samuel Kucherov, *Courts, Lawyers and Trials Under the Last Three Tsars* (New York, 1953), in his analysis of the Zasulich trial, produces evidence of its consequences, including the decline in the use of the jury trial, that proves Wallace's prediction correct.

it had been restored to her and she was faced with the task of what to do with it.

News of the "not guilty" verdict hit the crowds in the streets like a bomb explosion. They cried out in joy and disbelief as they mingled with the spectators coming out of the courtroom radiating their excitement. The shouting and singing could be heard for blocks.

Russian citizens may have greeted with joy the jury's verdict in the case of the State versus Vera Zasulich. His Imperial Highness, the Autocrat of All the Russias, did not. Tsar Aleksandr II, anticipating the possibility of an outcome of the trial unacceptable to him, had issued an order for Vera's rearrest. In obedience to his Sovereign's command, Count Palen, the Minister of Justice, sent a printed order to the public prosecutor to detain Vera Zasulich in the Preliminary Detention Prison under guard. The order arrived too late.

At about seven o'clock in the evening, Vera Zasulich came out of the Court House and was met with wild bursts of cheering. She was picked up and carried in triumph on the shoulders of several young men to the nearby prison to pick up her things. A little later she stepped out of the building with a woman friend and got into a waiting carriage which, with difficulty, made its way slowly up the street. Excited young people walked alongside and happily talked to Vera and her companion.

Suddenly armed gendarmes rushed in from a side street. They fanned out, shouting orders for the people to disperse. It became apparent that Vera was to be rearrested. Suddenly a shot was fired, then another. The young woman sitting in the carriage with Vera was hit in the hand and was rushed, bleeding, into a nearby apothecary shop. There were screams and the crowd fell back. A third shot was heard and a young man who had been running beside Vera's carriage fell to the street, killed instantly.

Thinking the woman who had been shot was Vera, many crowded around and inside the apothecary shop. In the confusion her carriage rushed forward. Another carriage, filled with policemen, drove alongside and ordered Vera's driver to stop. He whipped the horses and, in the nearly empty street, raced ahead. He made several sharp turns, at one point when he could not see the police carriage behind him, he stopped to let Vera jump out, then raced on, the police carriage still in hot pursuit. Vera hid in an alleyway for a time, then carefully made her way through the dark streets to a friend's home. She was kept well hidden for several weeks, never for long in one place, by people who took risks to provide shelter for her. As she later commented, they were not radicals and for them she was a curiosity, something completely outside their experience. She felt lonelier with them than she had in the Preliminary Detention Prison.

An important decision Vera Zasulich had to make was whether to leave Russia. She received a message from a woman revolutionary friend who had been sentenced to five years in the mines of Siberia in the Trial of the 193. Ignore those who try to persuade you to leave Russia, she advised, because if you do you will be only a "retired heroine." However, when the Tsar's order for her rearrest was made public and searches for her were being carried out all over Russia, she decided to go to Switzerland. Schemes and rumors of how she was to be smuggled out of Russia proliferated. It seemed as if everyone wanted to help, including a general who offered to escort her, disguised and documented as his wife. The most fanciful of the rumored schemes involved the Grand Duke Konstantin, the Tsar's younger brother, who was supposed to harbor a deep animosity toward the autocracy. He would, it was said, disguise Vera with a red wig, outfit her as a society lady, and put her on a first-class coach to Berlin. Rumors of this plan were so prevalent the police conducted daily searches of the luxury coaches of all trains leaving Russia. They apparently ignored or made only routine checks of the fourth-class carriages, one of which Vera Zasulich boarded on May 17 with a group of peasants. She and the two Russian radicals accompanying her wore peasant dress and were not detected.

They arrived safely in Berlin where utmost caution had to be taken because the old emperor, Wilhelm I, with his fraternal feeling for Emperor Aleksandr II, would have liked nothing better than to extradite the "wanted" Zasulich back to Russia, into the hands of the tsarist police. Vera and her companions had expected to meet Russian emigré radicals living in Berlin who would make arrangements for the last leg of their journey to Switzerland. When they arrived they found, to their dismay, that one of the several would-be assassins who appeared on the scene after the Zasulich shooting, Karl Nobiling, had the day before made an attempt on the life of Emperor Wilhelm I. All Berlin was excited and the Russian emigrés, frightened and agitated, expected police raids any moment. This left Vera Zasulich and her companions on their own. They took refuge in the parks where they stayed until they were finally able to board a train for Switzerland.

In Switzerland, Vera had to remain in hiding for fear of extradition. A French socialist who had fled France after the fall of the Paris Commune in 1871 consented to take her in. She would be safe with him because in Switzerland private homes were inviolable.

The day after Vera's arrival in Geneva a French emigré who had been an officer of the Paris Commune died. Socialists from all over Europe came to the funeral. Journalists, with their antennae out, quickly picked up hints that Zasulich, who had become internationally famous, was in Geneva. Her exact location was not revealed, for Vera had already begun the life of a Russian radical abroad, which was a constant play in concealment. Nevertheless she began to receive invitations to appear at anarchist rallies in Paris, and to make statements for and against socialists in Germany and elsewhere. A naturally retiring person who, as her French host observed,

Къ дѣлу В. И. Засуличъ.

МИНИСТЕРСТВО

ЮСТИЦІИ

~~~~~

КАНЦЕЛЯРІЯ

С Т О Л Ъ

~~~~~

Марта 31 дня
1878 года

~~~~~

№ 4843.

~~~~~

С.-Петербургъ.

Господину Прокурору С.-Петербургской Судебной Палаты.

ГОСУДАРЬ ИМПЕРАТОРЪ 31-го сего марта ВЫСОЧАЙШЕ повелѣть соизволилъ: дочь отставного капитана дѣвицу Вѣру Ивановну Засуличъ взять подъ стражу и содержать ее въ домѣ предварительнаго заключенія впредь до особаго распоряженія.

Прошу Ваше Превосходительство сдѣлать распоряженіе о немедленномъ приведеніи таковой — ВЫСОЧАЙШЕЙ воли въ исполненіе.

Министръ Юстиціи

Статсъ-Секретарь Гр. ПАЛЕНЪ.

Управляющій канцеляріей Бар. КОРФЪ.

Tsar's Order for the rearrest of Vera Zasulich
Reprinted in *Byloye*, **no. 11, November 1906, p. 278.**

CONCERNING THE CASE OF V. I. ZASULICH

MINISTRY
of Justice
———
CHANCELLORY
Office
———

March 31
1878
———
No. 4843
———
St. Petersburg
———

To the Public Prosecutor of St. Petersburg

Palace of Justice

HIS MAJESTY THE EMPEROR on the 31st day of March IMPERATIVELY commands that the daughter of the retired captain, the maiden Vera Ivanovna Zasulich, be put under guard and kept in the House of Preliminary Detention pending further instructions.

I ask Your Excellency to order the immediate execution of the SUPREME will in this matter.

Minister of Justice

State-Secretary Count PALEN

Director of the Chancellory Baron KORF

English Translation

"would not waste herself on revolutionary cries and shouts but would engage in conscientious reflection and arrive at her own decisions," she refused all such invitations.

Those who sought to further their own causes by use of her name did not understand that she hated her fame so much it made her gnash her teeth. She would never succumb to what she called "public posturing." She was not the advocate of any doctrine and said, "My notion of anarchism was as vague as my notion of social democracy." She ascribed her ignorance to deficiencies in the Russian educational system and to tsarist censorship which curtailed the circulation of information. Until she knew more and studied more she would not write or speak out. Someday she would but not now.

To clear her mind, to prepare her soul for a new life, Vera went with a comrade to walk in the Swiss Alps. There, surrounded by snow-covered peaks, climbing the grassy slopes, she found herself in another world. "My intense feeling of freedom grew stronger with each passing hour. I was liberated from everything that oppressed me—from people, but most of all from myself. All my unresolved questions and painful thoughts disappeared."

Zasulich's shot at Trepov and her spectacular trial caught the attention of the Russian people and of people far beyond Russia's borders. As G. Valbert wrote in the May 1878 issue of the *Revue des Deux Mondes:*

> [Europe] completely forgot Bismarck, Lord Beaconsfield [Disraeli], Prince Gortchakoff, whether or not the Congress of Berlin would meet, in its concentration on Vera Zasoulitch and the strange judicial venture of which she, until a few weeks ago a completely unknown girl, was the heroine.

But an air of mystery surrounded this heroine. In the widely circulated police photograph she was enveloped in a long, dark-grey cloak scalloped around the hem, called a *talma.* A black shawl covered her hair. Her profile, white against the blackness, made her look as dramatic as an opera star.

Knowing almost nothing about her, everyone imagined Zasulich in his or her own way. Some saw her as a poetic young girl, sweet and pure as an early Christian martyr. To others she was the nemesis of revolution, a revolver in one hand and a red flag in the other, her lips mouthing slogans of terror. The silence she maintained about herself, the secluded life she led after she fled Russia, her dedication to self-contained intellectual endeavors, did nothing to shed light on the mystery of Vera Zasulich. But the record of her early radicalism was there. If State Prosecutor Kessel, had done a more thorough investigation of Vera Zasulich's past, he could have punctured holes in her lawyer's presentation of her as a political innocent. By the time she shot Trepov she had served a long apprenticeship in the Russian revolutionary movement.

Vera Zasulich grew up on the estate of her mother's relatives who took her in at age three. She became the only charge of an old governess who had educated several generations of the family's daughters. She taught Vera poetry and religion (that dwelt exclusively on the most gruesome aspects of death), French and German. She lost no occasion to instill in the child the feeling that the two of them were "outsiders," unwanted and unloved by the large family they lived with as dependents. As Vera saw herself, she was scolded by her relatives every time she asked a question, never affectionately held or kissed, never called pet names, abused by the servants. She was even whipped—"lightly," she said—laid out on a bench in the bathhouse and held there while she tried to wiggle off. She became convinced she was indeed an alien. She did not belong. She longed only to escape.

A ray of light brightened Vera's gloomy life when she was about eleven years old. On the estate there appeared a copy of the New Testament. During Lent, Vera was asked to read a chapter aloud every day. Her aunts, her governess, all of the children and their nurses sat around to listen. At first Vera did not like this task, but as she read she began to realize Christ was completely different from the frightening God her governess taught her about. Christ was good and kind in a way the child could understand. Why had his followers betrayed and abandoned him? Alone Christ was judged, alone he sacrificed his life. Night and day Vera dreamed of ways to save Christ from his terrible fate. She said that a few years later she gave up her faith in God and eternal life, but her vision of Christ the Redeemer, the one who sacrificed himself for others, remained with her always. She believed "there are times, there are entire ages, when there is nothing more beautiful and desirable than a crown of thorns."

The unhappy child reached her teens and felt the harsh nudge of fate pushing her toward the only future the family could see for a girl in her social position—two years in a young ladies' boarding school to prepare her for the exam she must pass to become a licensed governess. Then would begin the lowly life of living in other people's homes, teaching other people's children—a prospect Vera loathed. She concentrated on how to escape this terrible fate, and thought "If only I had been a boy, I could have done almost anything." And then "the distant specter of revolution appeared, making me equal to a boy. I too could dream of action, of exploits." She too could sacrifice herself in the great struggle against the evils of Russian society.

When the fifteen-year-old Vera came to Moscow to go to school, her two older sisters were living there with their husbands and were deeply involved in radical circles. They were all eventually arrested and exiled. Visiting the homes of her sisters and going with them to meetings and lectures, Vera met political extremists, heard revolutionary ideas discussed, and had access to forbidden literature. Later, when she was taking courses in St. Petersburg, she said that in the radical circles she frequented there, she was far better-read than her companions. In her student days in both Moscow and St. Petersburg she engaged in the illegal activities of teaching workers to read and doing routine tasks in the underground press.

The lawyer Aleksandrov in the trial of Vera Zasulich infused with high drama every facet of her life he chose to elucidate. In reality, her life pattern, set during the years of imprisonment and exile, was a lonely vigil of the mind, sparked by the occasional book or journal that came her way which she read and reread, always analyzing every word. But early in the fifth year of her life as a prisoner and exile, Vera saw an opportunity to change all that. And she grabbed it. The police moved her to Khar'kov and arranged for her to enroll in a medical training course to qualify her as a midwife. She soon met several local revolutionaries, and noticing that police surveillance had become rather slack, she decided to throw off the routine of reporting every week. Nothing happened. So she took the plunge. She became an "illegal." She joined the ranks of underground Russia.

By the time Vera Zasulich joined the underground her sense of the injustice of her years of imprisonment, exile, and hounding by the police, as well as the injustice she had seen heaped on others, had bred in her a terrible hatred of the tsarist police and the whole Russian autocratic system. She was looking for an alternative, and like many women of her time and class, found it in the optimistic ideas of the rural socialism of the *narodniki*. The word *narod* means people, and the *narodniki* were the Going-to-the-People people. By the mid-1870s the *narodniki*, Russia's educated youth—students, teachers, wives, and daughters of gentry households, and young professionals—had become a mass movement. By the thousands, in the famous summer of 1874, they left their classrooms, homes, and jobs to follow the call Russia's émigré radical publicists (Herzen, Lavrov, and Bakunin) had been proclaiming for years.[8]

> *Khodite v Narod!* (Go to the People!) You, the privileged few, have an obligation to repay "the people," the peasants and workers, who have slaved in degradation and misery for you and your kind for generations. Educate them! Prepare them—and yourselves—for the Revolution, for that great redistribution of the land, for the social regeneration to come when the autocracy will topple and our people will be freed from their chains.

---

[8]Aleksandr Herzen (1812–1870), a talented writer on social issues, too radical for the Russia of Nikolai I, emigrated in 1847. For many years he published in England *Kolokol* (The Bell), illegally circulated and very influential in Russia. Peter Lavrov (1823–1900), an army officer whose *Historical Letters*, published in 1868–1869, admonished the privileged and the educated that they had an obligation to the people to establish a just social order. He escaped abroad in 1870 and soon began to publish first a journal then a bi-weekly newspaper *Vperyod* (Forward) with the same message. Michael Bakunin (1819–1872), called the father of revolutionary anarchism, was imprisoned for his ideas; he escaped from Siberia to the West, where he was an ardent advocate of anarchism and revolution.

This message showed the way for the sons and daughters of Russia's gentry to assuage the guilt that lay on them for the sins of their ancestors. But there was more. Russia's poets and publicists, idealizing the peasant, taught them that in the ancient Russian institution, the peasant commune, lay the nucleus of an ideal socialist society—a new utopia. "Nihilists"[9] they were called, by Russians and by Western journalists. They picked up the word from Turgenev's 1862 novel *Fathers and Children,*[10] whose iconoclastic hero, Bazarov, was labeled a "nihilist."

When Vera Zasulich joined the underground, in appearance and personal habits she fit the popular image of the *nigilistka,* or girl "nihilist." The *nigilistka's* blue spectacles testified to her intellectualism, her cropped hair and plain unadorned dress were proof of her repudiation of the ribbons, ruffles, feathers, parasols, hoops, and crinolines of the world of the pampered, helpless young ladies of high style and fashion.

Rosaliya Bograd, later the wife of G. V. Plekhanov, never forgot her first meeting with Vera Zasulich in the Khar'kov railway station in 1875. Rosaliya, feeling herself terribly radical and liberated, was going off by train to St. Petersburg to become a *kursistka,* as young women students were called. Looking at Vera she realized how tied to her gentry background she was by her dress and the clothes she carried in her suitcases, so carefully packed by her mother with lots of underwear, starched blouses, long skirts, stockings, and handkerchiefs. Her first glance told her Vera had abandoned such trappings.

> Vera wore a shapeless grey outfit that might be described as a good-sized piece of linen in the center of which had been cut out a hole for her head and on the sides two holes for her arms. This piece of linen was held in with a narrow belt, but its edges hung down on all sides, fluttering in the wind. On her head was something—not a hat, but more like a *pirog*—made out of cheap grey material. On her feet were wide, clumsy-looking boots that she later explained to me had been specially made for her according to her own design. Her linen body covering, of course, had no pockets, so in place of a handkerchief she simply picked up the edge of one of the hanging corners of the material.

Vera had the reputation of always being so deeply immersed in her thoughts that she paid no heed to her appearance, yet Rosaliya's description proves she cut a striking figure. She herself left evidence in an autobiographical

---

[9]The word *"nihilist"* was from the beginning a misnomer for it implied negativism, and while Russia's radicals of the 1860s and 1870s did flout many of the traditional beliefs and values of contemporary Russian society, the dynamic force motivating all their activities was their positive approach to the new, idealistic society of the future, where freedom and equality would prevail.

[10]English translations of Ivan Sergeevich Turgenev's *Ottsy i Deti* (Fathers and Children) almost always render the title erroneously as *Fathers and Sons.*

Vera Ivanovna Zasulich

sketch that she planned very carefully the costume she would wear to shoot Trepov, knowing she would be photographed in it and that the photograph would receive wide publicity.

Soon after she entered the underground, Vera Zasulich left Khar'kov and went to Kiev. She arrived at a time when Kiev's revolutionary circles were the most radical in Russia. It was in Kiev, in the face of increasing numbers of arrests, exilings, imprisonment, and hangings of *narodniki* youth for the "crimes" of trying to teach peasants and workers to read, and of printing and distributing illegal literature, that a new organization, called *Zemlya i Volya*[11] (Land and Freedom), began talking and writing about striking back at the tsarist police with "disorganizing acts."

---

[11]*Zemlya i Volya* was not a political party (though it is sometimes called a party). It consisted of many loosely held together local groups sharing more or less common goals of agrarian socialism and opposition to autocracy.

Vera went to Kiev to join *Zemlya i Volya* but instead fell in with some young people, living in a communal dwelling, who had formed their own organization, the *Yuzhniye Buntari* or Young Rebels. Lev Deich, a tall, bespectacled, black-bearded, twenty-year-old medical school dropout, came to the *Buntari* soon after Vera joined. He found the four young women and six men a lively group whose animated conversation, joke telling, and singing of Russian songs went on until well past midnight as they drank tea and snacked on sausage, cheese, and other *zakuski*. It seemed to him God was taking good care of the Kiev *Buntari!*

Vera Zasulich and Lev Deich, whose daring revolutionary exploits over the next three decades became legendary, soon became lovers. Obviously fascinated by her, Deich later wrote that in Vera's *Buntari* days she was a strong, healthy, well-built country girl, not beautiful but with a face lighted up by her large, expressive grey eyes which reflected her innate intelligence. Everyone liked her for her constant concern for others, her infectious good nature, and her ready laughter. Buoyant and cheerful, she was affectionately called Marfusha by her companions. She was very unassuming but had a naturally loud voice and punctuated her conversation with shouts and large gestures that were very amusing. Her insatiable curiosity, her constant reading, and her previous revolutionary experience put her intellectually head and shoulders above the other members of the group, but she never tried to impose her opinion, always listened attentively to others, and willingly accepted and worked to carry out group decisions.

Although the thousands of arrests in the summer and fall of 1874 had almost wiped out the Going-to-the-People Movement, the Kiev *Buntari* in 1875 and 1876 were still tied to that movement's *narodniki* ideas. But they had gone one step beyond in their determination to defend themselves if they were threatened with arrest by the police. They acquired revolvers and learned to shoot them. They drew up manifestos stating the "rights of the people." In the summer they went to live in nearby villages with the aim of "educating" the peasants and fomenting a peasant uprising.

Vera Zasulich, dressed in peasant garb and posing as a wife or as a sister of one or another of her male comrades, went on several occasions to live in a village. She worked diligently at being a peasant *baba*, but her efforts at cooking were a disaster and she could not convincingly carry out the essential household and field tasks demanded of a peasant woman. As for educating the peasants, speaking Russian with a Moscow accent, every time she opened her mouth she sent her Ukrainian peasant neighbors into gales of laughter which she heartily joined. She was, of course, having her own troubles with Ukrainian speech which she found difficult to understand. But worst of all, she was always buried in a book, in an era when peasants not only could not read but had seldom seen and were highly suspicious of anyone who could.

The *Buntari* enjoyed getting together to tell stories and jokes about their peasant experiences, but Vera, eventually discouraged by the lack of success of their efforts in the villages, decided to leave Kiev. With one of her comrades, Masha Kolenkina, she went to St. Petersburg. There the young women worked briefly for an illegal printing press and Vera spent some time in the country with one of her sisters.

The year was 1877. Aside from news of the terrible Russian losses on the Russo-Turkish war front, the chief topic of conversation in St. Petersburg was trials: The Trial of the Demonstrators on the Square of Our Lady of Kazan in January; in March, the Trial of the 50 (sixteen of them young women whose crime was propagandizing and teaching factory workers to read); in October, the Trial of the 193 (the remnant of the more than a thousand Going-to-the-People young men and women arrested, interrogated, jailed, held in "protective detention," or put under police surveillance in 1874). The 193 were not tried in open court before a jury, but in secret by the judicial arm of the Imperial Senate. Nevertheless, speeches of the accused and their lawyers leaked out. To Vera and Masha, and to great segments of the literate Russian public, the Trial of the 193 displayed in horrendous detail the cruelty and injustice of the tsarist autocracy in its relentless attempt to destroy Russia's idealistic youth.

The two young women, on their own, decided to act. As soon as the Trial of the 193 was over, (with the aim of not jeopardizing the fate of the accused in any way) they would shoot two Tsarist officials: Zhelekhovsky, the hated prosecutor in the Trial of the 193, and Senator Zhikharev who had declared war on the Going-to-the-People propagandists and had ordered the arrest of thousands. Then came news of Trepov's order to have Bogoliubov beaten. As was usual in the case of scandalous acts of tsarist officials, there was much guarded talk in drawing rooms and on street corners condemning this latest outrage. For Vera Zasulich and Masha Kolenkina, it simply strengthened their decision to act. There was only one change in their plan: they substituted Trepov for Zhikharev.

The Trial of the 193 came to a close on January 23, 1878. That same evening Masha and Vera drew lots to determine who was to shoot whom. The next morning, after a night in which Vera was troubled by nightmares, the young women went out early into the streets of St. Petersburg, each armed for her bloody deed. While Vera succeeded in her mission, Masha did not. Even though she offered a generous bribe to the lackey at the door of Zhelekhovsky's office, she was turned away, and left without detection.

When Vera Zasulich left Russia, it lay heavily on her conscience that she had failed to make the supreme sacrifice she had intended—to give up her life for the crime she had deliberately committed. Her acquittal had returned her life to her, her burden was to use it well. Her inclinations were intellectual, bookish; her demeanor was modest, but she had an overwhelming passion—devotion to the revolution. She believed that only by overthrowing the autocracy would the Russian people achieve the general happiness and well-being that was their right and her goal. She had no well-thought-out political philosophy—only a thorough knowledge of the novels, poetry, and polemic tracts Russia's writers had produced to bemoan Russia's fate. She was acquainted with some of the works of a few European social philsophers, including Jean Jacques Rousseau and John Stuart Mill. Also, she had no plan of action.

However modest the real Zasulich was, the image of Zasulich the Terrorist loomed large across the horizon. Political murder was not new, and there were many examples of it in the nineteenth century. Lincoln was shot. Several attempts were made on the lives of Queen Victoria and Napoleon III. Vera Zasulich was often compared to Charlotte Corday, who killed Marat the French revolutionary leader. But Zasulich's shooting of Trepov was different. Her motive was different and the public reaction to her deed was different.

The assassin of a public figure is ordinarily a loner or part of a small conspiratorial group whose motive is to kill a hated tyrant or rival and who, once the deed is done, disappears from the scene. But Zasulich's motive, was not to kill a man, nor was it hatred of the man she shot. She was simply determined to shine the light of publicity on a system permeated with injustice. Her deed was done in the Russia of 1878, where the ignorance, corruption, cruelty, and abuse of power that existed on every level of society was well known, but because of the absence of freedom of speech, press, and assembly, went unchallenged. Fear of speaking out, of opposing authority was a tradition in Russia, and was perpetuated by the oppressive presence of the tsarist bureaucracy with its heavy arsenal of armed might aimed at any and all who might think of reforming or changing it. The success of her daring act in penetrating that armor, and the enthusiastic approval of the public, guaranteed it would have consequences of which Vera Zasulich never dreamed, and, as it turned out, strongly disapproved of.

Vera Zasulich did not act as a member of a conspiracy or a party, but she was a representative of a broad political movement of the best educated and dedicated Russian youth, the *narodniki,* who were at that moment seeking a more effective way than Going-to-the-People gradualism to change the tsarist system. Her shot at Trepov beamed out the potent message: Terrorism works! "A weapon no army, no police force, no legion of spies can stop," exulted Russia's radicals.[12] Zasulich's "propaganda of the deed" appeared to accomplish more in an instant to demoralize the tsarist government and

---

[12]A phrase from a pamphlet by the *Zemlya i Volya* terrorist advocate N. Morozov, quoted in O. V. Aptekman, *Zemlya i Volya,* Rostov-on-Don, 1907, p. 182.

arouse positive public opinion than had been achieved by years of "propaganda of the word," youth demonstrations, and the curses of countless victims tormented in penal servitude and exile. Vera Zasulich had begun the modern revolutionary tactic of political terrorism.

Beyond the circles of Russia's reform-minded youth, the general public reaction to Vera Zasulich revealed a characteristic of the Russian soul which had been demonstrated time and again in Russian history, and had played an important role in the rise of political terrorism there: veneration of the person who sacrifices everything, including his or her own life, not to redress a personal grievance, but for some higher purpose.[13] Ilya Repin, Russia's great realist painter, commenting on this characteristic, noted that in every Russian there is a strain of the heroic and a scorn of death—and the strength of this lies in not being afraid to die. When the one who demonstrated this kind of self-sacrifice was a young woman the veneration seemed to have no limits.

During the spring and the summer following Zasulich's shot at Trepov, one assassination or attempted assassination followed another as police officers were shot and stabbed when they attempted to arrest Zemlya i Volya activists for real or suspected criminal activity. The climax was the spectacular killing of General Mezentsev, the head of the Third Section (the secret police), in St. Petersburg as he walked with an aide on Mikhailovsky Square on the morning of August 4, 1878. He was stabbed by Zasulich's friend Sergei Kravchinsky. Kravchinsky jumped into the moving carriage of an accomplice and sped away, undetected, to a safe haven abroad. Timed for release the day of the murder, Kravchinsky's pamphlet "A Death For a Death" warned:

> For each political activist hanged by the government, a tsarist official will die.[14]

It was but a short step to transform the primitive concept of "A Death For a Death" into a full-fledged philosophy of revolution that made political terror a vital revolutionary tactic, and that transformation was not long in coming.

As more and more embittered veterans of Zemlya i Volya gradualism armed themselves with brass knuckles, guns, and knives, persuasive indi-

---

[13]Examples include Feodosia Morozova, a seventeenth century noblewoman who suffered torture, exile and death because she refused to accept changes in religious ritual imposed by the Tsar, and the Decembrist Women who in the early nineteenth century sacrificed everything when, in support of their revolutionary husbands, they joined them in prison and exile in Siberia. These women have remained heroines to the Russian people.

[14]The death Kravchinsky avenged was that of a Zemlya i Volya printer named Kovalski who was arrested, court-martialed and hanged in Odessa on July 1878. Kovalski's crime: operating a secret printing press and resisting arrest.

viduals began a push for a switch in revolutionary methods and aims. They said, in effect:

> Too long and with too little success have we worked for the goal of social revolution from below, for a people's uprising to achieve peasant commune socialism. We have learned from our experience that social change is impossible under the tsarist system. Let us change our goal to political revolution, to the overthrow of the tsarist regime. Concentrate revolutionary activity in St. Petersburg (and other cities) and use organized terror against tsarist officials, including the Tsar himself. Terror will weaken the government by eliminating key figures who are running it, demonstrate to "the people" that the autocracy is vulnerable, and encourage wide popular support for the political party of the individuals who sacrifice themselves for our goal of freedom.

"It is *narodnaya volya*,[15] the people's will!" the terror advocates said. They called those who wanted to stick to Going-to-the People gradualism *Derevenshchiki,* or Villagers.

Zemlya i Volya leaders, threatened with a split in their pitifully small ranks (thinned out by constant arrests, hangings, and exiling), called a conference in an attempt to heal the breach. One by one in June 1879 they filtered into the resort town of Voronezh. In their summer clothes and straw hats, carrying parasols and picnic baskets as if going on a summer outing, they rowed in small boats to an island in the Voronezh River where they argued and debated. The enthusiasm of the terrorist faction, with its plans for action, headed by a plan to kill Tsar Aleksandr II, frightened and excited and won support among even dedicated Villagers.

A staunch opponent of terrorist action was Vera Zasulich's friend George Plekhanov, famous as the red-bearded orator who had electrified the demonstrators on Kazan Square in 1876. He had become an active agitator among factory workers and was editor of *Zemlya i Volya* publications. George Plekhanov vigorously opposed the shift to political revolution:

> You cannot create a parliament at the point of a gun! Revolutions are not created by terrorists. Revolutions are the business of the masses. History creates the conditions for revolution, not a handful of terrorists.

Plekhanov's arrogance and unwillingness to compromise when the *Narodnaya Volya* leaders said they would continue to provide funds for propaganda among "the people," combined with the excitement generated by the *Narodnaya Volya* program, caused his Villager comrades to desert him. In an angry mood Plekhanov abruptly left the conference.

In the meantime, in Switzerland, Vera Zasulich's connection with Russia's revolutionary movement was revived when Lev Deich, just escaped

---

[15]*Volya* also means freedom, thus enriching the term *narodnaya volya.*

from prison in Kiev, and IA. V. Stefanovich, a former Kiev *Buntari* comrade, arrived in Geneva. Trying to adjust to a new life in an alien land but still tied to events in Russia, they argued about the increase of terrorism in their homeland. Vera expressed concern because each terrorist act, including her own, led to heavy government retaliation and the loss of revolutionists to prison, exile, and the noose. She still believed that in Russia where there was no legal way to control corrupt and cruel officials, terror had to be used as a defense weapon. But she saw that a revolutionary party concentrating its resources and energy on terror would become an elite organization separated from the workers and peasants. To her a true revolution would occur only when an informed people was sufficiently aroused to rise in rebellion.

Zasulich, Deich, and Stefanovich decided to risk arrest by sneaking back into Russia to support Plekhanov and attempt to restore *Zemlya i Volya* gradualism. Arming themselves with false passports and disguises, they arrived in St. Petersburg in the summer of 1879 where most of the Voronezh delegates had reassembled and the debates were continuing. A few villagers came over to the side of Zasulich (whose prestige was high in revolutionary circles), Plekhanov, Deich, and Stefanovich, but the result was to split, not unite, *Zemlya i Volya*. Two parties emerged: *Narodnaya Volya* (the People's Will), and the Villager party which called itself *Cherny Peredel* (Black [soil] Repartition).

Cherny Peredel had little support and inadequate funds because it was shortchanged in the division of *Zemlya i Volya* resources. Apprehensive because of heavy police surveillance, its leaders voted in January 1880 to send Plekhanov, Zasulich, Deich, and Stefanovich abroad until calmer times prevailed in Russia. They departed just in time, for within hours the police confiscated their printing press and arrested almost every member of the party remaining in Russia.

Narodnaya Volya, with its vigorous leadership and positive program of action, attracted youthful volunteers, gained notoriety and financial support, and went from one spectacular assassination to another—climaxed by the killing of Tsar Aleksandr II on March 1, 1881. Lev Deich said that despite their opposition to this kind of terror, he and Vera were so excited by the assassination of the Tsar that only lack of funds prevented them from returning to Russia and joining what at first appeared to be the triumphant finale of "the people's" struggle to end tsarist autocracy.[16] Even the most skeptical, Deich said, believed the new Tsar Aleksandr III would have to grant a constitution. But they were wrong. A regime of massive repression was launched by the new Tsar which transformed Russia into a prototype of the modern police state and within a few years succeeded in destroying

---

[16]Stefanovich did go back to Russia at this time and joined *Narodnaya Volya*.

the *Narodnaya Volya* Party organization in Russia, even though scattered groups of adherents to the cause managed to survive.

One result of the repression was that for more than a decade the Russian emigrés in Europe were almost completely cut off from their homeland. Crossing the border became almost impossible and the smuggling of illegal literature became more and more difficult.

The question was, what were the young 1880 emigrés like Zasulich, Deich, Stefanovich, and later Axelrod and a few others, who in Russia had been "revolutionary disorganizers," and Plekhanov, a spellbinding soapbox orator, going to do as emigrés in Switzerland? Funds from their families in Russia and collections from Russia's radical groups came infrequently. The new emigrés were ill-prepared to earn a living and were virtually penniless. As for political conviction, they had a burning desire to save Russia, but had experienced the failure of their agrarian socialist theories to gain much support among peasants and workers. They witnessed students and intellectuals as well as soldiers, sailors, and even workers swelling the ranks of the *Narodnaya Volya*—then it too was destroyed.

Arriving in Geneva in January 1880, settling into cheap, sparsely furnished rooms, with almost no money to buy food, or wood or coal for their stoves, they went to the public library during the day and spent their evenings in a tavern. When the Russians came into the library, the good-natured librarian gave up trying to keep order. And she never succeeded in collecting from them the small fee that was supposed to be paid by readers for heat, lights, replacement of lost books, and new purchases.

In the Café Armand, huddled near the stove, they read the newspapers including the Russian *Obshchina* (Society), a Bakunist paper, and Peter Kropotkin's anarchist *L'Avantgarde*. They drank countless glasses of tea with heaping spoonfuls of sugar and carried on hot political discussions until dawn

Vera Zasulich had become a chain smoker, rolling her own cigarettes. As she talked, wildly gesticulating, she scattered ashes over her blouse, her companions, and into her glass of tea. The *Narodniki*, she said, had been aware only of the injustices of the tsarist system, and setting out to correct them had won moral victory after moral victory over despotism but had not succeeded in changing it nor the lives of the Russian people. Their ideological base was inadequate, she concluded. What the revolution needed was a revolutionary theory based on an understanding of the economic and social forces of Russia. The revolution also needed consistent workers—not heroes seeking danger for danger's sake in their effort to further the cause of freedom.

Plekhanov's dedication to village commune socialism was also weakening. He had begun to reread Marx whose ideas he had rejected when he first encountered the Russian translation of *Das Kapital* in 1872. Winding up his efforts to edit a *Cherny Peredel* periodical, he urged his comrades to read and discuss the ideas of Marx and Engels.

The French tavern-keeper, Madam Gresso, widow of a French Communard, was a frugal woman, but she was kind-hearted and extended credit to the young Russians. Once in a while, one of them would have an article accepted by a journal for pay—then there would be a triumphal celebration. The tavern proprietor would be paid and they would have a rare real meal. Emerging from the café in the wee hours of the morning into the quiet streets of Geneva, they were usually singing Russian songs—a performance not appreciated by the stiff Genevans.

The emigrés sometimes attended Genevan socialist meetings. On one occasion the chairman looked at the Russians, sitting in a group, and said:

> Do you speak French? To speak at our meetings you must speak in French. So what do you want to say?

Vera Zasulich spoke French fluently, but, voluble as she was in private conversation, she was so bashful that in a public meeting she rarely uttered a word. Deich, who did not know French, got up, was recognized and said:

> Le Bourgeois fi, fi, fi, mais le proletaires O, O, O!

He sat down. All the Russians clapped.

Urged on by Plekhanov, who in emigration was becoming a scholar, his comrades were coming more and more under the influence of Marx. They were excited by the Marxist idea of the inevitability of revolution, the economic imperative that would with the development of capitalism force a bourgeois overthrow of the semi-feudal Russian autocracy and set the stage for the emergence of a revolutionary proletariat. This action would, in its turn, end bourgeois capitalism and usher in their long-hoped-for socialist society. It was as if a light had been turned on. Out of despair—new hope!

Zazulich, Plekhanov, and Axelrod concentrated their efforts on adapting Marxist theory to Russian conditions, which was not easy. Marx had based his ideas on developments in the most highly industrialized societies of his day, England and Germany, while Russia was one of the least industrialized states in Europe. But the new Marxists, ignoring their extreme poverty, their malnutrition, overwork, insufficient sleep, and frequent illnesses, turned out a steady stream of articles they submitted to European Marxist periodicals and printed in the short-lived Russian journals they themselves edited and published whenever they could scrape together a few hundred francs.

By 1882 they were confirmed Marxists, and the next year Zasulich, Plekhanov, Deich, and Axelrod formed the first Russian Marxist political organization, the Group for the Emancipation of Labor. Plekhanov, a brilliant dialectician, often called the "Father of Russian Marxism," was the leading theorist in the Emancipation of Labor Group, but he and the other emigrés were completely unknown. European Marxists poured scorn on their initial dialectical efforts. As Marx himself put it, these gentlemen are preparing for the leap into communism "by means of the dullest of dull doctrinaire views."

One member of the Emancipation of Labor Group was known every-where—Versa Zasulich! But she shunned fame, and was reluctant to write the letter her friends wanted her to write Marx. Finally she did it and received an immediate reply from Friedrich Engels, who addressed her as "dear heroic citizen" and, saying Marx was ill and would write to her later [which he did], went on to answer her question concerning the development of capitalism in Russia. So it was discovered when Vera Zasulich wrote to the socialist leaders of Western Europe, they were impressed; they took pains to answer her queries and engage in doctrinal discussions. That Vera Zasulich was one of them gave the early Russian Marxists a prestige they otherwise would not have had. Marx died soon after the beginning of the exchange of letters, but Zasulich continued to correspond with Engels. She translated some of his works from German into Russian and finally, at an international socialist congress in Zurich in 1890, she met him. Engels was charmed by Zasulich, and later, when she lived in London in the 1890s, she visited him often. They conversed (and corresponded) in French.

The financial state of the Emancipation of Labor Group was always precarious. There was never quite enough money to get an article or an issue of a journal printed, not to mention pay the rent and buy food. Deich, Axelrod, and Plekhanov knew that if the famous Zasulich would go to Paris and present their case to a few people, she could easily raise the small sums they needed. Modest and proud, she steadfastly refused to do it, though at last in 1883 Deich said in a letter to Axelrod, "If we don't get the two-hundred francs we need, she will surely go." But, he said later, she did not go.

Lev Deich masterminded the smuggling of Emancipation of Labor publications into Russia and kept up a few contacts between the handful of Marxist emigrés and the small, scattered radical groups of the underground. An unforeseen set of circumstances led to Deich's arrest and imprisonment in Germany in 1885 while he was making arrangements to smuggle yet another batch of illegal literature across the border to Russia. He had escaped from prison before and Zasulich was confident he could do it again. She managed to get a file and a supply of banknotes into his cell, but before he could use them he was extradited to Russia. Zasulich was frantic. Then she found out Melitina Visconti, a Russian student at the University of Geneva, was going home for a visit. Vera asked her to take a message to her lawyer Aleksandrov, asking him to defend Deich. Melitina carried out her mission, but before Aleksandrov could see him, Deich was transferred from the Peter Paul Fortress Prison to Odessa. Aleksandrov went to Odessa and took part in the trial, but Deich was brought before a military tribunal and sentenced to the Siberian *katorga* for thirteen years and indefinite exile after that. Heartbroken, and unable to think of any way to free Deich, Zasulich was in a state of deep depression for months and, some of her friends said, close to suicide. Deich and Zasulich wrote long letters to each other but she did not see him until he escaped from Siberia and returned to Europe, via Japan and the United States, in 1901.

Unlike the male members of the Emancipation of Labor Group who had families, Zasulich led a lonely existence after Deich's imprisonment. Depending on the Russian emigré Marxists as a surrogate family, she devoted all her bodily and intellectual strength to the Marxist cause. In a letter to Deich early in 1890 she said:

> Dear Brother.[17] I am living in this village in the Haute Savoie, France, where there is not a single Russian nor any of my French acquaintances. I have a tiny room exactly like the ones I usually rent in Geneva, an iron stove, great disorder, and all the rest, as always. I get up late, around ten, or eleven sometimes. I immediately brew coffee, very strong, with sugar if possible. I drink it then throw myself into my writing, stopping from time to time (whenever I'm having trouble) to roll a cigarette and pace around the room. I do this until 4 or 5 in the afternoon. Then I either go nearby for provisions, or, if there is anything remaining from the evening before, I'll cook a steak, eat, and lie down with a book for an hour—or longer, if I get carried away. After that I do not write. I think, rethink, correct, and rewrite. There's tea on the stove, and from time to time I sip some. At nine I have coffee again, and work until 2 A.M. Then I lie down with a book. . . .
>
> I don't talk with anyone for months on end (or only to myself, in whispers) except in shops to say "Give me a pound of this or that," or "Bonjour, madame." However, one visitor comes to me every day, and I always say a word or two to him. He is a big, shaggy, brown dog named Turk. He always knows when I have meat and invariably appears every half hour and holds up his paws until I give him a piece.
>
> I go to Geneva once a month. I go oftener if necessary. In Geneva I see George [Plekhanov] and we talk over articles and books. . . . So that is my life. I do not read the newspapers. I do not think about myself. What do I think about? Books and articles? Yes, much about them, both written and unwritten. And I hope you will read somewhere those that are published. You live with people, and I am very much interested in them, but I am in solitary confinement. I will try to write more often. With hearty kisses, your sister Sasha.

Zasulich was the devoted disciple and faithful collaborator of Plekhanov. For years when they lived in Geneva, or just across the border in France,

---

[17]In their letters Deich and Zasulich addressed each other as "Brother" and "Sister." She often signed her letters "Sasha," which, interestingly enough, was the diminutive of her sister Aleksandra Uspenskaya. In conversation Zasulich usually referred to Lev Deich as "Evgeny," one of his pseudonyms she seemed to like.

not a day passed that they did not confer together on ideas, theories, and plans. Under his tutelage she sharpened her polemic skills. Her articles on Marxism, her translations into Russian of Marxist and socialist literature in other languages, and her long reviews of current books appeared in issue after issue of Russian emigré journals (some of which she edited), as well as in German, French, and English Marxist publications.

Zasulich's respect for Plekhanov's mind did not prevent her from seeing and having to cope with the peculiarities of his personality. His rigid "scientific" structuring of Russian Marxist theory led him into pedantic abstractions far removed from reality, and his arrogant self-assurance that he, and he alone, had marked out the true path to revolution resulted in bitter quarrels with his fellow emigrés, who had their own ideas about Marxist "truth." Zasulich was constantly trying to patch up quarrels. Cajoling, flattering, soothing inflamed egos, toning down sharply worded letters and articles, she usually got the prima donnas to shake hands and make up.

She even took care of their bodily ills. In 1885, when Plekhanov had pneumonia and still had not recovered, the Swiss government, accusing him erroneously of being an anarchist, ordered his deportation. Leaving his wife and children in Geneva,[18] he and Zasulich went to France, where she nursed him back to health. She had to do monotonous copy work for a few francs a day to pay for his food and medicine, while neglecting herself. By the time she got back to Switzerland, she came down with pneumonia.

In her articles Zasulich often superimposed her own moral imperative on the rigid Marxist economic imperative. The result was a generally looser interpretation of Marx than that of Plekhanov and Axelrod. To her the revolution was not simply the dialectic of history decreeing inevitable class struggle; it was the path to freedom and well-being for the Russian people. It was the opportunity, through the solidarity of cooperative action (a Marxist political party), to free the people from the harsh reality of their economic exploitation and to emancipate their souls for the achievement for each person of the "highest value of life."

Aware of the potency of ideas, Zasulich could not accept the Marxist "law" that every social and political development is pinned to a specific economic change, causing a whole class to think in a certain way. In Rus-

---

[18]Rosaliya Markovna Bograd, with whom Plekhanov had been living before leaving Russia, did not accompany him to Switzerland in January 1880. She was pregnant and, completing her medical training, wanted to take the final exams and leave Russia as a licensed physician. She took the exams but when an investigation turned up the fact that she had been living with a wanted man, the medical school refused to give her a passing grade. She left Russia, joined Plekhanov, and by 1885 they had three children. In an attempt to ease their financial straits, Rosaliya resumed her medical studies in Geneva, passed the exams, and began to practice medicine about 1890. She and Plekhanov married in 1908, after he finally obtained a divorce from the woman he had married in 1876.

sia, though capitalist development was taking place, she saw no evidence and no possibility of class struggle between the bourgeoisie and the autocracy (which, according to Marx, must occur) because the two were tied together by a network of mutual economic relationships. And, looking realistically at the growing but still tiny Russian proletariat, she concluded the working class was neither inherently socialist nor revolutionary. Instead of class warfare, Russian Marxists should seek cooperation among groups opposing tyranny.

Axelrod and Plekhanov, concerned about Zasulich's expression of such "unscientific" ideas in print, decided to advise her to avoid writing articles involving Marxist theory. In a "Dear Vera" letter written in 1888, Axelrod subjected a manuscript she had sent him to severe criticism and concluded by urging her in the future

> to select subjects of a historical or descriptive nature; in a word, themes for which abstract thought, broad empirical knowledge, and the ability to use logical methods of developing ideas are not needed.[19]

If Axelrod and Plekhanov were the self-acknowledged theorists qualified to interpret Marxism scientifically in Russian terms, Zasulich, and later Lenin, were the practical realists, willing to use Marxism as a not necessarily scientific means to an end. Reading the "qualified interpreters" today is an exercise in dull irrelevance; Zasulich, however, who tempered Marxist theory with common sense, moral judgment, and shrewd observation of things as she saw them, reads like a prophet who had her finger on the pulse of time.

In 1894 Tsar Aleksandr III died in his bed. The new Tsar, Nikolai II, like his father, ignored the need for reform and concentrated on destroying all those attempting to work for it. The government, pushing for rapid industrial development and railroad building—financed by foreign loans—sought to raise funds by taxing more heavily the already over-taxed peasants, by increasing grain exports, and by keeping workers' wages low and their hours long. There was peasant and worker unrest; in general, the condition of the people became worse,. However, under the new Tsar, who lacked his father's iron will, the police-state atmosphere lightened somewhat and revolutionary activity stirred again in Russia.

Vera Zasulich, with her intuitive understanding of Russia and Russians, sensed the rising revolutionary spirit. Dismayed at her emigré comrades, for whom Marxism had become more a literary exercise than a revolutionary cause, she urged them to act, to create ties with the Marxist groups proliferating in Russia, and to bring into the fold the new crop of Russian revolu-

---

[19]P. B. Axelrod-V. I. Zasulich in *Literaturnoye Naslediye*, vol. 1, part 3. no. 4, pp. 234–36.

tionary emigrés arriving in Western Europe in large numbers in the late 1890s.

Both inside Russia, where small Marxist groups had appeared in a few cities, and in Europe, among the Russian Marxist emigrés, there was a push to form a Social Democratic political party. In Russia in March 1898, what was called the First Congress of the All Russian Social Democratic (labor) party was held in Minsk (most of the delegates were immediately arrested). Later in the same year the Russian emigrés in Switzerland, by then calling themselves the Union of Social Democrats, held their First Congress. A war of the printed word between the two new political parties soon got under way, as personality conflicts and doctrinal differences flared and appeared to threaten any prospect for harmony or unity.

Determined to patch up these differences, Vera Zasulich decided to go to Russia. With the new generation of Russian revolutionaries, her fame once again came into play. Although she had lived in exile for more than two decades, she was not forgotten in Russia. Members of the generation growing up in the 1890s and early 1900s remembered how as children they had listened wide-eyed to the tales their elders told about the revolutionary heroine Vera Zasulich, who had shot a cruel and corrupt official. Later, as gymnazium (high school) students, they read about her in stealthily circulated illegal books, such as Stepniak's (Kravchinsky) *Podpol'naia Rossiia* (Underground Russia). And they eagerly awaited the monthly arrival from abroad of forbidden Russian Marxist journals, published by the Emancipation of Labor group, which often contained articles by Vera Zasulich. One of this new generation wrote:

> The image of Vera Zasulich was for us, the youth, a living lesson in heroism. Every time we thought of her or discussed our reading of her articles, involuntarily we were transformed spiritually and morally, thanks only to our contact with the world of her ideas.[20]

Disregarding the fact that there had never been a revocation of the order for her arrest, issued by Aleksandr II in 1878, Vera Zasulich obtained an illegal passport in the name of Velika Dimitrievna Kirova and secretly arrived in St. Petersburg in December 1899. The excuse she gave for making the trip—"I must take a look at the muzhik (peasant) and see what his nose has grown like"[21]—proved her years of exile had not diluted her "Russianness" nor dimmed her *Buntari* days sense of humor.

---

[20]L. S. Fyedorenko [N. Charov], "Vera Zasulich," *Katorga i Ssylka,* no. 2 (23), Moscow, 1926, pp. 197–205.

[21]As Vladimir Nabokov put it in his book *Nikolai Gogol* (Norfolk, 1944, pp. 4–5), Russians are acutely nose-conscious. To them the nose is a funny thing and there are hundreds of proverbs and other sayings that revolve around the nose, not to mention Gogol's famous story *The Nose,* a veritable hymn to that organ.

One of the new Russian Marxists Vera met in St. Petersburg was Lenin, who had recently returned from Siberian exile and was soon to leave for Europe. An important outcome of this meeting was their decision to establish an emigré journal to serve as a unifying and organizational agent for all the Russian Social Democratic groups inside and outside Russia. That journal was the famous *Iskra*—its motto: "The Spark (*iskra*) That Lights the Flame." Of the six editors Vera did most of the work and loved it, because through *Iskra* she felt close to Russia again. Like several others of the old Emancipation of Labor Group, including Plekhanov, she fell under the spell of Lenin's dynamism. She hoped his concentration on organizing a framework for revolution would move the new Russian Social Democratic party into an active role in the revolution she felt was imminent.

Work on *Iskra* took Zasulich first to Munich, then to London, where she lived for several years with two young emigrés, Martov and Alekseev,[22] also editors of *Iskra*, and with various comrades who came and went, including Trotsky. Lenin once described this London commune as more than a house with open windows; it was a public thoroughfare through which everyone marched night and day. Martov could simultaneously write, smoke, eat, and converse continously with up to a dozen people. The big room on the first floor of the house, where they all gathered to smoke and talk, was in an eternal clutter. Zasulich won over all the new crop of Russian emigrés with her simplicity and friendliness and her willingness to discuss everything from the German Social Democrats and her ideas of the role of the Russian "liberals" in the revolution to "what it was really like" in the legendary days of the 1870s. When Nikolai Volsky said to her that he found Chernyshevsky's *What's To Be Done?* a dreary, tedious, and feeble book and could not understand how her generation could have been so inspired by it, her response was to first make sure he had really read the book. When he assured her he had, she shook her head and said:

> You don't understand it, you just don't understand it, and it's difficult for you to understand. Chernyshevsky was hampered by censorship and he had to write in allusions and hieroglyphs. We were able to decipher them, but you, the young people of the 1900s, don't have this knack. You read a passage in Chernyshevsky and you find it dull and empty, but in fact there is a great

---

[22]Iuli Martov, a Marxist in the 1890s and an early, close associate of Lenin, became a Menshevik in 1903 and continued as a Menshevik leader through the October Revolution. Exiled in 1920, he died in Berlin in 1923. Nikolai Alekseev was a medical student active in the revolutionary movement in the 1890s; arrested in 1898, he escaped, emigrated, and lived from 1900 to 1903 in London. He worked on *Iskra*, served in World War I as a doctor, participated as a Bolshevik in the 1917 Revolution, and served all the rest of his life as a Communist functionary.

revolutionary idea concealed in it. . . . There circulated for a long time a sort of key for clear understanding of things he was compelled to put only in a very veiled and opaque form. Today, you haven't got such a key and without it, you can't know Chernyshevsky.

Then Zasulich went on patiently giving Volsky examples of how "the key" opened up Chernyshevsky's obscure and confusing sentences.

The London Commune members took turns preparing dinner, and Krupskaya (Lenin's wife) said Vera rose to this new challenge by becoming a good housewife, carefully purchasing provisions when it came her turn to cook. Vera said once some English ladies came to call and, apparently searching for a subject of conversation, asked her how she cooked meat. She replied, "If I'm hungry I cook it ten minutes; if I'm not hungry about three hours." The ladies soon left and Vera did not see them again.

Zasulich never got over the old days of starving in Geneva, and as an "old lady" (of over fifty) she lived, ate, and dressed like a poor student. Trotsky said when they ate in a restaurant and she covered the thinnest slice of ham with a thick layer of mustard (a condiment she loved), they would say "Vera Ivanovna is feasting!"[23]

Lev Deich's return in 1901, as Vera headed into the most frustrating part of her life, may not have helped her failing health. Nevertheless, in the days of increasing political controversy when Lenin, the rising star in the Russian Social Democratic party, as well as her old friend Plekhanov, turned against her for a brief time, she could count on Deich's unwavering support inside and outside the crowded, smoke-filled rooms where the decisions often were made.

A second Social Democratic Party Congress began to be discussed; its major task would be reaching agreement on a party program. Being used as a basis for discussion was a draft program drawn up years before by Plekhanov. One item in this draft was the acceptance in principle of terrorist acts as a method of struggle against absolutism. Also, in Russia, another new political party, the Socialist Revolutionaries, who called themselves the heirs of the *Narodniki,* had adopted terror as a revolutionary tactic. Faced with the threat of a renewed outbreak of political terrorism, Vera Zasulich wrote an article, "Po Povodu Sovremennykh Sobytyi" (About Current Events), published in the April 1901 issue of *Iskra.* Breaking the unwritten rule of anonymity, she signed it with her own name to let the world know

---

[23]Sources for these details of Zasulich as the intellectual mentor and "mother confessor" of the London household of the *Iskra* staff, and as the in-fighter for her moral concepts in party councils appear in Nadezhda Krupskaya (Lenin's wife), *Memories of Lenin,* London, 1936; Leon Trotsky, *Lenin, Notes for a Biographer,* New York, 1971; Nikolai Valentinov (N. V. Volsky), *Encounters with Lenin,* London, 1968.

that the woman who started political terrorism nearly a quarter of a century earlier now condemned it in the strongest terms. She argued:

> Terror does not stimulate broad political activity, but in fact stifles it by exhausting society's energy as it rivets almost hypnotic concentration on terror itself.

> In the 1870s, when the Russian people were slaves with no means to combat injustice, terror was the only available way to call public attention to crimes committed by tsarist officials.

> It is true that the terrorist act excites the thirst for freedom that is so strong in Russian society. But it is a passive excitement. It is complaisant—something like the aesthetic appreciation of a theatrical performance.

> Some liberals shed sentimental tears over the heroic terrorist, but it never whetted their thirst for getting into political action. Between the liberal sympathizers and the terrorist there is a great gulf.

> As a matter of fact, only very few experienced people, exceptional for their energy, fearlessness, and conspiratorial skills, can be terrorists. But the terrorist deed makes such a strong impression the political party committed to it begins to see all other matters as trifles and by concentrating its energy on the acts of a handful of terrorist heroes reduces the supporters of freedom to impotence. All that is required of them is from time to time to cry out "Hurrah, Hurrah."

In addition to denouncing political terror for its ineffectiveness as a revolutionary tactic and proclaiming the actual harm "elitism" does by narrowing the revolutionary cause, Zasulich examined the moral problem of terror. She cited the conversation in Dostoyevski's *Brothers Karamazov* when Ivan asks Alyosha, "If all the people could be made happy and given peace at last by torturing to death only one small child, would you consent to do it?" Alyosha said no, he could not do it. Ivan continued, "And the people whose happiness would be assured by the sacrifice of this little victim, would they agree to it? Which one of them would kill the child?"

Obviously drawing on memory of her own assassination attempt and the experience of others she knew among the 1870s terrorists who had killed, she wrote:

> The terrorist hero is much admired in Russia, but to him alone falls the doing of the deed, the risk, and all the consequent suffering. Fortunate are the ones who are quickly executed. They escape the pangs of conscience. They escape the horrors of imprisonment, the years of solitary confinement and the executions of their comrades they must witness in prisons like Schlisselburg.

> Now, if there are those who still want to resume terror, let them ask themselves: What will they do in the time of terror? And how will they, during that time, pay for it?

The obvious answers to these questions were that they would do nothing, and they would not pay anything for it.

Zasulich saw Russia at the turn of the century as quite different from Russia in the 1860s and 1870s.

> Today the Russian people's desire for freedom is so great there is no cause for despair. No longer are the Russian people sunk in the kind of slavish existence they endured in the 1870s. Rising literacy, the increasing number of teachers, and reading rooms and libraries mean more people can read party manifestos and literature, more people can organize and struggle for necessary changes without the harmful stimulus of terrorist deeds. What is needed now is for all supporters of freedom, all enemies of the whip to understand that victory over autocracy is within their grasp.

The item on terror was dropped from the draft program of the Russian Social Democratic party.

But had Vera Zasulich abandoned, once and for all, the use of terror? A little more than a year after publication of the April 1901 article, what do we see in *Iskra* (no. 22, July 1902)? A story calling for a hero to take up the sword in behalf of the workers of Vilna, who were whipped on the order of Governor Val when they tried to demonstrate on May 1. May 1! The day of international worker demonstrations! In every city of Europe, workers marched through the streets carrying red banners, singing the "Internationale." But not in Russia, where the crack of the whip was still to be heard: flogging, a punishment devised for slaves.

> The police savagery carried out against the participants in the May Day demonstrations thunders for vengeance. . . . Not one class-conscious proletarian, not one sincere friend of the Russian proletariat has the right to be calm at this time, or to act as if nothing had happened.

And she quoted a poem:

> When nothing can help, then for him
> Remains only his sharp sword!

She concluded: "A selfless person could, on his own, decide to direct several bullets into Vilna's Upper Chamber! Eternal remembrance to the hero!"

The Second Congress of the new Russian Social Democratic party held in Brussels in 1903 witnessed Lenin's tactic of splitting the party and emerging as the leader of what he called the "Bolshevik" faction.[24] This was a

---

[24]The word *Bolshevik*, derived from *bolshe*, meaning "larger" or "majority," was chosen by Lenin for effect, since the "majority" vote he got in one balloting at the congress was a manipulated one and his opponents actually outnumbered his supporters. Lenin called his opponents *Mensheviks*, a word derived from *menshe* meaning "smaller" or "minority." A serious mistake his opponents made was to accept this designation.

split over the issue of party organization that Vera Zasulich could not patch up, nor could she as a party leader arouse support for her cause in debate at the Congress. An incoherent speaker, she would never bring even that small gathering to its feet yelling "Bravo!" In order for her to say anything in a public meeting she had to be worked up to a fever pitch, then paying no attention to formal procedure, she would get up all aflame, interrupt whoever had the floor, disregard the chairman, and hold forth. Her words were always original, her conclusions prophetic and she was often right— but seldom effective.

Zasulich's metier was the written word. In an article in *Iskra* (July 25, 1904) she said there had been no serious differences among the party members at the Congress. The split occurred because of Lenin's lust for power. Disregarding the existing party he simply created one of his own. She wrote:

> The party for Lenin—this is his plan—is the imposition of his will. It is not new, it is the idea of Louis XIV: *L'etat c'est moi*. Lenin's version is: The party it is I, Lenin.

She also criticized Lenin's interpretation of Marx in his 1902 pamphlet *What's To Be Done?* which, she said, opened up the possibility of revolution by coup d'etat instead of a true worker's revolution and was a violation of the Marxian premise that a bourgeois revolution must precede a proletarian revolution. Lenin's premature revolution could lead only to a permanent dictatorship by an elite over the masses.

In the seesaw battle for control of the Social Democratic party organization which came out into the open at the Second Congress, first Lenin was on top, and removed Zasulich and the "old" Marxists from the editorial board of *Iskra*. He observed that in the past she "may have saved Rome, but now she is not pulling her weight." Lenin could not stand intellectuals like her who wanted to drown the party in "moralizing vomit." In fact, he could not stand women, unless, like Krupskaya (his wife) and Inessa Armand (his alleged mistress), they spoke or wrote words he prepared for them.[25]

Soon, Lenin's opponents, whom he called "Mensheviks," won out and Vera was back editing *Iskra*, but this paper was shortly replaced by other journals and ceased publication. The Bolshevik-Menshevik split of the Russian Social Democratic party was not a clean break. Efforts to reunite the

---

[25] A surviving and amusing example of Lenin's patriarchal "instruction" of Inessa Armand appears in two letters he wrote to her, minutely criticizing the draft she had sent him of a pamphlet she was writing in 1915 for the working women of Russia. He reserved special and lengthy criticism of her treatment of the topic "free love." It is not surprising that Armand never completed the pamphlet. Versions of these two letters appear in a Soviet pamphlet, *V. I. Lenin on the Emancipation of Women*, Moscow, 1965.

two parts continued, but the disarray in the party's leadership left it unprepared for effective action in the Revolution of 1905. Among the Social Democratic leaders, Zasulich alone had been predicting revolution was near. Instead of the milestone toward the socialist revolution it could have been, the Revolution of 1905 was for the Social Democratic party a disaster of lost opportunities. It left the party in shambles for a decade.

Suffering from a lung ailment diagnosed as tuberculosis, Zasulich, with Deich, came back to Russia in 1905. Deich was soon arrested as an escapee from Siberian exile and without a trial was resentenced. He escaped en route to Siberia and spent the years until the 1917 Revolution in various European countries and in the United States.

Vera Zasulich continued to live a quiet life in St. Petersburg where she worked to support herself by translating French and English literature into Russian. Unable to exert her peacemaking talents on the Social Democratic leaders who had reduced the party to impotence by their factional fights, and plagued by ill health, Zasulich had practically retired from politics. She was provoked to action by attacks, first by Plekhanov, then by Lenin, on several of her closest colleagues who were advocating liquidation of the conspirational arm of the Social Democratic party, a move she had long favored. The conspirational apparatus created by Lenin was used for "expropriations" (mainly train and bank robberies) which kept the party in funds, and even though the party platform disavowed terrorism, it secretly cooperated with the Socialist Revolutionaries in political assassinations.

Zasulich wrote a series of articles in 1913 arguing the time had come for the Social Democratic party to abandon or liquidate its underground apparatus and its elitism. It should become a mass party of workers like those in every country of Western Europe.[26]

The battle over "liquidationism" had not ended when fast-moving events in the third disastrous year of Russia's participation in World War I led to revolution. Tsar Nikolai II was forced to abdicate in February 1917. Vera Zasulich welcomed what appeared to be the end of autocracy and the first step toward what she saw as a still far distant goal of the triumph of socialism.

No one was more aware than Zasulich that the Russian Social Democrats were not a mass party, and that the party's leadership, except for Lenin, was ineffective. That Lenin would try to take over the government of Russia, the way he had tried (and not succeeded) to take over the Social Democratic party, Zasulich might have suspected. That he would succeed was beyond her comprehension.

---

[26]Jay Bergman discusses this controversy in his article "The Political Thought of Vera Zasulich," *Slavic Review*, June 1979, and gives exact references to her articles and those attacking her, written by Lenin and Plekhanov.

Two months after the October Revolution which put the Bolsheviks in power (in the kind of coup d'état she had warned more than a decade earlier was Lenin's aim), Vera Zasulich wrote an attack on the new regime "Sotsialism Smolnogo" (The Socialism of Smolny), published in February 1918, in issue no. 4 of *Nasha Zhizn*. She branded the "men of Smolny" (Smolny Institute was Lenin's headquarters until March 1918 when the seat of government was moved to Moscow), that is, Lenin and his associates, as usurpers who had saddled Russia with an unbridled tyranny, had resorted to mass terror, had destroyed all freedom, and with senseless orders and restrictions thrown Russia into veritable chaos. All citizens who value freedom, she bitterly observed, have reason to oppose the new autocracy, but socialists most of all.

> At this moment there are no more ruthless enemies of socialism than the men of Smolny. They are not capable of converting capitalist into socialist production. They will only destroy productive industry. . . . Everything the hand of Smolny touches will be ruined.

The ruin of Russian industry would also ruin the proletariat, leaving the Red Guard as the only supporters of the regime.

> What kind of socialism is this? It is not socialism, it is the ruin of socialism. And not in Russia only. Our ruin will lead to the dawn of militarism in the whole world, which pushes into the misty distance any possibility of socialism.

In the spring of 1917 George Plekhanov had been greeted at the Finland Station as a hero when he returned to Petrograd (as St. Petersburg began to be called during World War I) after thirty-seven years in exile. Old and unwell, he soon found the fast-moving events quite incomprehensible. He attended a conference in Moscow in the late summer of 1917 where he felt he had been cast aside and abandoned, like old Firs at the end of Chekhov's play *The Cherry Orchard*. Plekhanov asked his host if he could take him up to the Sparrow Hills. He remembered it was there, high above Moscow, that the young Herzen and his friend Ogarev took a solemn oath, swearing to dedicate their lives to avenging the Decembrist martyrs who had suffered exile, imprisonment, and death at the hands of Tsar Nikolai I for their daring demonstration for constitutional rights on Senate Square in St. Petersburg on December 14, 1825.

Several days later, Plekhanov with a few friends he invited, including Vera Zasulich (who had recently reconciled her differences with him), were taken in automobiles to the Sparrow Hills. They gathered on a grassy slope and looked down on the city stretched out below. In the light of the late afternoon sun the hairpin bends of the Moscow River became a sparkling silver ribbon, and beyond it stood the jagged wall and white bell towers of the Novodevichi Monastery. The leaves of the limes and maples in the Neskuchny Garden were just beginning to turn yellow; the dark silhouette of the Donskoi Monastery cast its shadow; through the blue-grey haze appeared the towers, palaces, and churches of the Kremlin; and just outside the Kremlin wall loomed the gigantic gold, almost flaming cupola of Christ the Savior Cathedral.[27] Obviously moved by this sight, Plekhanov, becoming very pale, grabbed Vera's hands and said:

> Vera Ivanovna, ninety years ago, near this spot, Herzen and Ogarev took their vow. About forty years ago, in another place—do you remember?—you and I also vowed that the good of the people would be for us the highest law of our lives. We are now, obviously, approaching the end of our road. . . . While we still breathe, let us ask ourselves, let us look one another directly in the eye: Did we fulfill our vow? I think we fulfilled it honestly. Isn't it true, Vera Ivanovna, honestly?

Vera's face reflected her emotion as she dabbed away the tears.[28]

For the year and a few months she lived after the Sparrow Hills excursion, Vera Zasulich, observing the drama of the Russian Revolution in which many of the leading figures were her former male colleagues, might too have gone back in memory forty years to the time when she believed as she once wrote:

> The Russian women revolutionaries of the 1870s . . . achieved a good fortune seldom attained in history: the possibility to act not in the capacity of inspirers, wives, and mothers of men, but in complete independence as equals to men in all their social activities.

Had she really functioned as an equal with the men in the Russian Social Democratic party? Or would she have had to say again, as she did when she was a young girl:

> If only I had been a boy, then I could have done almost anything.

ANNOTATED REFERENCES

"Uznitsa" was written for the girls of the Trial of the 50 (February 21–March 14, 1877) first printed in *Byloye* in 1906, reprinted in V. Bogucharsky (V. Yakolev), *Aktivnoye Narodnichestvo Semidesiatykh Godov*, Moscow, 1912, p. 301.

Nikolai Ivanovich Tsilov, *Atlas Trinadtsati Chastey S. Peterburga s Podrobnym Izobrazheniem, Naberezhnykh, Ulits, Pereulkov, Kasennykh i Obyvatelskikh Domov*, S. Petersburg, 1849. An excellent atlas of old St. Petersburg.

Augustus J. C. Hare, *Russia*, London, 1885, gives a picturesque and detailed description of St. Petersburg as it was when he visited it in the early 1880s.

---

[27]Christ the Savior Cathedral was torn down to make way for Lenin's mausoleum on Red Square.

[28]Nikolai Valentinov (N. V. Volsky), "Tragediia G. V. Plekhanova" (The Tragedy of G. V. Plekhanov), *Novyi Zhurnal*, vol. 20, 1948, as an eyewitness describes in touching detail the scene on the Sparrow Hills above Moscow in 1917.

The description of the trial of Vera Zasulich in this chapter is based on Justice Anatoly Fyodoro-vich Koni's *Vospominaniia o Dele Very Zasulich* (Recollections about the Case of Vera Zasul-ich), Moscow, 1928. His detailed account of the trial includes quotations of interrogations, the lawyers' speeches, descriptions of the personalities involved, and critical commentary on the mood of the time.

The Trepov shooting was front-page news around the world. It first appeared in *The New York Times*, February 6, 1878, and items on Zasulich, including elaborately concocted scandals, continued to appear through June 1878. There were articles about her in many foreign journals, including *Revue des Deux Mondes*, vol. 27, May 1878, and the London *Contemporary Review*, vol. 32, June 1878.

Sof'ya Vasilevna Kovalevskaia, Russia's famous woman mathematician, a professor at the Uni-versity of Stockholm, wrote a novel entitled *Nigilistka* (The Girl Nihilist), Geneva, Switzerland, 1892. The colorful account of the courtroom scene is obviously modeled on the Zasulich trial and for this reason provides an excellent source for determining the appearance and the atmosphere of that occasion. An English translation of Kovalevskaia's novel is *Vera Vorontsoff*, Boston-New York, c. 1895.

Sergei Kravchinsky (Stepniak), *Podpol'naia Rossiia*, London, 1881 (English edition *Under-ground Russia*, London, 1883), contains a "profile" of Zasulich. *The Career of a Nihilist*, a novel he wrote in English, provides an excellent background for this period. Kravchinsky, one of the assassins of 1878 inspired by Zasulich, left Russia after he stabbed Mezentsev, and settled in London. A description of him and his work appears in Donald Senese, *S.M. Stepniak-Kravchinskii: The London Years*, Newtonville, MA, 1987.

The Bolshevik labeling of Zasulich as an "enemy of the October Revolution" has condemned her to obscurity in the Soviet Union, but for a short period after 1917, facts about her life as a revolutionary before she shot Trepov, and her life as an emigré afterwards, began to appear in the memoirs of 1870s *Narodniki* and turn of the century Marxists. Many of these were pub-lished in journals such as *Katorga i Ssylka* (Prison and Exile), *Golos Minuvshego* (Voice of the Past), a new series of *Byloye* (The Past), etc., and as pamphlets under the editorship of the All-Russia Society of Political Prisoners and Exiled Deportees. Among these are the memoirs of Zasulich's sister, Aleksandra Ivanovna Uspenskaia (*Byloye*, 1922, no. 18); Liubov Isaakovna Axelrod (the wife of P. B. Axelrod), *Etiudy i Vospominaniia* (Sketches and Reminiscences), Leningrad, 1925, contains 10 pages of memories of Zasulich.

After Zasulich's death on May 8, 1919, Lev Deich published several articles about her includ-ing *Byloye*, "Vospominaniia V. I. Zasulich," no. 14, 1919, pp. 87–107; *Golos Minuvshego*, "Pamiati Ushedshikh," no. 5–12, Maia-Dekabr, pp. 199–210; and "Yuzniye Buntari," 1920–1921, pp. 44–71. He told the story of their emigration to Switzerland in "Nasha Emigratsiia v 70kh Godakh," *Vestnik Evropy*, Kniga 7, Iiul' 1913, pp. 172–198. In vol. 2 of *Za Polveka* (Half a Century Ago), Berlin, 1923, Deich gave many details about Zasulich in her *Buntari* days and tried to evaluate her terrorist act.

The major source of information on Zasulich, the Emancipation of Labor members, and their activities, is the six volumes of documents edited by Lev Deich: *Gruppa "Osvobozhdeniye Truda,"* iz archivov G. V. Plekhanova, V. I. Zasulich i L. B. Deicha, Moscow, n.d. In this collection are many recollections of people who knew these emigrés well, including Rosaliya Markovna Bograd (Plekhanova), Sbornik 3, pp. 82–87; Melitina Aleksandrovna Visconti, Sbor-nik 2, pp. 149–59; Ts. S. Burevich-Martinovskaia, Sbornik 2, pp. 161–67. N. Kuliabko-Koret-ski, in his article "Moi Vstrechi c V. I. Zasulich" (My Meetings with V. I. Zasulich), Sbornik

3, pp. 68–81, relates many piquant details of the Zasulich trial, including Zasulich and her lawyer Aleksandrov's dislike for each other and their disagreement about how to present her case. He wanted her to appear in court in fashionable dress. She refused. Noticing she bit her fingernails, he insisted she refrain from doing it during the trial. He told her juries always consider nailbiters guilty. She took heed of that advice. Zasulich's "Dear Brother" letter to Deich quoted in this chapter appears in Sbornik 5, pp. 91–94.

Until near the end of her life, when she wrote three brief autobiographical sketches, Zasulich wrote nothing about herself. An exception was an unfinished account of the Nechaev affair, dated 1883, that Lev Deich found among her papers in 1922. He published it in *Gruppa "Osvobozhdeniye Truda,"* Sbornik 2, pp. 22–72. One of her autobiographical sketches, "Iz Vospominani o Pokushenii na Trepova" (From my recollections about my attempt on Trepov) appeared in *Byloye,* kniga 14, 1919. In 1931 a pamphlet published in Moscow, Vera Zasulich, *Vospominaniia,* contains the two articles noted above, and in addition, two other autobiographical sketches. This work is heavily footnoted, with "corrections," and much pertinent and extraneous detail by the compiler B. P. Kosmin. An English translation of selections from these sketches appears in *Five Sisters, Women Against the Tsar,* Barbara Alpern Engel and Clifford N. Rosenthal, editors and translators, New York, 1975.

As a prolific Marxist polemist, Zasulich produced dozens of articles, commentaries, and translations that were published in European and Russian emigré socialist newspapers and periodicals. This material has never been collected, although during a period of relative freedom of the press in tsarist Russia following the Revolution of 1905, a partial collection of her works was published in two volumes (nearly 800 large pages of fine print): *Sbornik Statey* (Collection of Articles), St. Petersburg, 1907.

During the Khrushchev "thaw" a small book containing six of Zasulich's articles of literary criticism was published: *Stati o Russkoy Literature,* Moscow, 1960. The 39-page introduction by R. Kovnator is the nearest thing to a biography and analysis of Zasulich's work that has appeared in the Soviet Union. In I. N. Kurbatova's book, *Nachalo Rasprostraneniia Marksisma v Rossii* (The Beginning of the Spread of Marxism in Russia), section 3 of chapter 2 is a 29-page discussion and brief survey of a few of Zasulich's writings up to 1900.

Vera Zasulich's shooting of Trepov continues to be briefly referred to as one of the momentous events of Russian revolutionary history. Vera Zasulich, the political theorist and literary critic between 1880 and 1905, rarely gets even a footnote in history. The most thorough attempts to evaluate Zasulich's political thought are three doctoral dissertations (the first two are unpublished): Rita Mae Cawley Kelly, "The Role of Vera Ivanovna Zasulich in the Development of the Russian Revolutionary Movement," University of Indiana, 1967: Jay Bergman, "Vera Zasulich and the Politics of Revolutionary Writing," Yale University, 1977 (Bergman's article "The Political Thought of Vera Zasulich" was published in *The Slavic Review,* June, 1979); Wolf Geierhos, *Vera Zasulic und die Russische Revolutionäre Bewegung,* Munich and Vienna, 1977.

2

A Tale of Two Women

Raging wind lashed tree branches to the ground, stripping off spring leaves and blossoms. Rolling claps of thunder reverberated through the city. Flashes of lightning put into stark silhouette the gold spire of the Sts. Peter and Paul Fortress Cathedral across the wild waves of the rising River Neva, and threw bursts of light into the windows of the dim chapel of the Winter Palace where tapers burned at each end of the open golden casket bearing the body of the dead Tsaritsa, Maria Aleksandrovna, wife of Aleksandr II.

Dressed in the white coronation gown she had worn twenty-five years earlier, her wasted face lightly veiled with costly lace, the Tsaritsa lay under á golden canopy lined with ermine, on a catafalque covered with scarlet velvet rising in the center of the flower-filled chapel. The heavy scent of flowers and death would have been overpowering but for the damp, rain-drenched air of the spring storm that came in gusts into the dark corridors of the Palace.

If the storm did not abate, plans for the next day's elaborate funeral ritual would be jeopardized. In this ceremony, the body would be taken from the Winter Palace, across the river, to the Peter Paul Fortress Cathedral for burial alongside the Tsars and Tsaritsas interred there from the time of Peter the Great.

In late morning the rain stopped. The sky brightened, but a wild wind continued to blow. Crossing the wooden floating bridge would be hazardous, but when the three-gun salute from the Peter Paul Fortress boomed out at exactly twelve noon, the funeral cortege began to file slowly through a double line of infantry soldiers standing at attention on either side of the quai. Leading the procession were gorgeously dressed subordinate military and civil officers, followed by the standard bearers of the crowns, scepters, orbs, and escutcheons of "all the Russias": Vladimir, Novgorod, Smolensk, Kazan, Siberia, Astrakhan, Volhynia, Podolia, Kherson-Taurida, Rostov, Yaroslavl, Georgia—on and on they came. Next were black-clothed priests and majestic bishops wearing Byzantine miters and chasubles that allowed only their faces and hands to show and made them look like moving icons. Choristers marched, chanting the cadenced service of the dead as the bells of the city's churches tolled out mournful dirges, and military bands added the rat-a-tat-tat drumbeat of solemn marches.

Nature's violence which broke out at the Tsaritsa's passing contrasted sharply with the quiet life she had led from the time she came to Russia from the tiny German state of Hesse-Darmstadt as a seventeen-year-old princess to marry the heir to the Russian throne. In Russia, where war and violence raged like the storm over the city of St. Petersburg on the night of May 26, 1880, the Tsaritsa seemed to live in a charmed circle, completely absorbed in her family of six sons and a daughter and the many charities she sponsored. Reduced to little more than skin and bones by tuberculosis, the fifty-six-year-old Empress passed away quietly in her sleep. Some questioned whether she died of wasted lungs or of a broken heart after the Tsar, insensitive to her feelings, moved his mistress into the Imperial Palace. He even considered a divorce, but gave up the idea when it became clear the price would be renunciation of the throne.

Chanting choirs, marching bands, and members of the Holy Synod preceded the magnificent funeral coach of white and gold; it bore the body of the Tsaritsa in an open coffin surrounded by pages carrying lighted torches. Immediately behind rode the tall bearded Tsar Aleksandr II, still handsome at sixty-two, dressed in the purple and silver uniform of the Circassian Guard, mounted on a cream-colored horse caparisoned with black and gold trappings. By his side and to the rear came eighteen Grand Dukes, the Crown Prince of Germany, the Archduke of Austria, Prince Alexander of Hesse, Prince Aleksandr of Bulgaria, Prince Waldemar of Denmark, and representatives of other nations. They wore uniforms of bright reds, blues, and purples and rode horses harnessed in glittering gold and silver. Behind them, in black carriages, dressed in deep mourning, rode the Grand Duchesses, foreign queens and princesses, and the dead Tsaritsa's ladies in waiting, followed by hosts of uniformed civil and military personnel.

More than six thousand people marched or rode in the funeral cortege. Many thousands of soldiers and officers of the guard stood at attention along the route, and tens of thousands of onlookers crowded the streets to observe the glittering procession. The two women who were to have the most influence on the remaining months of Aleksandr's life and the course of Russian history were neither in the procession nor among the street throngs.

One was Katerina Dolgorukoya, nominally lady in waiting to the Tsaritsa

Princess Katerina Dolgorukoya in 1866

Maria Aleksandrovna, actually the mistress of Tsar Aleksandr II who had borne him four children out of wedlock. She did not ride in the mourning carriage with the other ladies in waiting. The beautiful, chestnut-haired, thirty-year-old woman sat alone, hidden by the damask curtain of a window of her apartment in the Winter Palace. As the funeral carriage passed she made the sign of the cross and moved her lips in prayer. She knew that— at last—her long exile from public life and society was at an end. Before her now loomed the marriage vows the Tsar had promised her would come "eventually" when, nearly fifteen years earlier, he had taken her as a schoolgirl from the Smolny Institute, the fashionable school for "noble maidens" founded by Katerina the Great. There was even (dare she hope?) the prospect she might wear the Imperial Crown and become Tsaritsa of all the Russias!

The other woman, petite, blonde, blue-eyed, twenty-seven-year-old Sof'ya Perovskaya, was a nine-year veteran of revolutionary circles, and, as a member of the Executive Committee of the newly formed, secret *Narodnaya Volya* (People's Will) party, deeply committed to its immediate objective: the assassination of Tsar Aleksandr II.[1] Sof'ya Perovskaya, when asked by Sergei Ivanov why terror occupied such an important place in the *Narodnaya Volya* party program, explained:

> The first shot ran out—Vera Zasulich's shot. That shot was not for revenge. It was retribution for violation of human dignity, and everyone understood that, but retribution by an individual is insufficient to achieve the aims of Russian political terrorism. The *Narodnaya Volya* party has elevated it [terror] to a systematic method of struggle, as a powerful means of agitation, as the most effective and impressive way to . . . hold over the government the sword of Damocles, to compel it to yield and to make concessions. All other ways are closed to us, closed by the government itself, yes, and not only to us.[2]

Continuing, Sof'ya pointed out that she herself and many of her comrades, only after much wavering, decided they had to leave the *narodniki* propaganda circles and take up terror because it was the only way to break through the thick wall of autocracy against which all their peaceful efforts had been wrecked.

During the first eight months of its existence, the Executive Committee of *Narodnaya Volya* planned six attempts on the life of Aleksandr II. Four of them did not materialize. Two did.

An explosion on November 19, 1879 derailed the train approaching Moscow on which the Tsar was thought to be traveling from the Black Sea resort of Livadia to St. Petersburg. In preparation for the attack, *Narodnaya Volya* activists had bought a house alongside the railroad tracks. Sof'ya Perovskaya and a male comrade lived in it, posing as husband and wife, while relays of party workers tunneled out from the basement to mine the tracks. On the fatal day, Sof'ya was selected to watch for the approaching train.

---

[1]Besides their intense but different interest in the Tsar, the two women had other things in common: each belonged to the titled Russian aristocracy and each had an ancestor who had been wedded to a ruling Romanoff. In fact, three Dolgoruky women had been betrothed to Romanoff tsars (one of them, Marie, to Michael, the first Romanoff tsar), none surviving long enough to have children. Aleksei Razumovsky (from whom the Perovsky family sprang), though of Cossack origin, was the husband of the ruling Tsaritsa Elizaveta, daughter of Peter the Great.

[2]Sergei Ivanov, "Iz vospominaniy o 1881 gode," *Byloye*, no. 4, April 1906, pp. 236–37.

She gave the signal to detonate the charge. The explosion derailed the train and killed a number of people, but, misinformed by their team of observers down the track, the Moscow conspirators had blown up the second of three trains in the tsarist entourage. The Tsar was on the first train which rolled safely into Moscow.

An even more spectacular attempt was the February 5, 1880, Winter Palace explosion. It was carried out by a *Narodnaya Volya* working man,[3] Stepan Khalturin, with the help of the Executive Committee. Having secured a job as a carpenter in the Tsar's St. Petersburg residence, the Winter Palace, each day for weeks he carried into the workmen's dormitory (located in the Palace basement near the floor of the dining room) small bags of dynamite. He hid them under the pillow of his bunk, then, as the amount accumulated, in his trunk. At the precise hour the Tsar was accustomed to dine, Khalturin set off the charge. The explosion lighted up the sky and could be heard for blocks. The Tsar was not in the dining room, having tarried in his study with his guest of the evening, Prince Alexander of Battenburg.[4]

Two days later, on February 7, 1880, came the *Narodnaya Volya* Proclamation:

> We declare once more to Aleksandr II that we will carry on our struggle so long as he refuses to use his power to the benefit of the people, so long as he does not permit the calling of an All-People's Constituent Assembly, completely free to follow the will of the voters. Until the first step is taken to free the land, the question before us remains the same and we must do what we have to do.

> We appeal to all Russian citizens to help us in this struggle against the senseless and inhuman despotism under whose pressure all the best efforts of the fatherland are ruined.

These attempts did not kill the Tsar, but *Narodnaya Volya* with its attention-grabbing explosions and proclamations seized the initiative. Again the message was "Terror Works!" The Tsar was forced to act.

Aleksandr II was a monarch who liked to review troops, redesign their uniforms, play whist with his cronies, and dally with attractive women. He preferred to put off decisions, to have a commission appointed and pigeon-hole its recommendations. But he could be pushed into action, as he had been in the first years of his reign, when, following the disastrous Crimean War, the bonfires of peasant insurrections were erupting all over Russia. After several years of hesitation he finally acted—not from any desire for

---

[3]Members of the Executive Committee, especially Perovskaya and Andrei Zhelyabov, were, with some success, making an effort to recruit workers to join *Narodnaya Volya*.

[4]There are several versions of the Tsar's escape: Battenburg's train was late, the Tsar was dining in the Yellow Room, not the main dining room, etc. Eleven people were killed in the explosion and fifty-six were injured. Khalturin's role in the plot was not discovered.

reform, but from fear of revolution. Aleksandr II made his famous statement, "Better change from above then revolution from below," and issued the *Osvoboditel'nyi Ukaz* (Emancipation Proclamation) of 1861 that ended serfdom. There quickly followed edicts modernizing Russia's archaic courts and universities and reviving the ancient elected units of local government, the *zemstva*.[5]

Then, worried that these reforms might jeopardize the most sacred principle of Russian government, "pure" autocracy, Aleksandr II (already being called the Tsar Liberator) began permitting his reactionary ministers to burden his reforms with limitations and restrictions. The Tsar never saw the ferment of Russian society—which his reforms helped bring about by starting the process of modernization—as anything the gendarmerie, the army, and the secret police could not handle by tracking down dissidents and jailing, exiling, and hanging them. By early 1880, the *Narodnaya Volya* railroad derailment, the Winter Palace explosion, and the threats of still more political terrorism proved the bankruptcy of this approach. The Autocrat of all the Russias had narrowly escaped assassination twice in three months and the perpetrators were still at large. The monarchy had to act.

A rational person looking at the disarray and the incompetence of the tsarist government in February 1880—completely out of touch with what the population wanted and needed—would have advised some kind of elected popular representation in the administration. In fact, just such a plan (the election of representatives by local government units, the *zemstva*, to the Imperial Council), had been drawn up years before. For two decades, time after time when crises arose, it had been dug out of the files and routinely considered. Each time the Tsar rejected it, as he did again in February 1880. Instead of this "constitutional change" (a forbidden term in the Tsar's presence), Aleksandr II followed the advice of his son, the Tsarevich, who said that nothing new was needed. A single official should be given the power to coordinate existing agencies to make them more efficient. The result was the creation of a new position: Supreme Commander for the Defense of the Social Order. To fill the job, the Tsar chose Count Mikhail Loris-Melikov, an Army officer of Armenian origin who had won fame in the recently ended Russo-Turkish War by taking the impregnable Fortress of Kars, and, with that victory, restoring Russia's badly battered military prestige.

Loris-Melikov, a newcomer in the councils of state, was an unorthodox choice. To St. Petersburg reactionaries he was a wild-eyed liberal, for he had made a few administrative reforms as governor of Khar'kov (a position to which he had been appointed after the assassination of Prince Dmitri

---

[5] The singular of this word is *zemstvo*; *zemstva* is the plural.

Kropatkin, the Khar'kov governor, on February 9, 1879).[6] Liberals expected Loris-Melikov to initiate the constitutional reforms they saw as needed to undercut the growing appeal of the revolutionaries. To *Narodnaya Volya* members, Loris-Melikov was the double-faced governor of Khar'kov whose "liberalism" consisted of making empty gestures. He showed his "openness" by secretly supporting the journal *Glasnost,*[7] a short-lived socialist weekly, while efficiently rounding up "socialist" activists and ensuring them speedy trials and harsh sentences.

At first Loris-Melikov seemed to infuse life into the moribund tsarist government. Among his innovations was the press conference. Calling together newspaper editors and reporters, he grandiloquently introduced himself as the head of a "Dictatorship of the Heart"!

The new Dictator's popularity zoomed when he foiled an attempt on his life. The assault occurred as he walked on a St. Petersburg street soon after his arrival in the city in February 1880. The attacker fired three shots at Loris-Melikov, but the bullets were deflected by the fur on his coat. Springing on his assailant and wrestling him to the ground, Loris-Melikov turned the miscreant over to the police and saw to it he was immediately tried. The man was executed two days later in the first public hanging in St. Petersburg in fifty years.[8] The scaffold built especially for the occasion was left standing on the Semenovsky Field as a reminder to future would-be assassins.

The *Narodnaya Volya* Executive Committee immediately disclaimed any connection with this assassination attempt. Indeed, the party, for its own reasons, had temporarily suspended its plotting against the Tsar or any other high officials.

Loris-Melikov worked on two fronts: one was direct and forceful action against the revolutionaries; the other was attempted persuasion of Aleksandr II that he—as Tsar, the absolute autocrat—should himself decree the changes in the government that the revolutionaries proclaimed could only be made by "the people's representatives."

The Tsar consented, unwillingly, to a few changes. These included the elimination of the Third Section (the secret police) and the transfer of that group's function to the Ministry of the Interior which Loris-Melikov was to supervise. He also permitted Loris-Melikov to force the resignation of several of his most reactionary ministers. The press censorship was relaxed slightly, and an unpopular salt tax was eliminated. However, this was not

---

[6]The assassin was *Zemlya i Volya* activist, Grigory Goldenberg, who was not detected and later that year joined *Narodnaya Volya.*
[7]Sergei Ivanov recounted Loris-Melikov's rumored backing of *Glasnost* in "Iz Vospominaniy o 1881 Gode," *Byloye,* no. 4, April 1906, p. 231.
[8]The attacker was I. O. Mlodetsky. An article about his execution, "Kasn' Mlodetskogo" by A. Engel'meyer, appeared in *Golos Minuvshago,* 1917, nos. 7 and 8.

the kind of change the public had expected. It was not what was needed to move the tsarist government off the narrow track of repression. Loris-Melikov, as had ministers before him, dusted off the old plan to grant to the zemstva the right to select delegates to the Imperial Council. This action would enlarge the council, an ancient aristocratic body with a purely advisory function in lawmaking, and transform it—without any grant of power—into a body of representatives of "the people." The laws would continue to be made as they always had been in Russia, that is, by the Tsar issuing an ukaz (an order or decree). It was a far from radical change, but Aleksandr II, with his instinctive aversion to any kind of popular participation in government, did not give his approval.

Then, in May 1880 came an event that changed everything: the death of the Tsaritsa, Maria Aleksandrovna.

Scarcely a month later, in deepest secrecy, Tsar Aleksandr II, who had long wanted to make his mistress, Katerina Dolgorukoya, his wife "before God," ordered a palace priest to perform the marriage ceremony, in violation of the rules of Church and State that decreed a one-year mourning period for a royal spouse.

The Tsar's marriage did not remain secret for long. Gossip at the Imperial Court, in high society, and even among the common people, enlivened every gathering—and the mood was general disapproval. The assumption made was that the beautiful young Katerina Dolgorukoya would not be satisfied with being just the wife of the Tsar, and that the infatuated Aleksandr II would like nothing better than to see her standing at the head of the red staircase in the Kremlin in Moscow, wearing the crown of the Romanoffs. In addition, it seemed to be common knowledge that the Tsar had ordered the Kremlin Archives to search out Peter the Great's ukaz for the coronation of his second wife (an illiterate peasant serving girl who, after his death, reigned briefly as Katerina I), expecting to use it as a model for the coronation of his own Katerina.[9]

Loris-Melikov was observed "growing livelier and merrier." He saw the doors that had closed on his effort to gain acceptance of his constitutional plan beginning to open. He now had a potent argument, based not on demands of state but on dictates of the heart. He told Aleksandr II the devastating effect of the unpopular coronation could be offset by a grand gesture of conciliation to the people. What better gesture than Loris-Melikov's constitutional plan? Loris-Melikov struck a bargain with Katya: she would promote his plan with the Tsar; he would promote her project to become Tsaritsa. They succeeded to such an extent that by mid-February 1881, only the

---

[9]Elizabeth Narishkin-Kurakin, Under Three Tsars, New York, 1931, p. 70. Alexandre Tarsaidzé, in his book Katia, New York, 1970, says Katya told her nephew, Boris Berg, the Tsar consulted the Kremlin Archives and also had her try on the crown (pp. 234–35).

year-long mourning period for the dead Tsaritsa, which would end in May, barred accomplishment of the dual project.[10]

In the meantime Loris-Melikov's Tsar-pleasing attack on revolutionaries was intensifying, with arrests, trials, and sentencing of men and women whose crimes were largely printing and distributing "illegal literature"— those brochures, broadsides, and obscure journals detailing gross miscarriages of justice. The Trial of the 16 (October 25, 1880) zeroed in on *Narodnaya Volya* activists, a move made possible by the revelations of Grigory Goldenberg, the assassin of Prince Dmitri Kropotkin, after his arrest in November 1879.[11] Of the five death sentences, two were carried out.[12] Aleksandr Kviatovsky and Andrei Presniakov, both members of the Executive Committee, were hanged on November 4, 1880. They had been arrested in July 1880, and as long as there was hope they would not be hanged, the *Narodnaya Volya* Executive Committee had kept their plans to assassinate the Tsar on hold. The hanging of the two served as a go-head signal. The next issue of the journal *Narodnaya Volya* announced: A Declaration of War. Highly secret and intense effort now concentrated on the operation: Death to the Tsar!

On another front, various elements of Russian society (especially in St. Petersburg) were increasingly restive because none of the reforms Loris-Melikov's Dictatorship of the Heart seemed initially to promise had come about, even though rumors that something was about to happen continued to circulate. What the public did not know was the existence of Loris-Melikov's "constitutional plan" nor how close it was to being put into effect. In early February, the Tsar, in a surprise move, ordered the court mourning period shortened. It would end February 19.

Loris-Melikov speeded up preparations to submit his plan to the Tsar's advisors, and on Sunday morning March 1, Aleksandr II asked Loris-Melikov to bring it to him for his signature. On that same morning, in another part of St. Petersburg, the members of the Executive Committee of *Narod-*

---

[10]Constantin de Grunwald, *Le Tsar Alexandre II*, Paris, 1963, p. 339. W. E. Mosse, *Alexander II and the Modernization of Russia*, London, 1958, says the initiator of the plan of using Katya in this project was Aleksandr Abaza, the minister of Finance (p. 170).

[11]Goldenberg was told that by revealing all he knew about his comrades and their activities he could bring about constitutional reforms which the tsarist government was prevented from doing only by the continued terrorism of the revolutionaries. He was assured no harm would befall the people he identified. After weeks of testimony, his interrogator left. Goldenberg soon realized the enormity of his betrayal and hanged himself in his cell; but the result was that almost all the *Narodnaya Volya* activists had been identified and linked to the terrorist acts they had perpetrated.

[12]The question of why so many more death sentences were issued than were actually carried out is discussed by William C. Fuller, Jr., *Civil-Military Conflict in Imperial Russia: 1881–1914*, Princeton, 1985, chapter 6.

naya Volya were completing preparations to meet their deadline for the assassination of Aleksandr II on March 1.

Only if Aleksandr II lived would Katya's romantic dream come true. Only if he died, thought Sof'ya Perovskaya, could her goal be achieved.

Of the six women and ten men who were the Executive Committee of the *Narodnaya Volya* party in 1880, none was a more ardent revolutionary or more committed to "Death to the Tsar" than Sof'ya Perovskaya. Unlike many of her comrades who explained, often at length, why they had become revolutionaries, Sof'ya left no written record of why she chose the "path of dynamite" which took her so far away from her aristocratic origins. After her death, reminiscences about Sof'ya's deeds, personality, thoughts, and even her conversations were recorded by her associates. Some of them also expressed ideas about why and how she became a revolutionary; others speculated on why she turned to terrorism.

The earliest explanation, and the one most often cited, is an unhappy childhood in a family dominated by a tyrannical father. At age seventeen she rebelled against him and left home, never to return. This analysis appeared in a twenty-four-page biography published in London (in Russian) within a year of her death,[13] even though the anonymous author admits that after an eight-year acquaintance with Perovskaya "I know little of her life. I know only what I saw and heard from her friends; from her I heard almost nothing." Others observed her habitual silence about herself and also attributed it to her unhappy girlhood and her refusal to complain about it.

Quite another version of Perovskaya's family life appears in Sof'ya's brother Vasya's Memoirs.[14] He pictures the four Perovsky children growing up in a happy household, full of affection from both parents who loved and respected each other. He attributes the changes in his father's mood, when Sof'ya was in her teens, to ill health and his shattered career—a sharp contrast to the record of success of his brother, his uncles, and his famous father.[15] Vasya admits Sof'ya left home on bad terms with her father, but recounts that when the tsarist government conducted a massive round-up of Going-to-the-People youth in 1873 and 1874, Sof'ya was arrested (January 5, 1874), charged with the crime of appearing before the workers of St.

---

[13]*Sof'ya L'vovna Perovskaya*, Krasny Krest Narodnoy Voli, London, 1882.

[14]V. L. Perovsky, *Vospominaniia o Sestre* (Reminiscences about My Sister), Moscow, 1927, originally published in *Katorga i Ssylka* in three installments in 1925.

[15]His depression was occasioned by his dismissal as governor of St. Petersburg province in 1866 when the radical student Karakozov succeeded in getting through supposedly tight security and fired several shots at Tsar Aleksandr II. The implication was that the governor was derelict in his duty. The careers of five members of the Perovsky family, including Sof'ya's grandfather Lev Alekseevich, are listed in the 1890 edition of the *Entsiklopedicheskiy Slovar'*, St. Petersburg, vol. 23.

Petersburg as a preacher of new ideas, and clapped into a dark and dirty cell in the grim Peter Paul Fortress Prison. After several weeks Sof'ya called on her father for help. Vasya says that without even asking why she was in prison, he went immediately to police headquarters to talk with Count Peter Shuvaloff, chief of police and his former regimental colleague. Shuvaloff promised to see what he could do. Within two days after Lev Perovsky paid a 5,000 ruble bail, he was notified to come to police headquarters. He waited in the reception room for a few minutes, then Sof'ya was led in by two gendarmes. Neither Sof'ya nor her father could hold back their tears as they ran to each other and embraced.

This was not the first nor last time, according to Vasya, that Lev Perovsky interceded for his daughter. For the next four years, while hundreds and hundreds of Going-to-the-People youth languished in prisons and jails all over Russia, Sof'ya's legal position was "an accused person living in freedom"; literally, she was out on bail on her father's surety. As for Sof'ya's mother, Varvara Stepanovna, Vasya portrays her as her daughter's refuge, always welcoming her in times of crisis, always providing the moral support from which Sof'ya derived her strength.

Unjust imprisonment, very common in the 1870s in tsarist Russia, caused many a Russian youth to turn to the path of revolution. Sof'ya's brief stay in the Peter Paul Fortress Prison in 1874 was not her first incarceration. In 1871, soon after she joined the St. Petersburg Chaikovsky Circle, which was a brother-and sisterhood of talkers, dialecticians, and comrades who endlessly argued about the moral aspects of revolution, Sof'ya and several other members of the circle were arrested, jailed, and charged in the case of young Nikolai Goncharov, the son of a general. His crime was printing forty copies of a revolutionary sheet in his own home. Police investigation turned up no evidence the Chaikovskists were connected with this incident, so they were freed. Goncharov was sentenced to six years in prison.

Evidence that her first prison experience affected Sof'ya deeply is implicit in the only record, in her own words, on the subject of becoming a revolutionary. In the Trial of the Six, in March 1881, to a question by the prosecuting attorney she replied that she became a revolutionary in 1872 (soon after her unjust prison experience).

In the 1860s and 1870s, Russian intellectuals at home and in exile wrote tirelessly portraying Russia as a land of suffering, crying out to be saved. This literature, illegally circulated and widely read, appealed to the apocalyptic strain in the Russian character and inspired many young women and men to enter the ranks of the revolutionaries. Was Sof'ya Perovskaya one of them? Her Soviet biographer, Elena Segal,[16] following this line of thought,

---

[16]Elena Segal, *Sof'ya Perovskaya*, Moscow, 1962.

speculates that her first encounter with dissident ideas may have come during a trip she took with her mother to Geneva, Switzerland, at age twelve, to visit her uncle, Peter Perovsky, who was very ill. The year was 1865, a time when radical Russian emigré writers worked in Geneva, and Sof'ya, a precocious youngster, may have become aware of them and their ideas. She may have learned about 1860s *nihilism* when, in 1866, the *nihilist* student, Karakozov, shot at the Tsar, because of the traumatic effect this event had on the Perovsky family. Having to move out of the grand official governor's residence, Lev Perovsky tried to keep up the appearance of power and wealth, renting a fine house, hiring servants, entertaining lavishly—and soon faced bankruptcy. It was decided then that Madame Perovskaya and the girls, Sof'ya and her older sister Masha, would go to the Crimea to live on one of the Perovsky estates, Kilburine. For three years their home was the spacious manor house that had belonged to Sof'ya's grandfather. His interest in Greek antiques was reflected in the furnishings of the house, which also had a well-stocked library of his books.

Soon after Varvara Perovskaya and her daughters arrived in the Crimea, they were joined by the girls' brother Vasya, suspended from the university for taking part in a student demonstration. He came laden with forbidden books which they all read and discussed. This was a turning point in Sof'ya's life. Reading these books, discussing and arguing over them, stirred up in her an intense desire to learn more. She wanted to study the same subjects as Vasya.

When Lev Perovsky came to the Crimea in the summer of 1869 and sold Kilburine to help pay his debts, the family moved back to St. Petersburg and Sof'ya began attending the recently opened Alarchinsky classes for young women.[17] Suddenly she was in a new world, the world of stimulating ideas, in the company of young women who with their short hair, blue glasses, wide hats, plain short skirts, and white blouses looked, acted, and talked differently from the people she was accustomed to.

Sof'ya found the Alarchinsky classes as exciting as attending the theater. She was soon recognized by her professors as having remarkable mathematical and scientific ability and there was talk of her going to the Technological Institute, but courses there were still not open to women.

The Tsar's 1862 edict liberalizing the curricula of Russian universities and expanding the admission of students strictly forbade student organizations, publications, or demonstrations; yet in St. Petersburg and other cities, every

---

[17]In St. Petersburg in the spring of 1869 the first women's courses opened, called Alarchinsky because they took place in the No. 5 Men's Gymnasium (high school, or university preparatory school) near the Alarchina Bridge on the Fontanka Canal. The hours were 6–9 in the evening. The classes were taught by some of the best professors of that time. The subjects were physics, mathematics, geometry, Russian language, and pedagogy.

student boarding house had its loosely organized "circles" of young men and women reading forbidden books, debating radical ideas, and writing forbidden essays and broadsides. Few could resist the temptation to join this aspect of student life. Through her reading and discussions with other students, Sof'ya Perovskaya was being drawn into what was considered "revolutionary activity" in the Russia of Aleksandr II.

Sof'ya's place of refuge when she walked out of her father's house in 1870 was the home of her closest school friend, Sasha (Aleksandrovna) Kornilova, and Sasha's three older sisters, which had become a gathering place for students. Late into the night the rooms of this big house overflowed with young people engaged in endless debates on socialism, workers' rights, women's education, and the land problem as they sat in clouds of tobacco smoke, drinking tea and eating quantities of *zakuski*. To poor students, living far from their homes on a pittance, the food and tea at the Kornilovs represented the height of luxury. The widowed father of the Kornilov sisters was a rich porcelain manufacturer who gave his daughters free reign in their personal lives.

Through the Kornilov sisters Sof'ya met the remarkable group of men and women who soon came to be called by the name of one of them, Nikolai Chaikovsky, the Chaikovsky Circle. This circle became the most famous and influential of the youth groups of the 1870s. Its eloquent members, including the offspring of titled nobility and families of wealth and power, accepted the pretty eighteen-year-old Sof'ya Perovskaya as a bright novice and she soon became a serious debater and resourceful logician. She participated in the discussions which finally led the Chaikovskists to a loose consensus: political revolution was far into the future. The current task for Russia's educated youth was to work for social change, to uplift the abysmally low level of the lives of the Russian people—the peasants and the cruelly exploited workers in Russia's primitive mills and factories. These privileged youth had an inescapable obligation to Go-to-the-People—to serve them, to educate them and be educated by them, to learn their needs, and to teach them that even in backward Russia they had human rights.

In St. Petersburg the Chaikovskists were content to remain talkers, engaging in little activity beyond distributing books and pamphlets to students, but as Chaikovsky circles spread to other cities, and as the call to Go-to-the-People gained momentum, young people began to move. In ever larger numbers they went to the people, in the countryside and in factories, in transports of selflessness, dedicated to carrying out their mission as a labor of love.

One of them, in the summer of 1872, was Sof'ya Perovskaya. A friend left a description of her as she came into a village on the Volga near Stavropol, at that time a small town about 150 miles south of Kazan. Wearing a wide straw hat, her flaxen hair sticking out in two short braided bunches on either side of her healthy pink cheeks, her eyes sparkled in anticipation. Strong and graceful, she was not very tall and was wearing a white home-spun blouse, with wide men's trousers pulled up and cinched in with a leather belt. She had on men's boots, and as she walked along the road a pack of children ran after her shouting, "A *barynia* (an upper-class lady) wearing pants! A *barynia* wearing pants!"[18] Sof'ya Perovskaya had "gone to the people." But what to do? What did this young *barynia* wearing pants know about peasants? She and Sasha Kornilova had read a little about peasants and their problems in books, but this did not prepare her for what she saw.

Sof'ya decided to attend the classes held during the summer for girls in the region to prepare them for the exam they had to pass to qualify as teachers in the almost nonexistent elementary schools. After a few weeks she took the teacher qualifying exam and easily passed it. In the meantime she began to assist the local *zemstvo* doctor who taught her how to vaccinate for smallpox. She became proficient enough for him to give her a license, and with that Sof'ya set out for the surrounding countryside. She took with her a local girl she had met in the teachers' training class who knew the peasants, their customs, and their prejudices.

Peasant mothers grieved over the toll of children's lives lost every year to the dread disease of smallpox, but they feared innoculation as a deadly sin, a mark of the devil. It was not easy for two girls, one of them a strange *barynia*, to approach these somber, apprehensive, ignorant women and convince them there was no sin in vaccination, and that it would save their children's lives.

The children were curious. Sof'ya soon found she could gain the confidence of the mothers by winning over the children. She even overcame their fear of the needle by giving them candy and little cakes she always carried in her pockets. Sof'ya and her companion walked from village to village, from *izba* (hut) to *izba*. They slept on the floor on straw mats and ate peasant food—buckwheat and cabbage. The only available examples of Sof'ya Perovskaya's own writing are four letters she wrote during and immediately after her Stavropol experience. She expressed her horror at the deathly torpor of peasant life, the misery of it. She was overwhelmed by her helplessness. "I want to wake them up from their half-dead sleep, but I haven't the knowledge. I haven't the means."[19]

It was a shock for Sof'ya to learn that soon after she left, gendarmes appeared. They fanned out over the villages and settlements where she and

---

[18]"Sof'ya Perovskaya v Stavropole. Vospominaniia M. S. Karpovoy," *Katorga i Ssylka,* March, 1925, pp. 231–234.
[19]"Neizdannye Pis'ma S. L. Perovskoy" (Unpublished Letters of S. L. Perovskaya), *Krasnyi Arkhiv,* vol. 3, 1923, pp. 244–50.

her young assistant had worked, looking for the two "criminals" they said had been teaching revolution. Village schools were searched, textbooks were removed, and soon the schools were closed and the teachers dismissed.

But she did not give up. In the fall Sof'ya went to a village near Tver (present-day Kalinin) where she and another Chaikovsky Circle girl taught in a people's school. By the summer of 1873, when Sof'ya went back to St. Petersburg, she had forsaken formal education. The house she rented on Saratovskaia Street, on the Viburg side (near the factory district), became the headquarters of the Chaikovsky Circle. She spent most of her afternoons and evenings near the Nevsky Gate talking about socialism and people's rights to factory workers as they came off their jobs. Her co-worker, Sergei Sinegub, noticed that each day when she appeared the number of workers gathered round her became larger. Her pleasant voice and ready laughter, her persuasive language, he said, not only convinced her listeners, but fired them with enthusiasm and a sense of duty to work for the rights of the people. She was, in fact, creating the first organization of St. Petersburg factory workers.[20]

Abruptly, her work was halted. She was arrested and jailed. Soon almost all her Chaikovskist associates were in prison or had gone into exile. The tsarist government's massive 1874 round-up of Going-to-the-People youth had begun. Through her father's influence, Sof'ya avoided prison, but she did not avoid the spiritual turmoil that came with the destruction of her intellectual base, the Chaikovsky Circle, and the disappearance behind bars or into exile of her friends and co-workers.

Limited in what she could do in this time of unrest, Sof'ya sought and received permission from the authorities to take a *feldsher* course in Sinferopol, after which she worked as a physician's assistant in hospitals and in a Red Cross barracks until June 1877.[21] At this time she was called back to St. Petersburg to stand trial in the famous Go-to-the-People Trial of the 193. She rented a little house which, as before, became a meeting place for dissidents. She was soon a leader in a new network of radical youths, *Zemlya i Volya* (Land and Freedom). The Chaikovsky circles had been open organizations; *Zemlya i Volya* was secret. It operated a secret press, and while still

---

[20]Sergei Silovich Sinegub, *Zapiski Chaikovtsa* (Memories of the Chaikovskists), Moscow 1929.
[21]Her service in the Red Cross barracks was a detail brought out in the Trial of the Six in 1881. Her service was in the time of the Russo-Turkish War, and although there is no evidence of it from her or her friends, Sof'ya must have witnessed some of the terrible mistreatment of the common soldiers which her friend Anna Korba also observed as a volunteer nurse. Korba said this experience was one of the things that turned her into a confirmed revolutionary. A. P. Pribyleva-Korba, in her autobiography in the *Entsiklopedicheskiy Slovar* (Granat), vol. 40, Moscow, 1926.

expressing adherence to Going-to-the-People education and propaganda aims, some of its members were beginning to advocate terror as retaliation against tsarist officials for specific injustices, vowing to use force to resist arrest.

Sof'ya visited the accused who were being moved into the St. Petersburg Preliminary Detention Prison in preparation for the Trial of the 193. Many of them were her former associates. She heard their horror stories of nearly four years of imprisonment, which had been substantially reduced by death-dealing epidemics, scurvy, and suicide, the number originally scheduled to be tried.

When the Trial of the 193 finally opened in October 1877, Sof'ya Perovskaya was one of the first called before the court. She resolutely refused to testify. By her tactic of silence, she frustrated the authorities who had expected to use her testimony to help convict the others. She was given a temporary reprieve and released, again on her father's bail. She was not ready to join the terrorist faction of Zemlya i Volya, but anger similar to that which drove Vera Zasulich to shoot Trepov was triggered in Sof'ya by an action of the Tsar. Alarmed at the jury's exoneration of Zasulich on March 31, 1878, he ordered the light sentences handed down by the Senate Court in the Trial of the 193 in January to be changed to severe ones. Sof'ya was particularly infuriated by an order to fetter in irons three resentenced men and to take them to Khar'kov for incarceration in that city's Central Prison.

Sof'ya's response was not an assassination attempt; it was a jail break. Her effort to free the political prisoners of Khar'kov Central Prison was one of the spectacular events of the year 1878. Lack of means and insufficient staff doomed it to failure and left Sof'ya distraught. She was convinced that with a little more daring they could have brought it off. An unexpected dividend was publicity the attempted prison break received, revealing the dark horrors inside the prison's walls. Public indignation was aroused, evoking a flood of sympathy for the forgotten, suffering inmates and for the undiscovered heroes who tried to free them.[22]

The Khar'kov prison break attempt revealed Sof'ya Perovskaya's skill as the organizer of a conspiracy and her commitment to action, to risk taking, to willingness to expose herself, to sacrifice life itself to reach a decided-upon goal.

Narrowly escaping from Khar'kov, Sof'ya boarded a train headed south. Soon she was in the Crimea taking refuge with her mother who was then living on another Perovsky estate there. Shortly after she arrived, the police came to take her back to St. Petersburg, not for the Khar'kov action (her role in the attempted prison break was still undetected), but because, as one of

---

[22]One statistic made public was the report of the prison's chaplain that in one year two hundred of the prison's five hundred inmates died of scurvy.

the 193, she had been resentenced to exile in the far north, near the White Sea. After tearful good-byes, she went with two policemen to begin the train trip to St. Petersburg. Determined not to let herself "fall into the tiger's mouth," she escaped her captors, and arriving in St. Petersburg, immediately obtained a false passport. She became an illegal and never again used her own name. She entered the Empire of Darkness, the Russian underground.

The course of events was serving as a magnet, pulling Sof'ya Perovskaya closer to the dread specter of terror. The decision finally came in the wake of the Voronezh Conference called in the summer of 1879 to work out a program to heal the split that was threatening to destroy *Zemlya i Volya*. Its membership was pathetically small in number and faced with overwhelming tasks. The record of the conference shows that Perovskaya argued for unity to a point beyond feasibility. The split finally came and she had to decide.

It is hard to imagine the difficulty of this decision for Sof'ya Perovskaya. Should she join the group calling itself *Narodnaya Volya*, whose members were committed to political revolution using organized terror as a tactic, or should she stay with the remnants of the Going-to-the-People group, now calling itself *Cherny Peredel* (Black [soil] Partition), sometimes also called "the Villagers"? Her sympathies were with the Villagers, but when she repeatedly asked, "What are you people doing?" one of them put it in a nutshell:

> We cannot do much in this climate of fear and reprisals to educate the peasants and workers, but ours is a long-term effort. So why don't you go abroad, then come back to Russia when things settle down and we can take up our work again?

"No! No!" cried Sof'ya. "I will stay here and perish with my comrades in the struggle."

In striking contrast to the Villagers, *Narodnaya Volya* spokesmen presented their plans and their stirring manifestos with vigor and enthusiasm. The most eloquent of them was Andrei Zhelyabov, who at Voronezh emerged as one of the new party's most important leaders. He had first seen Sof'ya Perovskaya when they were both among the accused in the Trial of the 193. He met her again in Khar'kov where he had an opportunity to observe her organizing ability. He was determined to coopt her as a member of the Executive Committee of *Narodnaya Volya*. Until 1879 Zhelyabov's work in radical circles in his native area, the Odessa region, had been as a propagandist. A recent convert to terror, at Voronezh he argued long and hard with Sof'ya. He did not convince her. She seemed to have an instinctive aversion to terror. "That woman! You can't do anything with her!" he is quoted as saying.

The debates between the Villagers and *Narodnaya Volya* continued after the Voronezh Conference, and many of them took place in Sof'ya's apartment in St. Petersburg. Sof'ya's natural tendency to side with those she considered wronged was noted by Maria Kovalevskaya. She observed Sof'ya becoming angry when, in a hot debate, George Plekhanov, the erudite, gentry dialectician of the Villagers, expressed his disdain for the eloquent Zhelyabov, of peasant origin, with cutting sarcasm. The next day, when Sof'ya saw Kovalevskaya, she referred to *Narodnaya Volya* as "our group."[23]

It was Zhelyabov who, the day after she made her decision, came before the Executive Committee to announce triumphantly that Sof'ya Perovskaya had joined *Narodnaya Volya*. It may have been this announcement which gave rise to the widely held assumption that Sof'ya turned to terrorism because she fell in love with Zhelyabov. There is, however, much evidence of her turning away from *narodniki* gradualism before her intense debating sessions with Zhelyabov. Her two attempted prison breaks in Khar'kov were not without violence, and she participated in the Moscow train explosion plot to kill the Tsar before she joined *Narodnaya Volya*.

Sof'ya Perovskaya's first dramatic act, leaving her father's house, was, in retrospect, a small step compared with her decision to join *Narodnaya Volya*. Almost as climactic was joining her life to Zhelyabov's. Her first biographer said, and many repeated it, that Sof'ya had an aversion to men (attributed to animosity toward her father), considering them morally, and in all else, inferior to women.[24] Despite what everyone who knew her said was her loving nature, despite her easy comradery with her male Chaikovskists and *Zemlya i Volya* friends and the men she had lived with in false marriages for conspiratorial purposes, she had never been anything more than a committed party worker with any of them. It appeared that in taking on the self-denying profession of dedicated revolutionary, up to her twenty-sixth year, Sof'ya Perovskaya imposed on herself a celibate life. Then she fell in love, impetuously in love with a man who returned her ardor in full measure; the flaming intensity of this love deepened by the impending doom they both knew they faced.

Andrei Zehlyabov was an unusually handsome man. Tall, well-built, with dark, reddish hair and a curly beard he lovingly cared for and was very proud of, he was eloquent and brilliant of mind, but not a bookish intellectual. He was a doer, not a prince, like Kropotkin, who wrote learned trea-

---

[23]Quoted in David Footman, *Red Prelude*, New Haven, 1945, p. 106.
[24]Sasha Kornilova said that in her late teens Sof'ya became intensely interested in "the woman question" and thought seriously of becoming an equal rights advocate, but got involved instead in revolutionary movements. "Perovskaya i Osnovanie Kruzhka Chaikovtsev," *Katorga i Ssylka*, 1925–1926, nos. 20–22.

tises in prison; not a *dvorianin*, or landed gentleman, like Plekhanov and most of the Chaikovskists. He was a self-made man of the people. He loved to sing and dance and had a huge capacity for enjoying life. He seemed to like everybody and both men and women were attracted to him. Born a serf twelve years before emancipation, he was rescued from the lowly life of his family—house serfs for generations—by a landowner who paid for his education. He later obtained a small government stipend enabling him to attend the University of Odessa where he became a student leader. Involved in student demonstrations, he was expelled. He worked as a tutor and teacher, joined radical circles, was an effective propagandist among urban workers, and was arrested several times.[25]

The romance of two people as far apart in social origin as Sof'ya Perovskaya and Andre Zhelyabov could have had no reality outside the frenzied atmosphere of a Russian revolutionary circle like *Narodnaya Volya*. Even Turgenev, whose novels are peopled with characters accurately drawn from Russian life in the 1860s and 1870s, did not go so far as to have one of his high-born heroines fall in love with a peasant. The most venturesome of them, Yelena in *On the Eve*, fed up with her upper-class, do-nothing-but-talk admirers, fell in love and went off—not with a peasant, but with the revolutionary Insarov, like herself a member of the gentry, but a Bulgarian!

While Sof'ya Perovskaya had accepted terror as a revolutionary tactic, she clung to the belief that *Narodnaya Volya* should not abandon "the people." She considered concentrating on terror alone—as some party activists wanted to do—a negative approach. Zhelyabov accepted her reasoning, and since both of them were excellent organizers and recruiters, they carried on the double responsibility of planning attempts on the Tsar's life and expanding *Narodnaya Volya's* supporters and influence.

Narodnaya Volya planned and carried out attacks that took their toll of innocent victims. There is much evidence that Sof'ya Perovskaya shed tears over the victims of the tsarist police state. There is no evidence she wept over the victims of the terrorists' dynamite. Just as her military ancestors, in their conquests of vast territories for the tsars, looked on battlefield dead with equanimity, Sof'ya saw innocent victims of the terrorists falling, as she herself was ready to fall, as soldiers in the battle for rights of the people. Theirs was a necessary sacrifice, a part of the price that had to be paid for freedom.

---

[25]Zhelyabov had married the daughter of one of his employers, a civic-minded sugar factory owner who employed him as a tutor for his children. Zhelyabov's wife, who loved music, gave up her piano and tried to live the life of a radical, but it did not work. When it became clear to Zhelyabov that he was on the path of becoming a professional revolutionary, he insisted on a divorce. Broken-hearted, his wife took their son, went back to her father's home, and resumed her family name.

In the scenario projected by *Narodnaya Volya*, their assassination of the Tsar would end terrorism—government terror and revolutionary terror. The party, tiny though it was in numbers, would be in an effective bargaining position, with the whole tsarist government in complete disarray. In their moment of triumph, a vast army of *Narodnaya Volya* sympathizers would rally to support their program, forcing the new Tsar to give the people a voice in the government.[26] The call would go out for the election of a constituent assembly by a free and universal vote. The downtrodden people of Russia would, at last, win their rights.

Sundays in St. Petersburg were military parade days. Few things appealed to Tsar Aleksandr II more than reviewing colorfully uniformed troops marching, or mounted cavalry trotting in public squares or in vast riding academies—the pride of St. Petersburg. On Sunday morning, March 1, 1881, Aleksandr II was very happy. He had learned the night before that the police had arrested a man who refused to identify himself, but who the police were sure was Zhelyabov. He had been identified by Goldenberg as the chief conspirator of the new revolutionary party, *Narodnaya Volya*. Now, Loris-Melikov had come with the document he had prepared for his "constitutional plan," to which even the Tsarevich, who opposed all reform, had agreed. Aleksandr II came to Katya to tell her he was about to sign it.

I hope it will make a good impression and that Russia will take it as proof that I mean to give them all that I can.

Then he made the sign of the cross, and said "Tomorrow it will be in all the papers. I have ordered it."[27]

The Tsar had little enthusiasm for the projected governmental change, but it was not too high a price to pay for the *ukaz* he hoped would soon follow, making his beloved Katya the Tsaritsa of all the Russias.

The Tsar prepared to leave for the Manege, the riding academy between the Street of the Engineers and Italianskaya Street, to review the colorful mounting-of-the-guard ceremony. He promised to follow Katya's advice to avoid Malaya Sadovaya Street and the Nevsky Prospekt, because—according to what she considered well-founded rumors—they had been mined by the revolutionaries. Saying he would be back in good time for a walk in the Jardin d'Été, he embraced her, and left the Winter Palace at 12:15 in a small, closed, armored carriage drawn by his fast Orlov trotters. There were

---

[26]Anatole Leroy-Beaulieu, in volume 6 of his *The Empire of the Tsars and the Russians* (English translation, London, 1903–1905), reported on *Narodnaya Volya's* financial resources, saying that while no exact figures were available, the people he talked to believed the contributions in the late 1870s and early 1880s ran into the millions, which indicated wide public sympathy.
[27]This is Katya's version of what was said, as it appears in Victor Laferté, *Alexandre II, Détails Inédits sur Sa Vie Intime et Sa Mort*, Geneva and Paris, 1882.

six Cossack outriders and a seventh armed Cossack sitting on the box with the coachman. Three police officers followed in two sleighs.

News of Zehlyabov's arrest was a blow to the members of the Executive Committee of *Narodnaya Volya* whose members were hard at work to meet the assassination plot deadline of March 1. The effect of the news, was to harden their determination. Zhelyabov had relied mainly on a land mine laid under Malaya Sadovaya Street. The conspirators had rented a store on that street and opened a cheese shop. Laboriously they had tunneled from the basement out under the street. Malaya Sadovaya, just off the Nevsky Prospekt, was often traversed by the Tsar when making his regular Sunday trip to and from the Manege to inspect the mounting-of-the-guard ceremony. For weeks the *Narodnaya Volya* plotters worked at their digging. They successfully foiled several police inspections and fended off curious neighbors, but—as poor shopkeepers—sold very little cheese.

Sof'ya Perovskaya, aware of the failure of planned mine explosions in several other assassination attempts, was ready to rely on a back-up plan. In an emergency meeting the day after Zhelyabov's arrest the Executive Committee agreed to charge the mine under Malaya Sadovaya and to go to work immediately to assemble four of the new-type, small, nitroglycerine bombs developed by Nikolai Kibalchich, the party's technical genius. He, Sof'ya Perovskaya, Vera Figner, and two other plotters worked feverishly all night in Vera Figner's flat assembling the bombs.

On Sunday morning March 1, dressed neatly as she always was, the exhausted Sof'ya came out of the building carrying a small package. Walking along the street covered with a thin layer of new-fallen snow, she soon found a droshky, or horse-drawn cab, for hire, got in, and sat down, carefully cradling in her lap the paper bag containing two bombs. Russian terrorist women carried fulminate of dynamite around like society ladies carried cosmetics; nevertheless, Sof'ya feared that at any moment the lurching of the vehicle over the uneven cobblestones might jostle the bombs and set off a premature explosion.

Sof'ya arrived safely at the conspiratorial flat of Gessya Gelfman, where the four bomb throwers were already assembled. They had spent the day before practicing by throwing rocks in an open field. Sof'ya picked up an envelope and hastily drew a crude map of the area of the Manege, placing crosses at the points where she wanted the bomb throwers to stand. She herself would be at the corner of Italianskaya Street and Mikhailovsky Square to observe the Tsar's movements after leaving the Manege. If the Malaya Sadovaya explosion missed the Tsar's carriage, or if he did not take that route, she would pull out her large white handkerchief and go through the motions of blowing her nose. This would signal the bomb throwers to move into their second-line positions along the Katerinski Canal. By the time Sof'ya completed her instructions, Kibalchich appeared with the remaining two bombs.

The little group went out into the streets of St. Petersburg. Each of the four men, dressed in rough peasant gear and wearing a fur cap, was carrying a small paper parcel. Because she had been observing the Tsar's comings and goings for weeks, Sof'ya knew it was too early to go to their stations, for if they stood too long in one place they ran the risk of attracting police attention. They went to a cafe and slowly drank tea.

At the Manege the Parade of the Guard came to an end with three ringing regimental commands of "Atten'shun!" Then in unison the young recruits shouted, "Long live the Tsar!" Aleksandr II, splendid in his uniform of the Guard Sappers, stood up, saluted, and cried out: "Good health to you, my sons!" He walked from the Manege to his carriage for the short drive to the palace of his cousin, the Grand Duchess Katerina.

At 1:45 the Tsar left the Grand Duchess's palace, stepped into his carriage, and ordered his coachman to return to the Winter Palace along the Katerinski Canal esplanade. Usually a busy thoroughfare, it was thought to be safe because it was bordered by the Quai on one side and the wall of a park on the other. When she saw the carriage turn into the Street of the Engineers, Sof'ya signaled the bombers to move to the Katerinski Quai.

As the Tsar's coachman reached the clear stretch of the avenue running along the Quai to the Mikhailovsky Palace, he loosened the reins and snapped his whip. The horses swept off at such a fast trot the Cossack outriders broke into a gallop to keep up. In front of the carriage the only people visible were a boy dragging a basket in the snow along the Quai, two or three soldiers, and a young peasant, wearing a fur cap, carrying a small parcel.

At the moment the imperial carriage reached the fur-capped peasant, he tossed his parcel under the horses' feet. An immediate explosion threw up debris, struck the back axle of the carriage, felled a Cossack escort, and hit the boy with the basket, who began to scream.

As the Tsar got out of his carriage to inquire about the injured man and the boy, the frightened horses dashed off with the coachman hard-put to bring them under control. To questioners the Tsar said, "I am unhurt," and cries of "God be praised" were heard. But when one of the police officers urged him to get into his sleigh and leave at once, the Tsar thanked him but refused, and continued to walk along the Quai where the bomb thrower was being held by two policemen. Katerina Dolgorukoya later accused the police, the Cossacks, and several officers of gross negligence in their failure at this point to protect the Tsar.

A second bomb thrower standing at the parapet of the Quai saw the Tsar walking toward him. He waited an instant, then dropped his bomb at Aleksandr's feet. It went off with terrific force. Through the flying snow, smoke, and debris the Tsar could be seen lying in the street, both legs shattered, his uniform in shreds, bleeding profusely from wounds all over his body. The bomb thrower also was lying fatally injured in the snow, as were more than a dozen others hurt in the blast, some of them already dead. Before losing consciousness the Tsar ordered that he be taken to the Winter Palace at once. He was put in a police sleigh and rushed off to the Palace where he died within the hour.

The deed was done. The two men with unused bombs looked on in horror. One of them rushed with the crowd that assembled in the wake of the second explosion and, seeing the Tsar had been fatally injured, found his human instincts taking over as he helped lift the dying man onto the sleigh.

Sof'ya Perovskaya did not linger. She made her way to the empty backroom of a nearby cafe where a fellow conspirator and a student waited for her. Around two o'clock she opened the doors and walked silently in. On her face was a controlled expression of sadness, but she was so tense she was able to speak only in short, abrupt phrases. She said she thought they had succeeded. The Tsar, if not dead, was seriously injured. Rysakov, who threw the first bomb, was in the hands of the police. She feared Kotik (Grinevitsky), the second bomb thrower, was dead.

The most articulate of the revolutionaries, Vera Figner, wrote that she learned from excited talk in the streets shortly after the explosion that the Tsar was dead. She rushed with the news to her comrades who had agreed to stay in their quarters that day until informed of what happened:

> When I came in I was so overcome with excitement I could scarcely stammer out that the Tsar had been killed. I wept. Others did, too. We could hardly believe the somber nightmare, which for decades had crushed young Russia, was ended. All the horrors of the prisons, the exilings, the executions, the atrocities inflicted on the hundreds and thousands of our people, the blood of our martyrs—all was atoned for at this moment by our spilling of tsarist blood. A heavy burden had been taken off our shoulders. Reaction was at an end. The new Russia was in the offing. In that solemn moment all our thoughts centered on our hopes for a better future in our country.

By four o'clock the members of the Executive Committee had gathered in Gelfman's conspiratorial flat. All shared Vera Figner's confused sentiments of relief, excitement, almost disbelief.

The leaders of Narodnaya Volya had brought off a spectacular blow against the autocracy. Now they had to alert the Russian people that it was time for them to take the next step. The Secretary wrote out a draft of the first proclamation. The members, including Sof'ya Perovskaya, discussed and soon approved it.

> Today March 1, 1881, the death sentence of Narodnaya Volya was carried out on Aleksandr II, a glorious demonstration that the Russian people have the means to break even the eternal despotism of the Romanoffs. . . . Now only the active struggle of all honorable citizens against despotism can move Russia out onto the path of freedom and independence.

The final draft was immediately taken to the Narodnaya Volya secret press for printing and distribution. Then began the discussion of the points that must be included in an announcement to all the Russian people of the *Narodnaya Volya* program of action and its proposals to the new Tsar, Aleksandr III.

While the Executive Committee spent the night putting together words, the tsarist police were assembling guns. By morning the city of St. Petersburg had become an armed fortress. Thousands of Cossacks had been ordered into the city and were in place to guard all roads and railroads, to check everyone entering or leaving the city. Streets were blocked off. House-to-house searches were in progress. Tsarist officials cast aside all other considerations of government to concentrate on the annihilation of the party of Aleksandr II's assassins, its leaders, its followers, and its sympathizers. Thousands were arrested. The new Tsar, Aleksandr III, fearful for his life, moved to a palace in nearby Gatchina where barricades were put up and moats dug as measures of protection. The people of St. Petersburg cringed in apprehension. As frightened spectators they witnessed a grand drama of threats and counterthreats by the government and the revolutionaries.

The city of St. Petersburg was a doleful sight on the morning of March 2. The lamps, housefronts, balconies, and windows were covered with strips of black and white cloth. A clamp-down on newspapers virtually stopped normal means of communicating anything except official bulletins, but the battle of words in pronouncements and proclamations by both sides was in full swing. Keeping pace with the official press releases were the rousing manifestos of the underground press, which appeared as if by magic tacked to kiosks, lamp posts, and postal boxes in every street and square in the city declaring *Narodnaya Volya's* determination to continue the struggle against tyranny as long as it took to achieve their often-repeated aims of freedom for the Russian people.

> To the Russian Workers!
> To the Peasants!
> To Western European Society!
> To the Russian People!

Daring party workers were in the streets posting these notices in all parts of the city. Others were carrying bundles of them to provincial towns and cities in all corners of Russia. Determined that *Narodnaya Volya* achieve its projected aims that were to follow the assassination of the Tsar, Sof'ya Perovskaya worked day and night, losing herself in continuous activity.

Within a few days the party's "Open Letter to Aleksandr III" was circulated. After a statement of condolence it said to the new Tsar:

> You have lost your father. We have lost not only our fathers, but our brothers, our wives, our children and our dearest friends. But we are ready to suppress personal feelings, if it be demanded, for the welfare of Russia. We expect the same from you.

The letter declared the late Tsar's vigorous policy of trying to repress revolution by hanging the innocent and the guilty, filling the prisons, and populating the remote regions of the Empire with political exiles had failed. In fact, the policy had expanded the ranks of the revolutionaries and brought the country to a state of pauperism and ruin. If the new Tsar continued this policy the results would be even more dire.

The message to the new Tsar was that there were only two exits from this hopeless situation: one, revolution which cannot be avoided by punishing revolutionaries; the other, voluntary transfer of supreme power from the autocracy to the people. There was no reply from Aleksandr III. Pushed by his reactionary advisers who demanded he flaunt his autocratic power, he later defined his position in a manifesto proclaiming:

> The Voice of God commands us to place ourself with assurance at the head of the Absolute Power. . . . we shall preside serenely over the destinies of our Empire, which henceforward will be discussed between God and ourself alone.[28]

The significance of these words was clear. Fear gripped the hearts of St. Petersburg citizens who had long secretly sympathized with the revolutionaries. Now, they retreated into silence and sycophancy.

The desertion of Russian society, and the sheer numbers of tsarist punitive forces drove the *Narodnaya Volya* Executive Committee, which alone knew the limited personnel and resources at its disposal, into retreat. Some, including Vera Figner and Sof'ya Perovskaya, urged an aggressive stance, a final fiery flare. They argued for an immediate attempt on the new Tsar. Vera wanted to keep the still-undiscovered cache of explosives under Malaya Sadovaya Street in readiness for the first time Aleksandr III traversed it. When she was overruled by her comrades, she shouted: "You are cowards!"

In defiance of the Executive Committee, Sof'ya Perovskaya took time from her heavy schedule of party activities to seek out laundresses and milliners who worked in the Winter Palace in her search for information about the new imperial family that would be essential for her secret plan to eliminate the new Tsar.

The public, in an atmosphere of strained expectation, was in a state of

---

[28]The manifesto was issued not in response to *Narodnaya Volya,* but at the urging of the new Tsar's friend and adviser, the Procurator of the Holy Synod, Konstantin P. Pobedonostsev, who was fearful Aleksandr III might be influenced by appeals coming to him from prominent Russians. Lev Tolstoy's famous plea for an imperial pardon to those being tried for assassinating Aleksandr II received wide acclaim beyond Russia's borders. *Narodnaya Volya's* proclamations appear in *I Marta 1881 goda, Proklamatsii i Vozzvaniia Izdanniye Posle Tsareubistva,* Petrograd, 1920. Aleksandr III's manifesto appears in *K. P. Pobedonostsev i Ego Korrespondenty,* Moscow, 1923, Vol. I, p. 52.

apprehensive excitement. The government dared make no plans for the coronation of Aleksandr III who remained in hiding behind barricades in Gatchina. Sof'ya Perovskaya was constantly thinking of schemes to free Tarass[29] (Zhelyabov) but her ideas for a prison break got lost in the chaotic discussions of party business, with members of the Executive Committee becoming more frenzied as one after another they were being picked up by the police. Fearing arrest, they began to leave St. Petersburg, with some crossing the border into Western Europe.

At the outset neither Zhelyabov, already behind bars before the assassination, nor Sof'ya Perovskaya, going from one hiding place to another as she tended Party affairs from early morning until late at night, was implicated in the Tsar's murder. The only person involved in it who had been arrested was the eighteen-year-old artisan, Rysakov, the first bomb thrower. And except for what concerned his own assigned task, Rysakov had been kept in ignorance of all aspects of the Party's terrorist activities. But in prison he panicked and began to talk. He identified Sof'ya as the woman who directed the assassination. She was already on the wanted list since Goldenberg had given the police information about her role in the 1879 Moscow train derailment. Soon copies of a mug shot of Sof'ya were distributed to police and to informers all over the capital.[30]

A newspaper "extra" appeared on the streets of St. Petersburg on March 3. Newsboys shouted "New telegram about the evil assassination!" "Zhelyabov Declares His Role in the March 1 Affair." Why did he do it? Sof'ya understood. She knew Zhelyabov believed theatrical effect was an important way to influence the public. The death of the Tsar was great drama. The accused in the court trial must not be the teenage raw recruit Rysakov. The most articulate and dedicated of the *Narodnaya Volya* activists must lay their lives on the line and stand trial. It was a God-given opportunity to climax the drama of regicide. The courtroom was a stage, and there—before the world—would be paraded the party's ideas, aims, and justification of its deeds. Then the final act—martyrdom on the scaffold.

Within the confines of the Winter Palace, another woman was going through a different kind of martyrdom. Katerina Dolgorukoya was often in hysterics as she mourned the loss of the Tsar, her lover and protector, and surveyed the ruins of her dream of becoming Tsaritsa. She was surrounded by the hostility of the royal family and the gloating of the new Tsar's ultra-reactionary officials, relishing their unexpected capture of power. Overnight they tore up the Loris-Melikov "constitution" with the approval of the new

---

[29]After reading Gogol's *Tarass Bulba,* Zhelyabov talked so much about it his friends started to call him Tarass.

[30]It is this grim photograph which has given posterity such an unflattering image of a woman her contemporaries described as always smiling and very pretty.

Tsar, who had agreed to it the day before when he was Crown Prince. They soon forced Loris-Melikov to resign and he went back to the Caucasus in disgrace. Katerina was in a hopeless position. She had suddenly become a *ci-devant,* a "has been." As far as tsarist society was concerned she was a "non-person." The new Tsar, Aleksandr III, gave Katya a month to leave the Winter Palace. She had the means to stay, but she decided to leave Russia. She took her children, who had been legitimized with the name Yurievsky, an ancient family name of the Romanoffs which the Tsar had bestowed on Katerina and their children after their marriage. With an entourage of tutors, governesses, a doctor, nurses, Russian cooks and their assistants, footmen, maids, a coachman and three dogs, Katya's party with all its trappings filled several cars of the Nord Express. She journeyed first to Switzerland, then to France, where she lived as the Imperial Widow of the Tsar, always insisting she be addressed as "Your Highness."

In the days following the assassination of Aleksandr II, Sof'ya Perovskaya, deeply in love with a doomed man, was clinging to straws. She could have gone abroad or into hiding, but unless Zhelyabov had a chance of escaping, she would stay to share his fate. She was physically exhausted, mentally drained. It was becoming more difficult for her to find a place to sleep a few hours at night. Sometimes she had no money for necessities and she refused to spend on herself the party funds she was still making the rounds to collect. One day, needing medicine, she asked Vera Figner to lend her fifteen rubles. She said her mother (at that time ignorant of her daughter's role in the Tsar's assassination) had sent her a silk ball gown (of all things!) and she was sure her dressmaker would soon be able to sell it for enough to repay Vera!

Sof'ya Perovskaya still had connections in high places. One day Rina Epstein arrived in St. Petersburg from abroad. She had shared Sof'ya's apartment until that September day in 1880 when she moved out and Zhelyabov moved in with his false passport identifying him as Sof'ya's brother. Rina received a message that Sof'ya wanted to see her. She did not know Sof'ya was involved in the assassination and assumed she wanted her help to go abroad, as getting people safely over the border had become Rina's speciality. Not at all. "It is impossible to leave the capital at such an important moment," said Sof'ya. "There is too much to do."

What Sof'ya wanted was for her young friend to go to an important government official, a general who could be trusted, to find out from him exactly what Zhelyabov's situation was. Rina agreed. She said she had a dress elegant enough to wear for an official visit and would go to the general's office at ten o'clock the next morning. Impatient as Sof'ya was to have whatever information the general could give about Zhelyabov, she told Rina the earliest she could see her the next day was six o'clock in the evening because she had seven appointments in opposite ends of the city which would keep her busy all day.

Rina had her interview with the general. She arrived at the house where she was to meet Sof'ya at six. She became more and more worried as the minutes and the hours slowly passed. Finally, at nine o'clock the doors opened. Sof'ya came in, pale and exhausted. The daughter of the house brought in a samovar and went out leaving the two young women alone. Without any circumlocution Rina told Sof'ya that the fate of Zhelyabov and other participants the police expected to round up soon in this case was death on the scaffold. There would be a trial but it would be for appearances only. After hearing the general's information about the trial, Sof'ya threw all caution to the winds. She appeared on the streets of St. Petersburg on foot and riding in open horse-drawn cabs every day, with no effort at disguising or shielding herself.

Mikhailov, designated the "third bomb thrower,"[31] who had carried his bomb onto the Katerinski Quai on March 1 but did not have to use it, was identified by Rysakov and arrested, as were Gessya Gelfman and Kibalchich. While admitting their own deeds, none of them, under questioning and possibly torture, named any of their comrades or co-workers. The police picked up Sof'ya Perovskaya on March 10 as she was riding in a cab on the Nevsky Prospekt.

Sof'ya's friends agreed that a letter, long thought to have been written by her to her mother just before her trial, represented her calm acceptance of her fate.[32]

---

[31] Ignati Grinevitsky was the second bomb thrower, whose bomb killed the Tsar, and also himself. The fourth thrower, Ivan Emelianov, was not arrested until after the Trial of the Six. He was tried in the Trial of the 20 in 1882 and sentenced to the Siberian *katorga*. He was released in 1902 and died in 1916. Nikolai Sablin, who had occupied the conspiratorial flat with Gessya Gelfman and was involved in the March 1 plot, committed suicide when the police, with information given them by Rysakov, descended on the flat March 3.

[32] In a letter Sergei Kravchinsky (Stepniak) wrote to Vera Zasulich, dated Milan, Spring 1882, he said he had just finished a brochure on Sof'ya Perovskaya (it later appeared as a chapter in his book *Underground Russia*) and thanked her for sending him what was purported to be Sof'ya's last letter to her mother written in prison just before her trial, saying "The letter is simply wonderful. Perovskaya, of course, did not write it, but the author (or better the authoress, for it was undoubtedly written by a woman) obviously knew Sof'ya well. . . . We are all indebted to the writer of these notes—whose words are simply pearls; they so accurately portray Sof'ya's destiny and come so close to depicting her genuine greatness." *Gruppa Osvobozhdeniye Truda* iz archivov G. V. Plekhanova, V. I. Zasulich i L. D. Deicha, sbornik i, pp. 218–21. A page of the handwritten original of the letter is reproduced in V. L. Perovsky's *Vospominaniia o Sestre*, Moscow, 1927. This correspondence seems to indicate that Vera Zasulich and Lev Deich wrote the Red Cross biography of Perovskaya, published in London in 1882.

My dear, adored Mama: The thought of you oppresses and torments me always. My darling, I implore you to be calm and not grieve for me, for my fate does not afflict me in the least. I shall meet it with complete tranquility, for I have long expected it. And I assure you, dear Mama, that my fate is not such a mournful one. I have lived as my convictions dictated, and it would have been impossible for me to have acted otherwise. [33]

She went on it this vein at some length, then asked her mother to carry out "a little commission" for her:

Buy me some cuffs and collars—the collars rather narrow and the cuffs with buttons, for studs are not allowed to be worn here. Before appearing at the trial I must mend my dress a little, for it has become much worn here. Goodbye until we meet again my dear mother . . .

Your own Sof'ya

March 22, 1881.

At about the time of the date on this letter, the police arrested Sof'ya's brother Vasya, and they soon appeared at her mother's door in the Crimea with an order that she proceed to St. Petersburg at once. They gave her 150 rubles for the trip. She left for the capital immediately. This order was not an act of kindness by the authorities to permit Varvara Perovskaya to say farewell to her daughter; it was a last-ditch attempt to unseal the closed lips of Sof'ya Perovskaya who was refusing to reveal the identity of her *Narodnaya Volya* comrades or the party's non-member supporters.

Upon her arrival in St. Petersburg, Madame Perovskaya was instructed to go directly to the Ministry of the Interior, where she promptly found herself seated across a table from Loris-Melikov who said:

I must inform you that the Tsar himself orders you to use all your influence to persuade your daughter to give you the names of her accomplices so that we may bring to an end this spilling of blood.

To which Varvara Perovskaya replied:

My daughter from earliest childhood has displayed such independence that she will never give anything to anybody on order. She will respond only to kindness and persuasion. She is a mature person and she clearly understands what she has done. Therefore, no order of this kind can influence her.

Whereupon, Loris-Melikov threatened her, saying her son Vasya was under arrest and she should consider what could be done to him if she did not obey the Tsar's orders. She replied that she understood all that, but reiterated neither he nor the Tsar could expect any information from her or Sof'ya. Still, Madame Perovskaya pleaded for permission to visit her daughter.

---

[33]The full text appears in the chapter on Perovskaya in Kravchinsky's (Stepniak) *Underground Russia.*

The next day a message was delivered to Sof'ya's mother at her hotel, informing her of the time and place of the meeting she had requested. She went to the prison and was led by a guard into a room with four chairs. Standing in the room were two police officers. Sof'ya was brought in. Mother and daughter silently embraced. They were told to sit in two chairs side by side, while a police officer sat opposite each woman, their knees almost touching. They exchanged a few words, mostly Sof'ya's entreaties to her mother not to grieve. The visit was soon over. Varvara Perovskaya was permitted one more visit, and again they sat silently together side by side, opposite the policemen, Sof'ya with her head in her mother's lap.[33]

On Thursday, March 26, 1881, the court building on Liteiny Prospect was surrounded by police and gendarmes, but unlike the Vera Zasulich trial, the public was not admitted to the Trial of the Six. This was not a jury trial. It was a trial by the Court of the Imperial Senate. The presiding justice, Fuchs, lacking the independence of Judge Koni, agreed to end the trial in three days with a conviction, to silence any effort on the part of the accused or the lawyers defending them to use the trial as a forum for their party's ideas, and to impose rigid censorship on the six representatives of the Russian and foreign press who were permitted to attend.

At 11 o'clock in the morning, the trial of the two women and four men indicted in the murder of Tsar Aleksandr II opened. The defendants represented a cross-section of Russian society: Gelfman, daughter of a Jewish merchant; Kibalchich, the son of a priest, and a scientific genius whose main concern at the trial was to get some kind of assurance that his most important invention, a flying machine, would be built and put into operation; Mikhailov, a workingman; Perovskaya, an aristocrat; Rysakov, a middle-class artisan; and Zhelyabov, of peasant origin.

Dominating the square, whitewashed courtroom was a full-size painting of Aleksandr II, draped in black and white. The dead Tsar stood as if presiding over the trial. Besides the eight judges, the prosecuting attorney, a few court officials (including the four attorneys assigned by the court to defend the prisoners), and the authorized representatives of the press, few people were permitted in the courtroom. The accused, all wearing black prison robes, were brought in. They walked between two rows of gendarmes and were seated in the dock. They began excitedly to talk to each other but were immediately stopped. The London *Times* correspondent described each prisoner. He noted Rysakov's youthful face, with deep-set eyes under bushy brows and long, fair hair brushed back over his neck. Gessya Gelfman was

---

[34]Vasya Perovsky in his memoir, *Vospominaniia o Sestre,* says that when he returned from Siberia in 1885 his mother told him these details about her prison visits with Sof'ya and her meeting with Loris-Melikov.

Sof'ya Lvovna Perovskaya (Photo 1881)

Gessya Gelfman

a tiny woman of dark complexion and black frizzled hair; she smiled a lot when looking at or conversing with her fellow prisoners. Sof'ya Perovskaya was small and delicate-looking, with a good figure, pale features, blue eyes, and blonde hair neatly arranged in a chignon. The correspondent commented on her calmness and self-possession. He saw Zhelyabov as a tall, thin, handsome man, his bearded face with regular features notable for its fierce and determined look. Mikhailov was large, heavy-set, and looked like a Russian peasant. Kibalchich, tall and thin, had sharp features, dark hair and wore a small beard and moustache.

The prisoners were charged with belonging to a secret society, named in the indictment as the Russian Social Revolutionary Party, whose aim was the overthrow of the tsarist government and the existing social order. They were charged with making several attempts on the life of His Late Imperial Majesty, and finally with his murder.

Many witnesses for the prosecution were called, and Muraviev, the prosecutor, took more than five hours to present the case against the accused. He spoke in grandiloquent phrases, tracing the heinous crimes of the revolutionaries and their movement. He accompanied his passionate words with sweeping gestures; he screamed, he wept. He sketched the revolutionary career of Sof'ya Perovskaya from her first transgressions as a propagandist in 1872 to the Tsar's assassination.

> We must imagine a political plot. We must imagine this plot is to use the most cruel, the most revolting means. We must imagine that a woman participates in this plot, that she becomes the head of it, that she takes on herself the carrying out of all the details of the assassination, that she, with cynical cold-bloodedness, assembles the explosives, sketches the plan, and orders where each person is to stand, that this woman becomes the soul of the plot, that she runs to look at its consequences, standing only a few steps from the place of villainy to admire what her hand has done. Such a woman is utterly devoid of any ordinary sense of morality.

Muraviev demanded the death penalty for all of the six without exception:

> Cast out by men, accused by their country, may they answer for their crimes before the Almighty God!

Only Muraviev and Sof'ya Perovskaya were aware at the time, though neither showed it by the slightest sign of recognition, that they had, as children of neighboring families, been playmates.

No one of the four court-assigned defense attorneys spoke more than fifteen minutes in behalf of his client. They did little more than make feeble efforts to persuade the judges to lighten the penalty the prosecutor had demanded. Zhelyabov refused the services of an attorney, demanding to make his own defense. It is difficult to determine what he actually said, for the official record of the trial was not made public until 1906, and gives evidence of having been heavily censored (the record of the long sessions of the three-day trial contains only 262 pages). Foreign correspondents, warned that their dispatches would not be permitted to go on the wires until approved by court officials, could send out only sketchy bits and pieces of information.

Censorship destroyed Zhelyabov's projected scenario of courtroom drama played out for all the world to see. His words and the words of his comrades, which he hoped would explain to the Russian people and to the world why Russia's talented, dedicated youth had chosen the path of terror, never got through. Despite the censorship, the London *Times* correspondent was able to convey a few of Zhelyabov's adroit challenges of the prosecutor's charges, including his repudiation of Muraviev's portrayal of the Populists as nothing but base murderers:

> Look back over the last ten years. We have not always advocated political murder. We were at first peaceful propagandists, but through oppression and persecution we were at last obliged to recognize the government as our greatest enemy and our views were thereby materially changed. The government made us revolutionaries. We had to defend ourselves. We thus came to adopt violence.

In the official court record Sof'ya Perovskaya is quoted as giving her occupation as "revolutionary activist." To each question put to her about her role in the March 1 assassination and the November 19 Moscow derailment of the train in the Tsar's entourage, Sof'ya Perovskaya calmly answered she was guilty. She further said as a member of the *Narodnaya Volya* party and as an agent of the Executive Committee she agreed fully with the party's principles and its program, but she said:

> Many, many accusations have been thrown at us by the prosecutor. I do not speak of the accusations of acts I am guilty of; I have consistently admitted all of those. But the accusations of our immorality, brutality, and contempt for public opinion—it is these accusations I deny. Anyone who knows our life and the circumstances in which we have worked will not accuse us of immorality or brutality. They know we have worked early and late in our dedication to the well-being of the people.

Her only other plea was for Gessya Gelfman, who she said had been occupied only with distribution of party propaganda, and even though her apartment was used by the party for conspiratorial purposes, Gelfman was not involved in any way in the plot against the Tsar's life.

At the close of the late-night session of the third day, the Trial of the Six came to an end. All six were condemned to death by hanging. Because she belonged to the nobility, Sof'ya's sentence had to be passed upon by the Tsar himself.

Varvara Perovskaya, feeling she could not bear to attend the trial, did not ask permission; but she did request to see her daughter after the trial was over. She was informed by the authorities that once the death sentence was passed the condemned person was considered dead. A visit was, therefore, not possible.[35] After this cruel answer the poor woman left her hotel to seek the comfort of a visit with her brother, an official in the Institute of Natural Science. His children greeted her with a tender welcome, but her brother, fearful of his own fate, asked her to leave. Broken-hearted, Varvara Perovskaya left St. Petersburg for the Crimea.

On April 3, around eight o'clock in the morning, the black-garbed condemned, except for Gessya Gelfman who shortly after the trial made it known she was pregnant,[36] were marched out of the grim Trubetskoi Bastion of the Peter Paul Fortress. With their hands and legs fettered, they were loaded into two heavy carts. Each was securely tied to an iron bar behind a high seat with his or her back to the horses. Zhelyabov and Rysakov were in the first cart, Sof'ya between the two other men in the second. On each chest hung a placard with the words "Tsar Killer" in large black letters.

Preceded by a cart filled with soldiers and police and followed by a cart with priests and coffins, the carts with the prisoners rumbled noisily through the prison gates. Accompanied by marching drummers, whose loud and monotonous rhythm would drown out any words the condemned or the crowds might utter, they went through the streets of St. Petersburg where lines of soldiers stood between them and the tens of thousands of people gathered there. The Trial of the Six had been secret. Now the regicides were on public display. Were the crowds friendly or hostile? Government spokesmen said the general mood was satisfaction that justice had triumphed, but others said there were everywhere shouts of encouragement as the carts passed. All except Rysakov, who was on the verge of collapse, sat erect and looked straight ahead as they rode through the thronged streets. The black hoods of the prison gowns nearly covered their faces except for that of Sof'ya Perovskaya. She sat defiantly straight, her high, broad forehead and the delicate profile of her upturned face clearly visible. Had Sof'ya's ancestor, Count Vasili Alekseevich Perovsky, the determined and resourceful general who led the conquest of the huge steppe region above Turkestan in the

---

[35]Kravchinsky (Stepniak), in his correspondence with Vera Zasulich (Gruppa "Osvobozhdeniye Truda" . . . sbornik I, pp. 218ff.), reported the widespread belief that since the prisoners were allowed no visitors after being sentenced to death—a privilege always granted to prisoners about to die—they were subjected to torture in an attempt to force them to name accomplices and supporters. In his book Underground Russia, in his chapter on Perovskaya, he states as a fact that they were tortured. He also has Madame Perovskaya's request to see her daughter, after she was sentenced, granted. She was instructed to arrive the morning of April 3, and it was arranged so she got there just as the prison gates opened. She saw her daughter, fettered in chains, on her way to the gallows. Vasya Perovsky, in his memoirs, specifically denies this ever happened.

[36]Soon after the birth of her child, Gessya died in prison. Her baby daughter was taken to an orphanage where she soon died. Gessya's husband, Nikolai Kolotkevich, was a member of the Executive Committee of Narodnaya Volya. He was arrested in January 1881 and tried in the Trial of the 20 in 1882. He was condemned to death and died in prison in 1884.

1850s, ridden any more proudly than she through the streets of St. Petersburg when he came to lay the fruits of his military prowess at the feet of
Tsar Nikolai I? By her stern, calm bearing, Perovskaya was making hers a
triumphal journey.

The carts made their way southward to the large, barren, Semenovsky
Field, still covered with piles of snow that began to melt as the sun's rays
penetrated the morning fog for the beginning of a beautiful day. In the center
of the parade ground was the rough wooden scaffold, painted black, that
Loris-Melikov had left standing after the execution of his would-be assassin.
The execution, badly bungled by the drunken peasant executioner (some
foreign correspondents called it butchery), lasted twenty-five minutes as
each of the condemned was hanged in turn. The bodies were put into rough
wooden coffins, piled into the carts, and guarded by Cossack outriders,
taken for ignominious burial in the prisoners' graveyard in the distant suburb
of Preobrazhenskoe.

A fighting proclamation was *Narodnaya Volya's* response to the hanging
of the five on April 3, 1881, which removed two of its most capable leaders,
Perovskaya and Zhelyabov. The executed comrades had carried out the task
they had taken upon themselves to do for the people, but since the goal for
which they had sacrificed their lives had not been achieved, *Narodnaya
Volya* would continue the struggle against tyranny.

Two women, born into the Russian aristocracy, could have had brilliant
marriages and lived out lives of ease in the highest ranks of St. Petersburg
society—at least until 1917. One of them, Katerina Dolgorukoya, abandoned her youth, her beauty, her family, all worldly pleasures, and her
place of first rank in the aristocratic world of her birth for a life of luxurious
imprisonment in the inner chambers of the Winter Palace as the mistress of
Aleksandr II. She was convinced she was carrying out a noble purpose of
bringing happiness to a melancholy monarch and encouraging him to make
concessions "to the people." The other woman, Sof'ya Perovskaya, abandoned a similar heritage for the turbulent life of a revolutionary, and in the
end sacrificed her life to what she believed to be the cause of freedom for
her country.

Katerina Dolgorukoya, known in Russia in her lifetime to no more than
a handful of people, was forgotten in her native land almost as soon as
she left Russia after the assassination of Aleksandr II. The memory of Sof'ya
Perovskaya was kept alive for over thirty years by members of the Russian
revolutionary movement who knew and admired her, and included accounts of her activities in their memoirs, first published in the underground
press in the 1880s and 1890s, then, after 1905, in legally printed books and
journals, many of which were reprinted after 1917. In the Soviet Union,
Sof'ya Perovskaya has become a legendary revolutionary figure. Her name
and a few facts of her martyrdom appear in Soviet textbooks, encyclopedias,
and in several inadequate biographies. There is today in Leningrad, Sof'ya

Perovskaya Street, not far from Zhelyabov Street, near the Katerinski Canal. In museums of the revolution all over the Soviet Union, faded pictures of Perovskaya hang alongside those of other famous revolutionaries, although Stalin ordered the banner "Death to Tyrants" that hung over the photographs of Perovskaya and Zhelyabov in the Leningrad Museum of the Revolution to be ripped off. In the Soviet Union, Sof'ya Perovskaya's action against the Tsar is mentioned, her struggle for freedom is unknown.

The hanging of Sof'ya Perovskaya, the first woman in Russia to be executed for a political crime, made a terrible impression in Russia and abroad. At the time of her death, Ivan Sergeevich Turgenev was moved to write and dedicate to her his prose-poem *Porog* (Threshhold):

> I see a huge building, in the front wall a narrow door, which is wide open; beyond it stretches a dismal darkness. Before the high threshhold stands a girl—a Russian girl.
>
> The impenetrable darkness is breathing frost, and with the icy breeze, from the depth of the building, comes the sound of a slow, hollow voice.
>
> "O you! waiting to cross this threshhold, do you know what awaits you?"
>
> "I know," answers the girl.
>
> "Cold, hunger, hatred, derision, contempt, insults, prison, suffering, even death?"
>
> "I know."
>
> "Complete isolation, alienation from everyone?"
>
> "I know. I am ready. I will bear all sorrow and miseries."
>
> "Not only if inflicted by enemies, but by kindred and friends?"
>
> "Yes, even by them."
>
> "Well, are you ready for self-sacrifice?"
>
> "Yes."
>
> "For an anonymous self-sacrifice? You shall die, and nobody, nobody shall know even whose memory is to be honored."
>
> "I want neither gratitude nor pity. I want no name."
>
> "Are you ready—to commit a crime?"
>
> The girl bowed her head.
>
> "I am ready to commit a crime."
>
> The voice paused a while before renewing its questioning.
>
> "Do you know," it said, at last, "that you may lose your faith in what you believe now; that you may come to feel that you were mistaken and have lost in vain your young life?"
>
> "I know that, also. Nevertheless, I will enter."
>
> "Enter, then!"
>
> The girl crosses the threshold, and a heavy curtain falls behind her.
>
> "A fool!" gnashed someone outside.
>
> "A saint!" answered a voice from somewhere.[37]

---

[37] *Porog* was published September 25, 1883, in an illegal *Narodnaya Volya* flyer. It does not appear in any of the editions of Turgenev's collected works. It was republished in *Russkaia Istoricheskaia Biblioteka*, no. 6, Literatura Partiy Narodnoy Voli. It also appears at the end of Nikolai Petrovich Asheshov, *Sof'ya Perovskaya. Material Dlia Biografiy i Kharakteristiki*, St. Petersburg, 1921.

ANNOTATED REFERENCES

The London *Times,* June 7 & 8, 1880, printed a detailed account of Tsaritsa Maria Aleksandrovna's funeral. The English court was in mourning because the dead Tsaritsa's daughter was married to Queen Victoria's son, the Duke of Edinburgh.

Sof'ya L'vovna Perovskaya, Krasny Krest Norodnoy Voli (24 pages), London, 1882 was the earliest biography. S. M. Kravchinsky (Stepniak), *Underground Russia. Revolutionary Profiles and Sketches from Life* (in English), London, 1883, has a chapter on Perovskaya. The book was published later in Russian, and over the years the chapter on Perovskaya was published separately in several languages.

Heavily censored accounts of the Trial of the Six were printed in the Russian and foreign press. The London *Times* account appeared April 9, 1881. The official record of the trial, *Protsess 1go Marta 1881go goda,* was published in St. Petersburg, 1906. A collection of twelve proclamations of the time appears in *1 Marta 1881 goda,* Petrograd 1920, edited by N. S. Tiutchev.

Peter Alekseevich Kropotkin in his *Memoirs of a Revolutionist* (first published serially in the *Atlantic Monthly,* September 1898 to September 1899), New York and Boston, 1899, lovingly sketched Sof'ya Perovskaya in her Chaikovsky Circle days.

Vera Figner, *Zapechatlennyi Trud* (The Unforgettable Effort), Moscow, 1921, in the first volume, devotes a chapter to Perovskaya and describes her own reactions to March 1, 1881.

V. L. Perovsky's memories of his sister appeared in book form as *Vospominaniia o Sestre,* Moscow, 1927.

Nikolai Petrovich Asheshov's *Sof'ya Perovskaya, Material Dlia Biografii i Kharakteristiki,* Petersburg, 1921 is a collection of quoted excerpts from all the reminiscences and memoirs available to him in 1919. He did a similar collection on Zhelyabov.

David Footman, *Red Prelude. The Life of the Russian Terrorist Zhelyabov,* New Haven, 1945, is the best source of information on Perovskaya in English.

Soviet Biographies are: Elena Segal, *Sof'ya Perovskaya,* Moscow, 1962, which has a good bibliography and E. Pavliuchenko, *Sof'ya Perovskaya,* Moscow, 1969.

Of the many books written on Katerina Dolgorukoya's life with Aleksandr II, the most informative is by Tarsaidzé, the most curious and interesting by Laferté.

Victor Laferté, *Aleksandr II, Détails Inédits sur Sa Vie Intime et Sa Mort,* Geneva and Paris, 1882. The identity of Laferté is unknown, but the source of the information was Katerina Dolgorukoya, and she "reveals all."

Alexandre Tarsaidzé, *Katia, Wife Before God,* New York, 1970. One of his main sources of information was Boris Berg, Katya's nephew, who knew her well.

Princess Marthe Bibesco (Lahovary), the prolific French novelist, wrote *Katia,* London 1939. Her fictionalized account was used as the basis for the French film *Katia,* directed by F. A. Algazy, starring Danielle Darrieux and John Loder.

There is no satisfactory biography of Aleksandr II, including the "official" two-volume *Imperator Aleksandr II, Ego Zhizn' i Tsarstvovanie* (Aleksandr II, His Life and Reign) by S. S. Tatishchev, St. Petersburg, 1903. Two later biographies are Constantin de Grunwald, *Alexandre II*, Paris, 1963, and E. M. Almedingen, *The Emperor Alexander II*, London, 1962.

3

Vera Figner and the Betrayal
of *Narodnaya Volya*

Kronshtadt. Front door to the Russian Empire!

Before the smoke of cannon fire cleared from his war of conquest with Sweden, Peter the Great began building at the exposed edge of his domain a new capital city, St. Petersburg—Russia's "Window to the West." To protect it, in 1703 he created a chain of forts stretching across the Bay of Finland, with the massive, three-sided tower on the barren sliver of land—eight-mile-long Kotlin Island—as its epicenter. On the island, in 1710, he founded the walled city of Kronshtadt, the "crown city," as a fortress and a place to house military officers, soldiers and sailors, and the growing community of shipbuilders, mechanics, and provisioners of the naval base.

Every Russian ruler, following Peter's daring example, strengthened Kronshtadt and its semi-circle of forts to block the Bay of Finland at a line fifteen miles to the west of St. Petersburg. Thick granite walls surrounded the island, jutting out like daggers into the grey waters of the Bay. Forbidding circular stone batteries of gun emplacements, rows of cannon, and ever-more-heavily fortified bastions loomed out of the mist and over the ice and snow in winter when the Bay was frozen—a grim warning to any who might dare think of testing the strength of the mighty Russian Empire.

Kronshtadt. Should it ever weaken, not only the capital of the Russian Empire would fall; the path to all of north and central Russia would be wide open, and Romanoff rule would end.

On a cold, sunny morning in mid-March 1881, two uniformed naval officers and a comely, well-dressed young woman came out of an apartment house on Litovskaia Street in St. Petersburg. They carried heavy bundles and packed them into a hired carriage. When all was stowed away, they got in and ordered the driver to the railroad station where they took the train for the short ride to Oranienbaum (now Lomonosov), eight miles down the coast from St. Petersburg. At the Oranienbaum station, they got into a horse-drawn car running on rails down to the dock where they boarded a naval steam launch. It made its way through the ice-clogged waters of the Bay and within a half hour chugged into a landing below the fortress city of Kronshtadt. Again they loaded their bundles into a hired carriage, then drove into the city through the center gate of the triple-arched entry of the thick citadel wall.

The carriage went along Aleksandrovskaya Street, through the square, past the statue of Peter the Great. On every street and in every square were soldiers and sailors. Colored service ribbons pinned to the grey coats of the army officers' uniforms blew in the wind. They passed the naval barracks on Pavlovskaya Street; the songs of a company of sailors rang out as they marched toward the gateway of the city on their way to naval exercises where sniper fire could be heard, beyond the wall, along the shore line.

The carriage stopped in front of a row of officers' houses. The packages were carried in by naval orderlies, and the two officers and the woman quickly followed. The woman was Vera Figner. The packages contained dynamite, salts of fulminic acid, guns, and illegal literature. They also held the hectograph on which *Narodnaya Volya* proclamations had been duplicated for distribution after the St. Petersburg printing press was dismantled to avoid confiscation by the police following the March 1 assassination of the Tsar. Kronshtadt; the strongest bastion of the Empire, its army and navy units headed by the Tsar and members of the royal family. Could this be a haven for Vera Figner in whose apartment was assembled the bomb that killed Tsar Aleksandr II?

That the Kronshtadt military force was peppered with revolutionary circles was a well-kept secret in 1881. Zhelyabov and Perovskaya had initiated the strategy of allying *Narodnaya Volya* and the military. A leading role in recruiting was played by Vera Figner, Anna Korba, Sof'ya Perovskaya, and other women of the Executive Committee. A dozen or more highly respected, patriotic officers with brilliant careers ahead of them and with companies of soldiers and sailors under their command, had joined revolutionary circles. Meeting several times a week they read illegal literature, discussed socialist revolutionary ideas, drew up programs of action, and listened to propaganda speeches by *Narodnaya Volya* activists. Some officers participated in the conspiracy to assassinate Aleksandr II. Others helped form revolutionary circles among the students of the Artillery Academy. They even brought explosives to the classes they were teaching and proceeded to prepare their men for the coming revolutionary struggle.

At the same time common soldiers, sailors, and workers on Kronshtadt were responding to the revolutionary call. Their enthusiasm was heightened

by the "great deeds" of *Narodnaya Volya* martyrs. The March 1 assassination brought a deputation of Kronshtadt soldiers to their officers with the
proclamation: "We are ready to appear at any moment, fully armed, before
the Winter Palace and within a quarter of an hour reduce it to ruins."

Nowhere in those March and April days was Vera Figner safe, but the
military brass of Kronshtadt was ready not only to provide a temporary refuge but to consider with her, as a leading representative of the Executive
Committee, the burning question of the day—should they begin a general
uprising? Should they act to take advantage of the opening the Tsar's assassination had made in the strained fabric of autocratic rule?

Loathing tsarist orders to shoot and coerce young people whose actions
seemed to them in no way criminal, sickened by what they saw during the
Turkish War of tsarist official brutality toward common soldiers and sailors,
many officers in tsarist military units were ready for Vera Figner's message.
Nor were they immune to her beauty. She stood before the men gathered
in her borrowed officer's quarters in those March and April days, her wil-
lowy figure well set off by the severe lines of her long-skirted, simple blue
suit with its white, stand-up collar and satin bow at the neck—a model of
elegant femininity. Her face was a perfect oval, her thick ash-blonde hair
was piled in a braid on top of her head, or worn in a heavy chignon at the
nape of her neck. But the fine features of her lovely face were strong. The
firm mouth and the level gaze of her big brown eyes conveyed the auda-
cious pride of a woman and a fighter. Quick of movement, cheerful of coun-
tenance, the tones of her rich contralto voice were low, musical, and persuasive:

> Russian Officers! Great moments in history, like the one we are living in,
> demand decisive responses. In such a moment no one can be politically neu-
> tral. You cannot comfort yourself by saying you will just fulfill your duty, for
> the question is "What is duty?"

> There on the wall is the time-honored motto of the Russian Army: "Glory and
> Honor." This motto was handed on to you as a heritage from your predeces-
> sors and it must be passed on by you, unstained, to future generations. Of
> what does an officer's honor consist? Can he preserve his honor by spilling
> the blood of his fellow citizens? Is it honorable for an officer to be an oppres-
> sor? As military officers you are duty bound to defend the people. Can you
> then raise your weapons against them?

> You must decide these tough questions. You cannot remain neutral.

> Russian officers! Stretching out before you are two paths. You can stand with
> the liberators of our people or you can be their hangmen. And let him who
> wavers remember the foul path he must tread if he chooses to serve tyranny.
> He must deaden his conscience, spit on human dignity, blind himself to the
> shootings and beatings by the mercenary police, and be ready to order his

Vera Figner 1878

troops to shoot innocent people at the first signal of every rapacious district police officer. He must fill the prisons with fighters for the people's rights and roughly choke every honorable voice, every independent thought.

Say "No!" to this. Join the people! The people's legions will knock the weapons from the hand of the tyrant. In the open war with tyranny which is at hand, the true officers will carry the flag of the people. To them we say: To you is entrusted the fate of the masses. The unstained hands of citizen officers will write the history of the future with their heroic deeds. Only the people's legions can be true to the lofty motto "Glory and Honor."

In the gigantic battle between the revolution and tyranny—join us! Who is not
with us is against us. It is we who will win![1]

Naval Lieutenant Nikolai Sukhanov rose to say that plans were going ahead
for "a military insurrection division" which would instigate not just demonstrations but an armed uprising. The prospects for success were good, he
said. Meantime the task was to fight with propaganda, to distribute revolutionary proclamations on every square and highway of Russia. Revolutionary circles were being established and activated in military installations all
over the Empire, a veritable revolutionary network, with direct lines of communication to the centers in St. Petersburg and Kronshtadt.

Vera Figner did not mention it, but she and her listeners well knew Russia's first revolutionaries were army officers: the Decembrists, shot down by
Tsar Nikolai I, court-martialed, hanged, or exiled to the *katorga,* hard labor
in the mines of Siberia, for their daring to organize and to demonstrate for
a constitution on a snowy December day in 1825 on St. Petersburg's Senate
Square. These men, the flower of Russian society, were brutally punished
by the Tsar, but were revered as heroes by the Russian people. Bards and
poets related in song and verse their exploits of bravery and self-sacrifice.
In the 1880s an officer could join the revolutionaries with the thought he
was following in the footsteps of Russia's honored heroes of old.

Vera Figner's days on Kronshtadt were filled with feverish activity. A single word from her would have set off a military uprising, but serious problems prevented action. There was no money. Police surveillance in St. Petersburg had immobilized the regular collection of funds from party
members and sympathizers. Then there was the uncertainty of link-ups with
the revolutionary military and civilian party units in other parts of the Empire. Worst of all, execution and imprisonment of most of that fearless band
of revolutionary leaders had left *Naronaya Volya* an army without strong
and cohesive generalship, without most of the men and women who had
worked as a team in making decisions for more than two years. Together
they had succeeded with their terrorist acts and propaganda in focusing the
attention of the nation and the world on the bankruptcy of tsarist rule.

In an effort to close the leadership gap, Lieutenant Sukhanov and his
colleagues were working on a plan to free the *Narodnaya Volya* leaders
imprisoned in the Petropavlovsk Fortress. To procure the funds needed for
bribes and other expenses, they decided to rob the Kronshtadt Bank. In the
interim the officers contributed hundreds of rubles of their own money to

---

[1] Of the many background materials consulted for this reconstruction of Vera Figner's speech,
the source of the words is "Ispolnitel'niy Komitet Ofitseram Russkoy Armii," dated August 24,
1881, *Literatura Narodnoy Voli,* St. Petersburg, 1905, pp. 908–12.

keep the party going. Party proclamations were being duplicated on the hectograph brought from St. Petersburg, but soon the officers got a printing press assembled on Kronshtadt and began teaching sailors how to use it.

After Easter, Vera Figner was called to Moscow where a remnant of the Executive Committee, three women and five men, had settled, thinking it safer than St. Petersburg. There they recruited several new members and continued to churn out proclamations threatening that assassinations would continue, that terrorism would not end until the autocracy began the establishment of free institutions.

Except for ceaseless police activity, the tsarist government was paralyzed. The police, on the defensive because they had failed to protect the Tsar from his assassins, were in a zealous frenzy, picking up suspects by the hundreds, imprisoning, exiling, and hanging them. In the reigning chaos, no one was certain of the real strength of the revolutionaries. The authorities were so unsettled by fear of when and where the terrorists might strike next they dared not make plans for the coronation of the new Tsar, who remained a virtual prisoner in his palace outside St. Petersburg. He was inaccessible to anybody, even to his own ministers. The Russian public, like the sea after a storm, was still being buffeted about by the waves of recent events.

The Executive Committee of *Narodnaya Volya* decided Vera Figner should go to Odessa to spur the revolutionary military circles in the Black Sea area to greater activity. She would make contacts to prepare for the arrival of Lieutenant Sukhanov who was expected to forge links between the military circles of the north and south. She was also to examine the situation of the Odessa revolutionaries, numerically one of the largest and, traditionally, one of the best organized groups in Russia, left leaderless and in disarray by widespread arrests and executions in the wake of the March 1 assassination.

Figner had many friends in Odessa, for the party had sent her there in 1879 and again in 1880, with Sof'ya Perovskaya, to work on a project to assassinate Aleksandr II in Odessa. The plan was abandoned when his travel arrangements changed. She was greeted by old comrades, but found the city under a pall of fear. The tsarist military prosecutor of Odessa and Kiev, General Strel'nikov, was engaged in an orgy of persecution and killing. Guilty or innocent, it made no difference to him. "Better arrest nine innocent people than let a single guilty one escape," he was fond of repeating.

Vera Figner's military contact was Lieutenant Colonel Mikhail Ashenbrenner, a much-decorated veteran of the Turkish War, whom she had met in 1880 and had found difficult to communicate with. She decided either he was not used to female society or did not like it. This must have been her own misconception, for Ashenbrenner in his memoirs described himself as entranced with Vera Figner's beauty and poetic charm when he first met her accidentally at a friend's apartment. He said she had a magnetic quality that was inexpressibly exciting.

Ashenbrenner invited Figner to come to a secret apartment for a meeting. There she found assembled the whole command of his infantry regiment. She was struck by the difference between these men and the officers of the north with whom she had been working. The northern officers were dashing young men about her own age, elegant and venturesome, ready for any risky adventure. In contrast, these solid, established soldiers, all ten or more years her senior, apparently liked to read illegal radical literature and meet together to discuss ideas of freedom, socialism, and the future transformation of Russian society. They were well informed, they were good talkers, but not one of them had ever engaged in any kind of revolutionary activity.

Diplomatically, but with fire in her eyes, Vera Figner sharply attacked their inactivity. It was not enough, she said, to rent an apartment secretly and to talk among themselves. Why were they not conducting propaganda among their own men? Why were they not making contact with the naval officers of the Black Sea Fleet? Why were they not going out to the military installations in other cities to set up revolutionary circles where there were none—and she named several such places. As always happened, the men were greatly impressed with Vera Figner's beauty, her message, and her tactful but firmly spoken words. By the time she finished speaking they were ready for action. She left, satisfied she had stirred them up and prepared the way for Lieutenant Sukhanov's imminent arrival.

Then came an unexpected blow: On April 28 Lieutenant Sukhanov was arrested. Vera Figner, accustomed to working in the tightly knit brotherhood of the *Narodnaya Volya* Executive Committee, whose every member would have died rather than reveal a party secret or an associate's identity, was not prepared for the penetration of a government spy, an informer, into the ranks of her military colleagues. There had been a few betrayals in the past, by people on the party's periphery; and the raw recruit, young Rysakov who threw the first bomb on March 1, had broken under the relentless interrogation of the prosecutor Dobrzhinskyi. Fortunately for the party, Rysakov knew very little and could identify only a few people. Up to the spring of 1881 no spy had penetrated the party's inner circle.

Who was the spy? There was not a clue.

Immersed in the tasks at hand, Vera Figner and her colleagues did not spend the time and effort needed to ferret out the traitor. There was, of course, the possibility Sukhanov had accidentally fallen into the hands of the police. Vera knew and constantly warned that the elaborate precautionary measures the revolutionaries had perfected over the years were given way, and that carelessness alone was causing arrests.

Then came several more arrests—of army officers in St. Petersburg and two more of Vera's naval officer colleagues. Other naval officers were saved for the time being by spring maneuvers which took the Kronshtadt officers and men out to sea.

Sukhanov's mission was assigned to another officer who came south, accompanied by Anna Korba. Following Figner's leads and cooperating with the now active Major Ashenbrenner, they went to work on expanding military circles dedicated to revolution, recruiting members, and stepping up revolutionary propaganda on military bases and in the cities where they were located. In the Caucasus Anna Korba converted a whole regiment to the cause.

Narodnaya Volya, committed as it was to terrorism against tyranny, took pains to dissociate itself from acts of violence abroad. The president of the United States, James A. Garfield, was fatally injured by an assassin's bullet on July 4, 1881. His assailant was not a political radical but a mentally deranged man who said he wanted to make Vice President Chester Arthur president to save the Republican party. When the president died of his wounds in September the Executive Committee of *Narodnaya Volya* sent an open letter of sympathy to the American people along with a statement that they considered it their duty in the name of the Russian revolutionaries to protest his assassination.

> In a country where personal freedom guarantees the full possibility of an honest struggle of ideas, where a free people not only make the laws but elect the rulers—in such a country political murder as an instrument of political conflict is an expression of that very spirit of despotism from which it is our aim to extricate Russia. Violence can be justified only if it is directed against violence.

More than half a year had passed since the assassination of Tsar Aleksandr II on March 1. That the assassination would be a clarion call to the numerous and influential silent supporters of the freedom movement to pressure the tsarist government to grant reforms proved to be an erroneous assumption, yet *Narodnaya Volya* continued its threats and propaganda attacks on the government.

Returning to Moscow from her mission to the south, Vera Figner met with the Executive Committee, its new members outnumbering the old. They immediately launched into a discussion of what to do next. She put on the agenda a request for authorization of an "action" in Odessa. Seeking their support, she told the committee of the desperate complaints being received by the Odessa *Narodnaya Volya* against General Strel'nikov, the military prosecutor of Odessa and Kiev. The General, considering himself the leader of a war against sedition, was making massive searches and arrests. Week after week, hundreds were rounded up, imprisoned, tortured, exiled, or hanged. His treatment of the Jews of Odessa was a continuous pogrom, but hardest hit were members of *Narodnaya Volya*, not only being arrested, denounced, and hanged but vilified by Strel'nikov as common criminals trying to hide behind the false banner of freedom. Figner argued that the Executive Committee owed it to their comrades Strel'nikov had hanged, they owed it to their party he had slandered and undermined, they owed it to the suffering people of Odessa, to order Strel'nikov's execution. She said Strel'nikov knew his life was in danger. Many had threatened to kill him. He was well guarded, but in Odessa she said a successful attack on his life could be made.

The Executive Committee accepted Vera Figner's proposal. She left at once for Odessa. It was the beginning of December. She trailed Strel'nikov for weeks and passed on her information to two young men, experts in explosives whom the party had recruited (one of them, Khalturin, had blown up the Winter Palace dining room in 1880). Since the Moscow Executive Committee did not send the funds they promised, Vera raised money for their getaway horse and carriage.

On March 15, Vera Figner left Odessa for Moscow. Three days later the scenario she had planned for shooting General Strel'nikov was carried out. Shot in the back of the head as he sat on a bench on Odessa's famous Primorski Boulevard, taking in the beautiful scene of the Black Sea stretching out below, he died instantly. But the gunman found it hard going through the crowd that gathered at the sound of the shot. He finally reached his comrade in the getaway carriage, but it was surrounded and they could not move. The police arrived and the two men were arrested. Within four days they were tried and hanged.

Narodnaya Volya's proclamation of triumph said the hangman Strel'nikov had been shot for his role as executioner, carrying out the criminal tsarist policy of violating the rights of the people. The shooting was an ominous warning to tsarist officials that *Narodnaya Volya* was still a force to be reckoned with. There were warnings that the head of the secret police, Sudeykin, was next on their hit list.

In Moscow Vera Figner was assigned a room occupied by local party members in the tiny, wretched apartment of a teacher who spent her days trudging from house to house giving lessons to children. The teacher's nanny, who lived with her, was an ancient crone, bent nearly double, toothless, and half-blind. She wandered about the rooms, hitting the floor with the stick she leaned on, ceaselessly mumbling the ominous phrase, "There's trouble ahead. There's trouble ahead. I feel it in my bones. There's trouble ahead." And, as Vera Figner laconically said, "Trouble came." Arrests in Moscow were a daily occurrence. No one knew who would be next. Those who could left the city, several for destinations abroad. *Narodnaya Volya's* illegal press was discovered. Several more of its members were arrested.

By mid-April no member of the Executive Committee was left in Moscow—except Vera Figner. And she was a veritable prisoner in the poor teacher's apartment. She could not receive visitors and she dared not go into the streets. She decided she had to leave Moscow. She chose Khar'kov as her refuge. She knew that in Khar'kov there was a local *Narodnaya Volya* party whose members she thought could be relied on and who had the potential of being activated. Khar'kov was a provincial town. There were few intellectuals there, or other groups who might be prospective sympathizers or supporters of *Narodnaya Volya,* but it seemed to offer a safe haven, a base of operations from which Vera could go out to other centers to recruit and to activate.

Soon came another blow. News arrived of the arrest in St. Petersburg and Kronshtadt of the few remaining members of the Executive Committee and the flight abroad of the rest of them. By mid-June 1882, only one member of the committee remained in Russia: Vera Figner.

Vera Nikolaevna Figner *was* the *Narodnaya Volya* Executive Committee.

What now were the party's resources? Figner asked herself. There was, first of all, the party's formidable reputation, which the killing of Strel'nikov had reinforced. The Strel'nikov murder multiplied the tsarist government's fears, making it more difficult for the police to assess the party's strength. The new tsar remained uncrowned. During tentative preparations for a coronation illumination in Moscow, a *Narodnaya Volya* activist, who had assisted in the cheese shop mine operation on Malaya Sadovaya Street, was found among the workers, and plans for the coronation were halted indefinitely.

Another *Norodnaya Volya* resource was the number of experienced party workers scattered all over Russia who, although they had never been members of the Executive Committee, had been active in various other ways. From her Khar'kov base Vera Figner had been traveling the length and breadth of European Russia, from Azov to Minsk, to Tambov, Saratov, Novorossiysk, Nikolaev, Tiflis, Poltava, Kiev, and many other cities, recruiting, always recruiting.[2] She left in her wake dozens of new circles, with hundreds of idealistic young women and men anxious to assume active roles but lacking training, guidance, and seasoning.

There were the three printing presses in Moscow, Minsk, and Vitebsk that had been closed down to escape detection. When the opportunity arose they would be used again. The distribution of proclamations and pamphlets

---

[2]Norman M. Naimark, *Terrorists and Social Democrats: The Russian Revolutionary Movement under Alexander III,* Cambridge, Mass. and London, 1983, says that despite the fact that nearly 6,000 women and men were arrested, and most of them exiled, in the years following Alexander II's assassination, Vera Figner did a remarkable job of reviving and setting up new revolutionary circles all over Russia. It was these circles which in the years of black reaction under Aleksandr III did much to keep the revolutionary movement alive.

was the only way to keep the public informed of "the truth" of Narodnaya Volya activities, its program, and its ideas. Party literature smuggled in from abroad did not meet the need.

With these resources and her own indomitable will, Vera Figner was convinced she could rebuild the Executive Committee to its former strength and refocus the party toward political revolution and a guarantee of rights for the people. She decided to bring several military officers into the Executive Committee on the assumption the party would benefit from their training and experience in the difficult decisions ahead. She persuaded several high-ranking officers to go on leave so they might single-mindedly devote themselves to party activities. Officers on leave could presumably escape the moral dilemma they faced when, continuing to serve in the Tsar's armed forces, they were actively opposing tsarist autocracy!

One of these officers was Sergei Degaev, a professional soldier and artillery officer. He had gone on leave when recruited in 1880 by Zhelyabov, who had kept him on the periphery of Narodnaya Volya activity. Degaev had been arrested after the March 1 assassination but was quickly released, even though he had been one of the "diggers" in the cheese shop mine operation under Malaya Sadovaya Street. He was disliked, even distrusted, by several Executive Committee members, including Anna Korba who had been recently arrested and was behind bars. But when he came to Khar'kov, sought out Vera Figner, and offered his services, she responded to him as an old confederate. She was soon confiding in him and sending him on secret missions to military bases and party circles all over Russia.

Party affairs seemed to be proceeding well enough to start up the underground Narodnaya Volya press. Odessa, now that Strel'nikov had been removed, appeared to be the place to do it. Degaev, Figner decided, was the man to put in charge.

In October 1882, Vera Figner received through an intermediary, the well-known critic and publicist Nikolai Mikhailovsky, an offer to negotiate a truce with the tsarist government. The offer was purportedly being made by a highly placed person in the tsarist establishment. Mikhailovsky said she was being addressed as head of the party, because the government was exhausted from the struggle with Narodnaya Volya and wished peace. It was ready to step onto the path of reform, but could not take that step under the constant threat of revolutionary terror. The only obstacle to reform was terror. Stop terror and reforms would be decreed at once.

The specific proposal was for Narodnaya Volya to announce publicly its agreement to stop the terror until the coronation of the new Tsar, Aleksandr III. In return for keeping this agreement, at the coronation the government would issue a manifesto guaranteeing full political amnesty, freedom of the press, and freedom for peaceful socialist propaganda. As proof of its sincerity the government was willing to make the first move; it would immediately free one of the many *Narodnaya Volya* leaders being held in the Peter Paul Fortress Prison in St. Petersburg. The person suggested was Isaev, a man in the lower ranks of the party hierarchy, with whom Vera Figner had at various times lived in the same apartment, posing as his wife.

Vera Figner was incredulous. Was this victory? Or was it a trap? Was it possible that a year and a half after the killing of Tsar Aleksandr II the tsarist government had finally been brought to its knees? Was the *Narodnaya Volya* party, now a mere shadow of its former self, accomplishing what *Narodnaya Volya* at full strength had failed to do? Distrust of the tsarist regime was so thoroughly ingrained in Vera Figner she could only register suspicion and alarm. She remembered the occasion three years earlier, when clever interrogation by a police official persuaded the imprisoned Executive Committee member, Grigory Goldenberg, to talk by appealing to his patriotism. His information had then been used to search out *Narodnaya Volya* leaders, arrest, try, and sentence them to death, exile, and imprisonment. What guarantee was there that the promises of freedom being made by the "highly placed" person would ever be carried out? What was to prevent the government, using the information *Narodnaya Volya* would have to reveal in the negotiations, from setting in motion official actions with the aim of unraveling thread by thread what was left of the party? What would prevent the ferreting out, arrest, and execution of every active agent?

Vera Figner could understand the proposal in only one way. It was a trick. "Freedom of the Press." "Amnesty." "Constitution." "Reform." Words, mere words!

Mikhailovsky raised a question of his own. "Is *Narodnaya Volya* able at the present time to carry out an effective terrorist program?"

In all honesty, Vera could only bow her head and say, "No."

"So, if you accept this proposal, what have you to lose?"

"Everything," thought Vera Figner. Everything she had done with almost superhuman effort to rebuild *Narodnaya Volya* and its Executive Committee. Opposing thoughts raced in her head, but assuming an outward calm she instructed Mikhailovsky to tell the "highly placed" person to negotiate with L. Tikhomirov and Natalia Oloviannikova, two members of the old Executive Committee who were living in Europe. This would be a play for time and would leave Vera and the new Executive Committee in Russia free to accept or reject the outcome of the negotiations abroad, whatever they might be.

Of the negotiations in Europe, Vera heard nothing. She received no communication from Tikhomirov or from her emissary Neonilla Salova. Only after her imprisonment did Vera Figner learn that in the negotiations initiated in Europe, the stakes got very high. The tsarist spokesman was authorized to offer millions of francs if the *Narodnaya Volya* exiles would convince the Executive Committee in Russia publicly to renounce terror and begin negotiating the terms of a truce. Then, suddenly, all negotiations stopped. The emissaries from the "highly placed" person were ordered to return to Russia immediately or face charges of treason.

Vera's plans to reactivate the *Narodnaya Volya* press started out well. Degaev moved to Odessa in November 1882 with his wife. Vera sent three trusted fellow workers to help the couple, and soon the presses began to roll.

On December 20, Vera learned the police had raided the print shop, impounded the press, and put Degaev, his wife, and his three helpers behind bars.

The abrupt end of the attempt to revive the *Narodnaya Volya* press was a heavy blow. She later wrote:

> It is painful to recall that dark time which began with this event. I saw all my work come to naught. Lost were five people in Odessa. Added to them were recent arrests in St. Petersburg and Kronshtadt. I was persistent but it all seemed to be in vain. Yet I could not retreat. Too many young people still were looking to me with hope, getting from my continued faith and work for our cause, moral support for their own dedication.

> My circle of comrades was broken, lost. I remained alone. Like the eternal wanderer of Eugene Sue, I was treading a crooked path, and I could see no end to it.

> I was living a double life: one external—for people; one internal—for myself. Outwardly I had to retain a quiet, cheerful face. And I was cheerful. But in the quiet of the night I was almost overcome with sadness. Is this the end? I asked myself. My end? The party's end? Then in the morning I would again put on my mask and go to work.

On January 23, 1883, Vera received an urgent message from a good friend asking her to come at once. Vera walked rapidly to the secret address and went in. As she stepped through the door she stopped in amazement. Before her stood Degaev, pale and distraught, with the face of a man tortured with worry. He had made a daring escape from his police escort, he said, as they were taking him from Odessa to Kiev. He did not know what happened to his imprisoned colleagues and had no idea who would have betrayed the printing press to the police. His main concern was over the fate of his wife, still in custody.

In the weeks that followed Vera freely transmitted to Degaev important information about party and member activities. One evening Degaev asked, "Vera, do you feel safe here in Khar'kov?"

"Absolutely," she replied, then added, jokingly, "unless the traitor Merkulov meets me in the street."

In a manner conveying deep concern, Degaev asked Vera about her daily routine. Did she follow a regular schedule of going out each day? Did the house she lived in have an exit as well as the entrance at the front gate? Without hesitation Vera answered all these questions, appreciating his attention to her safety.

On February 10, 1883, Vera Figner walked out at her habitual hour— eight o'clock in the morning, the time when women paramedical students were going to their classes. Her strategy was to lose herself among them for she carried a passport with a false name, identifying her as a medical assistant, or feldsher, student. She had gone scarcely ten steps when she looked up and saw Merkulov. He recognized her, of course, but did not grab her. Glancing sideways she could see no police. She continued to walk very fast, straight ahead. Calmly she sized up her situation and quickly concluded there was no escape—no passageway through a yard, no nearby safe apartment or house she could dash into and out of by a back way. What was in her pockets? A notebook with two or three names, a postal receipt for money sent to a party member in Rostov. These had to be destroyed. She began tearing paper and dropping it piece by piece. As she approached a little square at whose edge lived a couple she knew, two gendarmes appeared and grabbed her before she could dash in. They tossed her into a waiting sleigh and within minutes she was in the police station.

In a separate room an inexperienced woman began to search Vera. Before she got to her pocket, Vera put what was left of her incriminating paper into her mouth. The woman screamed. Two police officers rushed in and grabbed Vera by the throat, but she opened her lips in a wide smile to show she had swallowed whatever it was she had in her mouth.

Early the next morning, accompanied by two gendarmes, Vera Figner boarded a train bound for St. Petersburg. During the day-long trip she tried to find the answer to the puzzle of her sudden arrest, but could not figure out who had betrayed her. News of Vera Figner's arrest preceded her arrival in St. Petersburg. The Minister of Justice, informed by telegram, was overjoyed. Aleksandr III was told and exclaimed, "Thank God! At last that terrible woman has been arrested."

When she arrived in St. Petersburg on a Saturday evening, Vera was locked up in a local police station and ignored by officials for several days. Then she was taken to the office of the Third Section, the tsarist secret police. As she entered the building she was led through corridors packed with people, from high officials to lowly clerks. They crowded in to gape and satisfy their curiosity about this legendary woman whose name they whispered as she passed.

Soon she was escorted into the large, high-ceilinged office of an upper-echelon police officer, the minister of Internal Affairs, Count Dmitri A. Tolstoy, came in followed by the assistant minister (until recently director of the police department), Viacheslav K. Pleve.

Pleve, a coarse, corpulent man, spoke first. Pointing to a row of straight chairs along one wall, Pleve ordered Vera to sit down, then proceeded to lecture her. He said all the young people the police were taking into custody every day would never have been arrested if they had not been impressed with her enthusiastic example. "So now," he said, with a look of scorn on his face, "are you still so enthusiastic? Or are you glad you were arrested because you are tired of what you are doing?"

In contrast, the minister of Internal Affairs was refined and acted like a worldly, well-educated man. Tactful and soft in manner, he wanted to draw her into conversation on political matters; but she avoided this, saying her views would be better explained in court.

Figner considered Count Tolstoy senile and stupid, but he was good-natured. Looking at her, he exclaimed, "What a modest appearance you have. I expected someone entirely different." Then he talked on and on about classical education and how the revolutionaries opposed it. He got to the subject of political assassination in general and tsar killing in particular and said, "What did you accomplish by this? You kill one tsar and his place is taken by another." His manner was that of a grandfather reprimanding his grandson. Then he said, "What a pity we do not have more time. I would win you over." Not wishing to leave him the last word, Vera said, "I also regret we haven't the time. I think I could turn you into a Narodnaya Volya supporter."

Vera's little joke was repeated throughout the chancelleries. Upon her first meeting with the Imperial Prosecutor Dobrzhinskyi, he made her laugh with the question: "Do you really think you could win Count Tolstoy to your faith?"

She answered, "Why not?"

Vera was soon taken across the Neva River to the immense, grim Peter Paul Fortress Prison, the Russian Bastille. Wide and flat, surmounted by a tall, tapering spire, its gates opened into endless somber vaults, with sentinels standing at intervals, dimly lighted by the images of saints holding tapers in the niches of the walls. In cell Number 43 she sat for nearly two years awaiting trial.

At the beginning she was often called to the prison administration office for questioning. She told them she saw no need for all this questioning because she had no intention of hiding any of her revolutionary activities up to March 1, 1881. As to what happened after that, she said she would never reveal anything. She said, "Bring paper and ink to me in my cell and I will write down everything I know."

This is how Vera Figner came to write an autobiographical sketch which was soon being circulated and read like a novel by officials high and low, one of them her divorced husband, Aleksei V. Filippov, who had become a member of the Ministry of Justice.

One day a tall, handsome old gendarme general with a sympathetic face came to her cell. He introduced himself and, before she could stop him, took her hand and kissed it. "You are a good person," he told her, "Your misfortune is that after you got married you didn't have children." He had come to tell her of plans for the trial. She asked whether the government intended to launch a huge trial. She was thinking of the hundreds of officers who were implicated in one way or another in revolutionary organizations. He told her the trial would be confined to fourteen people, and of those, only six were military officers. He added that they could, of course, have brought dozens to trial.

Days, weeks, and months passed. The year ended and another began. Vera was left alone, completely alone. In the silence, the awful truth crowded in. This was the end. Not only had her role in the political struggle come to an end; life itself would soon end—on the scaffold. As she reviewed her life for the official record, past events of a personal nature flooded into her mind. She thought especially of her mother, whom she had not seen for many years; of her three sisters, every one of them suffering imprisonment, exile, illness—all caused by the revolutionary careers they had undoubtedly been influenced to follow by her example. What a contrast to their two brothers, both wealthy professional men: one an engineer, the other a famous opera singer.

Finally Vera's mother and her sister Olga (the only sister living in freedom at that time) were given permission to visit her for twenty minutes every two weeks. Bi-weekly they dutifully came and sat behind bars, with guards on either side. Far across a huge room behind an iron fence sat Vera, who wept each time she saw them. She wanted desperately to kiss her mother's hands, to feel the touch of her soft fingers on her face. No, to meet face to face, to touch was against the rules.

Spring came. Vera longed to see a flower. Just one flower. She dreamed of the clusters of flowers that bloomed in the spring along the streets of St. Petersburg. Olga brought a hyacinth for Vera. She pleaded with the guard to let her sister have the flower. No, he was adamant.

In the spring of 1884, after more than a year of isolation from officials, Vera was called to the prison office. There she saw again the tall, old gendarme general who had visited her many months before. Imperial Prosecutor Dobrzhinskyi was with him. They were, with grave faces, sitting behind a table on which lay big, bound notebooks.

Opening one of the notebooks, Dobrzhinskyi put the pages covered with writing in front of Vera and asked, "Do you recognize this handwriting?"

"No," She replied,

Then Dobrzhinskyi turned several pages and showed her a signature: Sergei Degaev, 20/11/82.

November 20! "This must be a mistake," Vera thought. "The printing press in Odessa was seized December 18, and the comrades were indicted December 20."

Dobrzhinskyi then showed her page after page covered with the same handwriting, report after report to the police, each signed with the same signature: Sergei Degaev. Absolute proof lay before Vera that her trusted comrade, her friend Degaev, had been turning over to the tsarist police everything he knew about the *Narodnaya Volya* party. Not only were all the major activists named, but even the least significant people were identified and located. All the important secrets and sources of the party's strengths and weaknesses were fully revealed. Everything had been put under a bell glass. His treason had fed the leaders of the party, high and low, into the police maw: Sukhanov, Anna Korba, Ashenbrenner. On and on she read the names of her betrayed comrades.

Now Vera understood why suddenly she had heard no more of Mikhailovsky's "highly placed person" and the truce between the government and *Narodnaya Volya*. After Degaev engineered his false arrest in Odessa in December 1882 and went on to betray Vera in Khar'kov, and in his reports revealed the weakened position of the party, what need was there for the government even to pretend to make concessions?

Vera was stunned. Degaev! Degaev did this! She paced back and forth while the general and Dobrzhinskyi quietly turned the pages of the notebooks. When she finally sat down, Dobrzhinskyi began to pull from a pile of papers sheet after sheet and hand them one by one to Vera. Each contained the testimony of a southern military officer. Each one began with the words: "Repenting my errors, I inform the authorities . . ." And so "repented" thirty-five men, including the chosen few in whose strength and character Vera had believed so firmly she had enlisted them in important party activities. All those men, who had promised that at the call of the Executive Committee they would advance with guns in their hands, that they would sacrifice their lives for the cause of the people, all those men who had given their word of honor to fight on the barricades, had confessed they "were mistaken," they "had erred."

Which was worse? The collapse of will of the military comrades or the betrayal of Degaev? This double blow shook Vera Figner to the core of her being. Degaev, whom she had trusted, had lied, pretended, and deceived. He pumped out information in order to betray. He flattered and twisted his intended victims. The police arrested him only to mask his treachery; his "escapes" were a sham. Beginning with treason, he went on to become a provocateur. He used his friends and professional associates in the military establishment to draw men into the revolutionary movement only to betray them!

Vera wanted to die. But she had to live. "I must live. I must appear in court—that high, concluding act of every revolutionary. As a member of the Executive Committee, I must speak for it. I must fulfill my last duty. I must do what is expected of me. I must share the fate of my comrades Degaev betrayed."

To survive until the trial, Vera had to crowd out of her mind the revolution for which she had lived and worked for nearly a decade. She must, all day, every day, without rest, occupy herself in some kind of work. She took up study of the English language. She had a rudimentary knowledge of English, but now she threw herself so completely into her study of it that within two weeks she read Macaulay's *History of England,* and went on reading voraciously. "Books were my salvation," she said.

On September 18, 1884, the fourteen accused were taken before the regional military court. There the act of indictment was read to them.

All the people in the Trial of the Fourteen had been betrayed by Degaev, but his name was not mentioned in the indictment nor later in the court proceedings. At the military court on that September morning, Leont'ev, the court-appointed lawyer for the defense of the fourteen, whispered to Vera Figner, "Sudeykin is dead. Degaev did it and escaped." This news was terribly confusing. Degaev had killed a major foe of *Narodnaya Volya!* Yet he had betrayed her and how many other party leaders? She could make no sense of it.[3]

On Saturday, September 21, at ten o'clock at night, the accused were taken separately from the Peter Paul Fortress Prison to the House of Preliminary Detention which was attached by a labyrinth of underground corridors to the Circuit Court building on Liteiny Prospect. On Monday morning Vera Figner was led into the courtroom where her thirteen co-defendants were already sitting in the prisoners dock, two gendarmes standing beside each prisoner with naked swords at their sides. Vera could hardly hold back her tears. Could these thin, wan people, with looks of despair on their waxen, yellow faces, after months of preliminary detention, be the comrades who, when she last saw them, were vigorous, cheerful people, full of the joy of living?

---

[3]Not until 1906 did accounts of Degaev's treachery begin to appear. They revealed the combination of Sudeykin's manipulation of Degaev for his own purposes of winning the Tsar's approval (and a high office) because he was arresting so many terrorists, and Degaev's use of Sudeykin's protection to eliminate *Narodnaya Volya* leaders so he himself could become head of the party. Hatred and guilt finally drove Degaev to kill Sudeykin. He fled to the United States where he earned a Ph.D. at Johns Hopkins University, served as Dean of the College of Engineering at the University of South Dakota, went on to a position at the Armour Institute of Technology, and died in Bryn Mawr, Pennsylvania in 1921 (his American wife taught at Bryn Mawr College). Lev Deich's *Provokatory i Terror,* Tula, 1926, contains articles Deich published earlier. *Byloye,* no. 4, April 1906, has an article on Degaev by Anna Korba, and in the same issue "Degaevshchina (materialyi i dokumenty)."

The witnesses filed in—the experts on explosives, the attorneys from the Imperial Prosecutor's Office, the defense lawyers. This was not a jury trial like that of Vera Zasulich; it was not an open trial like the Trial of the Six in March, 1881, it was a closed, court-martial trial with no representatives of the press or the public. The audience in the courtroom was exclusively bureaucrats from the prosecutor's office and the Department of Police. Leading prison administrators were there, as was Minister of Justice Dmitri N. Nabokov, and Minister of the Interior Count Dmitri Tolstoy. Vera's mother and her sister Olga had also gained admission.

Everyone stood at attention as the judges walked in and sat down. Then, speaking in a boring monotone, the court secretary read the act of indictment. The crimes and illegal activities of Vera Figner alone made a long list. There followed the accusatory testimony of witnesses. Neither the accused nor the defense lawyers made any attempt to refute the evidence. The verbal sallies of the prosecution against the accused were rather mild, though the prosecutor general made a thrust at Vera Figner, asking rhetorically how she, a well-educated woman of the gentry, could have such an insatiable thirst for blood? He concluded by demanding the death penalty for them all.

Vera Figner had refused the services of a defense attorney, saying she would speak for herself. The general defender, Leont'ev, commenting on the prosecutor's question about Vera Figner's thirst for blood, said she was a person who so passionately loved truth that for the sake of that love, did not draw back from the necessity of spilling blood. The "public" of bureaucrats in the courtroom listened attentively as he ended with the words, "As for the sentence that awaits Vera Figner, she does not expect nor does she want either mercy or leniency."

On the fourth day of the trial came the moment Vera Figner described as the most memorable of her life. The presiding judge turned to the prisoners in the dock and said: "You the accused: To you belongs the last word!"

The dispirited prisoners, certain of being condemned to death, knew these words would be their last public utterances. The chance to speak gave them the opportunity to show their real character, to give moral justification for their deeds, to express their deep convictions, and publicly to say all they wanted to say, all they ought to say, all they must say. And if this last opportunity was not grasped—at once—it would be lost forever.

Physically and spiritually exhausted by events and by twenty months of solitary confinement in the Peter Paul Fortress, Vera Figner was nonetheless ready. During sleepless nights she had ceaselessly worked to put her thoughts in order in anticipation of this moment when she would carry out her last duty to her dead comrades, to those still in prison and in exile, to the ruined party, and to the future generations of revolutionaries she was sure would arise.

Names of the condemned began to be called. Several of her male comrades rose and began to speak, only to have the presiding judge curtly admonish them that they were not speaking "to the point at issue" and tell them to sit down.

Vera Figner heard her name called. She stood up. The courtroom suddenly became quiet—unnaturally quiet. She lifted her head and found all eyes turned on her. Like an electric shock, this concentration of attention touched off a flow of words. Her striking beauty, which physical exhaustion had not obscured, her low musical voice, and the message she conveyed held her listeners, including the presiding judge, at rapt attention for more than half an hour—with no interruptions.

The court scrutiny of my actions begins with 1879. The prosecutor in his speech expressed surprise at how many actions I engaged in, as well as the kinds of things I did. But these crimes, as well as all the others, have their history. They are firmly linked to all that happened before in my life. During my preliminary detention [twenty months] I often asked myself: Might my life have gone in another direction than it went? And might it have ended any other way except on the bench of judgment? Each time I had to answer: No.

I began my life in the most favorable circumstances. . . . My family was well-off, enlightened, and loving so that I never experienced the struggle which so often takes place between the old and the new generations. I never knew material need, never had to worry about a crust of bread, or the problem of achieving economic independence. When at seventeen I finished my studies at the Institute [the Women's Institute in Kazan], for the first time I began to see that not everyone was living in such comfort as I was. The idea that I had an obligation to the masses burst into my head when I realized I belonged to a cultured minority. It was an obligation placed on me to the rest of the population, the uncultured masses who live from hand to mouth, sunk in hard physical labor, entirely deprived of what is usually called the blessings of civilization. The striking contrast between my position and theirs made me realize I had to create an aim in life that would enable me to go down to the suffering masses and benefit them.

From the Russian journalism of the time and from the women's movement, which was at its height in the beginning of the 1870s, I found the solution to my problem. It became clear to me that by becoming a doctor I could fulfill my philanthropic aspirations. The Women's Academy in Petersburg opened about this time, but it was, and still is, so weak as to keep it hovering between life and death. Since I was firmly committed to my goal of becoming a doctor for the socially deprived, I decided I must go abroad [for training].

And so, significantly reshaping my life, I traveled to Zurich, Switzerland, and entered the university. Life abroad was very different from that in Russia. The things I met with there were entirely new to me. What I had learned and seen in Russia did not prepare me for these things, did not prepare me to evaluate correctly all that confronted me. . . . Furthermore, I went abroad at a time when contemporary events in Paris [the Paris Commune, 1871] and the revolution in Spain were calling forth strong responses in the world of the workers of the West. I was soon introduced to the doctrine of socialism. . . . I took to socialism almost instinctively. Socialist ideas seemed to be only an extension of the philanthropic notions that sprang up in my mind earlier. A doctrine promising equality, brotherhood, and general human happiness dazzled me. I did not see Europe's workers' movement as a product of Western European life. I mistakenly considered its teachings applicable to all times and all places.

Influenced by these ideas and events, I joined the first revolutionary circle [of Russian women students]. My sister Lidiia [who, with Vera's husband, Aleksei Fillipov, accompanied her to Switzerland] also belonged.

In a few words Vera told of the weakness of this circle. The young women's ideas of socialism and revolution were immature. They joyfully looked forward to the worldwide revolution they visualized as coming very soon. They saw the masses, in their poverty and degradation, as instinctively socialistic, just waiting for the spark of socialist propaganda to ignite the flame. The ruling minority would soon become aware of the impossibility of struggle with the masses and would concede to their demands. The possibility of bloodshed never occurred to these naive revolutionaries.

Vera said she stood apart in the circle because she was an inherently conservative person who did not make a decision quickly; but once she made it, only with great difficulty did she relinquish it. The revolutionary circle of Russian women students in Zurich did not remain active for very long. Most of its members, some after two, some after three years at the University, decided to return to Russia in the spring of 1874, Vera elected to stay in Switzerland to complete her medical studies.

Soon the girls who returned to Russia were in prison. They had arrived when the "Going to the People Movement" was in full swing and decided to do their bit to spread the word which they believed would awaken the Russian people from their torpor. At a time when most of Russia's populist youth were going to the countryside, they found jobs in Moscow factories to make contact with workers. Their aim was to teach them to read and to bring the message of socialism they had learned abroad. Their arrest, their months in prison, their trial (the famous Moscow Trial of the 50), and sentencing to the *katorga* made a terrible impression on Vera.

When a plea came from friends in Russia to return to take up the work of her imprisoned, former fellow-students, Vera was ready to consider it. She had already completed her medical training except for the final formalities of getting the degree. (Sometime before this she had separated from her husband who had returned to Russia to resume his legal career.) Thinking matters over, she decided her desire for a medical degree, her ambition to use the title "Doctor," was sheer vanity. Could she not treat Russian peasants without it?

She found that the question was not whether she *could* treat the peasants, but whether she would be *permitted* to treat them. She went to the country and became a *zemstvo* feldsher (local medical assistant).

Never anywhere but in Russia would I have been subject to persecution. In fact, elsewhere I would have been considered a useful member of society. Very soon I found a whole league had formed against me, led by the head of the Gentry [Council] and the director of the district police, joined by official and unofficial persons down to the village police and the district clerk. They spread a steady stream of false rumors about me—that I had no passport, that my diploma was a fabrication, and so forth. When the peasants did not want to make an unprofitable deal with a landlord, they said it was my fault. When the District Assembly lowered the wages of the district clerk, I was to blame. They made private and public inquiries about me. When the district police officer came to the village where I lived, several peasants were arrested and in the inquiry my name came up. There were two denunciations of me to the governor of the province, and thanks only to the intercession of the chairman of the *zemstvo* administration, I was momentarily left in peace. But I was living in the midst of a police-spying atmosphere. People were afraid of me. The peasants who sought medical attention had to walk through back yards to reach the place where I lived.

I finally had to ask myself: What can I do under such conditions? . . . I had come to this rural district to study the situation, to learn what peasants them- selves thought, what they hoped for. No one had any factual incriminating evidence against me. There was none. It was that they could not believe a person like me, who did not lack education, would settle in the village without some sinister, ulterior motive. I was simply being persecuted for my spirit, for my attitudes.

She said it had become impossible to make contact with the people, even to carry out routine medical services the peasants would lack completely without her. Unwilling to give up, Vera began to wonder if she was making mistakes which could be avoided if she moved to another place and tried again.

I resisted relinquishing my long-cherished goal. For four years I had studied medicine motivated by the idea that my life's work would be among peasants. From my own experience and from information I gathered from others I could only conclude that the problem was not my personality nor the conditions in a particular place. The problem was that there was no political freedom in Russia.

Up to that time Vera said her approach had been social altruism, but experi- encing personally for the first time the "inconveniences of our way of gov- erning," it became clear to her that the basic problem was the flaws in the Russian form of government.

At that time I had two options: I could take a step backward, go abroad and become a doctor—but there I would be a doctor not for peasants but for the rich, which I didn't want to do; or I could use my energy and strength to remove the obstacle which had shattered the aim to which I had committed myself.

At first she refused to join the secret, illegal political party, *Zemlya i Volya*, but when she was driven from her goal of practicing medicine for the people, she changed her mind. Later when the party split, she joined *Narodnaya Volya*, accepted its commitment to terror, and became a member of its Executive Committee.

> My experience led me to the conviction that the only way the existing order could be changed was by violence. There was no peaceful path along which I could go. As you know, we have no freedom of the press. Even to think about the spread of ideas by the printed word is impossible. If there had been any element of society to point out to me another path except violence I would have chosen it, or at least tried it. But I saw no protest coming from anywhere—not from the representatives of justice, not from the *Zemstva*, not from the municipal or any other existing corporate bodies. There was not even any literary influence speaking up for change in Russian life. All this led me to conclude that the only way out of the terrible situation in our country was by means of acts of violence.

> Once I took that path I followed it to the end. I always demand consistency in people and in myself. I expect words to harmonize with deeds, and it seemed to me that if I accepted in theory the path of violence, I had the moral obligation to participate directly in the violent actions undertaken by the organization I belonged to. Under such compulsion I took part in many of them because I could not in good conscience draw others to participate in violence if I myself did not. . . .

> This is the explanation of that "bloodthirstiness," of those acts which appear so frightful, so callous, so incomprehensible, if it is not remembered that they were prompted by motives which seem to me honorable.

> For me the most vital point of the *Narodnaya Volya* program was the destruction of the absolutist form of government. Personally I did not care whether the regime which replaced it was a republic or a constitutional monarchy. One can dream of a republic, but only that form of government a society is ready for can become a reality. . . . The most important thing was to create a political atmosphere in which people could develop their capacities to the full and apply them to the benefit of society—for it appears to me that in our system such conditions do not exist.

Vera stopped speaking. The presiding judge asked, "Have you said everything you wanted to?" "Yes," she replied. Utterly exhausted, she sat down. Her last duty done, a great peace flooded her soul: a peace, she thought, like that which comes just before death.

During the brief adjournment following Vera's statement, the defense lawyers came to shake her hand, and her comrades in the prisoners' dock furtively whispered their congratulations. Her speech had made an impression on the prosecutors and the judges as well. The Minister of Justice leaned over to ask the defense attorney, Leont'ev, to give him a steno-graphic copy of her words.

Sitting on the prisoners' bench, with an armed guard on either side of her, Vera was overwhelmed with a feeling of freedom—freedom from duty to her country, to society, to the party. She said to herself, "I had become only an ordinary person, a daughter to my mother, a sister to my sisters, who alone stood beside me in the midst of the general ruin."

The judges filed back into the courtroom. The sentences were read. Death by hanging for Vera Figner and seven of her comrades, including the six military officers. The others received sentences of varying lengths in the *katorga.*

From the time of the open Trial of the 50 in March 1877, through the Trial of the 193 in 1879, Vera Zasulich's jury trial the same year, the Trial of the 20 in 1882, and the Trial of the Six in March 1881, the words the revolutionaries and their lawyers spoke in the courtroom were printed in newspapers in Russia and abroad—not always in their entirety, and often distorted by censorship. The Trial of the 14 in September 1884 was differ-ent. No word that the trial was scheduled to take place appeared in the press; no word of the proceedings was printed in newspapers in Russia or abroad. Vera Figner's words reached only the courtroom audience. Selec-tions from her speech were printed in the underground press in 1886, but not until 1906 was it printed in its entirety in the Socialist Revolutionary party periodical *Byloye,* along with the memoirs of several other participants in the trial.

The change in treatment Vera got as a prisoner condemned to death be-gan very soon. On Monday after the trial, prison guards came to take her from the House of Detention where the relatively lax rules had allowed her to sit alongside her mother and sister and exchange tender caresses. She was wearing the delicate underclothing and a lovely, light-blue silk dress her mother had brought her. She carried a box of French bonbons and in a paper bag some beautiful Duchess pears. Arriving at the Peter Paul Fortress Prison, she was taken to her old cell, Number 43, where she lay down on her cot with its double mattress, two soft pillows, and a nice coverlet, and went to sleep.

She was awakened by the grinding of the key in the lock of the heavy iron door of her cell. Two prison officers and a guard stomped in. Before she had time to stand up, one of them began reading from an official docu-ment a list of regulations to be applied at once. The first was the issue of condemned prisoner garb. They took her to another cell, empty except for a woman prison attendant standing in front of a pile of filthy rags. The men left. The woman stripped Vera naked, dropping her lovely blue dress and underthings to the floor, even removing the gold chain round her neck—a gift from her mother. From the rags, she pulled out a coarse peasant shirt, with sleeves so long they covered Vera's hands, and a dirty canvas shawl.

Around her legs the woman wound rough linen cloths, then threw over Vera's head a thick wool skirt. Finally, she flung on her shoulders the regulation heavy, grey wool prison coat with the yellow *tuz* (a diamond-shaped patch) on the back.

Almost overcome by the smell of the grime and sweat left in the unwashed clothing by previous wearers, and bowed down by its weight, Vera could scarcely move when the guards came to take her back to cell Number 43. What a change she found! The mattress, pillows, and coverlet had disappeared from the cot, replaced by a bag of straw and a piece of an old blanket. On the table, instead of her white earthenware pitcher was a rusty, crumpled tin can. In the morning, instead of tea she was given hot water with black bread so hard she found it difficult to eat. Her request for books from the prison library, which had kept her alive during her twenty months of preliminary detention, was denied. Instead, a guard brought her a copy of the New Testament. In childhood the gospels had fascinated her, but at this point in her life they left her cold. For want of anything else to do, she began to read words and phrases of scripture and mechanically translated them into German and French, while clinging to her own God, her own religion. She defined it as the religion of liberty, equality, and fraternity. "For the glory of that religion I was ready to endure everything."

The old prison doctor, a kindly man, made his rounds on Saturdays and usually joked with his charges, including Vera whom he had been seeing weekly for almost two years. He came into her cell and looked at her in disbelief. Apparently at a loss for words he said, "Are you well?" A strange question, Vera thought, to ask a person condemned to death.

Eight days passed. Then in the evening Vera heard the grinding noise of opening and closing prison doors. A key turned in the lock of her door and an old general, the commandant of the prison, came in with an inspector. He took out an impressive-looking document and in a loud voice slowly read:

> His most gracious majesty, the Emperor, has ordered your death sentence changed to life imprisonment at hard labor.

Vera asked herself,

> Did I expect they would execute me? No, I didn't. But if the death sentence had been carried out I would have died in full control of myself. I was ready for death. I was hardly overwhelmed with enthusiasm for it, but my strength was exhausted and I preferred quick death on the scaffold to the slow death of life imprisonment, the inevitability of which I was clearly aware.

The execution of Perovskaya, the first woman hanged on the scaffold, had taken place only three years before and made a terrible impression in Russia. This event, Vera reasoned, accounted for the change in the fate of the two women, herself and Ludmila Volkenshtein, sentenced to death in the Trial of the Fourteen.

Two more days passed. On October 12, guards and gendarmes came to Vera's cell and subjected her to the final humiliation. They fastened fetters to her legs and arms. She was marched out of the prison, through two lines of soldiers, to be taken she knew not where.

Thus began the time when the clock of life stopped.

Vera Figner and several other prisoners, each in chains, were put into separate cubicles on a motor launch which headed into the Neva River and made its way, mile after mile, to the north. Long before the five-hour trip was over, Vera began to suspect their destination: Shlisselburg! Russia's grimmest prison. The thirteenth-century dungeons of the ancient Fortress of Shlisselburg, on an island in the farthest reaches of the Neva, had recently been rebuilt expressly as a torture chamber for the new crop of political prisoners. Entering it, prisoners were told; was the equivalent of death— slow dying in oblivion, completely cut off from every outside human contact, and as completely isolated from fellow prisoners inside as strictly enforced rules could achieve.

From earliest childhood Vera Figner had been made aware of her unusual beauty. Once when they were small children, her mother had read to Vera and her brothers and sisters tales from a collection of legends about the rulers of the ancient Russian state of Muscovy. One told of the handsome young Tsar, Mikhail Feodorovich who, when it came time to wed, sent out to the four corners of his realm an order to his nobles to bring their marriageable daughters to the capital city, to Moscow, to the Tsar's palace. From far and near the fairest of the fair came. As they paraded before the Tsar, he chose the most beautiful of them all for his bride.

This story fired the imagination of the child Vera. She began to imagine when she grew up and the Tsar's ritual of choosing a bride took place, she and all the lovely girls of Russia would parade before him and he would select her, Vera Nikolaevna, as the most beautiful of them all. She would become the Tsaritsa, wear a crown of diamonds and rubies, and be dressed in silver and gold.

Years later Vera remarked:

In real life I never became a Tsaritsa, ruling an empire, but I had a realm, and I was named a queen. In Shlisselburg there were only two women, Ludmila Volkenshtein and me, and our fellow prisoners called us queens. But I was not dressed in purple velvet and white ermine, but in a rough, grey woolen coat with a yellow ace on the back.[4]

---

[4]Another aspect of her prison look that Vera might have mentioned was the loss of her crowning beauty—her long, luxuriant hair. Upon entering Shlisselburg she, like all Russian prisoners, had her hair cropped. She expressed her awareness of how that detracted from her appearance when she described (in *Zapechatlenniy Trud*, vol. 2, pp. 180–81, how she felt when confronted by an elegantly dressed Petersburg official she had encountered during her trial, who came into her cell on a routine inspection tour in 1885.

She reigned twenty years, in the darkness of a small bare prison cell, existing in the perpetual numbing silence broken only by the awareness of comrades being hanged in the prison yard, by the screams of the suicides and the muffled groans of those suffering fatal diseases, or those with gagged mouths being led off to the punishment dungeons.

> A new life began—a life amidst deathly silence, that silence in which you always listen for something, that silence which little by little overpowers you, envelops you, penetrates into all the pores of your body, into your mind, into your very soul. How dreadful it is in its dumbness, how frightening in its soundlessness and in its unexpected interruptions. Gradually between it and you creeps a sensation of the closeness of some kind of mystery; everything becomes unreal, puzzling, as on a moonlit night, in solitude, in the shadow of a still forest. Everything is incomprehensible. In this silence the real becomes vague and unreal, and the imaginary seems real. Everything is tangled up, confused. The day—long, grey, wearying—in its idleness is like sleep without dreams, but at night you have dreams so bright and glowing that you have continually to assure yourself that they are only dreams.

Her revolutionary career over, Vera Figner stubbornly clung to the realization she had become a symbol of the Russian Revolution—its past and its future. This realization gave her courage, kept her alive, kept her sane, though often her sanity by only a hair's breadth hung in the balance. She constantly repeated to herself:

> Have courage, Vera, and be firm! Be resolute. Do not fear. Do not fear. In this mysterious stillness, behind these deaf stones your comrades are invisibly present. It is not you alone who are suffering; they too are suffering. Think of them. They are invisible, but they are here. You do not hear them but they are here. They watch over you; like disembodied spirits they guard you. Nothing will happen to you, nothing will happen to you. You are not alone. You are not alone.

In the mid-1890s, after the prisoners had been deprived of all reading matter for thirteen years, a new director of the prison gave permission for the circulation of books and journals, and for the receipt of letters from close relatives twice a year. After more than a decade of living without hope in the utter darkness of a stale dungeon, it was as if day had dawned, as the written word brought in the light of the outside world.

One day as Vera Figner was going through an 1895 issue of the magazine *Russkoe Bogatstvo*, she began to read a poem signed only with the letter "M." As her eyes scanned the lines she could hardly contain her excitement. When she got to the last stanza tears of happiness coursed down her cheeks. She realized that "M" was Mikhailovsky,[5] and that he had addressed this poem to her, with no idea of whether she would ever see it.

---

[5]In 1918 N. S. Tiutchev informed Vera that the poem was not written by Mikhailovsky, but at his request by Verkhoiantsev.

When agonizingly and painfully
Your heart is gripped with anguish,
When your eyes involuntarily glisten
With hot tears,
With brow bent
Thinking in silence,
Remember, in our country
You are recalled with love.

In moments of somber sorrow
Live! With hope!
You will arise to a new life!
You will be able to love again!
Not all your dreams are destroyed.
Not everything is buried.
And know, my friend, the angry storm
Did not destroy everything.

Fate does not always bring disaster,
Night does not endure forever.
Day is close by, and before the break of dawn
The shadows will go away.

Vera Figner exulted, "From behind the walls of the fortress my voice still got through to my friends, and over the heavy barriers of stone flew their words of love to me."

And *Narodnaya Volya?* The party to which Vera Figner had dedicated her life? From the bits of information that got through to the prisoners from those brought to Shlisselburg after 1884, she could only conclude the party was dead—killed by its own weaknesses and the cruel reaction of the reign of Aleksandr III. Was the revolutionary voice really silenced? Had the stillness of the graveyard settled over Russia?

Much as she suffered year after year from the harsh regime, the numbing idleness, the terrible isolation of prison life, Vera reacted with shock and anger when on the evening of January 13, 1903, prison officials came clanking along the corridor and stopped at her door. Unlocking it, the prison commandant strode in, holding up in a theatrical gesture an official paper he read out to her: His Majesty, the Emperor, in answer to your mother's entreaties, has ordered your sentence of life imprisonment changed to a prison term of twenty years. The date of your release will be September 28, 1904.

Vera wrote later, in the second volume of *Zapechatlennyi Trud,* that she was stunned, outraged that she had been granted a favor by the imperial power she hated.

It must be some kind of mistake. . . . Didn't my steadfast, strong-willed mother, without tears, without showing the slightest weakness, see, one after the other, two of her daughters taken off to Siberia, and didn't she give me her word never to ask any kind of moderation of my sentence? . . . I didn't want mercy. I wanted to continue to share my fate with my *narodovol'tsi* comrades.

For those twenty years the world had been closed to her, all human ties broken. Her fellow prisoners had become her family, her homeland, everything.

What Vera did not know, having been permitted no correspondence with her family for over a year and a half, was that her mother was dying of cancer. Learning this, Vera's reproaches turned on herself. A flood of memories of her mother crowded in. It had been her mother who had laid the foundation, while Vera was still a child, for her spiritual development. And after the years in which Vera had neglected her mother, beginning with leaving home in an early marriage, study in Switzerland, followed by years of illegal revolutionary activity—despite all this, it was her mother who stood by her during two years of imprisonment in the Peter Paul Fortress and during the harrowing days of her trial. Vera concluded, "Nothing, absolutely nothing have I given her in my whole life . . . only grief." All she could do was get down on her knees and implore forgiveness. And, she wrote, in answer to her prayers, she received the words, "A mother's heart does not know chagrin."[6]

Vera Figner walked out of Shlisselburg on September 29, 1904. Actually, she stumbled out. The ground seemed to be shifting beneath her feet and she had to be supported to keep from falling. For the first time in twenty years she was addressed by a prison official not as "Number eleven," but as Vera Nikolaevna." She was put on a motor launch for the trip back to St. Petersburg where, once again, she entered the Peter Paul Fortress Prison. Her nerves shattered, physically debilitated, wearing threadbare prison garb, and feeling like an old woman at age fifty-two, she was, after a few days, granted a brief visit with her sisters and her brother Peter. It was a painful meeting. Vera's sisters, who she remembered as young girls, had become stolid matrons, mothers of families; her brother, a handsome, successful engineer, had been a ruddy-cheeked, beardless boy when she last saw him. And she—so long separated from human contact—could only sit where her brother placed her and look at him while he gripped both her hands in his.

Vera left Shlisselburg, the world of the half-dead and only with great difficulty did she come back to the world of the living. Her detailed description in her book, *Posle Shlisselburga* (After Shlisselburg), of her condition after twenty years of solitary confinement and the agony of her mental and physical readjustment is a remarkable, almost clinical, account. She

---

[6]Her mother died November 15, 1903, almost a year before Vera was released from Shlisselburg at the end of September 1904.

achieved her rehabilitation only with the strong support of her three sisters and two brothers. A few of her comrades of the old days who were still living sought her out, as did some of the new generation of revolutionaries. Most of them were members of the Socialist Revolutionary party which had come onto the Russian revolutionary scene several years before her release from Shlisselburg, and like the *Narodnaya Volya,* had many women leaders.

Within two weeks Vera was transported to a frozen, Arctic Circle prison village in the Province of Archangel. She suffered from the cold, angina, and general malaise. Again four walls, and silence—the awful silence. Little by little, as if through a thick fog, she became aware of what was going on in Russia: war with Japan in the Far East; Bloody Sunday in St. Petersburg when the Tsar gave orders to shoot into a great, unarmed crowd of men, women, and children marching in a peaceful demonstration; turbulence everywhere as workers, peasants, the bourgeoisie, intellectuals, and professional people more and more boldly were organizing and making demands.

Through the ceaseless efforts of her youngest sister, Olga, Vera was moved to a village where there was a doctor, and finally in June was granted permission to visit her aunt in the area of her old home near Kazan. Below Yaroslavl, Vera traveled by boat down the Volga. The broad river, the flat fields, the wide expanse of sky—this was the land of her childhood, the land she dreamed about in those endless days of dark isolation in Shlisselburg. It was a bittersweet homecoming. Her beloved aunt was waiting for her with open arms, the estates of her sister Evgeniya and her brothers, with their generous hospitality, were nearby. She visited her mother's grave and the family estate—the old home where she and her sisters and brothers were born and grew up—but wherever she went there also went the police who observed her every move twenty-four hours a day. The land and the villages were poorer and more pitiful than they had been when she last saw them a quarter of a century before. Crops looked withered and thin, the land seemed to have lost its productivity. Everywhere she saw tumble-down huts, the people still illiterate, still beset with drunkenness, wearing rags, bearing the heavy imprint of years of beating and slavery. The land had been impoverished by the tsarist government policy of exporting grain, no matter what the cost to the rural economy, to create the gold reserves needed to finance the building of railroads and industry.

Ironically, in the turbulent years of 1905 and 1906, Vera Figner found herself in the uncomfortable position of a landowner, surrounded by—and failing to understand the mood of—peasants on the verge of action. Their demand was not for revolution, nor socialism, nor representative government, nor education. No! They were urgently voicing the age-old peasant demand for land: division of the land, individual ownership. And those who had land wanted more. Vera suffered terrible chagrin when her refusal of what she regarded as a peasant's unreasonable (but actually very petty) re-

Vera Figner, Nizhni-Novgorod, 1906

quest resulted in his setting fire to her ancestral home. Living nearby, with several servants, in a house her brother had recently built on his estate, Vera was alerted in the middle of the night by the village fire bell. She stood at a darkened window and watched the flames and clouds of smoke rise in the night air as the great house with its outbuildings, its ancient willow trees and gardens turned into blackened cinders.

It was not long after the fire that Vera Figner asked herself: How can I live? For whom? For what? But at this point she decided she must live, must create for herself a new life. Life in the country was depressing. The police surveillance—still in full force a year and a half after her release from prison—she felt was a threat not only to her but to her family and friends. She decided to go with her sister to Nizhni-Novgorod. It was no better. Feeling herself a nervous wreck, she could not sleep, could not relax; every sound was like a blow.

> The prison experience disfigured me. It followed me in my relation to society, to people; it made me react with the sensitivity of the mimosa which causes it to wilt at every touch.

Vera finally accepted the invitation of her brother Nikolai, the famous opera singer (for whom Tchaikovsky wrote *The Queen of Spades*), to provide whatever financial resources she needed to begin life anew in Europe. She left Russia in 1907, soon settled in Paris, and gradually achieved the composure necessary to take up a new career as a writer. Her first article, written while she was still in Russia, at the request of V. L. Burtsev, editor of the influential emigré journal *Byloye*, was a tribute to her fellow Shlisselburg prisoner, Ludmila Volkenshtein.[7]

Once settled in Europe, Vera Figner, in a steady stream of articles, wrote what she knew of the Russian revolutionary movement, of the revolutionary activists of the eventful years of the 1870s and 1880s, and of conditions in Russia's prisons and in Siberian exile. In 1910 she founded the Paris Committee to Help Russia's Political Prisoners, and spent much time and effort fundraising. Her booklet *Les Prisons Russes* was published in Lausanne in 1911.

With her fluency in French and German, Vera Figner soon became a popular lecturer. Hundreds of people crowded into halls in many cities of Europe to hear her. In 1914, she was in Switzerland. A friend told her a Russian emigré called V. I. Lenin was scheduled to speak at a meeting in Montreux.[8] She went and found about twenty people there, mostly Russians, none of whom she knew. Lenin got up and gave a long technical speech on the imperialist phase of capitalism, which, he said, inevitably led to war that in every land would be followed by civil war and revolution. He left immediately after the speech so there was none of the lively discus-

---

[7]*Byloye*, no. 3, March 1906. Volkenshtein became widely known when a piece she wrote in 1896, while in transit on police order from Shlisselburg to Sakhalin Island (5,000 miles away), "13 Let v Shlisselburgskoy Kreposti" (13 Years in Shlisselburg Prison), was published in an emigré journal, then in 1900 as a 72-page pamphlet in London. It publicized for the first time conditions in the prison. On January 10, 1906, Volkenshtein was shot down in Vladivostok when army units were ordered by the governor to open fire on a peaceful demonstration of men, women, and children.

[8]This is Vera Figner's only reference to Lenin in the six volumes of her collected works. It appears in volume 3, pp. 422–23. She made several references to Lenin's brother Aleksandr Ul'ianov who was hanged in the prison yard of Shlisselburg in 1887, convicted as a member of a plot against the life of Aleksandr III.

sion Vera had become accustomed to in the *narodniki* circles of the 1870s. She remarked that Lenin and his talk made an unfavorable impression on her, but she did not, like Vera Zasulich, openly oppose him or his ideas. Zasulich, as an emigré, had become a political theorist and had long clashed with Lenin on theoretical grounds. Figner, on the other hand, was an astute commentator on the passing scene, and once said in a letter to her brother that her writing "goes well only when it comes from the heart, not from the mind."

Vera's brother Nikolai made arrangements in 1915 with the tsarist government for his sister's return to Russia. These arrangements went awry when official messages got misdirected, with the result that as soon as she crossed the border from Bulgaria to Russia she was arrested and clapped in jail in Kishenev. The young woman warden who searched her did not recognize the name Vera Figner, though she said she knew of the great opera singer named Figner. Vera was transported in fetters to St. Petersburg and again imprisoned. Intervention by her famous brother and three sisters soon secured her release. She was given permission to choose a place to live, under police surveillance, provided it had no university and no strategic military installations. She chose Nizhnii-Novgorod, where one of her sisters lived. In wartime, the government, with more pressing matters at hand, did not make a big issue of the case of the sixty-three-year-old Vera Figner. In 1916 she was permitted to live in the capital, now called Petrograd. She did not engage in political activity, but as an "old revolutionary" greeted with "joy, sorrow, and anxiety" the revolution in February 1917, which toppled the tsarist government she had once fought so vigorously.

ANNOTATED REFERENCES

The fullest source of available information on Vera Figner is her published writing about herself and her contemporaries. Most of what she wrote and published, beginning in 1907, in European and emigré Russian journals, was collected and published in Moscow, 1928–1929, in six volumes: *Polnoye Sobraniye Sochineniy* (Complete Collected Works), in the Historical-Revolutionary Library Series of *Katorga i Ssylka*. The first title (volumes 1 and 2 in this collection), *Zapechatlennyi Trud* (The Unforgettable Effort), and volume 3, *Posle Shlisselburga* (After Shlisselburg), were first published in 1921–1922, and republished in the six-volume collected works. These volumes are an autobiographical account of Figner's life, from her childhood through her painful readjustment to life after her more than twenty years of imprisonment in solitary confinement. Volume 4 is a reprint of Figner's first book, published in 1920, *Shlisselburgskie Uzniki* (The Prisoners of Shlisselburg); volume 5, *Ocherki, Stat'i, i Rechi* (Sketches, Articles and Speeches); volume 6, *Pis'ma* (Letters).

Zapechatlennyi Trud has been translated into several languages, including French and German. A much-abridged English translation called *Memoirs of a Revolutionist* was published in 1927 and reissued in 1968. Selections from *Zapechatlennyi Trud*, in English translation, appear in *Five Sisters, Women Against the Tsar*, Barbara A. Engel and Clifford N. Rosenthal, editors and translators, New York, 1975.

Vera Figner wrote an autobiographical essay that was published in 1926 in the *Entsikloped-icheskiy Slovar*, Russkogo Bibiliograficheskogo Instituta Granat., volume 40.

Two Soviet biographical sources are E. Pavliuchenko's 36-page introduction to the 1964 edition of *Zapechatlennyi Trud*, and Iraida Evgen'evna Matveeva's 68-page pamphlet *Vera Figner*, Moscow, 1961. Short essays under Vera Figner's name appear in all editions of the *Bolshaia Sovetskaia Entsiklopediia* (The Great Soviet Encyclopedia). In 1934, a 142-page abridgment of *Zapechatlennyi Trud* titled *V Borbe* (In the Struggle) was published in Moscow. It is profusely illustrated with photographs.

A biographical sketch of Figner by Richard Stites appears in *The Modern Encyclopedia of Russian and Soviet History*, edited by Joseph L. Wiecsynski, Academic and International Press, 1976.

There are two books on Kronshtadt: V. V. Vladimirov, *Kronshtadt*, Kiev-Khar'kov, 1899, and A. V. Shelov, *Istoricheskiy Ocherk Kreposti Kronshtadt*, Kronshtadt, 1904. Both have photos and maps. A description of the trip from St. Petersburg to Kronshtadt in the 1880s appears in a document on the execution of Naval Lieutenant N. E. Sukhanov, *Byloye* (London), no. 1, 1900.

"Voennaia Organizatsiia Partii 'Narodnoy Voli,'" *Byloye*, no. 8, August 1906, is an official 1883 tsarist government report on the distribution of *narodovol'tsy* propaganda among military personnel, with attention to the large role played by Figner. The report also described Vera Figner's stay in Kronshtadt in March and April 1881 and the plans to rob the Kronshtadt Bank, which she does not mention in her memoirs.

The most extensive description of the Shlisselburg experience appears in the second volume of Vera Figner's *Zapechatlennyi Trud: Kogda Chasy Zhizni Ostanovilis*. But the details are even grimmer in M. IY. Ashenbrenner's "Shlisselburgskaia Tiur'ma za 20 let, ot 1884–1904 g. Vospominanii," *Byloye*, (new series). St. Petersburg, vol. 1, no. 1, January 1906. This article was published as a pamphlet in Berlin, 1906, and was included in his book *Voennaia Organizatsiia Narodnoy Voli i Drugie Vospominaniia 1860–1904* (The Military Organization of Narodnaya Volya and Other Reminiscences 1860–1904), Moscow, 1924.

Two other publications on Shlisselburg are Ludmila Volkenshtein, *13 Let v Shlisselburgskoy Kreposti* (Thirteen Years in Shlisselburg Fortress), a 72-page pamphlet published in London, 1900. In 1906 it was brought out by *Novyi Mir* in St. Petersburg with a foreword by Vera Zasulich. Simon O. Pollock's book on Shlisselburg, *The Russian Bastille*, was published in Chicago in 1908. Vera Figner's 36-page booklet, *Les Prisons Russes*, Lausanne, 1911, contains information on Shlisselburg.

In addition to Vera Figner's full description of her arrest and trial in the first volume of *Zapechatlennyi Trud*, the trial is described by A. A. Spandoni, one of those tried in the Trial of the 14, "Stranitsa iz Vospominanii" (A Page from My Recollections), *Byloye*, no. 5, May 1906. The text of Figner's speech before the court appears in "K Biografii Very Nikolaevny Figner," *Byloye*, no. 5, May 1906. (The heading for the speech is erroneously dated January 27, 1884; the correct date was September 27, 1884). *Byloye*, no. 7, July 1906, published "Iz Pokazaniy V. N. Figner" (From the Testimony of V. N. Figner). This was the autobiographical account she wrote for the authorities while awaiting trial in the Peter Paul Fortress Prison.

The Strel'nikov assassination is described in the first volume of *Zapechatlennyi Trud*. Additional information appears in "Protsess 17ti Narodovol'tsev v 1883 godu" (Trial of the 17 Members of *Narodnaya Volya* in 1883), *Byloye*, no. 10, October 1906, and in M. Drei's article "Strel'nikovskyi Prostsess v Odesse v 1883 godu po Lichnym Vospominaniiam" (The Strel'nikov Trial in Odessa in 1883 According to Personal Recollections), *Katorga i Ssylka*, 1924, no. 2 (9).

Accounts of Nikolai Mikhailovsky's meeting with Vera Figner in Khar'kov in October 1882 appear in the first volume of *Zapechatlennyi Trud*, and in Mikhailovsky's *Vospominaniia* (Recollections), published in Berlin, circa 1902. Figner wrote a detailed response to Mikhailovsky's account in a review of V. IA. Bogucharsky's (V. Yakolev) *Iz Istorii Politicheskoy Bor'by v 70kh i 80kh godov XIX veka, Partiia "Narodnoy Voli" eë Proiskhozhdenie, Sud'by i Gibel'* (History of the Political Struggles in the 1870s and 1880s, the Narodnaya Volya Party, its Birth, Life and Death), Moscow, 1912, She criticized Bogucharsky for accepting Mikhailovsky's version of the incident and undertook to correct the record once and for all. Her review appeared in *Russkoe Bogatstvo*, no. 11, November 1912.

An account of a meeting Vera Figner addressed in London's South Place Institute on June 23, 1909, with quotations from her speech and a description of the enthusiastic response by the audience, appeared in the July 1909 issue of *Free Russia* (London). The text of the speech is included in volume 5 of her collected works, pp. 435–44.

Impressions of Vera Figner by Lidiia Dan (wife of Menshevik leader Feodor Dan), a friend of Figner's niece, Vera Sakhanovich, were recorded in a 13-page typescript, "Iz Vstrech s Veroy Nikolaevnoy Figner" (Of My Meetings with Vera Nikolaevna Figner) by the Inter-University Project on the History of the Menshevik Movement, New York, 1961. As might be expected, Lidiia, of a younger generation, did not look upon Figner with the adoration invariably expressed by her contemporaries.

Vera Figner was one of the most remarkable women of her era, yet there is no adequate biography of her in Russian or any other language. Sources of information on her life in the Russian language are plentiful. She wrote voluminously and was much written about. Quantities of this material are available in print (mainly in Russian periodicals of the 1920s), but the wealth of documentary material locked away in Soviet archives awaits the future biographer who gains access to it and the freedom to use it.

4

Babushka, Apostle of Terror

Just before the Christmas holidays in December 1904, Katerina Konstantinovna Breshko-Breshkovskaya came as a guest speaker to Wellesley College. She had been invited to address the students in French 11-12 and their
friends. Announcing her lecture, the December 14 *College News* called her
"a woman revolutionist of noble birth and spirit who has come to America,
after twenty-five years spent in exile in the mines of Kara and the wastes of
Siberia."

A real Russian revolutionist on the Wellesley campus! It was an exciting
prospect. The plan for the French classroom as the meeting place had to be
abandoned. The event was rescheduled for the College Hall Chapel.

As the announced hour of 3:30 approached, excited women students, in
their striped shirtwaists and wide-belted, long sweeping skirts, many with
braids hanging down their backs, converged toward the chapel doors.
While waiting for them to open the women chatted and looked, as usual,
at the reproductions of Raphael paintings flanking the doors. Those coming
down the broad College Hall stairways, with their carved banisters, saw
beyond the large windows on each landing a snow-covered south lawn and
barren tree branches creaking in the strong north wind on that icy, sunny
Thursday afternoon.

The chapel doors opened and the crowd entered the large, balconied
auditorium with a high apse over the vaulted east end, on which the words
"non ministrari sed ministrare" were engraved. Here, from the low, square
platform, the poet Longfellow had read his sonnet to the first Wellesley students in 1875. Here in the intervening years, Oliver Wendell Holmes, Matthew Arnold, Dr. Lyman Abbot, Frances Willard, William Dean Howells,
Julia Ward Howe, Booker T. Washington, Ernestine Schumann-Heink, and

many other men and women, famous in their day, had spoken or performed.

Meantime the "Barge," the all-purpose college carriage, drawn by two shaggy brown horses, was approaching the pillared porte-cochere of College Hall. It was bringing from the Wellesley train station Katerina Breshkovskaya[1] and her escorts, Vida Dutton Scudder, professor of English, who had accompanied her from Denison House, the south Boston settlement where she was staying, and Professor Henriette Louise Colin of the French Department.

In the chapel the women were still jockeying for seats, with much scraping of high-backed chairs on the wooden floor, when up the left aisle walked Professors Colin and Scudder with a tall, sturdily built, pleasant-looking, white-haired, sixty-year-old woman. She wore a short, nondescript black cotton dress with a narrow, white muslin collar, and over her shoulders a woolen shawl. This was the woman known all over Russia as *Babushka Revolyutsii*, Grandmother of the Revolution.

After Professor Colin's brief introduction, Katerina Breshkovskaya began to speak in French, as Professor Scudder translated. The Russian woman's expressive, mobile face, her clear blue eyes, her well-modulated voice and impassioned flow of language immediately caught and held the attention of her audience. She spoke of the issue she said was dearest to her heart: the education and the enlightenment of Russia's eighty-million peasants. She was not ashamed to plead for the financial help of Wellesley students in this monumental task. She did not make her plea in vain for the students responded with generous contributions to a fund they immediately set up "for the printing of books for Russian peasant schools."

Six months before the peaceful scene of Katerina Breshkovskaya lecturing in the Wellesley College Hall Chapel, and later sitting in the cosy Faculty Parlor sipping tea and conversing with eager students, an event occurred in St. Petersburg to which she did not allude. Count Viacheslav von Pleve, the tsarist Minister of the Interior, one of the most powerful and hated men in Russia, was at 9:50 A.M. on Thursday, July 28, riding in his official armored carriage drawn by two fast black horses, along heavily trafficked Ismailovsky Prospekt, on his way to the Baltic railroad station. There he would board the train to Peterhof (the imperial summer residence) for his weekly conference with Tsar Nikolai II. Near his carriage, on bicycles, in cabs, and on foot, were secret service men, detectives, and police. Suddenly, as Pleve's carriage slowed at an intersection to let a one-horse *droshky* cross the avenue, a young man wearing a brown overcoat and a railroad official's cap

---

[1]In America her name always appeared in print as Catherine Breshkovsky, and she herself signed letters to her American friends "Catherine."

Katerina Breshko-Breshkovskaya

dashed up to the scarcely moving vehicle, threw a small black object into the carriage and cried out, "Long live freedom!"

Instantly there was a deafening explosion. Clouds of black smoke rose as the armored carriage disintegrated. Paving stones, reduced to rubble, and flying pieces of debris filled the air. The wounded horses, with dangling harness and wheels in tow, ran wildly. It was a scene of mad confusion as the sidewalks began to fill with a crowd of onlookers. Before their eyes, in the middle of the street, were the mangled corpses of Pleve and his coachman, and the prone figures of wounded passersby. To one side lay the still breathing body of the assassin, Yegor Sergeevich Sazonov.

The half-dozen terrorists who carried out this act of violence in St. Petersburg were operatives of a conspiracy plotted far away from Russia, well in advance of the event. The plotters, members of the Battle Organization of the newly formed illegal Socialist Revolutionary party, were in Geneva, Switzerland—once called the Murder League on Lake Leman's shores. Katerina Breshkovskaya was a ranking member. It was she who recruited to a career of terror Boris Savinkov, the brilliant coordinator of the Pleve and other spectacular assassinations. Even in America, Katerina Breshkovskaya received daily communications from Geneva, including secret details of the death in Moscow, near the Kremlin wall, on February 5, 1905, of the Grand Duke Sergei Aleksandrovich, governor of Moscow and uncle of Tsar Nikolai II. His carriage was blown up in a bombing directed by Savinkov.

Katerina Breshkovskaya was introduced to the American public by George Kennan in an article, "A Ride Through the Trans-Baikal," that appeared in the May 1889 issue of Century Magazine. It was one in a series Kennan was sending back during his investigation of the Russian prison system in Siberia. In 1891 the Century Company published the articles in a two-volume work, Siberia and the Exile System, that immediately became popular in the United States and in Europe. Kennan related how he chanced to meet Breshkovskaya in October 1885 in Selenginsk, a Buriat village of wooden huts in the desolate valley of the Selenga River, lying between ranges of stony, barren, brown hills with no trees except in the higher slopes of the distant mountain chain marking the Mongolian border. She had been sent there as a "forced settler" after completing two prison terms in the gold mines of Kara and several punitive years near the Arctic Circle.

Kennan described Katerina Breshkovskaya as a woman in her mid-thirties (when he saw her she was actually in her forties). Her dark hair, cut short in prison, was streaked with gray, and her strong intelligent face showed traces of much suffering, but "neither hardship, nor exile, nor penal servitude had been able to break her brave, finely-tempered spirit, or to shake her convictions of honor and duty." Kennan saw her as a warm, sympathetic, attractive, educated woman. His prediction was that in the God-forsaken spot where she was being held prisoner, long before her penal term was over, she would die of privation, leaving only an unpainted wooden cross in a desolate graveyard beside the Selenga River to mark the fact she had once existed. This prediction contrasted sharply with her conviction that she and her fellow revolutionaries would triumph in the end in their struggle for liberty for the Russian people. Her parting words to him were:

> Mr. Kennan, we may die in exile, our children may die in exile, and our children's children may die in exile, but something will come of it at last.

Kennan wrote that the example of that woman raised all his standards "of courage, of fortitude, and of heroic self-sacrifice."

Whether, midst the horrors Kennan detailed in his description of the Siberian *katorga*, his account of Katerina Breshkovskaya's plight made much of an impression on the American public is questionable. She did, however, disprove Kennan's prediction of her early end, for within the decade she returned to Russia to enter again the ranks of those struggling against tsarist tyranny.

Katerina Breshkovskaya was often asked why she became a revolutionary, and she had a ready answer: Life in the place, the time, and the circumstances she was born very early planted the seeds of revolution in her heart. She looked at the luxury in which she, her parents, her brothers and sisters, and neighboring gentry lived on their great country estates, in palatial homes surrounded by beautiful parks and gardens. They had dozens of uniformed servants—nursemaids, governesses, and tutors; their language was French, not Russian; their tables groaned with delicacies, and fortunes were spent on champagne alone for great feasts. They dressed in silks and furs, fine imported woolens and cotton lawns. The contrast between all this and the miserable existence of the serfs was so striking it seared her soul and gave her no rest. Ignorant, often diseased and hungry, the peasants were ill-clothed and slept on vermin-infested straw in their tumbledown huts in the squalid villages scattered over the countryside. All the squandered wealth enjoyed by the gentry was at the expense of the oppressed peasants. They were scolded, they were whipped, they were sent to Siberia at the whim of their masters for the least fault. Their wives and daughters were taken to serve the master and his sons as concubines. As early as the age of eight, Katerina Verigo (her family name) looked with horror at the humiliation and suffering she saw all about her beyond the gates of the family mansion.

In her girlhood Katerina was helpless to right the wrongs of Russian society, but at age nineteen she saw a way out. Tsar Aleksandr II had not only emancipated the peasants in 1861, but had issued other reforming edicts. One of the most far-reaching was the "opening up" of the universities.

The thirst for education among Russia's youth in the 1860s was so great, and had gone unsatisfied for so long, heedless of the restrictions tsarist officials imposed on all the new educational institutions and on students, schools sprang up everywhere: *gymnazii* (high schools) to train young men for the universities, and boarding schools and pedagogical institutions for girls—the most famous established by Tsaritsa Maria Aleksandrovna herself. The upper-class youth of both sexes flocked to schools in St. Petersburg, Moscow, Kiev, Kazan and Odessa.

Katerina Verigo decided an education would show her how to help her country and its people. She persuaded her father, whose liberal inclination stemmed from family traditions that harked back to eighteenth-century French ideas once popular in Russia, to let her go to St. Petersburg to become a *kursistka*.

In 1863, with much excitement, trunks were packed and Katerina and her older sister, Natasha, accompanied by their mother, boarded the train in Chernigov, bound for St. Petersburg. Katerina said Natasha's objective was to "see the world," while her own was to "learn about the world."

The train had not gone far when into their compartment came young Prince Peter Kropotkin, handsome in his grey officer's uniform. Not yet the revolutionary anarchist he later became, still a favorite of Tsar Aleksandr II whose aide he had been from his teens, he had gone on active duty in the Army and was returning to St. Petersburg from an official mission to Siberia. Kropotkin spoke enthusiastically to the travelers of his hopes for Russia. Now that the Tsar Liberator had decreed reforms, Russia's gentry youth, as enlightened educated citizens, would have the all-important job of putting the reforms to work. He spoke eloquently of his hopes for Russia. Prince Kropotkin's words thrilled Katerina "like fire." Their conversation became so animated that Katerina's mother, constantly drilling her daughter in "lady-like behavior," admonished her to lower her voice.

Katerina's mother, of the Goremykin family—one of the most prestigious in Russia—had been educated at the famous Smolny Institute, established by Katerina the Great for the daughters of the nobility. She had many connections in the highest circles of St. Petersburg society. She left her daughters with a titled family when she returned to Chernigov. The arrangement did not last long. Katerina got a job as a tutor and began a life of three years of "freedom" in the capital city. The lectures for women she attended, given illegally by professors outside university walls, were exciting, as was her association with radical students and young officers.

Concerned about their daughters, far away in St. Petersburg, Olga and Konstantin Verigo tried in vain to get them to come home. Finally, Madame Verigo hit upon a plan to get them back. She wrote the girls that she was opening a boarding school for the daughters of the local gentry and wanted them as teachers. Natasha decided to return, but Katerina stayed on until her father wrote that her mother was ill and she was needed at home.

Katerina went home, but agreed to stay only on the condition she be given her "independence." At this point in her life independence meant the right to use the money she earned as a teacher of the daughters of the rich to set up a free school for peasant children. Her father gave his consent and helped her carry out her plans.

Katerina started a "village school" which soon came under the jurisdiction of the local *zemstvo* and involved her in politics. The elected *zemstvo* assemblies (ancient institutions, moribund until reactivated by Aleksandr II's reforms in the early 1860s) were authorized to establish, and fund by local tax levies, cooperative peasant banks and hospitals, to build and provide upkeep of roads, bridges, and peasant schools. It was also decreed that one-third of the delegates to each *zemstvo* assembly be elected by peasants—a privilege few thought they would ever try to use or if they did, would docilely vote as the landlords told them.

With great enthusiasm Katerina began to work zealously on two fronts. She tried to persuade young aristocrats from neighboring estates to assist her in her school or to set up schools of their own. Then, because she had studied peasant rights when she was in St. Petersburg and found they did exist, in ancient laws and in some of the new laws of Aleksandr II, she arranged gatherings of peasants to inform them of their rights. She especially emphasized the peasant right to elect representatives for the *zemstvo* assemblies.

Katerina's parents, concerned that their daughter's ideas of "freedom" were taking her close to, or beyond, the limits of what tsarist authorities would permit, decided to call a halt. At this point she took the route to freedom from parental control followed by many young Russian women of her day: she got married.

> I looked over my neighbor Nikolai Breshkovsky, a young, well-educated, studious landowner, and said to him that if he agreed to put his strength and talents to the service of cultural work among the peasants, I would marry him. I said that I had committed myself unconditionally to this work and would marry only on condition that I have full freedom to do my cultural work.

Nikolai Breshko-Breshkovsky, a broadminded, well-educated young man from an old noble family of Polish origin, recognized Katerina's demands as reasonable and accepted her offer. In 1869, with her family's approval Katerina married Nikolai, and the girl, Kati Verigo, became *dvorianka* Katerina Breshko-Breshkovskaya. The young couple immediately set to work on various projects, including a peasant bank and an agricultural school to teach peasants better farming methods.

Gatherings of peasants were arranged. Katerina had a clear, strong voice and proved to be an effective speaker, aided by her knowledge of Russian. As an early gesture of protest against her French-speaking family, she had learned Russian from the household servants who were of village origin; she could talk to the peasants in words and phrases they understood. As some of her associates later noted, her personality radiated a moral authority, and she had a power of persuasion given by nature to only a select few.

In Chernigov, peasants flocked to vote for liberal and reform-minded candidates as judges, arbiters, and delegates to local *zemstvo* assemblies. Many were elected. The new judges went to work at once on local problems and began to defend peasants' rights. One of them, a man Katerina had persuaded to run for office, cleared up in three months eight-hundred cases that had been clogging the docket for years. Several *zemstva*, backed by newly elected officials, went about setting up schools, savings banks, and libraries.

The conservative landlords, ousted from their longstanding control of the province, were first astonished, then alarmed. They saw the end of their time-honored sources of graft and were horrified at the thought of having to pay taxes for peasant schools, banks, and libraries. Their representatives hurried to St. Petersburg. They pounded the doors of the Ministry of the Interior. "Conspirators against the government are at work in the land," they shouted. "The peasants are becoming unruly."

There was a quick response. Tsarist officials, already apprehensive over the actual working of the Aleksandr II reforms, first removed from office the "conspirators," sending some to Siberia without trial. Others, like the Verigos and the Breshko-Breshkovskys, were put under strict police surveillance. Katerina's father, Konstantin Verigo, was deprived of an honorary office he had held for years, and she and her husband were ordered to close their schools and cease their efforts to "agitate" the peasants. "We want no apostles here," the governor of the province told Konstantin Verigo.

From this experience Katerina learned to see the tsarist government as a system of corruption whose existence depended on continuous exploitation of the peasants and intimidation of the citizenry by spies and the secret police. Her effort at peaceful change was stopped. She was not ready to stop, but was uncertain of what to do.

About that time an event occurred that Katerina Breshkovskaya said changed her life. In St. Petersburg in July 1871, sixty-four Nechaevists, members of Sergei Nechaev's revolutionary group, the People's Revenge, went on trial in open court. The Ministry of Justice decided full exposure of the Nechaev affair, which involved murder and foul play by Nechaev, would strike a fatal blow, not only against these misguided youthful followers of Nechaev, but against the very idea of revolution. Therefore, the verbatim stenographic record of the fiery speeches of the defense lawyers and the statements, full of revolutionary fervor, made by the prisoners in court were published in full each day in the *Pravitel'stevennyi Vestnik* (Government Messenger). Even Nechaev's "Catechism of a Revolutionary " and several of his incendiary proclamations were printed. Thus, inadvertently, the tsarist authorities provided a short course in the most extreme radicalism of the day that many a Russian youth grasped with fervor and excitement.

Every day the *Government Messenger* came by post to the Breshkovsky estate, and every day Katerina impatiently awaited its arrival. She devoured the speeches, the proclamations, and the "Catechism" which called the revolutionary

> a doomed person. He has neither his own interests, nor affairs, nor feelings, nor attachments, nor property, nor even name. Everything in him is absorbed by a single exclusive interest, by a total concept, a total passion— revolution. . . .

> The revolutionary is a doomed person. Merciless toward the state . . . he does not expect the least mercy toward himself. . . . [He is engaged in an] implacable life-and-death struggle. Every day he must be ready to die. He has to train himself to withstand torture.[2]

The "Catechism" stated that for the revolutionary there is no other goal except the complete liberation and happiness of the people, and, convinced that this goal can be achieved only by "an all-shattering revolution of the people, must work to incite them to massive rebellion." In addition, officials harmful to the revolution "must be destroyed. Their sudden and violent death can inspire the greatest fear in the government, and depriving it of clever and energetic figures, paralyze its power."

Of her reaction to all these radical pronouncements, Katerina Breshkovskaya said:

> just the way a traveler who has lost his way in the dark is shown by the sunrise which direction to go, so to me suddenly everything became clear. I saw many things. One of them was that I had a mission—a mission to go out and reveal the truth to the people, to teach them how they could become supporters of the coming revolution. If carrying out that mission meant breaking the law and running the risk of imprisonment or the gallows, I was ready for it.

But before crossing that threshhold she decided to make one more attempt at legal reform. "It is a poor patriot," she said, "who will not make every effort to use the legal means of his government before rising against it." She went on a round of personal visits to the landowners in the area who had shown an interest in improving the lot of the peasants on their estates by establishing schools or cooperative workshops and had, as a result, suffered the humiliation of having them closed down on order of government officials. Her message to these "progressive" landowners was: "Don't stop. Continue and expand your efforts. Challenge the blind and corrupt tsarist officials."

The response was uniformly negative. The landowners refused to risk bringing down on their heads tsarist punitive measures. Disheartened and discouraged, Katerina came back to her home. It was her last effort at legal

---

[2]Philip Pomper, *Sergei Nechaev*, New Brunswick, 1979, contains quotations from the "Catechism," pp. 90–94.

reform. The time had come to give up everything she owned and dedicate herself to the struggle for rights and freedom for the people. This decision created a crisis in her personal life.

> I was twenty-six years old [actually in 1873 when she left her husband she was twenty-nine]. My husband, like me, had a whole life before him, and therefore, I thought it only fair to speak frankly. I asked him if he was willing to suffer exile or death in the cause of freedom.

He was not willing. Katerina saw her husband as a man of noble character who was not ready to undergo the sacrifice that life as a revolutionary would bring. He, like her father, was a liberal who believed reform could eventually be achieved within the law. Katerina and her husband and father represent the two major tendencies in nineteenth- and early twentieth-century Russia: the daring revolutionary and the timid liberals.

Overcome with grief, Nikolai Breshko-Breshkovsky urged his wife to stay. Her parents also tried to persuade her to change her mind, reminding her she had a duty to her unborn child. But, with an aching heart, and with the knowledge that her devotion to the cause of freedom would endanger not only herself but her child and the members of her family, she left.

Katerina went to Kiev, which was a seething volcano of revolution. Her ill and recently widowed sister Olga welcomed her. Olga sympathized with the revolutionary cause and had many radical friends. Seven or eight of them, mostly students, shared Olga's basement apartment, living together as a family—as did many other student groups in Kiev and all other university cities. They were known as the Kiev Commune, and as new members crowded in, they soon had to move to larger quarters. In preparation for the revolutionary action they expected to take, the young idealists lived on plain fare and engaged in endless debate on aims and tactics.

Katerina's experience working with peasants, her qualities of leadership, and the fact that she was several years older than most of the Kiev Commune members put her in the forefront of revolutionary activity. She wrote colorful descriptions of the meetings of eager young people gathered secretly in smoke-filled rooms late at night, "packed together as closely as in a church at Easter." But seeing in the Kiev youth what she felt was excessive zeal, inadequate organization, and insufficient acquaintance with the realities of peasant life, Katerina became restless. She decided to go to St. Petersburg to observe the situation there. She found the capital city had become a lively center of revolutionary activity. Radical youth from all over the country were there to seek information and advice about Going-to-the-People. As in Kiev, Katerina found the gradualist Chaikovskist approach to revolution dominant, with its tendency to debate rather than to act, with its dedication to the idea that the mission of the intelligentsia was to educate the workers and the peasants. The problem was that she had learned from her own attempts at peasant education and legal reform that the gradualist approach to change was impossible under the tsarist system. As she put it, "I had to renounce my vocation [teaching], the creative work I love, to devote my energy to purely revolutionary ends, and, if necessary, to terrorist activity."

Her commitment soon led Katerina to approve and cooperate in an assassination plot, after meeting an old friend who was looking for volunteers to assist him in a conspiracy to start the revolution by assassinating Aleksandr II. Explosives placed in the Winter Palace would be detonated by a clock mechanism he had perfected. The plan was for him to remain in St. Petersburg to work out the final details of the explosion while Katerina and a companion, using assumed names, would go among the people and organize a revolt. The plot was aborted for lack of resources, and the plotters, undetected, did not become a terrorist group or party, but Katerina Breshkovskaya never gave up her commitment to terror as a necessary revolutionary tactic.

Before the winter of 1873–1874 was over Katerina had passed some of the tests laid down in Nechaev's "Catechism" for the revolutionary "as a doomed person." She had become an "illegal," living under an assumed name with a false passport. She had not only accepted the idea of "death to the enemies of the revolution," but had participated in a plot against the most powerful enemy of them all, the Tsar himself. With the birth of her son during her turbulent winter in St. Petersburg she faced another test: could she, as the "Catechism" demanded, "suppress all tender feelings of kinship and love in favor of total cold passion for the revolutionary cause"?

She had gone too far to turn back. She knew she could not keep her child. As she put it, she and other women revolutionaries chose to be fighters for justice, not mothers of victims of tyranny! Before her son's birth Katerina had asked her brother's wife, Vera, whom she loved and trusted, to take the baby and to rear the child as her own. Katerina took her son to Kiev where Vera, who had been ill, was living in the Kiev Commune. Vera recovered, and a carriage arrived to take Vera, with her husband, back to their estate. Passing the baby from her arms to Vera's and seeing the carriage drive away turned out to be a traumatic experience for Katerina:

> My heart felt torn into a thousand pieces. My feet were lame, my arms stiff. I could not move from the spot. I thought of the warning that had been given me when I first spoke of my wish to work for the peasants. While I was still a girl they said, "Wait! you will get married, and that will tie you down. Your young blood will be calmed, your running brook will become a quiet lake." And the time came when I was married, and I was conscious of no change in my spirit. I felt for the people's cause as strongly as ever—even more strongly. And then friends told me, "Just wait, you will have an estate of your own to care for, and that will take up all your time and thoughts." But my husband and I bought an estate, and no such result followed, for I could never let one

tiny estate outweigh the vast plains of all Russia. My spirit and my convictions remained the same. And with time came new counsel from friends. Now they argued: "Yes, you have remained unchanged by husband and home, but you will succumb to the command of Nature. With the birth of a child will come the death of your revolutionary ideals. The wings you have used for soaring high in the air among the clouds you will now use to shelter your little one." And I gave birth to a little one. I felt that in that boy my youth was buried, and that when he was taken from my body, the fire of my spirit had gone out with him. But it was not so. The conflict between my love for the child and my love for the revolution and for the freedom of Russia robbed me of many a night's sleep. I knew I could not be a mother and still be a revolutionist. Those were not two tasks to which it was possible to give a divided attention. Either the one or the other must absorb one's whole being, one's entire devotion. So I gave up my child.

In the spring and summer of 1874 thousands of young idealists left their revolutionary circles, study groups, jobs, schools, and homes to Go-to-the-People. Young men and women went into the villages as doctors, doctors' helpers, nurses and midwives, teachers, village scribes, even as agricultural laborers, blacksmiths, shoemakers, woodcutters, and cloth dyers to live in close contact with the peasants, to teach them and to learn from them their most pressing social needs.

Going-to-the-People appealed to Katerina Breshkovskaya. She knew the peasants' grievances and she knew how to approach peasant men and women. Dressed in peasant clothing she was entirely convincing, as many of her colleagues were not. In that memorable summer of 1874 she and a young man and woman formed a team and tramped the roads of the Ukraine. They explained to peasants, who recognized them as strangers because they did not speak the Ukrainian language, that they had come from another province where they had lost their land and were searching for work.

At gatherings they succeeded in arranging, the peasants listened to Katerina and were excited by her talk of "land and freedom," but when she identified the Tsar and tsarist rule as the cause of their distress and their unfulfilled demands for land, she did not convince them. To the peasants their ruler was the faraway, fairy tale Tsar who loved his peasants. They were his children. It was the soldiers and the landowners who abused the peasants, who lied to the Tsar about his peasants. When Katerina pulled a little book out of a pocket in her voluminous peasant skirt and began to read—always a simple story with a "lesson" of how some legendary simple person became a hero by resisting oppression and fighting for freedom—the peasants were astonished. Peasant women, and almost all peasant men, could neither read nor write. Some became suspicious. Word would mysteriously get to the authorities that revolutionaries were in the vicinity. Warned in time, Katerina and her co-workers would disappear into the Underground, only to resurface in yet another peasant village. But before the summer was over, in the village of Tulchin, she did not get away in time. She was arrested and clapped into a large, filthy rural jail in Podolia, filled to capacity with Going-to-the-People youth and a few criminals.

Claiming to be Thekla Kossaia, an illiterate peasant, Katerina was shifted around to several jails in different towns in the district where she observed the cruel treatment of women prisoners. "The air was filled with their screams and curses as the women were beaten." Not until she was taken to Kiev, some three months after her arrest, was Katerina confronted by people brought into court by the prosecutor who identified her. She still insisted she was Thekla Kossaia, but when the prosecutor threatened to send for her parents, she gave in. Her treatment in prison immediately changed for the better once she was identified as belonging to the nobility.

Katerina Breshkovskaya spent nearly four years in "preliminary detention" in Russian jails before finally, in October 1877, she was brought into court as the famous Trial of the 193 began in St. Petersburg. She might have gotten off with a light sentence, as most of the other women did, but when she appeared before the judge for sentencing, she took the occasion to speak out and made a strong statement on the unfairness and illegality of the procedure. Condemned to five years of hard labor in the mines of Kara, she was the first woman to receive such a sentence.

Toward the end of June 1879, those of the Trial of the 193 condemned to the Siberian *katorga* were dressed in convict clothing, fettered in irons, and in groups of ten led out of the Litovski Castle Prison in St. Petersburg at night—to avoid a demonstration by their many admirers and sympathizers. They were taken by train, first to Moscow, then to Nizhnii-Novgorod for debarkation on convict barges, with special compartments for the nobility, whose toilet facilities were a pail of water on the deck. Slowly they floated down the Volga to its juncture with the Kama River, where they turned gradually northward as they went up the Kama. Three weeks after leaving St. Petersburg they reached Perm. They were dirty, many of them sick, and half-starved. The officer in charge kept most of the money the prisoners were required to give him to buy their food, leaving them to exist mainly on hard black bread and water.

On July 20 began the trek on that *via dolorosa*, the Great Siberian Road. Each prisoner was loaded into a horse-drawn, springless wagon and seated between two armed gendarmes. Under great pressure to reach Kara, more than three thousand miles to the east and north, before the winter freeze set in in eastern Siberia in September, the horses were raced over rutted roads. They raised enormous clouds of dust that obscured the beautiful scenery they were passing through—grassy slopes of the Ural Mountains and prairie meadows filled with myriads of wild flowers. Hungrier and hungrier, dirtier and dirtier, they raced on, stopping only for a few hours of sleep on bare benches at filthy, reeking, vermin-infested, overcrowded prison stops for change of horses. Katerina wrote:

> Through the walls we heard the endless jangling of fetters, the moaning of women, the cries of sick babies. On the walls a mass of inscriptions—names of friends who had gone before us, news of death and insanity—some of them freshly cut. But one worm-eaten love poem looked a century old. For along the Great Siberian Road over a million men, women, and children have dragged . . . people from every social class, murderers and degenerates side by side with tender young girls exiled through the jealous wife of some petty town official.

On they went, through Krassnoyarsk and Irkutsk. They reached Lake Baikal where a steamer waited to take them across its stormy waters to Mysovaia. Siberian drivers met them there with crude carts. They reached Chita, Sretensk, then another steamer took them on to Us't-Kara.

Katerina was kept in Us't-Kara for only ten months because her four years of preliminary detention were subtracted from her five-year sentence, and she was not put to work in the mines but had to endure what she regarded as a worse punishment—enforced idleness. At the end of the ten months she was not released but marched, on foot, in a silent procession of convicts to Barguzin, a bleak prison area near the eastern shores of Lake Baikal. As they marched, except for the whipping of a strong wind, the only sound was the rattling of the chains which echoed like mournful bells in the icy air.

In Barguzin, cold and hunger were the prisoners' lot. By spring each year, from one-quarter to one-third of them had died of tuberculosis, typhoid fever, malnutrition, or failed attempts at escape; the woman suffered humiliation and violence, victims of the Cossack guards. The moral dissoluteness of the authorities, Katerina said, could not be described in words.

Seeing a few forlorn children there, Katerina proposed to start a school for them, but the police refused permission. She became more and more desperate. Finally, she and three young exiled student prisoners decided to escape. They made a successful getaway, then began the almost insuperable difficulties of reaching the coast—the goal being Japan—through what seemed to be endless chains of mountains. They walked and climbed and eluded the police for six hundred miles before they were caught.

As punishment for her escape attempt, Katerina was resentenced to the mines of Kara for four years and to forty blows of the lash. The prison authorities, apparently reluctant at that time to flog a female political prisoner, never carried out the flogging. When she was brought back to Kara she was surprised to find twenty other women political prisoners who had been sentenced to the mines. Delighted to have their company, she suffered to see one after the other of them die, until fewer than half remained.

At the end of four years in Kara, Katerina Breshkovskaya was marched on foot a thousand miles to the south and east to Selenginsk where she was put, under police surveillance as a "forced settler." That was where George Kennan found her in 1885. She said:

In dead Selenginsk I rotted eight whole years. In my heart burned a passionate wish to run away, but constantly shadowed by tsarist police, I was like a wild falcon in a narrow cage. I grew almost frantic with loneliness and to keep my sanity I would rush out in the snow shouting passionate orations, or, playing the prima donna, sing grand opera arias to the bleak landscape—which never applauded.

In 1892, nearly two decades after her first imprisonment, the authorities gave Katerina Breshkovskaya a "peasant passport" and the status of "banishment." She became a "free exile," confined to the Siberian penal area and, under rather loose police surveillance, free to move about. She made use of her new status to walk from one isolated settlement to another all across Siberia. In each place, with great care and caution, she gathered around her groups of people and spoke to them words of hope, assuring them the coming revolution would change their miserable condition. It was imperative, she told them, that they join the cause. Wherever she went secret circles of revolutionaries appeared, and she made converts of some of the leading citizens of Siberia.

In 1896, after she had endured twenty-three years of prison and exile, the tsarist authorities released Katerina Breshkovskaya and accorded her the right to live anywhere in the Russian Empire except the capital city and the Province of St. Petersburg. Returning to European Russia, she found the remnants of her family (her husband and her parents were dead) no happier to be with her than she with them. She said, "To them I was a woman deprived of all rights, a convict, a horror, and nothing could change this terrible fact."

She also met her twenty-three-year-old son, Nikolai Nikolaevich Breshko-Breshkovsky, who from babyhood had been told his mother was dead. Reared in the aristocratic circle of her brother's family, he was a conservative young man, already beginning to make a name for himself as a writer of popular fiction. When he learned the returned prisoner was his mother, he turned from her in revulsion and made it clear he never wanted to see her again.[3]

She soon resumed her old role as an "illegal" and took to the road. The tireless apostle of revolution, she had to get a sense of the mood of Russia. At first it was as if she had returned to a different country. For one thing, the cities of Russia were linked by a network of railroads. The railroads enabled her to visit many more places and see many more people than in

---

[3]Katerina's son became a well-known and prolific author of novels (28 titles appear in the New York Public Library catalog), continuing to write and publish (in Russian) as an emigré in Paris after the 1917 revolution until his death in 1943. Katerina Breshkovskaya's close friend George Lazerev said the subject of her son was too painful for her to talk about (in a letter to Irene Dietrich, October 30, 1934, on file in the Special Collection Department of the Wellesley College Library).

the 1870s when she had trudged on foot from village to village, from *izba* (hut) to *izba* on the alternately dusty or muddy roads.

The Russia she came back to had changed in another way. The literacy rate, while still one of the lowest in Europe, had risen, not only in the cities and towns but even in the countryside. In almost every village there were one or two peasants who could read, and Katerina Breshkovskaya saw an unsatisfied craving for education among the peasant youth. She also found the 1870s peasant worship of the Tsar was becoming the exception rather than the rule. No longer did peasants look upon political activists with fear and report them to the police. As one peasant said to her, "Its different now. We don't forget that Sof'ya Perovskaya, wearing *lapti* (peasant boots), walked in our village."

In 1896 rising peasant literacy and the changing peasant attitude presented Katerina Breshkovskaya with a double challenge: to recruit young people as propagandists, to carry the written and spoken word to them, and to print, or to import from abroad, illegal revolutionary literature.

With the sharpened perception of the returning exile, Katerina came into the stagnant Russia of Nikolai II and was shocked at the suffering villages and worsening peasant economy, the terrible condition of factory workers and the huge servant classes in the towns, the heavy punitive measures of the government against any element of the population which dared to make even the slightest real or suspected criticism of the tsarist regime. Seeing the general malaise and hearing the grumbling everywhere, she sensed in every fiber of her being that revolution, like a great tidal wave, was building strength in people of all levels of society across the endless expanse of Russia. The time was ripe for organized revolutionary activity. But her old associates, the 1870s radicals, were scattered or dead, and the old political groups were discredited and gone. She was confronted with a new time, new people, even a new language. She noticed the young people talked very fast, uninterruptedly, with poor pronunciation, in "the monotonous phrases of German marxism."

During Katerina Breshkovskaya's years in Siberia a new generation of revolutionary youth had appeared. She found them grouped in isolated circles in the cities and towns of Russia. They knew only vaguely about the 1870s *narodniki* and their ideas and traditions; the reactionary reign of Aleksandr III (which ended in 1894) had worked systematically to obliterate them. The youth of the 1890s, in search of a revolutionary doctrine, were reading Marx and the Marxian journals smuggled in from Germany and Switzerland—many of their articles written by Vera Zasulich, who remained a legendary heroine in Russia, and, living abroad, had become a prolific Marxist polemist.

Katerina Breshkovskaya was no theoretician, but she was an expert in sizing up a political situation and she believed in action. She was convinced that the doctrinaire Marxist philosophy with its urban orientation did not fit the needs and aspirations of Russia with its small, urban working class, at most two or three million, compared to nearly one hundred thirty million peasants. Despite this overwhelming fact of Russian life, Marxist theory projected the revolution as a proletarian mass movement with urban workers rising against the capitalist system and replacing it initially by a dictatorship of the proletariat to carry out a ruthless process of nationalization. Peasant ownership of land was considered capitalistic and was a feature of Russian life that would cease with the Marxist revolution.

To Katerina, not only the means but the final aims of the Marxists were wrong. A dictatorship, even if temporary, she equated with tyranny. As for the proletariat achieving the overthrow of the existing system, which was more patriarchal than it was capitalistic, this was patently impossible. She was convinced, as the 1870s narodniki had been, that only Russia's long-suffering, dissatisfied (and, at times in Russia's past, rebellious) peasants could be the shock troops of revolution. She also adhered to the narodniki belief that the revolutionary spark had to be struck by a relatively small group of informed, dedicated, self-sacrificing leaders who would propagandize and organize the people, and, when called upon, carry out acts of terror selflessly. A new world would come into being as a result of propaganda and carefully triggered violence—a different world from that visualized by the Marxists. Socialization of the land would be the first order of the day. Each peasant would be allotted his rightful share. Factories would be turned over to the workers. And each individual in Russian society, peasant and non-peasant, would be guaranteed freedom for every kind of personal, social, and creative expression when the tsarist government was replaced by a republic.

With these arguments Katerina Breshkovskaya sought out and engaged in hot debate with Russian youth professing Marxist leanings. She succeeded in winning many over to her narodniki agrarian socialist views. She found allies in her crusade as her former 1870s comrades began reappearing on the scene. In a steady trickle in the mid-1890s the stariki (the old ones) returned from Siberian exile, with a stronger commitment than ever to free the long-suffering people of Russia. In the depths of their souls the old fire was still burning, ready to leap into flame at the slightest encouragement. She tracked them down and stirred them into action. Finding one old returned narodnik reluctant to return to the thorny path of revolution, she told him, "It is shameful for you to settle down to peace and quiet. You'll die in disgrace, not like a fighter but safe in your bed. You'll be a coward, dying a vile dog's death."

Katerina Breshkovskaya, with her white hair, her political past, the quality of her mind, and the kindness and simplicity of her demeanor, charmed young people. She found that as a participant in and a survivor of the narod-

niki movement she was held in great veneration. She was at age fifty-two the "Old Revolutionary," and soon became universally known as *Babushka Revolyutsii*—Grandmother of the Revolution. She was so designated even in the files of the *Okhranka,* the tsarist secret police.

Most political parties have "founding fathers." The Socialist Revolutionary party (the S.R., or Esser party, as the Russians call it), which became Russia's only mass political party before 1917, had a "founding mother," or grandmother. Katerina Breshkovskaya laid the foundation in the years after 1896 when she hovered over all Russia, like the Holy Ghost of Revolution. She said:

> For six years railway coaches were my quarters. I gathered people together wherever I could: in peasant huts, in student attics, in the drawing rooms of liberals, on river barges, in forests, in village grist mills.
>
> I had to search out people cautiously, preserving the greatest prudence for their sake as well as mine. In order to found anew the party of people's freedom I had to go to many provinces, many towns and villages. I had to find out who could be relied upon among the intelligentsia, as well as among the peasants.

Soon after 1896 the name Katerina Breshkovskaya entirely disappeared in Russia but in every city, in every town and village, it would from time to time be whispered, "Babushka is here." "Babushka is here." "Do you want to see her?" "But you know . . ." and the speaker would raise fingers to lips to close them.

Part of Babushka's strategy was to put the young people she recruited to work. On Sundays and holidays, seminarians, high school, and technical school students manned hectographs and crude mimeograph copiers, turning out sheet by sheet the pages of revolutionary pamphlets they put together and sold for a few *kopeiki* to peasants and workers: "The Crooked and the Straight," "Conversations about the Land," "A Word about Truth," "The Will of the Tsar and the Will of the People." Beginning in Saratov Province, then spreading to Tambov, Samara, Perm, Khar'kov, Poltava and beyond, thousands of copies of pamphlets were duplicated, sold, and eagerly read. Sometimes peasants came to volunteer their help. Babushka said:

> My heart was overjoyed at the sight of a middle-aged, bearded peasant, carefully tracing out with hectograph ink the letters on the master sheet; then so carefully lifting off the copies, his eyes shining with happiness as one sheet after another piled up, anticipating with pleasure the distribution of the beloved little book through the whole locality and possibly the whole district.

Soon hectograph and mimeograph duplicating was supplemented by quantities of pamphlets smuggled in from abroad, enabling Babushka and her comrades to put into circulation what she called "People's Revolutionary

Lending Libraries," each "Library" containing several small books. To give the appearance of legality, printed on each one was this inscription:

> Printed with the approval of the Permanent Commission on Reading for the People. Recommended by the Teachers' Commission of the Ministry of People's Enlightenment for school libraries of the lower schools, for workers' free libraries, and for public peoples' reading rooms. Printed by the Ministry of People's Enlightenment, St. Petersburg. Passed by the Censor.

Babushka's labors dedicated to revolution and socialism, combined with the efforts of more and more like-minded leaders—many of whom she had recruited—increased the number of activists in socialist-revolutionary political groups in Russia's cities, towns, and villages to the tens of thousands.[4] Consolidation into an organized political party was inevitable despite the fact that political parties in tsarist Russia were illegal. Beginning in 1897 meetings of delegates from various cities, with the aim of uniting their groups, occurred every year, but not until 1901, at a conference in Saratov, was agreement on the Socialist Revolutionary, or Esser, party organization and program achieved.

One of the most important issues all Socialist Revolutionary groups faced from the very beginning was terrorism. A typical example of the dilemma, and Babushka's approach to it, came up at a meeting of revolutionary youth in 1899 in Grigory Gershuni's cramped, smoke-filled room in Minsk. The point under discussion was whether terror has a role in revolutionary strategy. Someone recalled the days of Narodnaya Volya terror in the 1870s and 1880s. Disagreement flared when a return to it was suggested. One man said he could not even imagine living if there was to be a repetition of those frightful, stormy times.

Babushka was then occupying a room above Gershuni's, and as the talk became more heated, he heard her footsteps on the stairs. He opened the door and asked her to join the group. Explaining the subject they were discussing, he asked her: Should there now be a resumption of Narodnaya Volya terrorism? With sadness in her face, she said:

> We in our time were tormented with this same question, and we said, in the words of the gospel: "Yes, this cup is surely being passed to us." And today

---

[4]The size of Esser membership is difficult to determine. As Oliver Radkey wrote, the statistics are "neither accurate nor complete," but he put the actual membership at the height of the party's development at 50,000, and those continually in the orbit of party influence at 300,000. This compared to the Marxist Social Democratic party's claimed 150,000 membership, which was divided into Mensheviks and Bolsheviks. Radkey goes on to say that the contribution of the Essers to the revolution cannot be measured by number of members; "its service was to inflame the spirit of revolt in the rural masses" The Agrarian Foes of Bolshevism, New York, 1954, pp. 62–64. Copyright © 1954 Columbia University Press. Used by permission.

also the answer will come the hard way. Again we go toward the plunge into the abyss; again we look into it, and the abyss gazes back at us. What it means is that terror is again inevitable.

In this statement Babushka spoke, as she often did, in parables. Her reference is to the Gospel of St. Matthew, chapter 26, which recounts that Jesus on the last night of his life, in the Garden of Gethsemane with crucifixion awaiting him at dawn, thrice cried out, "Father, if it is possible, let the cup [of self-sacrifice] pass from me." Then Jesus submitted to his fate, doing "not as I will but as Thou wilt."

In her speeches to young people, Babushka proclaimed that to carry out a terrorist act was a magnificent manifestation of civic honor. She argued that the government did not condemn, and, in fact, often promoted, officials who brought death and devastation to the people with their orders for beating with the knout, for shooting into crowds of peaceful demonstrators, for looking upon rape and robbery by troops sent into localities "to restore order" as normal procedure. It was only right that the Esser party form a Battle Organization to attack these officials. Such attacks would frighten and weaken the government and inspire the people to stand up and resist government abuses. The youth hungrily listened to Babushka, and more volunteered than could be given assignments.

Babushka's terrorist propaganda was an emotional appeal. The definitive theoretical justification was an article in the official Esser journal, *Revoliutsionnaia Rossiia*, no. 7, written by Grigory Gershuni, a young bacteriologist Babushka had recruited. He identified terror as a necessary part of the Socialist Revolutionary struggle, but emphasized it was but one weapon in the arsenal of party action and must be carefully planned and coordinated with other weapons. Nevertheless, the "daring blows of the fighting avant-garde striking at the very heart of governmental power infinitely strengthens the mass struggle."

The year 1901 began with student demonstrations in many cities to mark the fortieth anniversary of the February 19, 1861, *ukaz* freeing the serfs. In March, the twentieth anniversary of the assassination of Tsar Aleksandr II was celebrated and his assassins commemorated. Several peasant disturbances were put down by provincial governors with marked brutality. In this charged atmosphere, with the debate over political terror in revolutionary circles spilling over into widely read journals and illegal brochures, with the manifesto of the Socialist Revolutionary party itself specifying systematic political terror as an important tactic in the revolutionary struggle, it is not surprising that, without waiting for the party to act, an assassin shot and killed the minister of Education, Nikolai Pavlovich Bogolepov, on February 14. The terrorist was an ex-student, Peter V. Karpovich, recently returned from abroad. A few weeks later another youth fired four shots at the powerful and widely hated procurator of the Holy Synod, Konstantin P. Pobedonostsev, who survived unharmed. By the end of the year the Esser Central Committee agreed to the formation of the Battle Organization, with Gershuni in complete control. Its purpose: to secretly organize and direct terror weapons against carefully chosen tsarist officials.

The first official targeted for assassination by the Battle Organization was Dmitri S. Sipiagin, the minister of Interior, who had launched the campaign to arrest and exile student demonstrators and to send punitive expeditions into the countryside to quell peasant riots. The chosen assassin was twenty-one-year-old Kiev University student, Stepan Balmashev, recruited for the Battle Organization by Babushka. After several months of target practice and preparation for his assignment (sometimes joined by other recruits to terror), he killed Sipiagin on April 2, 1902. Balmashev's deed, for which he was soon hanged, marked the beginning of a campaign of political terrorism in tsarist Russia which continued and intensified for five years.

After directing the Sipiagin assassination, Gershuni moved to Kiev. His apartment became the Battle Organization headquarters. There secret meetings were held, with Babushka in attendance when she was not off propagandizing and recruiting. There quantities of illegal party literature were stored, false passports were made, and communications from abroad on secret matters were directed after the leaders of the Esser Executive Committee left Russia for a safer haven in Paris and later Geneva.

The renewal of political terror, student and worker demonstrations, and peasant disorders which were becoming more frequent, stimulated increased action by the tsarist government against political activists of all persuasions. Arrests, trials behind closed doors, jailings, exile, and hangings became routine events. On May 13, 1903, Gershuni was arrested in Kiev. He walked into a trap laid by a Battle Organization member he admired and trusted, Evno F. Azeff. Neither Gershuni nor any of the Esser Executive Committee suspected that Azeff had for several years been a member of the top tsarist secret police organization, the *Okhranka*. In a manner reminiscent of the actions of Sergei Degaev who betrayed Vera Figner and many *narodovol'tsi* in the 1880s, Azeff's twisted career involved masterminding Esser plots, then betraying the plotters.[5] He was so trusted by his Esser colleagues, that after Gershuni's imprisonment, he was appointed head of the Battle Organization.

One after the other, Esser leaders were picked up by the police. Many fled abroad, but Babushka still functioned as the ubiquitous, illusive outlaw recruiter for the activist ranks of the Esser party. As she tirelessly preached, the party had as its aim the socialization of the land and the freeing of the

---

[5]Azeff was unmasked by Vladimir Burtsev, editor of *Byloye* in 1908. His story was told by Boris Ivanovich Nikolaevski, *Azeff the Spy*, New York, 1934.

people from tyranny. She led the life of a homeless agitator, hunted by whole battalions of police and secret agents. Tales circulated everywhere of her clever escapes and the stupidity of the police. Dressed in simple, worn, peasant clothes, when she saw a gendarme approach, Babushka would drop to a squatting position and pull her shawl over her bent head. If the gendarme stopped to question her, she would look up with a vacant stare, effect a toothless smile, nod her head, and mumble. Or she would drop to her knees before a sacred image, an icon, or a shrine in the street, and pray, with her shawl drawn over her face and her hand lifted to cross herself. This was clever pretense but it was not mockery, for Katerina Breshkovskaya was deeply religious. From childhood she had identified herself with the Christian martyr Saint Barbara, who had suffered death at the hands of her family rather than give up her faith.

On one occasion, at a country house where she had been given shelter by friends, the police—hot on her trail—surrounded the place. It happened to be the cook's day off. Babushka fled to the kitchen, saw the cook's dress and apron hanging in the pantry, quickly put them on, and began to prepare dinner. Again the police were foiled.

The *Okhranka* put pressure on Azeff to stop letting Babushka make fools of the police and gendarmerie. She must, without delay, be arrested. Esser party headquarters had informed Azeff that Babushka was going abroad. He saw that all crossing points along the Russian-European border were staffed with extra police. Finally the authorities succeeded in trailing her to her place of departure. As soon as she entered the waiting room of the railroad station she saw policemen guarding all doors, carefully inspecting every person boarding the outgoing trains. She noticed a party of nuns standing nearby, stepped over, and began a conversation with the abbess. The abbess became so interested in the conversation she invited Babushka to the convent. Out she walked, past the police, surrounded by nuns.

Finally, at the end of May 1903, Babushka, expertly disguised, took passage on a steamboat in Odessa, crossed the Black Sea to Rumania in the company of a young Esser party member, and traveled to Geneva. She left Russia to escape arrest, but she also felt the need to urge the members of the Central Committee in Switzerland to act on certain party problems. She called herself the old political "Nana" and "Order Giver." Because the number of arrests of Esser activists in Russia was rapidly increasing, she warned that the party's resources of trained people there were being drained. Meanwhile, thousands of young Russians, many of them Essers, were in Europe as students or living in self-imposed exile. The result was the appalling situation of the Esser party leadership being stronger abroad than it was in Russia.

Why, asked Babushka, were the leaders in Geneva devoting their time to debating with each other, to publishing books and pamphlets on socialist theory, when their main job was the propagation of Esser party ideology among peasants and workers in Russia? Every day Russia was veering closer to revolution, she said. Political reality necessitated organizing, at once, all available forces, readying them to enter the battle against the old regime, to sacrifice their lives for a free Russia. This meant getting Russians in Europe to go home and become active revolutionaries. To this end, for two years, Babushka traveled from city to city. Young people crowded the meetings she held, listened eagerly to her message, and read the revolutionary literature she distributed. Many were persuaded to go back to Russia.

Okhranka agents trailed Babushka from Paris to Amsterdam, from Amsterdam to London, from London to Brussels, from Brussels to Geneva. They wrote long reports about the streets and houses where she reportedly had stayed. They speculated endlessly on her whereabouts and even surmised that perhaps she had "sneaked back to Russia."

Babushka represented the Esser party at international socialist meetings in various cities and attended the Second International in Amsterdam. In Paris she fascinated young French socialists. They found her French excellent, but said it was the language of their grandfathers and great-grandfathers. It was as if she had appeared as a guest from the eighteenth century.

On July 28, 1904, in St. Petersburg, Boris Savinkov, as leader of his team of Esser terrorists, successfully carried out his assignment to assassinate Pleve. In Geneva the leaders of the party celebrated, and their praise of Azeff, as head of the Battle Organization, was boundless. Babushka, who did not like Azeff personally, bowed her head to the ground, Russian style, before him.

Public reaction in Russia to the assassination of Pleve was a mixture of consternation and rejoicing. It put the Esser party in the forefront of the political scene, and taking full responsibility, the Central Committee announced:

> The death of Pleve is only one step forward on the path of freeing the people. The path is long and difficult but we have begun and the way is clear. Karpovich and Balmashev, Gershuni and Pokotilov [a chemist killed by an accidental explosion while preparing materials for the Pleve assassination], the unknown who assassinated the governor of Ufa have shown us the way. Judgment day for the autocracy is near. Long live *Narodnaya Volya* (the People's Will). . . . Death to the Tsar and autocracy.

An appeal to the citizens of the civilized world announced that

> Pleve was executed by members of the Fighting Section of the Esser Party as a man in whom were incarnate all the abominations and all the horrors of tsarism.

> We repudiate terrorism in free countries, but in Russia where despotism excludes all possibility of an open political movement . . . we are compelled to use the force of revolutionary truth against tyranny.

In the fall of 1904 Babushka and the other Esser party leaders in Geneva decided she should go to America to raise money among the large Russian Jewish communities in the east coast cities of the United States. Even though these people were thought to be very poor, they were known to be sympathetic to socialism and to the cause of revolution in Russia. Accompanying her was a young Jewish party member, Karl Zhitlovski, who would translate what she had to say into Yiddish in the meetings she would hold with small groups of Russian expatriates.

Esser leaders in Geneva were surprised when news reached them that Babushka had taken America by storm! After a short detention on Ellis Island she was ferried across New York harbor to Manhattan where the United League of New York Revolutionists gave her a welcome. Babushka responded by opening wide her arms and adopting America as her second *patrie*. Everywhere she went she made friends who immediately became her "children" and their children her "grandchildren."

When Katerina Breshkovskaya spoke to a capacity crowd at Fanueil Hall in Boston, on the platform with her were many notables, including two Harvard professors, Julia Ward Howe, and Henry B. Blackwell. Letters of greeting from the governor of Massachusetts and many well-known Americans were read. In New York she spoke to a packed house at Cooper Union. In Chicago, on two successive Sundays, overflow crowds came to hear her at the West Side Auditorium where she was wildly applauded. Women wept, hats were flung into the air, words of affection in five languages rained down on her. Hundreds pushed to the front to clasp her hand. In the New Pennsylvania Hall in Philadelphia she was carried around the hall on the shoulders of two strong men as the crowd shouted and sang. Journalists reporting on her public appearances in America testified they had never before seen such audience enthusiasm.

How was it that this Russian revolutionary, virtually unknown in this country, suddenly was able to attract such enthusiastic crowds and to command the attention of an impressive array of American establishment figures? Without underestimating the power of Katerina Breshkovskaya's personality, other factors help explain her phenomenal success in America.

One was the American thirst for information about Russia. Newspapers and journals provided coverage of the Russo-Japanese war, on-the-scene reports of political assassinations in Russia, student demonstrations, pogroms, and peasant violence. They also printed stories of recurring economic and political crises, miscarriages of justice, and maltreatment of political prisoners. But Americans wanted to know more. They went to hear Russian visitors, such as Professor Paul Miliukov, who in December 1904 was lecturing in Boston at the Lowell Institute on "Russia's Crisis." The old revolutionary Nikolai Chaikovsky (in whose name the 1870s Chaikovsky circles were formed) had toured the United States earlier in 1904, speaking to eager crowds.

Another reason for Katerina Breshkovskaya's success was that the American Friends of Russian Freedom, with its roster of members influential in literary and political circles, welcomed her, arranged speaking engagements, and introduced her to many well-known American public figures. She, with her unerring sense of what was important, valued these contacts. To accomplish her mission in America, which to her was more than raising money, she had to reach not only recent immigrants from Russia but "real Americans," people of influence and position.

Katerina Breshkovskaya's message to America was that the victory of the "progressives" (her euphemism for "revolutionaries"), in whose ranks were all elements of Russian society, over the cruel and oppressive tsarist regime, was so near that they needed to be able to count on friends abroad.

> It is not weakness or lack of success that leads us to come to you; it is the enlargement of our work and its success, almost beyond our expectations, that obliges us to appeal to the sympathy of free peoples for their help in this hour of decisive struggle, when the victory will bring happiness to the whole of our suffering country.

Katerina Breshkovskaya got expansive coverage in the press. Kellogg Durland's articles in the *Boston Transcript* were typical of the enthusiasm everywhere expressed for her:

> To look upon the face of this silver-haired apostle is like receiving a benediction. Her outward and inward calm are superb. Her hands are beautiful in their delicacy and refinement, despite the years in Siberia. Her voice is low and sweet, her smile winning and childlike. Only her eyes betray the suffering of the years. In repose her face is strong like iron.

There was an outpouring of poetry as America's bards sang her praises. Katharine Lee Bates, author of "America the Beautiful," ended her verses to Babushka:

> Clearer still thy voice goes ringing
> Over steppe and mountain bringing,
> Holy Mother of the free.

In America Katerina Breshkovskaya visited settlement houses in New York, Boston, and Chicago, where she met Lillian D. Wald, Jane Addams, Helen S. Dudley, and Ellen Starr. She charmed the children she met, as well as the adults. According to Alice Stone Blackwell (daughter of the American feminist Lucy Stone), who became a kind of secretary to Breshkovskaya while she was in America, she made as deep an impression on the rich and educated as on the poor and the ignorant.

Did her American friends know, or suspect, that Katerina Breshkovskaya was Russia's leading exponent of terrorism? When reporters met with her in New York, she was asked about her political connections and beliefs. The New York *Times* (December 21, 1904) printed her reply to one questioner:

> I do not know what you would call me here. Nothing very bad I think. But in Russia I am regarded as a revolutionist. All of us who work for the freedom and education and the economic improvement of the people . . . are named revolutionists, anarchists, nihilists by the government. . . . Some of us are for strong means, of course. What do you expect, monsieur, are we to be slaves always?

This was a cleverly worded diplomatic statement, sufficiently cryptic to baffle most Americans. In her interview with Ernest Poole she mentioned the Esser Battle Organization (translated as the "Fighting League") as the agency whose only function was to carry out terrorist acts. She added that few Russians believed in assassination, especially since the aim of the Esser Party was revolution by the whole people.

Those who knew or suspected Katerina Breshkovskaya's commitment to terrorism apparently were willing to condone terrorism—in Russia. Ernest Poole expressed no condemnation of it, and Alice Stone Blackwell went so far as to justify it.[6]

On Sunday, January 9, 1905, while Katerina Breshkovskaya was still in America, columns of workers and their families, carrying placards and a petition to the Tsar, and led by a priest, Father Gapon, marched peacefully toward the Winter Palace in St. Petersburg. Stopped by a cordon of troops and ordered to disperse, they refused. The troops fired point blank into the crowd, killing and wounding hundreds. This butchery gave the revolutionaries a rallying cry: "Bloody Sunday." As the weeks passed, disturbances multiplied all over Russia.

Babushka's American friends, seeing the trouble in Russia, urged her to stay in the United States where she would be safe. She was convinced the revolution in Russia she had worked for all her life had started and was impatient to get back. She left the United States as soon as she could and arrived at Esser party headquarters in Geneva, her first stop, in March. She spoke out against the slow-moving Esser party organization. In a meeting of the Central Committee, she said the day of aristocratic terror against carefully targeted officials was over. The time had come to bring onto the turbulent scene in Russia the terror of the revolutionary masses. "Send out our Esser leaders and propagandists to activate the peasants and factory work-

---

[6]In *The Little Grandmother of the Russian Revolution*, p. 108, Blackwell wrote: "Political assassination is rightly abhorred in America. But in Russia there is no possibility of obtaining justice by law, even for the most monstrous crimes. No subject has any legal rights as against the Tsar; and the Tsar's irresponsible power was delegated to a whole army of police and other subordinate officials, who oppressed the people at their pleasure."

ers," she cried. "Release that flood of mass terror and the tsarist regime is finished." Her proposals were voted down, and the Central Committee went even further; it put a ban on advocacy of mass terror.

With reluctance, Babushka submitted. Her acute awareness of the closeness of great events convinced her of the urgent need for people to be exhorted to revolutionary daring. She must return to Russia. The safest way to get across the border, she decided, was to walk. With two companions, one a student, the other a peasant, each with a goodly supply of dynamite concealed on his person, she eluded border guards and got safely into Russia in May 1905.

The turbulent year of 1905 was characterized by widespread disorders in Russia—spontaneous peasant outbreaks, violence in cities and towns, strikes, a mutiny in the Black Sea Fleet—with an impact so great it jeopardized law and order and the normal working of the tsarist system.

In 1873 Katerina Breshkovskaya had left her liberal husband and her liberal father and brothers, who chose to work legally within the tsarist system. Their way was too slow for her. In 1905, however, the liberals stole a march on the revolutionaries. Seizing upon the weakening of authority, groups which had up to then been nonpolitical because tsarism forbade political activity, began to coalesce into unions, to meet in congresses to draw up demands, and even to form political parties. They included doctors, lawyers, railway employees, teachers, journalists and authors, engineers, bookkeepers, members of zemstvo assemblies, women's emancipation groups, and many more. They were demanding not revolution but political rights which were within the power of the Tsar to give.

Liberal concessions or revolution? The Tsar had a choice. And he saw that by granting rights he could emerge from the crisis with tsarist police power intact. He issued the October 17 Proclamation, granting broad constitutional rights to the people and establishing a representative legislature, the Duma.

While some of the rights remained in effect, more or less intact, for several years, most of them were violated by the authorities as they went about reestablishing autocratic power. The First Duma (which the Essers boycotted) was soon dismissed, as was the Second Duma. Arrests, secret trials, and exilings were resumed in greater volume than before 1905. The Russian Army's punitive expeditions against peasants and police-inspired pogroms against Jews were the order of the day. Reaction with a vengeance. And the new liberal political parties were too weak and inexperienced to make themselves an effective opposition.

Babushka, who had no more faith in liberal reform of the tsarist regime in 1905 than she had in 1873, stuck to her conviction that the only way to establish representative institutions in Russia was first to destroy tsarism by revolution. To her the Revolution of 1905 was no revolution. So in 1905 she was back on the roads of Russia. On foot and by rail she went from place to place admonishing people to act. She completely electrified the young men and women who gathered around her. She breathed into them enthusiasm and longing for open battle, which, she promised, was not far away. She ended each talk with the words:

> Go and be daring. Sacrifice yourself and destroy our enemies. To the People! To Arms!

All publications of the Russian Socialist Revolutionary, or Esser, party carried the banner: "In Combat we Will Achieve Our Rights," symbolizing the acceptance of organized terror as a tragic necessity, given the tsarist government's power monopoly and the lack of legal means to oppose police and military oppression. Daring assassinations, or "executions" as they were called, were not designed to take the place of the mass uprising of revolution; they were to hasten it.

The targets of terrorist guns and bombs were always officials who had aroused popular hatred in a locality or on a national scale as the perpetrators of cruel and murderous deeds carried out in the course of their official duties. A terrorist act against such an official was regarded by great segments of the Russian people, already seething with unrest, as a punitive act, a just punishment rendered by a self-sacrificing revolutionary, not in accordance with existing law codes but according to a higher law. Esser party leaders believed people of all ages and all classes would identify with the political party of the assassins and swell the revolutionary ranks.

They knew that many young men and women were ready to sacrifice themselves to demonstrate their love of the people and their dedication to the free Russia revolution would usher in. They were ready to carry out any terrorist assignment, and when tried in the courts, to exhibit a proud apostolic determination to bear witness to their ideals.

Tsarist officials were targeted for assassination by the Geneva-based Battle Organization of the Esser party. Its decisions were transmitted to the regional groups, variously called Flying Squadrons, or Fighting Sections, in almost every city in the Russian Empire. It was up to these organizations to choose, with great care, the person or persons to carry out the assignment to kill and to take the consequences. Inflamed by the idea of revolution, convinced that the violent policies of the tsarist regime created the necessity for terror, young Russian women were drawn to the holy mission of sacrificing themselves for the cause like moths to a flame. To them, to kill meant to die. Only by giving her own life could the woman terrorist justify taking the life of another.

In 1906 Zinaida Konopliannikova spoke defiant words before the court that condemned her to death for the murder of General Min (who had, with great loss of life, quelled public demonstrations in Moscow). She expressed her joy at being privileged to die for the people. On the day of her execution in the grim Shlisselburg fortress, she walked with a buoyant step to the scaffold and placed the noose around her own neck.

Another young terrorist, the twenty-one-year-old music student, Evestolia Ragozinnikova, did not plead for her life at her court-martial the day after she shot and killed General Maximovski in October 1907. She expressed happiness at having sacrificed herself for the people. It was because of her love for mankind that she killed Maximovski, "the perpetrator of inhuman cruelties on countless victims." She proclaimed her death a triumph for herself and for the people. In the Esser clandestine press, paeans of praise poured out for "Tolia" and young people like her who "with child-like purity," with "naive, happy expressions on their faces" went to their deaths and thus sanctified the terrorist means determined by the Esser Party.

Women activists engaged in every aspect of the illegal Esser party's political and terrorist work, ranging from decision making in the governing committees to carrying out the dangerous tasks of making and transporting explosives and using them against targeted tsarist officials. As Katerina Breshkovskaya said, the women of the Esser party were soldiers and leaders and sacrificed themselves for the revolution they did not expect to see.

With tsarist punitive measures in full swing and terrorist acts by Esser activists multiplied, Gershuni's plan of using terrorism sparingly, as a weapon carefully controlled by a central organization, had broken down. Local executive committees of the party were choosing their own targets and some individuals were acting on their own. Mikhail Stakhovich, a deputy in the First Duma, said in May 1906 that in the previous three months 288 Russian officials had been killed by terrorists and 383 wounded. In that year Ivan L. Goremykin, one of the most reactionary men of Russia, and a relative of Katerina Breshkovskaya on her mother's side, was chairman of the Tsar's Council of Ministers. Writing of 1906, Breshkovskaya said:

> The enemies of the revolution thought to stop it by hanging and shooting and exiling. But there were not enough trains to transport the exiles. Of school teachers alone, 20,000 were exiled. . . . The school buildings were empty except at night when they were used for secret revolutionary meetings.

The lower classes were becoming politically activated, and peasants, laborers, soldiers, and sailors were being added to the widening stream of people being herded into Far North and Siberian exile.

In 1907 the third issue of *Zemlya i Volya*, the Esser party organ for peasants, carried a message from the party's Central Committee. It advised peasants that if the Second Duma was dismissed, they should prepare for battle.

> Get guns, there are plenty around, in government warehouses. Form fighting detachments to march under Esser party leadership. The aim of our battle will

be to call a constituent assembly and to strengthen the people by providing land and liberty.

In the same issue appeared an article by Babushka, describing in detail what had to be done to carry out a People's Rebellion. This included destroying telegraph and railroad communications (tearing up rails, chopping down telephone poles, and blowing up bridges), replacing officials on all levels of government with elected delegates of the people, dismissing the army, the police, and the gendarmerie, and substituting a people's militia and a people's police force. All land and property must be expropriated for redistribution, and new legal codes must be written. She emphasized the role of the peasants:

> You, the peasants, are the main strength of Russia. Without you there can be no success. You have the responsibility for the fate of Russia. All await your initiative. And woe to you, peasants, if now you remain deaf to this call, if again, unprotesting, you go back to accepting mortally wounding insult, if again you leave your children to the torment of hunger, ignorance, and starving.

Babushka was trying to persuade the peasants to take the initiative she feared the leaders of the Esser party would not, despite their printed call to the peasants to prepare to fight. She was right. The Second Duma was dismissed but the Esser leaders did not initiate a People's Rebellion. The peasants did not take the initiative, either. This failure to act was disappointing to Babushka, but it did not stop her from spreading her propaganda and recruiting for terrorism.

In 1907 the tsarist police were on a nationwide alert to arrest Babushka. She eluded trap after trap laid for her arrest. Finally in September, however, betrayed by Azeff, she narrowly escaped in Saratov, but was picked up in Simbirsk where she had gone to attend a peasant congress. She was taken to St. Petersburg and imprisoned in the Peter Paul Fortress. This arrest brought to an end Katerina Breshkovskaya's long career as a revolutionist. It was a serious blow to the Esser party which lost not only a leading ideologue and expert organizer of peasants, but the most fanatical of its champions of terror.

Imprisonment, exile, hanging—that was the lot of the Russian revolutionary in tsarist Russia. Babushka was ready for whatever punishment the authorities imposed, fully aware of the brutal tactics she had initiated and helped carry out against the government she was convinced must be overthrown before reforms could be made. She was sure that the tactics of terror and revolutionary propaganda had caused the spectacular growth of the Esser party and had so weakened the tsarist government that revolution was at hand. She was in a state of exaltation. As she sat in her cell she did not think about her own fate but about the imminent revolution, the advent of liberty, and the triumph of freedom in Russia: "In my mind I sketched all the events of the new history of Russia that I was living through. Not dream but reality."

Quite different was the reaction of the friends Katerina Breshkovskaya had made in America. To them she was a frail old lady who had devoted her life to all the right things—education of the peasants, and freedom and justice for the long-suffering people of Russia. She deserved to be honored, not jailed. When they learned she was being held in solitary confinement in the Peter Paul Fortress Prison, they went into action. Within twenty-four hours the New York Petition Committee was formed. Fifty prominent New Yorkers at once signed a petition protesting her imprisonment, took it to Washington, and presented it to the Russian ambassador, Baron Rosen. Letters and telegrams were dispatched to the Tsar. Petitions signed by political and professional people went to the minister of Interior, Peter A. Stolypin, the powerful chairman of the Tsar's Council of Ministers, requesting the Russian government in the name of law and humanity to let Katerina Breshkovskaya out on bail. There was no response. Isabel Barrows, the wife of the Reverend Samuel J. Barrows, a well-known clergyman, publicist, politician, and secretary of the Prison Association of New York, made two trips to Russia in 1909 in a futile attempt to free Babushka, or at least to get her out of prison on bail.[7]

In March, 1910 the old revolutionaries Katerina Breshkovskaya and Nikolai Chaikovsky were tried before a judge in the Third Division of the Sudebnaya Palata. During the two days of the trial no representatives of the press were admitted, but correspondents of foreign newspapers lined up outside the courtroom and got glimpses of the proceedings. One journalist, standing at a doorway as Babushka passed through the dingy, narrow courthouse corridor, reported what he saw:

> An old, white-haired woman [she was sixty-six years old] dressed in a worn black dress, walked past with dignity and with a radiant face. . . . Before her marched a soldier holding a naked sword, and behind her ten armed gendarmes.

In the courtroom, when the time for sentencing came, the old judge called Katerina Breshkovskaya before him.

---

[7]A curious outcome of Barrows's second trip was her being furtively permitted to copy some letters Babushka had written to her son after he came to visit her in prison. These letters appear to be tender outpourings of love to a long-lost son (they are reprinted in *The Little Grandmother of the Russian Revolution,* chapter 11). One of the documents in the Special Collections Department Breshkovsky file in the Wellesley College Library is a letter from George Lazerev to Irene Dietrich, October 3, 1934, explaining that since prison rules allowed no communication except limited correspondence with a close relative, Esser leaders hit on the device of letters between mother and son to get important information to and from Babushka. Her "Dear Kolinka" letters were coded messages to her Esser colleagues.

"What is your occupation?" he asked.

"My occupation?" she repeated. "I am a propagandist for socialism."

"What can you say to justify yourself?"

"I have nothing to justify. I do not deny that I have sought to end the cruel unjust tsarist regime. I have not changed in any way from the time you tried me in 1879. And you too have not changed at all. So judge me."

"You, Katerina Konstantinovna Breshko-Breshkovskaya, are judged guilty of crimes against the State and I sentence you to banishment in Siberia for the rest of your life."

The court could have freed Katerina Breshkovskaya, as it did her old friend Nikolai Chaikovsky. But his revolutionary career was minor compared to hers. It took the court an hour just to read the indictment against her. Death could, in the eyes of the court, have been a fitting sentence, but that would have made her a martyr. The authorities shrewdly avoided that. The laws of tsarist Russia permitted sentencing of prisoners to hard labor to age seventy. This form of martyrdom, too, they denied her. What the court did, with its sentence of permanent exile in Siberia, was to put her so far away from the centers of Russian revolutionary activity that she lost her place as a decision maker in the Esser Party.

In April 1910, Katerina Breshkovskaya was again on the road to Siberia—this time spanning the miles, as far as Irkutsk, via the Trans-Siberian Railway in a convoy of one hundred fifty political prisoners and one hundred convicts. Then came the nearly eight hundred-mile journey by foot and horse-drawn carts to Kirensk, a small town on a lonely island in the Lena River, some two hundred miles north of the northern tip of Lake Baikal. At Mansurka a crowd of young people went out to meet the convoy. One of them wrote:

> Among this crowd in grey coats under a grey sky and in the rain her [Babushka's] imposing figure struck everyone immediately . . . a full figure with rosy face (I paid special attention—there were no wrinkles), sparkling eyes . . . it seemed to me that since 1905, when I had last seen her, she had grown younger. She was in good spirits . . . and this after five days of an awfully hard journey, all the time passed in pouring rain, in a shaky cart, with the nights passed in barracks or around camp fires. Many persons would have been quite prostrated, but our Babushka looked as if she were at a student party.

Finally the two hundred fifty prisoners and their large convoy of guards arrived at Kirensk, August 17, 1910.

Always optimistic, Babushka noted that one good thing about having six gendarmes watch her every move, night and day, was that she did not have to be afraid of the wolves: She occupied herself with correspondence, much of it with the American women friends she had in the United States in 1904–1905. She was filled with constant wonder at the interest her "sons and daughters" in America showed her. They sent her money and clothing which she gave away to other prisoners and to the poor of Kirensk. They sent her books, magazines, and newspapers. She wrote essays on social issues, including the education of children, the destiny of women, psychology, the difference between the Russian and the American character, and on the arts and culture generally. She said she scrupulously avoided politics and was careful not to include in her letters or articles anything that the authorities could object to, but this did not prevent the police who guarded her from swooping in from time to time and taking away her papers.

Katerina Breshkovskaya had received her apprenticeship in writing witty, newsy letters from prison in Siberia during her first confinement there in 1879. At that time she corresponded with members of her family and tried to convince them it was all a kind of lark. Now she again filled her letters with happy bits of information about her life and made light of her "little ills"—such as losing all her teeth and getting cataracts. These were cured, she said, during a summer she was sent for punitive reasons several hundred miles farther north into very rugged country and had to spend most of her days and nights in the open air.

After being out of newspaper headlines in the United States for more than three years, in December 1913 and January 1914, Katerina Breshkovskaya was back in the news. Even the Russian press reported that the seventy-year-old prisoner, in a daring escape attempt, had fled her place of exile. Dressed as a man, carrying £20 in English money in her pocket, five days after she was found missing she was riding in a carriage with a male companion along the Yakutsk main highway (the only path open in that part of the world in December). They were stopped and identified by the Irkutsk Chief of Police. A squad of fifty police was called out to escort them back to Kirensk where punitive measures awaited them—in Babushka's case, confinement in a prison hut for sixteen months. Found guilty later of infractions of prison regulations, Babushka got her chance to commune with the white bears when she was exiled for a time hundreds of miles to the north, in Bulun, near the Arctic Ocean. But, except for personal letters to her friends, the outside world heard nothing of Katerina Breshkovskaya until February 1917.

ANNOTATED REFERENCES

Although Katerina Breshkovskaya, a good raconteur, often told and wrote the story of her early life, she admitted in a letter (May 3, 1915) to Alice Stone Blackwell, "I do not know my own history. . . . The details of my material life interested me so little I do not remember them clearly." This may explain why each telling of her story differs. Two versions are available in English: The first 110 pages of The Little Grandmother of the Russian Revolution, edited by Alice Stone Blackwell, Boston, 1919; and in Hidden Springs of the Russian Revolution, edited by Lincoln Hutchinson, Stanford and London, 1931.

Autobiographical accounts in Russian include: (1) "Vospominaniia Propagandistki" (Reminiscences of a Propagandist), *Obshchina* (commune), an underground journal, no.7, 8–9, 1878, reprinted in *Byloye*, no. 4, May 1903, London. (2) "Babushka o Samoy Sebe" (Babushka, About Herself), an account she said she wrote on the train returning from Siberia in 1917. Published in the newspaper *Neva*, no.22, June 23, 1917. It was later published as a 16-page pamphlet by Narodnaia Vlast, Petrograd, 1917. (3) Three articles in the New York *Novyi Zhurnal*, "Rannie Godi" (Early Years), Kniga 60, June 1960; "Kak Ia Khodila v Narod" (How I Went to the People), Kniga 62, December 1960; and "1917yi god" (The Year 1917), Kniga 38, 1954.

Biographies:
V. G. Arkhangelski's Russian language *Katerina Breshkovskaia*, Prague, 1938. Jane E. Good and David R. Jones, *Babushka: The Life of the Russian Revolutionary Ekaterina Breshko-Breshkovskaia (1844–1934)*, Newtonville, Mass., 1989. Jones also wrote a Duke University master's thesis on her and a long biographical essay in *The Modern Encyclopedia of Russian and Soviet History*, edited by Joseph L. Wieczynski, Academic and International Press. There are brief biographical sketches of Breshkovskaya in the tsarist *Novyi Entsiklopedicheskiy Slovar'*, St. Petersburg, circa 1906, and in all editions of the *Bolshaia Sovetskaia Entsiklopedia*, though with each edition the sketch grows shorter, and in all of them she is characterized as an enemy of the revolution.

Voluble as Katerina Breshkovskaya was about her early years (those years were similar to those of hundreds of other *Narodniki*), she wrote almost nothing about the unique part of her career—the years between 1896 and 1907 when she was traveling the length and breadth of Russia determined to organize scattered radical underground groups into a united militant political force of skilled propagandists and non-Marxist socialist revolutionaries. Writing by others who touch on this aspect of her life include Alexander Kerensky, "Katherine Breshkovsky, 1844–1934" *Slavonic and Eastern European Review* (London), vol.13, no. 38, January 1935; and his "Zhizn' Kateriny Breshkovskoy, Zhivaia Istoriia Tselogo Stoletiia" (The Life of Katerina Breshkovskaya, the Life History of a Whole Century), in the archives collection of the Hoover Institution on War, Revolution and Peace, in the file "Katherine Breshkovskaia." Viktor Chernov, *Pered Burey* (Before the Storm), New York, 1933.

Stepan Sletov, *K Istoriy Vozniknoveniia Partiy Sotsialistov-Revoliutsionerov* (About the History of the Rise of the Party of the Socialist Revolutionaries), Petrograd, 1917. D. Perris, *Pionery Russkoy Revoliutsiy* (Pioneers of the Russian Revolution), St. Petersburg, 1906.

General Aleksandr I. Spiridovich (Chief of the *Okhranka* of Kiev and later Nikolai II's Chief Security Officer) wrote two books that reveal a good deal about Breshkovskaya: *Revoliutsionnoe Dvizhenie v Rossii v Period Imperii, Partiia Sotsialistov-Revoliutsionerov i eë Predshestvenniki 1886–1916* (The Revolutionary Movement in Russia in the Imperial Period. The Socialist Revolutionary Party and its Predecessors), Petrograd, 1918. Also his *Histoire du Terrorism Russe 1886–1916*, Paris, 1930. The Russian edition of Spiridovich's history of terrorism was published in Petrograd in 1918. All copies were immediately confiscated by the Bolshevik government and the book did not see the light of day until the French translation came out in 1930.

There is much unpublished material by and about Katerina Breshkovskaya in the United States. It includes letters, postcards (mostly from her in Siberia to her American friends), photographs, manuscripts, etc. The largest collection is in the Hoover Institution on War, Revolution and Peace at Stanford University. Small collections of documentary materials by and about her are in the Manuscript and Archives Section of the New York Public Library, and the Special Collections Department of the Wellesley College Library.

During Breshkovskaya's two visits to the United States, first from December 1904 to February 1905, and again in 1919, she received wide coverage in newspapers and magazines.

An article by Isabel Barrows in the April 16, 1910, *Outlook* (New York) is largely quotations from a letter written by Nikolai Chaikovsky describing his and Breshkovskaya's trial that took place in St. Petersburg a few weeks earlier.

Several American women who in 1904–1905 were impressed with Babushka wrote about her in glowing terms in their reminiscences: Vida Dutton Scudder, *On Journey,* New York, 1937. Lillian D. Wald, *The House on Henry Street,* New York, 1915, and *Windows on Henry Street,* Boston, 1934. Isabel Hayes Chapin Barrows, who in addition to her many articles about Babushka published in the New York *Outlook* and in newspapers, included information on her in the biography she wrote of her husband, *A Sunny Life,* Boston, 1913.

Part II

TWENTIETH-CENTURY WOMEN CONTINUE THE FIGHT

5

Maria Spiridonova Crosses
the Threshhold

With horror I now read fairy tales,
Not those we all know from childhood,
Oh no! I am aroused by what comes
Through the frightening rustle of the morning newspapers!
                                    —Konstantin Balmont

Onto the windswept wooden platform of the Borisoglebsk railroad station
on a snowy morning in January 1906, marched a detachment of Cossacks
wearing high astrakhan caps and red-epauletted, olive-drab uniforms. Each
had a sheathed short sword and a *nagaika* (whip) at his belt. Their presence
was a sure sign that an important tsarist official would depart on the noon
train for Tambov. As train-time neared, people with bags and bundles began
to assemble on the platform and in the waiting room. A delicate, rosy-
cheeked gymnazium (high-school) student appeared. She wore a brown,
full-skirted, ankle-length uniform, her black braid hanging down her back.
She stepped up to the ticket window and purchased a second-class ticket
to Tambov. School books buckled together with a strap hung over her shoulder, and she smiled as she stuck her hands in a muff which matched her
white fur cap.

The train steamed in. Passengers got off. The Cossacks, joined by blue-
coated gendarmes, began to line up across the platform. They stood in front
of an empty, maroon-colored, special, first-class car with the gold-em-
bossed tsarist double eagle insignia emblazoned near the doors.

People who had been waiting kissed their friends and relatives goodbye
and boarded the train. The high-school girl lingered on the platform near
the steps of the second-class car standing next to the special car. At the end

Maria Spiridonova, age 20

of the station platform Gavril Luzhenovsky, governor of Tambov Province, resplendent in the uniform of a full general of the Russian Army, stepped from his carriage. The fair-complexioned, corpulent, but handsome young man had recently been appointed by the Tsar to lead a punitive expedition to "impose order" in Tambov Province. He had earned a reputation for doing his job with utter ruthlessness.

General Luzhenovsky walked across the platform toward the train between a double chain of close-standing Cossacks and gendarmes. The high-school girl stepped onto the platform of the second class car, turned, saw the general, and calmly pulled a revolver from her muff. She took careful aim. As two shots rang out, Luzhenovsky fell—mortally wounded. She lowered herself to the station platform and pumped three more bullets into him. Then she raised the gun to her own head, ready to fire the sixth and last

Maria Spiridonova in Prison, 1906

bullet, when the hand of a Cossack soldier grabbed her arm. The gun fell out of her hand. With a blow of his fist, he knocked her flat.

At the sound of shots people on the platform began to scream. They pushed and shoved, attempting to flee. Brandishing whips, the Cossacks hit people at random, including the train conductor. Two Cossacks made their way toward the girl sprawled on the platform. Her high-pitched voice could be heard above the din crying, "Shoot me. Shoot me." A Cossack seized her braid of hair, wound it around his arm and, lifting her in the air, hit her repeatedly in the face and on the breasts. He then flung her onto the platform where the lashes of the Cossacks' flailing whips fell on her full force.

Grabbing the now-unconscious girl by one leg, a Cossack dragged her down a short flight of stairs, her head banging each step, and flung her into an already moving horse-drawn sledge. Ahead and behind went police carriages filled with gendarmes and Cossacks. As the horses made their way at a fast clip along the rough, frozen road to the police station, the girl's body in the sledge tossed lifelessly and her unbound hair blew in the snow-laden wind. The people on the station platform assumed she was dead.

The girl was twenty-one-year-old Maria Aleksandrovna Spiridonova. She had volunteered to carry out the death sentence the Tambov Socialist Revolutionaries, or Essers, had passed on General Luzhenovsky in December 1905. She had dressed in a gymnazium uniform and assumed a girlish air to escape suspicion on the fateful morning of the shooting.

The Tambov Essers decided the execution of Luzhenovsky would be welcomed by the many people who had suffered at his hands in the villages and towns of Tambov Province. They also expected it to call the attention of a wide public to the excesses of tsarist punitive expeditions in Tambov and elsewhere, to encourage people to act, and, they hoped, to join the revolutionary cause.

To convince herself of the righteousness of the deed she was about to do, Maria went to the villages, talked to peasant men and women, and saw firsthand the havoc the general's forces had wrought in the area. She was horrified at what she heard and saw, and was burning to carry out the party's mandate.[1]

Maria trailed Luzhenovsky for weeks, looking for a time and place to shoot him without injuring others. After killing him she expected to die. Either she would save the last bullet in her gun for herself, and die with her victim, or the tsarist authorities would carry out her speedy execution. She expected her deed would become just another statistic in the bloody annals of Russia's political struggles.

It did not. A series of unforeseen events catapulted Maria and her cause from obscurity into the glaring limelight.

The first unexpected event was that she managed somehow, while under heavy guard in the Tambov prison, to write and get a letter delivered to her Tambov Esser comrades. In it she described the torture she was subjected to by her jailors.

When, after seventeen days, her family was finally permitted to visit her in the Tambov prison, one of her sisters succeeded in walking out with the letter secreted on her person. She immediately delivered it to the Tambov committee. The committee members read the letter in shocked horror. They realized they had a bombshell in their hands. They knew they must get it published at once—in a *Russian* newspaper.

Because the year was 1906, they had one advantage. The 1905 Revolution had forced the tsarist government to grant a Manifesto of Freedom on October 17, 1905. The freedoms "guaranteed" by the Manifesto were fast being withdrawn, but in January 1906 freedom of the press had not yet been entirely eliminated.

---

[1]William C. Fuller, Jr., in his book *Civil-Military Conflict in Imperial Russia 1881–1914* (Princeton, 1985), chapter 5, explores the reasons for the savage violence of the Russian Army and police against the populace in the 1905–1907 period and provides statistics on its severity.

The Essers offered the letter to newspaper editors in city after city. All refused to touch it. Editors feared to expose themselves to predictably severe retaliation by tsarist authorities. Finally, however, the editor of the liberal St. Petersburg newspaper *Rus* defiantly printed it in the February 12, 1906, issue.

"Dear Comrades," it began. "Luzhenovsky has taken his last trip!" Maria told how she trailed and shot him. She described the Cossacks whipping her and the people on the railway station platform.

In the police station I was undressed and searched. I was led into a cold room with a damp, dirty, stone floor. About one o'clock the assistant police officer, Zhdanov, and the Cossack officer, Avramov, came in and stayed, with brief interruptions, until eleven o'clock that night. They interrogated me and were such masters of torture Ivan the Terrible would have envied them. First Zhdanov hit my legs hard, then flung me across the room where Avramov awaited me. He stamped on my back and tossed me to Zhdanov who stepped on my neck and threw me back again. When they tired of this game they forced me to undress stark naked. They whipped me, shouting awful curses: then one of them said: "Now, our fine lady, make us a fiery speech!" One of my eyes was swollen shut and the right side of my face was torn and bleeding. They pulled on the skin and slyly asked: "Does it hurt, dear? Now, tell us who you are and who are your comrades." Naked and terribly abused, I was delirious off and on, and fearful I might reveal something.

In a conscious moment Maria gave them her name. She told them she was a Tambov Esser and assured them the public prosecutor there could identify her.

The name Esser called forth a storm of indignation. They pulled out hairs one by one from my head and asked, "Where are the other revolutionaries?" Receiving no answer they put out burning cigarettes on my body and said: "Cry out! Cry out! You scum." With the aim of making me scream they held my naked body with their heavy boots like a vise, and gave me "refined blows" as they called them. With terrible curses they said, "We can make a whole village howl, but this little girl has not cried out once, either at the railroad station or here. But you will cry out," they cursed. "We are enjoying torturing you, and we will keep it up during the night until we turn you over to the Cossacks." "No!" said Avramov as he grabbed me in a rough embrace. "First us, then the Cossacks!"

Maria was saved from mass rape by the Cossacks, which surely would have killed her, by the arrival of a telegram from the court magistrate in Tambov, the capital of the province, demanding that she be brought there, some one hundred miles distant, at once.

They ordered a train immediately. . . . [As we came out of the police station] the rough swearing of Avramov hung in the air. He cursed me frightfully. I felt the breath of death. Even the Cossacks standing there looked terrified. Avramov said, "Ah, lads! How melancholy you are." [And to me] "This rabble is dying with envy at our happiness!" Whooping and whistling, with flaring lust

in his shining eyes and flashing teeth, singing a loathsome song, Avramov
pushed me into a second-class car of the train. I begged for water. No water.
Avramov was drunk and his fondling hands hit and pulled me. From his
drunken lips came distasteful whispers: "What satiny breasts! What a tender
body." I had no strength to fight. No strength to push him away. . . . With a
strong swing of his boot he hit me on my squeezed together legs and loosened
them. I called the policeman sitting in the empty car. He was sound asleep.
Avramov stretched out toward me and fondling my chin whispered: "Why do
you grit your teeth so? You will break your pretty little teeth." . . . When I
came to, shortly before we reached Tambov, the officer's hands were still on
me.

Maria ended her letter saying she was in the Tambov prison, seriously ill,
often delirious, with no medical attention. This she said she gladly accepted
as the consequence of carrying out the death sentence on Luzhenovsky, the
hangman and torturer of peasants. She said she expected to die. "I will die
peacefully, with a clear conscience."

This letter caused an immediate sensation. One journalist wrote, "It filled
with horror and outrage the heart of every honorable Russian." From the
great cities to the villages and towns in the farthest corners of the realm,
people identified her suffering with their own. She became the living symbol
of "our oppressed, bloodstained, suffering people. Before you stands not
just the humiliated, handcuffed, sick Spiridonova; before you stands sick,
handcuffed Russia."

Rumors and reports of savage treatment of prisoners had circulated secretly for decades, and sometimes got published abroad, but never before
had there appeared in a Russian journal such a gruesome personal account
of torture by tsarist officials. And the victim was a young, educated woman
from an upper-bourgeois Tambov family! As one popular pamphlet put it:

> Imagine this pure maiden, of flower-like beauty, representing the highest cul-
> ture of Russia, imagine this young defenseless girl in the shaggy paws of dis-
> gusting animals, with the beastly foulness and beastly sensuousness of orang-
> utans.

The shock of Maria Spiridonova's letter continued to reverberate throughout
Russia.

Gradually more newspapers and journals, in Russia and abroad, printed
Maria's story and quotations from her letter. Her name became known everywhere. The public craved to know who this girl was, whose very name,
as one newspaperman put it, "no one had ever heard of two months ago
. . . but now stirs the hearts of millions of Russians." Reporters and special
correspondents descended on Tambov to interview Maria's family and
neighbors. Her friends testified to her intelligence, beauty, courage, purity
of soul, and high ideals. In the villages peasants were found cursing the
"killer Luzhenovsky" and praying in the churches for God to restore the
health of their savior, "Little Marusya" !

Maria's letter was dismissed by the semi-official St. Petersburg newspaper, *Novoye Vremya,* and the conservative press in general, as the raving of a psychotic written in a delirium ("an erotic delirium," according to the Petersburg *Vedomosti*). To learn the truth, the editor of *Rus* and the Union of Equal Rights for Women commissioned the distinguished journalist Vsevolod Vladimirov to interview witnesses in Borisoglebsk and Tambov. Vladimirov found their stories not only confirmed what Maria had written in her letter, but added further gross and bloody details.

The doctor who was finally allowed to attend Maria in the Tambov Prison gave a dreadful description of her physical condition. The man in whose office Maria had worked as a clerk for nearly a year said that when he was escorted to the prison to identify her, his immediate response was to deny that the human wreck on the prison floor was Maria Spiridonova. The Borisoglebsk doctor called to treat Luzhenovsky after the shooting also talked to Vladimirov and said when he had done what he could for the General, he prepared to go to the police station to attend Maria, but was expressly forbidden to do so.

Vladimirov's findings and his account of her trial were published in a series of articles in *Rus.* Selections were reprinted as a booklet, *Maria Spiridonova.* Across the striking black-and-white block print cover, her name is spelled out; below it is silhouetted the prone figure of a girl lying on a prison floor. Through the barred window above her, a body can be seen hanging from a gallows. The pamphlet cost a ruble (about twenty-five cents) and sold by the thousands. Two photographs of the young Maria before her encounter with the police were included. Readers could see what a pretty girl she had been. It was shocking to compare those images with the photo of Maria sitting behind the bars of a prison window, her wrecked face so swollen and scarred as to be scarcely recognizable.[2] After Spiridonova's death

---

[2]The authenticity of this photograph was questioned in the Russian emigré journal *Kontinent,* no. 28, 1981, by Ekaterina Breitbard in an article " 'Okrasilsia Mesiats Bagriantsem . . .' 'ili Podvig Sviatogo Terrora?'' (" 'The Moon was Colored Royal Purple . . .' or Is the Heroic Deed of Terror Sacred?''). Positive evidence refuting her contention appears in the American Boston *Transcript* reporter, Kellogg Durland's book *The Red Reign in Russia,* New York, 1907. Durland was permitted to visit Maria Spiridonova in prison by the new governor of Tambov, who wanted to prove to him she was not being badly treated. Durland described her as a very delicate, very bright but very ill girl who spoke French, German, and "a leetle English." Her face was hideously scarred and bleeding; in fact, her condition was so terrible the photographer friend Durland brought with him almost fainted. The St. Petersburg paper *Rech'* published two of the pictures the photographer took. The entire issue was confiscated, but not before someone got a copy and reproduced the photo on a postcard which circulated wildly. Vladimirov's booklet *Maria Spiridonova* printed four photos, which when compared with the one in Durland's book and in Steinberg's biography of her, were obviously taken at the same time. The Breitbard article contains a number of other conclusions based on insufficient or erroneous evidence.

sentence was commuted to life imprisonment, another popular account was published as a pamphlet called *Pytki i Sud* (Torture and Trial) that carried the story of her trial and contained a good deal of personal information about her.

In addition to the unusual circumstance of the wide publicity she received, another unforeseen factor helped to make Maria Spiridonova's fate different from that of other terrorists of her time, namely, the delay in bringing her to trial. A terrorist assassin in tsarist Russia was ordinarily brought before a court-martial immediately, and the death penalty carried out at once since there was never any problem finding the accused guilty.

Maria had been so physically abused by her captors it took two months for her to recuperate sufficiently to appear before a court. During that time the Russian authorities maintained a grim silence, but Maria's defenders were active and vocal. Committees were formed in Russia and abroad. The European Committee for the Defense of Maria Spiridonova was studded with the names of people internationally known at the time, including Georg Brandes, the Danish literary critic; the Countess de Noailles, the Rumanian-born French poet; and Louis Bertrand, the French novelist and biographer.

Petitions for leniency were drawn up and sent to the Russian government—one of them signed "The Women of France." Another stated that since 1881, when Sof'ya Perovskaya was hanged, no woman had been executed in Russia (the statement was not true but it made a good public rallying point). *Rus* printed the letter written by Maria Spiridonova's mother "To the Mothers of Russia," an appeal to them to recognize that her daughter had suffered enough to pay her debt to society. Demonstrations for Maria were held in Western European cities and money was raised for her defense. French students petitioned for her right to emigrate to France. Everywhere the cry was heard: "Snatch Maria Spiridonova from the claws of death."

On March 12, in a barracks-like room of the Tambov military headquarters, the court-martial trial of Maria Spiridonova opened at noon behind closed doors. Those present were the army generals serving as judges; two Army lawyers appointed by the court, one to prosecute, the other to defend the accused; the governor of Tambov Province, newly appointed to take Luzhenovsky's place; N. V. Teslenko, the Moscow lawyer retained by Maria's family to defend her; Maria's mother; and one of her three sisters.

Maria was led into the courtroom and seated in a chair near the long table at which sat the army officers and her lawyer. She had been brought in mid-morning from the prison on the outskirts of Tambov along the main street in a closed carriage filled with police guards. On either side rode a detachment of Cossacks on prancing horses. The streets were crowded with people hoping to get a glimpse of "Little Marusya."

In the courtroom, wearing the rough, blue canvas prison gown, several sizes too large for her, Maria looked even smaller than she was. She had tucked up the sleeves to free her hands, and her small emaciated, scarred arms stuck out, looking like the arms of a child. The pallor of her face contrasted sharply with the blackness of her hair, wound round her head in a braid. Her skin was waxy, her face puffy and marred by the unnaturally red spots of the wounds that had not healed. Only her eyes, with deep shadows under them, looked alive. They burned like spreading blue fire—evidence of an unquenchable inner radiance.

The only color in the stark room was the red of the epaulets and the straps across the chests of the officers' olive-drab uniforms, and the tiny square of blue sky showing through a high window. The only sounds were the quiet sobbing of Maria's mother and the papers being shuffled by the men conducting the case.

After several petitions from the defense were disallowed by the judges, two witnesses were called and questioned on factual details of Maria's murder of the general. Then two doctors testified. One had attended Luzhenovsky, who lingered between life and death for several days after he was shot; the other had tended Maria when he was called to the Tambov prison days after her arrival there. When he saw her, he said, she was scarcely alive. He confirmed she had indeed received all the injuries described in her famous letter—and more. He said that even at the time of the trial she could perceive only light and dark with one eye, that her hearing had been permanently impaired, and that she had contracted tuberculosis.

Maria's mother could not control her sobbing and walked out of the courtroom. The presiding general read the indictment. Maria listened intently, holding one hand cupped to her ear, for this was the first time she had heard it. The only preparation Maria had for the trial was an hour and a half conference with Teslenko who got to see her at all only by overcoming all kinds of obstacles put in his way by prison officials. At the end of the reading of the indictment the court began its interrogation of the accused. She rose unsteadily to her feet, and, grasping the back of the chair, answered questions put to her. Speaking in a high, clear, pleasant voice, she then made her own statement;

> Yes. I killed Luzhenovsky. I want to explain why. As commandant he covered himself with glory. The trophies he laid at the feet of the bureaucracy were murdered peasants, ruined farms, raped women, and beaten children.

At intervals her small frame shook with seizures of coughing. Each time, putting her handkerchief to her mouth, she wiped away blood, then continued. She named village after village and described one murderous act after another.

> Take, for example, Borisoglebsk. A quiet town. There was no disorder there. On October 18 a peaceful meeting took place. There were speeches—

speeches of hope that the new Manifesto of October 17, the Manifesto of Freedom, would improve the unfortunate conditions of Russian life. Luzhenovsky marched into this town, imprisoned all the speakers, and started arresting people at random, according to his drunken whim. And it did not stop there. He went into the countryside and in the course of two months killed two hundred peasants and jailed no one knows how many others. The wholesale raping of women and girls by Cossack soldiers resulted in many cases of people becoming crazed with fear and despair.

This method of taking care of the needs of the people—that is, by bullets and bayonets—was supposed to be changed by the October 17 Manifesto, but it was not. The Manifesto of Freedom was betrayed by officials like Luzhenovsky. And again the blood flows.

My heart was broken by the pain of it. I was ashamed to live, knowing what was being done in Russia's villages by Luzhenovsky in particular, and by the punitive expeditions in general. Therefore, when the Socialists Revolutionary party decided to execute Luzhenovsky as a protest against them, I approved. And I volunteered to carry out the deed.

After Maria's statement the lawyers presented summations. The argument of the court-martial prosecutor was not made public, but the defense statements of the Army lawyer and Teslenko were. When she got back to her prison cell, Maria wrote down from memory her own statement that she had delivered spontaneously. She gave it to Teslenko with instructions to publish it after her death, but he persuaded her to release it at once. The public, therefore, learned most of the details of this secret trial soon after it took place.

The young military defender pleaded that the life of this weak, tortured young woman, almost a child, be spared even though she was guilty by the letter of law. He was speaking, he said, as a military man to judges who were also soldiers, deeply engaged in the business of war, taught to look death in the eye and to inflict it on others. They all knew there was one thing an honorable soldier would never do, even in the heat of battle: that was to take the life of a woman. Looking into the eyes of the judges he said. "I want to believe, I do believe, that your hands, predestined for blows in open honorable war, will not sign a death warrant for this hot-headed, amazing girl, carried away with impossible dreams about the happiness of the people, dear to us all. Consult your consciences. I believe they will show you a way out, a way to lift the heavy burden of imposing the death sentence."

Teslenko's plea began with his statement that the case of Maria Spiridonova should never have come before a military court, bound as such a court was to impose the death sentence. A civil court possibly would have been receptive to his argument that Maria Spiridonova was justified in doing what she did. The accused, he said, should not be Spiridonova; it should be Russian society unable, even unwilling, to control official killers and torturers like Luzhenovsky.

> How do we live in this bloody fog, where all the great inventions of humanity—steam, electricity, the telegraph, and photography—are used every day to gather news from all corners of our land of torment and suffering?

He said Maria Spiridonova's crime was that she looked on that society and was indignant. She killed a killer. Teslenko presented her as the necessary avenging conscience of Russia. For the court to order the execution of Spiridonova would only inflict a new wound on top of the myriad of old, unhealed wounds and would produce a shudder of terrible pain in Russia and in all lands. What Russia desperately needed, he concluded, was not to extend the pain but to end it. The judges of this court had a great opportunity. He begged them to take advantage of it. He implored, "when you leave the courtroom and go into your private chambers to decide on the sentence; replace the raised sword by the olive branch of reconciliation. Spare the life of Maria Spiridonova."

The proceedings had lasted more than three hours. The presiding officer ordered everyone to rise. The judges filed out for deliberation. After a few minutes they returned. Maria was asked to stand, and the presiding general read out the sentence:

> Maria Aleksandrovna Spiridonova, for the crime of premeditated murder: Death by hanging.

Her face was calm as she listened to the sentence. It was what she expected, and what she wanted. She began to speak:

> Gentlemen of the court, look around you. Where do you see joyful faces, healthy, happy people? Nowhere. There aren't any. Even those on the side that is now triumphant are somber because they know their triumph will be short-lived for there is an unquenchable will to end oppression.
>
> I am leaving this life. It is easy to kill me. You can invent the most horrible ways to execute me, but you cannot kill the truth I bear witness to. Nothing can.
>
> Death I do not fear. Kill me. You cannot kill my faith in the coming happiness and freedom of the people, when the people's lives will be governed by truth and equality, when the ideas of brotherhood and freedom will not be empty sounds but will really exist. Oh, for that—truly—I do not regret giving up my life.

Then, as if she recalled the tortures she had endured, a nervous spasm shook her body. She regained her composure and was escorted out of the courtroom to begin the trip back to prison. Even larger crowds than those of the morning thronged the streets. News of the death sentence had already reached the people and as the heavily guarded police carriage went by, they shouted words of encouragement. Maria, her mouth set in a smile, nodded, as if greeting friends, to all those whose eyes met hers.

Maria Spiridonova, like the girl in Turgenev's poem, *Poroq*, had crossed the threshhold. Like her, she had been ready—to commit a crime. Like her, she wanted neither gratitude nor pity. She was ready for a nameless grave.

Today again the question raised by Maria's contemporaries might be asked: Who was this girl who spoke so eloquently in court against murderous officials, yet defended her own murder of a man as a just and righteous act? Those who knew Maria Spiridonova before one side of her face was shattered in the Borisoglebsk police station referred to her as beautiful. Her dark hair was long and luxuriant, her complexion fair, her eyes dark blue with long lashes. She had regular features, her short, upper lip giving her face an open, girlish look. But there was a decisive set to her mouth that gave evidence of a firm and determined will. Her small, lithe body seemed to vibrate with energy and boldness.

Maria, the eldest of five children, was born to an upper-middle-class family in the provincial town of Tambov, located in the broad, flat lands between the Volga and the Don Rivers. Her father owned a factory that manufactured parquet flooring, an important item in Russia where a highly polished parquet wood floor was a feature of almost every home, palace, and public building.

From her earliest years Maria was recognized as unusually intelligent and capable. She could read and write at age five, and when she entered school was always first in her class. She and her family assumed that her high scholastic record in the Aleksandrov Women's Gymnazium (high school) in Tambov would qualify her for admission to the women's courses in one of Russia's leading universities where she would prepare for a career in medicine, for she had decided to become a physician. But a year before graduation Maria was expelled and the high school administrators and teachers wrote "recommendations" which insured she would never get into another school.

The journalist Vladimirov, in his articles about Maria in 1906 in the newspaper *Rus*, portrayed her as an extremely bright girl who protested against the burdensome trivialities of the tsarist school system. Her struggle to maintain her individuality led the school authorities on a course of endless fault finding. Her school life became a day in day out running battle. Naturally eloquent, she would bring up topics and ask questions in her own way, not according to the rigid course of study or the textbook. Such behavior angered the teachers. What is more, whenever issues arose that students decided to protest, Maria was always ready to lead the confrontation with the administration or with classroom teachers. On one occasion she wrote and read to her classmates an amusing story which was, in essence, a scathing criticism of the school and its personnel. Word of this composition reached the administration and her expulsion was considered.

In her senior year, Maria became a leader in a group that called itself the "Comrades' Circle," with members from both the boys' and the girls' gymnazia. Their stated aim was "self-education, self-development, and the circulation, reading, and discussion of books." The books, needless to say, were not on high-school reading lists nor available in school libraries. At this time, students from the local theological seminary began protesting the mediocrity of their training, one of the reasons Orthodox priests were held in such low esteem in tsarist Russia. They drew up a petition demanding changes in their textbooks and curriculum. They also claimed the right to enter universities.

The Comrades' Circle decided to support the seminarians. Maria was chosen to attend one of their meetings to demonstrate that gymnazia youth were solidly behind the awakened consciences of the seminarians. News of her attendance at this meeting swept through Tambov like wildfire. To the Aleksandrov Women's High School administration, it was the last straw. Maria Spiridonova had to be expelled.

For some reason the authorities did not act immediately. Then the head of the school received a proclamation, signed by Maria, making demands for rule and curriculum changes in the girls' high school. The lady called Maria to her office and a stormy scene ensued. That same day papers for Maria's expulsion were signed.

To Vladimirov, this course of events was an indictment, not of Maria, but of the rigid, arid Russian educational system. "It was consciously based," he wrote, "on falsity in all things, on the hypocrisy and dry, stale, soulless formalism which causes much evil in Russia and cripples and corrupts our children."

When Maria's formal schooling ended, said Vladimirov, her education began. She began a zealous program of study at home, reading voraciously and writing voluminous letters and essays. For recreation she practiced the piano which she often played for the entertainment of her family and friends. But the greatest single educational influence on Maria was the drama of Russian life unfolding before her eyes during the years of her late teens.

Violence and bloodshed ran like red threads through Russian history, from the days of the Tartar conquests, through the reigns of Ivan the Terrible, Peter the Great, and their successors into the twentieth century. Having blundered into war with Japan in 1904, the Russians lost battles, a fleet, and tens of thousands of men in far away Manchuria. Discontent was rife in every level of Russian society. To efforts aimed at gaining needed reform by individuals or political groups, whether peaceful or militant, legitimate or subversive, the tsarist government responded with violence. When on Sunday, January 9, 1905, thousands of working people, carrying icons and banners with the Tsar's picture on them, marched in peaceful protest to the Winter Palace, military units were ordered to shoot. At least one hundred fifty were killed and hundreds injured. People in all walks of life were horrified.

Close on the heels of Bloody Sunday came strikes, sporadic uprisings all over Russia, and an increase in subversive activity by Russia's active but illegal political parties. It was a time when most of Russia was under "reinforced protection," or martial law. Provincial governors were ordered to lead punitive expeditions not only against subversion but suspected subversion. They were ordered to search out, arrest, and try suspects in field courts-martial and to use the death penalty freely.

Revolution appeared to be imminent. Katerina Breshkovskaya, the old revolutionary affectionately known as Babushka, who was recruiting for the Esser Party, wrote:

> It was easy to agitate in the period 1903 to 1906. The soil was thoroughly prepared and seeds germinated readily. The enemies of the Revolution thought to stop it by hanging and shooting.

Tsarist punitive measures, she said, only succeeded in inspiring great numbers of the youth of Russia to join the Essers because they advocated terrorist acts against tsarist officials to hasten the advent of revolution.

There is no available evidence to show exactly when Maria Spiridonova joined the Esser party, but it is quite possible she was one of the hundreds of young women recruited by Babushka. In any event, in March 1905, Maria Spiridonova took part in a street demonstration in Tambov, was arrested, jailed, then unexpectedly released a month and a half later. Her arrest caused her to lose the office job she took in 1903 after the death of her father. But she found that though she no longer had a job, she had a calling—she had become a revolutionary. It was a calling her self-education had prepared her for and one to which by temperament she was suited.

It is possible that Isaac Steinberg, Maria Spiridonova's friend, fellow Esser, and biographer had her in mind when he wrote that in Russia at the dawn of the twentieth century there was a magnetism in the very word *revolution*. It drew to it the best, the most idealistic, the most intelligent youth.[3] *Revolution* became a symbol for these youths to express their love of freedom and their love of the people of Russia. They would work for it and, if necessary, sacrifice their lives to it because the revolution evoked the vision of a beautiful future.

When Maria's activism led her to murder for the sake of the Revolution, her family and her comrades stood by her. Two of her three sisters were sent to prison after police found them carrying letters the imprisoned Maria

---

[3]Isaac Steinberg, *In the Workshop of the Revolution,* New York and Toronto, 1953.

had written. When asked by the American Boston *Transcript* correspondent, Kellogg Durland, how she felt having three of her daughters in prison, Maria's mother replied, "I am the proudest mother in all Russia."

Delivered back to the Tambov prison after the court-martial trial, Maria was greeted with sympathy by her fellow inmates who had developed a deep affection for her. She waited impatiently for the knock of the hangman on the door of her cell. Meantime the Tambov court had authorized an appeal of her sentence to a higher level: Lieutenant General Glazov, Commander of the Military District of Moscow. After two weeks his decision was delivered to the officials of Tambov. Her sentence had been changed from death to life imprisonment at hard labor in Siberia—the dreaded *katorga*.

True to her ideals, Maria found this change distasteful. She wrote

> I regret the reprieve of the death sentence, the change to life imprisonment. . . . it seemed to me my death could have social significance. . . . I hate autocracy so much that I do not want from it any kind of mercy.

Maria Spiridonova had been judged and sentenced, but interest in her case did not immediately die. There were insistent public demands that Avramov and Zhdanov, the officers she named as her tormentors at the time of her arrest, be brought to trial. Instead, tsarist authorities commended and promoted them. But they had been judged guilty in the court of public opinion. It was not surprising, therefore, that on Easter Sunday the murdered body of Avramov was found in the streets of Tambov. A month later Zhdanov met the same fate—both victims of vigilante justice.

Nor was Maria Spiridonova forgotten in Europe. When it became known she had been sentenced to life imprisonment in Siberia, people began to raise money to finance her escape. Vera Figner wrote that she had addressed a meeting of poor working women, mostly laundresses, in London in 1908, and found them thoroughly familiar with the facts of Spiridonova's case. They wanted to know more about her and were anxious to contribute their hard-earned pennies to her escape fund.[4]

In May 1906, Maria Spiridonova was removed from the Tambov prison and taken to Moscow where she was put in the famous Butyrki Prison. Through this prison every exiled prisoner from European Russia had to pass on his or her way to the Siberian *katorga*.

ANNOTATED REFERENCES

News of the shooting of General Luzhenovsky on the platform of the Borisoglebsk railway station appeared in the St. Petersburg newspaper *Novoe Vremia*, January 17, 1906, as one item in the regular column "Disorders," which day after day detailed the shooting and bombing of tsarist officials.

---

[4]*Posle Shlisselburga* (After Shlisselburg), p. 246.

Descriptions of Russian railroad stations, including those of small towns, appear in Poultney Bigelow's Diary, September 2–8, 1891. See Poultney Bigelow Papers, New York Public Library, Manuscript Division, Box 47.

Rus was a liberal daily newspaper published in St. Petersburg from 1903. It underwent repeated name changes as a result of censorship. On December 2, 1905, the censors closed it down. On December 5 it appeared with a new name, *Molva* (Rumor), but after January 17, 1906, it was again *Rus*. Closed March 21, 1906, for a few days it was *Molva*, then March 25 it became *XX Veka* (Twentieth Century).

Vsevolod Vladimirov, *Maria Spiridonova* s portretom i risunkami, s predisloviem ot Soiuza Ravnopraviia Zhenshchin (with portraits and sketches and a foreword by the Union for the Equal Rights of Women). Price: one ruble. The date and place of publication appear as "Moscow, 1905." The erroneous dating seems to have been a ruse to confuse the censorship—more severe for 1906 publications than for those of 1905. This 116-page booklet consists of selections from Vladimirov's investigative reporting published in *Rus* during February and March 1906. Vladimirov went to Borisoglebsk and Tambov to gather information from eyewitnesses to the shooting and its aftermath. This booklet takes the story through the trial and imposition of the death sentence in March. It contains a postscript reporting the revenge killings of Spiridonova's torturers Avramov and Zhdanov.

Pytki i Sud (Torture and Trial), St. Petersburg, 1906. This 72-page pamphlet is another version of the Spiridonova story, published by the journal *Narodnaya Beseda* (Talk of the People) after the commutation of Spiridonova's death sentence to life imprisonment. It quotes statements about her from other periodicals, including *Rus* and *Nasha Zhizn'*, and gives in considerable detail an account of her life as a student in the Tambov women's gymnazium.

During the year 1906 *Maria Spiridonova* and *Pytki i Sud* circulated widely in the Russian Empire. The Balmont verse at the beginning of this chapter appeared at the top of the first page of *Pytki i Sud*.

The biographical sketch of Spiridonova in *Bortsi za Svobodu* (Fighters for Freedom), Petrograd, n.d., but around 1915, as well as the material on her early life in I. Z. Steinberg's biography *Spiridonova, Revolutionary Terrorist*, London, 1935, are taken directly from the Vladimirov *Maria Spiridonova* and *Pytki i Sud* pamphlets.

Spiridonova's name does not appear in the first two editions of the *Bolshaia Sovetskaia Entsiklopediia*, but there is a brief sketch in the third edition, volume 24 (1976). A short biography appears in vol. 40 of the *Entsiklopedicheskiy Slovar' Russkogo Bibliograficheskogo Institute Granat*. A brief account of Spiridonova's life by Maureen Perrie appears in *The Modern Encyclopedia of Russian and Soviet History*, Joseph L. Wieczynski, ed., vol. 37.

6

Katya and Sanya Izmailovich, The Irrepressible Revolutionary Sisters

In 1905 Minsk was the pleasant provincial capital of tsarist Russia's western province of the same name (now part of Byelorussia). Its streets radiated out from tree-studded Cathedral Square through low-lying residential areas to undulating fields that stretched for miles. These fields yielded the grain that made Minsk an important commercial city of around one hundred thousand people. With its history of attachment to Lithuania and to Poland, Minsk had large numbers of Roman Catholics and Lutherans; almost half of its population were Jews.

On one side of Cathedral Square stood the Russian Orthodox Cathedral of Sts. Peter and Paul and the District Courts. On the opposite side was the palatial residence of the provincial governor. In the Governor's Garden, near the Roman Catholic cathedral and opposite the Lutheran church, a band played on summer evenings. Along the main business street were the Odeon Theater and the headquarters of the Fourth Army Artillery Corps whose commander in chief was Brigadier General Adolf Izmailovich.

The home of the Izmailovich family stood on a tree-lined residential street, behind a wrought-iron fence and ornate gate, at the end of a line of linden trees. Since the outbreak of the Russo-Japanese War in 1904, General Izmailovich, a widower, had been on duty in the Far East; his four daughters with their many servants had run the household.

To the Izmailovich home came two steady streams of callers. In one stream were well-dressed high officials, military men, and church dignitaries who went to the front door. They were ushered in by a uniformed majordomo, and received by the General's married elder daughter Mariya (called Manya) and her sister Evgeniya (Zhenya) in the formal drawing room where the walls were decorated with displays of ancient weapons and portraits of the tsars. The other stream of visitors came in the back door. They were men and women laborers, students, and the town's radical intellectuals. They were let in by a lowly servant girl and received by Aleksandra (Sanya) and Katerina (Katya), the general's revolutionary daughters.

Sanya and Katya's visitors had made General Izmailovich's home the headquarters of the Esser party of Minsk. There the Executive Committee met; there decisions were made on strikes, demonstrations and terrorist acts; there the activists who were to carry out party missions were selected and instructed. In the general's home were stored the Esser party's illegal literature—books, pamphlets, broadsides—its guns and explosives. In and out the back door went Sanya and Katya disguised as servants, vegetable vendors, ragged peddlers, or pig women as they made their rounds carrying out party business.

Most of what is known of the Izmailovich sisters' revolutionary activity is contained in two long letters Sanya wrote and smuggled out of the Siberian *katorga* in 1908. By some miracle these letters survived and were published in the journal *Katorga i Ssylka (Prison and Exile)* in 1923–1924. Several photographs of Sanya also survived and show her as a tall, slender young women in plain, high-necked dresses that swept the floor. Her face is delicately molded, her look is calm and thoughtful, her long, ash-blonde hair is pulled straight back from her forehead, revealing a widow's peak, and twisted into an unmodish bun at the nape of her neck.

A dark and poorly reproduced photograph of Katya shows her seated at a desk studying an open book, but conveys nothing of her character. She had the reputation of being quite different from Sanya. She was also tall and slender, but of a mecurial temperament—bright and gay one moment, pensive and reflective the next. She was a determined, persuasive speaker, and often acted spontaneously and not always wisely.

In Sanya's letters is a lively account of some of her, Katya's, and their comrades' deeds. Also touched upon are their hopes, fears, loves, hates— reflecting the mood of the young revolutionary segment of Russian society in the turbulent years of 1905 and 1906. Sanya's writing reveals her as an intelligent, articulate young woman deeply committed to the program of the Esser party and its revolutionary tactics, including terror.

Sanya makes only one reference to her life before 1906. She says she was a *kursistka*, or university student, in St. Petersburg, and was even then an Esser activist. She tells of hiding in her room a male party member named Karl who had escaped from prison and was being hunted by the police.

The story of the terrorist acts of the Izmailovich sisters begins in the revolutionary year 1905—the year Tsar Nikolai II issued the Manifesto of Freedom with its promise of freedom of speech, press, and assembly, and its provision for the immediate election of a legislature representing all the people. After this proclamation was issued there was rejoicing from one end of the Russian Empire to the other. A revolution had occurred—it seemed.

In Minsk, about eleven o'clock on the morning of October 18, a crowd—including many railroad workers—began to gather in the Minsk-Libavo-Romenska railroad station. Soon the growing crowd surged into the adjacent square. A big table was moved out of the station and put in the middle of the square. The chairman of the railroad workers stood on the table and read the October 17 Manifesto to the cheering crowd. It was decided to send a delegation of twelve men to Governor Kurlov with a petition to free a group of political prisoners being held in the local jail. Soon the governor came out on a balcony facing the square and was greeted with hurrahs.

Holding aloft an order to release the prisoners, a detachment of workers set off to the jail singing the "Marseillaise." When they returned the streets were lined with people waving red flags, and as the freed prisoners marched into the square enthusiasm reached new heights. Caps were thrown in the air, red kerchiefs waved, and the shout went up: *"Da Zdravstvuet Svoboda!"* (Long Live Freedom). People clasped hands and kissed each other in transports of joy. The freed prisoners got up on the table and made speeches. They were greeted with shouts of "Long Live the Red Flag!" A few shouts of "Long Live the Black Hundreds" were also heard.[1] More and more people were arriving. At the edges of the square, carriages with women and children appeared. Whole families were enjoying the unusual spectacle.

A fully armed company of soldiers still stood at the entrance of the railroad station. When voices in the crowd asked them to disarm, their captain ordered the men to leave, and the excited crowd shouted "Long Live the Army!" The captain was led to the table where he stood beneath the red flag being waved by a girl standing on the table, her unbound hair flying in the wind. The crowd's repeated shouts of "Hurrah!" cut through the air.

About this time the head of the gendarmerie arrested a man in the crowd, an actor. As people began converging on him, demanding that the actor be freed, the officer—in a panic—asked Chief of Police Norov what to do. Norov encouraged action in the name of the government, but the officer decided to free the actor. The crowd cheered.

Officials began to ask people to move down Mikhailovsky Street to a larger square. The flag-waving crowd surged along the street in a mood of celebration, scarcely noticing that two companies of soldiers had regrouped along the sides of the square, standing with fixed bayonets. The singing and cheering of the moving crowd continued. Suddenly, an order to shoot was

---

[1]The Black Hundreds were extreme rightist gangs driven to violence by religious and ethnic hatred and by opposition to all liberal reform.

given. Some soldiers shot into the air, but others fired into the crowd. The dead and wounded fell to the ground and the crowd turned into a wild, screaming mob. Everyone was trying to escape. The square quickly emptied. People ran along Mikhailovsky Street in a mad search for doorways and passageways in which to hide. Some kept running and were gunned down. When the shooting stopped fifty people lay dead or dying and nearly one hundred others were wounded. More than fifteen hundred were rounded up, held under guard, and eventually sentenced to periods of hard labor in Siberia. Though the Minsk bloodletting was not the only one that followed in the wake of the celebrations heralding the October Manifesto, it was regarded in many quarters as a national disgrace.

Shortly after the tragic October 18 event, a Congress of the Esser party of the Northwest region of Russia was held in Minsk. The delegates had received from the Esser party Central Committee in Geneva the order sent to all local battle organizations calling on them to cease terrorist activity. The Geneva decision had been taken in response to the Tsar's October Manifesto of Freedom. The order was read at the Minsk Congress. Members were asked to accept it by voice vote. Whereupon Katya Izmailovich stood up and in an impassioned speech accused the Central Committee of making a terrible mistake.

> Just at the moment when it is necessary to demonstrate what terrorism can do, the Central Committee decides to lay aside its most formidable weapon. It is a betrayal of the cause of the people. We must not submit to this order.

Katya succeeded in persuading the Congress to reject it.

Word of the Esser Congress reached Governor Kurlov who immediately inaugurated greater surveillance of known and suspected revolutionaries in Minsk. A watch was put on the Izmailovich residence, but Sanya and Katya had already moved out, taking their party paraphernalia with them and distributing it to the homes of working and professional people in different parts of the city.

Before the October Manifesto, Kurlov had carried out pogroms against Minsk's large Jewish population. Emboldened by the evaporation of the October freedoms and by news of pogroms in Odessa, Kishinev, and other southern Russian cities, he began a round of violent acts against Jewish merchants and householders. The Essers and workers staged a protest in the streets only to be dispersed by gunfire.

The Minsk Essers' demands for the prosecution of Kurlov and Norov as violators of the Manifesto of Freedom fell on deaf ears. The tsarist government rapidly recovering some of its ancient bravado, began reverting to its time-honored practice of suppressing the freedom of its citizens with guns. Every day more punitive expeditions were sent into the countryside. Even in Moscow the crack Semenovsky regiment was ordered into the streets to put down a peaceful demonstration with guns and much bloodshed. By year's end the October "freedoms" were becoming a memory. In Geneva the Central Committee of the Esser party reluctantly reversed itself and sent out the word: Resume terror. One of the first to be targeted for "execution" was Kurlov, Governor of Minsk. To carry out the deed the Minsk Essers chose Sanya Izmailovich and Ivan (Vasya) Pulikov.

Popular dissatisfaction with the tsarist government was returning. Revolutionary zeal was rising again to the boiling point as more and more of the country was put under martial law. Sanya and Katya, as the leaders of the Minsk Essers, formulated a plan to send out an armed group to attack trains carrying military hardware. Their aim was to disrupt army supply lines. They were also working on plans for the assassination of Governor Kurlov. Then from the Battle Organization in Geneva came an important assignment for Katya. She was asked to carry out the biggest assassination attempt yet assigned a woman—the "execution" of a much-hated national figure. Katya eagerly accepted the assignment, but only she, Sanya, and one other Minsk Esser knew the identity of her target.

Faced with responsibilities that should have been sobering indeed, high-spirited Katya was irrepressible. One day in late November 1905, as she walked along the main street of Minsk, her pockets filled with illegal literature and a revolver in her purse, she saw an impressive cavalcade approaching. It was the vice-governor in his shiny black carriage drawn by prancing horses, convoyed by a dozen armed and mounted police. Lying on the sidewalk immediately in front of Katya was an abandoned galosh. In a flash she lifted it on the toe of her pointed shoe and with a swift kick sent it flying into the path of the horses. The startled animals abruptly shied to one side, then broke into a wild gallop. The gendarmes and the vice-governor's carriage raced through the streets. An alarm was sounded. Pedestrians ran for shelter and shopkeepers noisily lowered their shutters. Katya nonchalantly continued her walk down the street. When upbraided by Sanya for needlessly exposing herself and the party by her idiotic prank, Katya was contrite and said the devil must have tempted her. She promised never again to give in to such temptation.

Not long after her risky street escapade, Katya was arrested. The police discovered her hideout in the rooms of a working-class family. In the inner councils of the Esser party, Sanya urged the immediate rescue of Katya from prison, giving as the reason the approaching deadline for her secret assignment. Party members agreed to give Katya's rescue priority. Once that was accomplished the execution of Kurlov should be carried out at the earliest possible moment.

Sanya and Vasya Pulikov had already moved into an attic room opposite Governor Kurlov's official residence, posing as husband and wife. They were spending a good part of each day observing the governor's every movement as they followed him about in the streets and looked down from their perch high above Cathedral Square that they called "The North Pole".

Meantime, the rescue of Katya proved easy. Sanya discovered that the new women's prison on the outskirts of Minsk, where Katya had been taken, was not well guarded. Katya gave a simple prearranged signal while she was throwing snowballs in the prison yard during her exercise period. The signal alerted her rescuers—five young men dressed as gendarmes waiting outside the wooden fence surrounding the prison.

One young "gendarme" pulled a bell at the gate. When the lone guard came to ask what they wanted, their spokesman said they had brought a prisoner. The guard opened the gate, the young men came rushing into the yard and walked out with Katya and another political prisoner. Though there was no need to do so, one of them turned and shot the guard. After pushing the gate shut they ran to the side street where Sanya sat holding the reigns of the horses harnessed to their getaway sleigh. Their happiness over the successful escape was marred by the unnecessary killing of the lone guard. Katya kept crying, "Why did you do it? Why this needless sacrifice?" Sanya also was upset and laid the blame for the young man's act to his excitement and inexperience.

The next problem was where to hide Katya until she could be sent out of town and on to her assignment. After about ten days of shunting her from place to place, her rescuers decided the furor over the prison break had subsided enough for her to make her getaway. Late one cold January night the pale Katya was disguised, much against her will, as a painted-faced, brightly costumed "lady of the evening." The sisters kissed each other goodbye, apprehensive they might never see each other again. Then Katya stepped into a stylish *troika* on shining runners and was whisked through the main street of Minsk by three fast black horses, in the company of male comrades dressed as military officers out on an evening spree. Undetected, they soon left the city streets behind, and sped along the highway for several miles until they reached a small railroad station. Here, after a change of clothing and a long wait, Katya boarded the morning train headed south.

In the snow-covered Cathedral of Sts. Peter and Paul, funeral services for an army officer were scheduled for January 14, 1906. This was the kind of event Sanya and Vasya had been awaiting. They knew Governor-General Kurlov would attend. As he left the cathedral there would surely be an opportunity to make the fatal attack.

As the funeral procession entered the cathedral, Vasya, carrying a bomb in a valise, and Sanya with a loaded revolver in her pocket, walked into the snowy churchyard. From the church came the deep and mournful sounds of the ancient Slavonic funeral chant, breaking the silence of the grey winter day. Outside, as damp snowflakes fell on them, Sanya and Vasya stood with

**Aleksandra Izmailovich,
after police "interrogation," 1906**

grimly determined faces near a straggling group of people gathered to watch
what they could of the ceremony and procession.

The music stopped; the coffin was being carried out, followed by mourn-
ers, and—what luck! At the church door Kurlov turned and was walking in
their direction. Beside him was Chief of Police Norov, also on the Esser hit
list. As the two officials approached them, Vasya pulled the detonator and
threw his bomb in their path. Sanya raised her revolver and fired.

To their horror the bomb rolled in the wet snow and came to a halt without exploding and the revolver shots went wild. Suddenly Vasya and Sanya
were surrounded by gendarmes. With a well-aimed kick, one policeman
felled Sanya while two others pinned her unconscious body to the ground.
Others grabbed and held Vasya. The two targeted officials, frightened but
unscathed, rushed toward Kurlov's waiting carriage, but Norov suddenly
turned with a revolver in his hand and fired a shot at Sanya. A retired army
officer standing nearby also shot at her. Their aim was as poor as hers, and
the bruised would-be assassins were dragged off, loaded onto a police
wagon, and carted to the police station where they were thrown into two
tiny dark cells. The police immediately began beating and torturing them,
trying to pry out of them their names.

Early the next morning a crowd of the yard servants of the well-to-do families of Minsk, rounded up during the night by the police, were placed in two long rows in the police station courtyard. Then Sanya and Vasya were brought out and stood against a wall to be viewed by the yard servants, and, it was hoped, identified.

Coming out into the light and seeing dozens of eyes trained on her, Sanya was mortified. One of her eyes was swollen shut and her ear ached from the continuous blows her captors had rained on her head. Her outer skirt was torn to shreds and her hair was matted and disheveled. She held up her torn underskirt with one hand and tried to shield her face with the other, only to have it pulled away by a guard who ordered her to "stand so they can look, you rotten piece of filth."

Sanya was recognized at once by her father's yardman and Vasya was identified by a policeman who had seen him when he was imprisoned in a roundup of demonstrators a few weeks before in Smolensk.

Flung back into her cell, Sanya collapsed, wondering what would happen next. In the late evening there was much stamping of boots and rough talk by their guards. Their cell doors were opened and Sanya and Vasya were led out of the police station. Surrounded by gendarmes carrying lighted torches, they walked through the empty streets of Minsk to the main prison. As they trekked through the eerie darkness, with the flames of the torches flickering against the snowy streets, Sanya and Vasya tried to encourage each other on the fate that awaited them, but they were sharply commanded to stop talking.

They reached the prison and were led into the dimly lit vestibule where they were given tea and bread—their first food in two days. After a long wait, prison guards came to take them to their cells. As she walked into a long corridor, Sanya heard behind her the rumbling of the iron gates of the prison. Glancing back, she saw them slowly close. She had entered the Russian prison world which was to be her world, with one very brief interruption, to the end of her life four decades later.

Sanya Izmailovich described coming into the Minsk prison as her entry into her true spiritual home. Walking behind the guard she noticed that all the windows over the closed doors of the cells were alight; from behind each one she could hear the continuous hum of women's voices. Settling into the tiny tower cell assigned her, she became aware of an unbelievable sound—singing!

> As one song ended, there began another. Song after song. And all so bright, cheerful, strong. I had heard these [revolutionary] songs hundreds of times— in student evenings in St. Petersburg, in the intimate circles of close comrades, in boats on the river and in the forest. But nowhere had they spoken so directly to me as now behind bars. . . . From somewhere sounded a bell. The comrades swung into the "Marseillaise" and the songs for that night came to an end.

Often in her account Sanya mentions the prisoners' singing. Singing revolutionary songs was a gesture of defiance by the political prisoners that tsarist authorities did not, or could not, stop.

Every day the prisoners were led into the prison yard for exercise. As they walked, greetings and information were exchanged. Sanya and Vasya, by order of Governor Kurlov, were put in solitary confinement and not permitted to walk in the prison yard, but Sanya's ground-level cell had a window opening on the yard so she saw and sometimes was able to exchange a few words with her many friends among the political prisoners. Her daily exercise consisted of walking to and from the prison office for questioning. As she was led through the women's corridor, even though they were forbidden to do it, the prisoners climbed to the small openings above the locked doors of their cells and tenderly spoke her name and wished her well.

> So dear, so close I felt to all of them. They were so far, far away from those animals [who beat and tormented her in the police station] that my soul yearned to meet them. What my tormentors tried to beat into my head with the butts of their guns, the kicks of their boots, the spit they showered on me was the false idea that all my comrades with whom I had walked on one path, toward one goal, were a mirage, a fantasy. I almost came to believe that there was actually only one real world, the world of those wild beasts with human faces, and that they would always have me in their power. Now I can throw away this nightmare, and so with irrepressible joy I have been able to revert to my beliefs, to my love of my comrades.

In this way Sanya Ismailovich first articulated a problem that troubled all the Esser women terrorists. The terrorist woman professed to love the people, all the people. She sacrificed herself "for the people." But who were "the people"? Were the officials she tried to kill, people? The policemen—those "animals" who tortured her—were they "the people"? Was she not in practice loving only her comrades? Was she not, in fact, denying that whole segments of humanity, because of their brutality, were people? Would the new world she was sacrificing herself to bring about eliminate brutality? Or was brutality as human a trait as love? Sanya returned to this problem over and over again, but upon her arrival at the Minsk prison she became preoccupied with other matters.

In her daily visits to the prison office Sanya was confronted with witnesses who gave sworn testimony to acts they said they had seen her commit. Most of these, she said, were laughable they were so far away from the truth. Her sister Manya was called as a witness and also one of their servants, the maid Tatyana. Before the deposition, with two guards present, the sisters were allowed a brief conversation. Manya said the family's first news of Sanya's and Vasya's deed was that she had been killed on the spot. Someone told them of seeing her, covered with blood, being carried away in a carriage.

Manya also said the Izmailovich house had been thoroughly searched for bombs or other incriminating evidence, but the police had found nothing.

Tatyana the maid sat with downcast eyes and would not look at Sanya. Sanya assumed Tatyana would be a hostile witness since she knew the girl went every Sunday to church to listen to the "hate humanity" sermons of a priest who was an ardent supporter of the Black Hundreds. She had been absolutely immune to all Sanya's and Katya's efforts to convert her to socialism. But Manya later told Sanya that Tatyana took one look at the battered, disfigured face of her mistress in the Minsk prison and was moved to tears. Tatyana spent hours crying and praying for Sanya. The attempt on the lives of the officials had a traumatic effect on the simple servant girl who could see no purpose in it. Tatyana kept repeating, "Bombs can only be used for one thing: killing people. That is wrong."

Sanya's "front parlor" sisters came to the prison as often as they were permitted. They were solicitous of her legal status as well as her health and general well-being. Sanya registered small concern for such matters, assuming she would soon be hanged. She kept repeating she wanted to die, to die bravely.

Shortly after Sanya arrived at the Minsk prison, after the lights were out and the evening singing ended, she heard the sound of rapping on her wall. This was her introduction to the prison language of wall tapping. Who was the unseen person trying to communicate with her? It turned out to be Karl, a fellow Esser she had first met in St. Petersburg in her student days when she had sheltered him in her quarters at a time the police were on his trail. Later when he came to Minsk she had worked with him in the Esser Party. She had seen him in the prison yard and he had nodded a greeting to her. Now she found that his cell was immediately above hers. They shared a wall and could converse with each other at will. In high-spirited contempt for the autocracy they hated, they chose a password to identify themselves to each other: "God Save the Tsar."

Sanya learned from Karl that the bomb Vasya had thrown at Kurlov was not defective. The police took it into the Governor's Garden where they detonated it with a large explosion. If it had gone off when thrown by Vasya, they and their two targets would have been blown to bits. Sanya's reaction to this news was that she no longer felt any hatred against Kurlov, but she was contemptuous of Norov for refusing to come to the prison as a witness, giving as an excuse that his life was in danger. She said the real reason was that he wanted to avoid answering questions that were sure to arise about his own shots fired at Sanya after she had been felled by the police.

On January 29, Karl rapped out the message: "Chukhnin has been shot." That message made Sanya leap with joy. She drummed on the wall, "Hurrah!"

It was as if an electric spark pierced my brain. Joy flowed through my whole being. It was not only that Chukhnin, Commander-in-chief and "Butcher" of the Black Sea Fleet was wounded; it was that I knew who did it. It was Katya! Katya, not just my sister, but my closest comrade in our party work. Katya, my most beloved friend.

The Essers had targeted Admiral G. P. Chukhnin for execution because he had become a symbol of tsarist cruelty. In November 1905 he had ruthlessly quelled a mutinous uprising in Sevastopol, the great southern naval base. At this time, several battleships in the harbor, including the Potemkin,[2] had mutinied. A naval officer, Commander Peter Schmidt, as a gesture of disapproval of the rising tide of reaction, defied his superiors and joined the mutineers. Schmidt declared himself Commander of the Black Sea Fleet and before he knew what was happening, became a national hero. From St. Petersburg came orders to Chukhnin to put down the mutiny. Chukhnin issued an ultimatum demanding complete surrender. It was ignored. He ordered the shore artillery and the battleships that had not rebelled to open fire. Almost at once the mutinous ships were in flames and ran up the white flag. The mutiny collapsed, leaving many dead and wounded. Sixteen hundred men were arrested, and in January 1906, Peter Schmidt and three other leaders of the mutiny were awaiting court-martial trials and almost certain death sentences (carried out in February).

Karl continued his tapping. "The papers say a young woman, presenting herself as Mariya Krupnitskaya, the daughter of a naval lieutenant, came with a request concerning her father's pension. She was admitted to Chukhnin's office at the Black Sea Fleet headquarters in Sevastopol. As he was reading the petition, she shot him, hitting him in the shoulder and stomach."

"What then?" impatiently asked Sanya. There followed a quick indistinct rap Sanya did not understand. "Go on," she urged. Karl replied, "I said it." "What did you say? Repeat." There was a pause, then the rapping—slow, ominous: "She is no more."

Karl knew the identity of Mariya Krupnitskaya, and could understand how stunned Sanya was. He continued, "Chukhnin ordered her shot. They took her to the courtyard and shot her."

Sanya could not comprehend. Katya was no more? Overwhelmed by almost unbearable pain and grief she could not sleep. She paced the floor, back and forth, across her tiny cell. The next morning the whole prison was

---

[2]The Battleship Potemkin has entered the consciousness of Western Europeans and Americans through Sergei Eisenstein's film *Potemkin* which—not entirely accurately—deals with a mutiny by sailors on the Potemkin that took place several months earlier (in June) in the harbor of Odessa. On that occasion the loss of life, casualties, and general destruction were much greater than at Sevastopol in November 1905.

abuzz with the news: "Chukhnin, the 'Butcher,' has been shot!" "The dirty dog got his!" No one except Sanya and Karl knew that Mariya Krupnitskaya was really Katya Izmailovich, and they kept the secret. Sanya read and re-read the accounts in the newspapers Karl smuggled to her. The five bullets Katya pumped into Chukhnin's body were not fatal, and every day the newspapers carried accounts of his recovery.

Sanya received Karl's letter of condolence, full of immense sadness and curses against the cruel fate that had befallen Katya—such a happy creature, so full of the joy of life. Why was it necessary for her to die? What a terrible waste!

Spurred by the hopelessness of Karl's letters, there came, like a ray of light into Sanya's soul, an utterly different conclusion:

> No! Katya's life was not wasted! My soul was suddenly filled with deep joy for Katya because I realized at last that she knew why she lived and why she died. I was moved to write a bright, triumphant hymn to her and I sent it to Karl, urging him to take back his curses and to understand the great beauty of her death.

It was left to Sanya to inform her sisters of the identity of Chukhnin's would-be assassin. They refused to believe it and kept repeating that they had received a postcard from Katya with a Rumanian postmark dated the day of the assassination attempt. They forgot how close the great Russian naval base of Sevastopol was to the Rumanian border. Sanya saw how difficult it was for them: one sister dead and another probably to die very soon.

About this time, news of the assassination of General Luzhenovsky appeared in the newspapers, along with a statement that the woman who shot him, Maria Spiridonova, had been killed. This too saddened Sanya, who had no premonition that the announcement of Spiridonova's death was premature or that she and this unknown woman would soon be thrown together for the rest of their lives.

One morning Sanya looked out her window to see an official and guards standing in the prison courtyard in deep conversation. One pointed to her window and, seeing her standing there, shook his fist and shouted, "Soon you will pay, you dog. Within five days you will hang." Sanya said she was not concerned about the threat of death, but her sisters hired a lawyer to defend her in the upcoming court-martial trial.

On a bright, frosty morning, the lawyer came to see Sanya, bringing the indictment for her to read. As she went over it, she suddenly stopped—horrified. In addition to hers and Vasya's name was that of a boy, Okhsenk-rug, a baker's assistant. He had been picked up two weeks after the attempt on Kurlov and was accused of throwing a bomb at Police Chief Norov, a bomb that did not go off. Sanya knew very well who had thrown that bomb and it was not Okhsenkrug. He was totally innocent and she was devastated by her helplessness to prevent his being brought to trial. She knew he would almost certainly be convicted.

For her defense, Sanya's lawyer advised her to call witnesses who could testify that it was the bloodshed on October 18, when Kurlov ordered troops to shoot into the crowd of peaceful demonstrators, that had moved the Essers to make him a target for execution. Sanya agreed and named a number of witnesses, some in prison, some "in freedom." It was a futile effort, for the court forbade any of them to appear.

The night before the trial Sanya and Karl admitted what each of them had felt for some time—they were in love. Tapped out on their adjoining wall went messages assuring devotion to each other and to the cause for which they lived and expected soon to die.

> The magic of our love was born in the silence of the night. The wall that was made to keep us apart brought us together whenever we wanted it. That cold dead wall sprang to life as if by the touch of a magician's wand and we turned the bricks into lute strings. How good life was! How good the struggle! How wonderful our love!

On February 16, the day of the trial, a prison trusty woke Sanya at 4 A.M. She dressed and was led to the prison office. After a long wait, Vasya and Okhsenkrug were brought in. Her outrage at the injustice being done this innocent boy dissipated her calm state of mind. Finally, sledges came to take them, separately, through the dark streets, accompanied by a whole troop of armed, mounted Cossacks, to the Fourth Army Artillery Officers' headquarters where the court-martial was to be held.

For five hours the three sat in a huge, silent, dark room, lined up along a wall, far from each other. Each was guarded by a soldier standing at rigid attention with a bared sword at his side. Sanya's lawyer came and brought them tea. A short time later Vasya and Sanya were led into a big bright hall with rows of seats and many portraits on the wall. In the front of the room was a long table for the judges. At either end was a chair, one for the defense lawyer and one for the prosecutor. As she walked in, Sanya saw her sister Manya standing, smiling at them. Near her was an old man with sad eyes. "My father," whispered Vasya.

The uniformed officers serving as judges filed in. When they were seated, everyone sat down except Governor-General Kurlov who stood, straight as an arrow, behind the chair provided him at the judges' table.

The indictment against the three was "conspiracy with intent to kill." Sanya and Vasya were tried first. Prosecution witnesses were called. All gave testimony against the accused. Sanya's lawyer, a brilliant attorney with wide experience defending revolutionaries, cleverly confused Chief of Police Norov on the witness stand so that he admitted shooting the prone, unconscious, disarmed Sanya when she was being held down by the two policemen in the churchyard. His vexation and embarrassment reduced him to stuttering and incomprehensible utterances. But this performance did not improve Sanya's hopeless position before the court, nor did the questioning of the retired officer who had also shot at her at that time.

In his statement, Sanya's lawyer dramatically proclaimed that in this very courtroom were officers of the regiment who ordered their men to shoot into the defenseless, peaceful crowd in the streets of Minsk on October 18. Why had they not been brought to trial for "intent to kill"? For "murder!" They had killed citizens of Minsk. After every point the defense lawyer made, the presiding judge, ruled wearily: The session of the court will proceed.

As the process droned on Sanya's glance wandered to the portraits on the wall. Suddenly she became rigid with astonishment. Over the heads of the judges hung a portrait of her father! There on the wall was General Izmailovich sternly listening to what was happening to his daughter!

The voice of General Kurlov brought Sanya abruptly out of her reverie. Kurlov was briefly questioned by her attorney. To Sanya, it seemed that Kurlov was embarrassed by the proceedings but was covering his embarrassment with great self-possession. Unlike Norov, he answered all questions with clipped military precision. Sanya gazed at him and thought:

> When we were "in freedom" we had so passionately stalked him. For whole days we followed his goings and comings, taking care to remain unseen by him and his guards. Now he stood not three steps away from us . . . and we were his prisoners. He had won. He was the victor.

Sanya noticed Kurlov kept his eyes averted all through the questioning, not once looking straight at the judges, the defense attorney, or the defendants. When he finished his testimony and was striding rapidly out the room past her, suddenly his eyes met hers. To her utter amazement, in that split second, she saw in them fear—pure animal fear. She wanted to shout: "He is not the victor!" That look from her intended victim was proof to her that they had not failed after all. They had reduced a cruel defender of autocracy to a frightened, insignificant animal!

Sanya and Vasya were each permitted to make a statement before the court. They concentrated on the crimes of Kurlov and Norov, with specific emphasis on the shooting of innocent people on October 18. When the prosecutor rose to make a brief, final statement, his voice gradually became a deafening shout: "According to the law, the judges can render only one sentence: Death!"

The judges solemnly filed out. They returned in a few minutes and the presiding judge asked Sanya and Vasya to stand. Then he read:

> Ivan Pulikov. For your premeditated crime of conspiracy to murder you are sentenced to death by hanging.

Aleksandra Izmailovich. You are sentenced for the same premeditated crime to death by hanging.

Neither Sanya nor Vanya flinched. This was the sentence they expected.

As her attorney took her arm to lead her out of the courtroom, Sanya spoke to remind him she wanted to give testimony in the case of Okhsenk-rug. The presiding judge frowned but reluctantly agreed to hear her statement. She said she knew who threw the bomb at Norov and that Okhsenk-rug had had nothing to do with it. He was not even a member of the Esser party nor in any way a revolutionary.

"Will you then give us the name of the guilty one?" asked the judge. Sanya replied, "Yes. His given name is Samson." She had decided to do this because she had learned from Esser sources that the police knew the given name of the comrade who had made the attempt on Norov.The judge asked, "What is his family name?" "That I cannot tell you," she replied. The judge then contemptuously waved her off with the comment, "The criminal's testimony is of no consequence."

As Sanya was led across the room to the doors she felt the mournful eyes of the few spectators and uniformed guards upon her and Vasya. As she passed her sister, Manya smiled and said in a loud whisper, "Nonsense. They won't hang you." Sanya knew that only with superhuman effort had Manya managed that smile. Sanya's fate was such a terrible worry to her sister that it was heartbreaking. Sanya wanted to embrace and kiss her.

> Vasya and I were such pitiful wretched creatures to those who with cold fear in their eyes gazed at us. We are to be deprived of our last possession, life itself. But we felt ourselves richer than all of them. . . . We possessed something they all lacked. We had our cause and we were dying for it.

Sanya and Vasya were led out of the Artillery Corps Headquarters about four o'clock into bright clear daylight. They were again loaded into separate sleighs for a fast ride back to the prison, surrounded by galloping Cossacks and mounted policemen. They rode through the usually crowded main streets of Minsk, but the streets were empty—no vehicles, no pedestrians, only mounted policemen at intervals along street intersections. Sanya saw a young man come out of a shop only to be waved back inside by a gendarme. Looking more closely she saw faces glued to shop and residence windows watching, smiling, and waving as the procession moved rapidly along. They passed through the gates into the walled prison courtyard and were led into the office where Sanya and Vasya grasped each other's hands. Vasya vowed he was glad to die for the cause, but with rising emotion he told Sanya she must live. He told her that she and Katya had brought light and love into his poor life and that his final thought would be of them and their important work. They kissed each other and Sanya watched as he was led off. She never saw him again.

Sanya walked behind the prison trusty along the corridors of the women's quarters. From behind the cell doors she heard voices asking, "What was the sentence?" "We got the rope," she answered. Soon after the door of her cell closed, the prison grapevine brought news of Okhsenkrug's death sentence. It was as if cold water had been dashed on Sanya's euphoria, but when it came time to exchange messages with Karl, they were of the happiness of love and death. They agreed that the more a revolutionary loved life, the more beautiful was death.

Sanya was told the sentence would be carried out soon. At any moment she expected the knock on her door that would begin the short walk to the gallows. But one day passed, then another, and another.

> The days flowed on, like the smooth surging waters of a deep river. The sun shone in a blue holiday sky. It was like a holiday, a great holiday. In my soul there was no commonplace thought, nothing petty, mean or ordinary. . . . [As] the consciousness grew in me that there was no time left, everything I had ever thought about or done was illuminated, became a hundred times clearer, more lucid, more significant. My nervous system seemed to have been transformed into another higher order, of a finer texture, belonging to a higher organism altogether. I experienced a remarkable, an extraordinary love for all my comrades, for all mankind, for the whole world. This love was reflected in my smile which never left my face, in the sensitivity of my body, in the almost uncontrollable excitement that came over me. . . . I seemed to have been transplanted to another atmosphere which intensified all tones and shades. I never loved life so much as in these days of brightness. The love, the radiance of my soul which was the foundation of this frame of mind did not cast off sadness, but it was a special sadness, a gentle, transparent serenity.

More days passed, and Sanya began to think of the coming of spring and the imminent victory of the revolution. And, involuntarily, something in her cried out: "I want to see it! I want to live! I want to see the victory—the victory of the hungry villages, of all the downtrodden. I want to see it! I want to celebrate it!"

On the eighth day after the trial, before sunrise, Sanya was awakened by the chirping of sparrows. She got up and went to her window to try to sort out her thoughts. Suddenly a shrill voice cut into the quiet darkness. She recognized it. It was Vasya. "Comrades, my father just came and told me my death sentence has been upheld." From the day they parted after the trial neither Sanya nor the other prisoners had heard anything from Vasya. Now these ominous words. The whole prison was immediately abuzz, and during the day the disquiet became palpable.

Vasya tapped out a parting message which a comrade in a neighboring cell wrote down; then it was copied and circulated:

> Durnovo [P. N. Durnovo was the tsarist minister of the Interior] says that in saving a burning house no one counts the broken window panes. I am only one of the window panes in the many-storied edifice of autocracy and capital-

ism that is on fire. I am happy to think the broken window pane that is my life will make an opening, and through it let there blow a tearing wind that will furiously fan the flames and make the old building at last crash down.

The next morning in the darkness before dawn, Vasya was taken into the prison courtyard and hanged. The prison was filled with unearthly sounds of groans, shouts, hysterical cries. Sanya, looking out her window, found herself shaking as with a high fever, almost unable to breathe. She felt cold, like a stone, and the thought kept beating in her brain: "I want to die in the light of the sun, not in the darkness of the night."

Once it was daylight, crowds began to gather outside the prison. The comrades inside and outside, began to sing the revolutionary funeral march: "Farewell brother, honorably you passed on. . . ." There were speeches. Black flags were thrown from the prison windows and picked up by men and boys who climbed onto the prison wall. Vasya's statement was read to those outside who took it down, then rushed off to print and circulate it. The speeches and singing went on all day.

Too far away to distinguish the words of the speeches, Sanya wept and felt she was alone with her thoughts of Vasya. She remembered a conversation she had with him two years ago. He told her he agreed with all the ideas of the Essers but could not be a member of the party because he did not believe in terror. "I understand the theory of terror," he had said; "I see the necessity of terror in Russia, but I cannot imagine myself killing a man. I may sometime cross the threshhold to practical acceptance of terror, but now I cannot be a terrorist."

Crossing that threshold was something every terrorist had to do. Sanya did not explain when or how it happened either to Vasya or to herself. But she implied that in Vasya's case, her and Katya's influence, and, ironically, the love they gave to this lonely, impoverished boy with such high ideals, had something to do with it. Vasya's last words to his comrades were proof he was convinced that his attempt to kill a hated representative of the autocracy had meaning and significance. Sanya whispered to herself, "Vasya was happy to die for the cause."

A proposed prison hunger strike as a protest against Vasya's death sentence failed because of lack of solidarity, but the uproar in the city of Minsk was soon felt in the prison. Cells were filled to overflowing with those picked up in house-to-house searches and street demonstrations, including a group of twelve- and thirteen-year-old high-school boys. On the fatal day, these students appeared at the entrance to their school and began marching up and down, carrying a black flag and singing the Esser funeral march. They refused to go to classes, were rounded up, loaded into police vans, and carted off to prison where they were kept for several days. The boy leader of the group, aware that Sanya too would soon be hanged, sent a special greeting from his classmates to "Brave Comrade Izmailovich!"

Several days passed. News came that Okhsenkrug's death sentence had been commuted to fifteen years of imprisonment at hard labor. There was speculation as to whether the authorities who reviewed the sentence might have been influenced by the printing of a letter in the liberal St. Petersburg journal *Rus* that contained Sanya Izmailovich's information on the innocence of Okhsenkrug signed by 140 inmates of the Minsk prison. The appearance of the letter caused the descent of a veritable army of prison inspectors on the Minsk prison to investigate the scandal of how such a letter could have been written, circulated and signed by so many inmates under the very noses of the prison's supposed rigid surveillance.

News that one of Sanya's sisters had gone to Vilna with an appeal to the appropriate authorities for a pardon for her did not please Sanya. For weeks she had been living in an elevated atmosphere of unreality—expecting death, wishing for death, yet unable to stifle the will to live. When the decision from Vilna finally came it was a commutation of Sanya's death sentence to exile and life imprisonment at hard labor in the Siberian *katorga*.

Sanya saw her reprieve as depriving her of the privilege of dying for the cause as Katya had, as Vasya had, and as had so many other revered Essers. She understood why, following their own code, her sisters had to try to save her life, but she, like Vasya and Karl, was convinced that the ultimate beauty of life for a revolutionary was the sacrifice of that life.

From the moment they realized they were in love with each other, Karl and Sanya had been faced with separation—whether she was hanged, or whether she was to live out her life in exile, they would soon be parted forever. They wanted above all else a meeting face to face. For days each had made repeated requests, but to no avail.

On the evening of March 8, Sanya was suddenly taken to the prison office and told she was leaving immediately for Moscow, the embarkation point for Siberia. Sanya asked if she could see Karl, and got no answer. Her sisters, Manya and Zhenya, were there to say goodbye. The three sisters sat at a table trying, without much success, to carry on a conversation. Suddenly the door opened and in walked Karl and a fellow prisoner who spoke up to say he had been elected by their comrades to bid Comrade Izmailovich goodby for all of them. As he made a little speech, Sanya stood up, uncomprehending, with her eyes riveted on Karl.

> We had both waited for this moment so passionately and now we were face to face—and had no words. It was as if I and he knew only the language of the wall . . . An unfathomable sadness was mixed with so much happiness we were struck dumb. What could we say when all around us were other people. They did not know about us . . . So we just looked at each other and smiled. Then, all of a sudden, he was gone.

Sanya's sisters also left so they could get to the railroad station in time to see her off and say a final goodbye. Sanya was then ordered to strip to her underwear. A prison trusty put on her the clumsy canvas skirt, the bulky jacket of the same material, the white neckerchief. Then she was ordered to put on the sheepskin overcoat with the yellow prison diamond on the back. The leg fetters of the prisoner going into exile in the *katorga* were fastened on. The prison garb was so heavy she could scarcely move.

With other prisoners being taken from the Minsk prison to Moscow for transportation to the *katorga,* Sanya was led into the dark foggy street lighted with hissing torches all around. The clank of the Cossacks' naked swords and the prisoners' fetters, the grinding of wheels as the unwieldy coaches filled with prisoners began to move, and the striking of the horses' hooves on the cobblestones made such noise the shouts, cries and singing of the prisoners crowding the open barred windows were almost drowned out. The procession made its way slowly through dark streets. Along the way Sanya's sisters in a sleigh passed them.

All approaches to the Moscow-Brest railroad station were cordoned off. Lines of police were holding back the people who had come to wave goodbye and shout encouragement to the deportees. As she boarded one of the two white prison cars, she heard voices calling, "*Do svidaniia!*" and "Come back soon!"

Sanya was apprehensive about the train trip. She expected rough treatment from the convoys and the guards. To her surprise, the convoys were polite and helpful. Once she got to her assigned seat, one of them told her to take off the heavy prison garb and make herself comfortable. Then she heard someone say "Ah, how unfortunate that bomb of yours didn't explode." She looked at the man who said it. He was a guard wearing the badge of a subordinate army officer. He continued, "My comrade was on the Square that day. He was passing when the bomb rolled to a stop and he desperately wanted to push it with his sword to make it explode!" This officer and a corporal continued to talk to Sanya almost all night, indicating their sympathy with and interest in the Esser Party cause. She began to have the illusion she was sitting with comrades. Only the unsheathed swords of the guards at the doors of the prison car brought her back to reality. but she had to smile. She had expected her convoys to be rough animals and instead she found they were comrades.

ANNOTATED REFERENCES

Aleksandra Izmailovich's story has been taken almost entirely from her two long letters, written in 1908 and published in 1923 and 1924, under the title "Iz Proshlogo" in *Katorga i Ssylka,* no. 7, 1923, and no. 8, 1924.

A description of the provincial city of Minsk in the *Novyi Entsiklopedicheskiy Slovar',* Petrograd, n.d., vol. 26, gives the population in 1914 as 106,673, 42% Jewish. The *Entsiklopedicheskiy Slovar',* St. Petersburg, 1896, gives the population as 83,880, with 43,658 Jews.

The description of the Izmailovich home and its division between the "front-parlor sisters" and the "back-door sisters" appears in a memorial to Ekaterina Izmailovich in *Znamia Truda,* no. 6, September 30, 1907.

The account of the October 18 event at the Minsk-Libavo-Romenska railroad station is based on the detailed description of it written by the Procurator of the Minsk District Court, A. P. Zubkov in his November 1, 1905, report to the Procurator of the Vilensk Chamber of Justice, L. A. Shulgin, printed in *Revoliutsiia 1905–1907 gg, Dokumenty i Materialy, Vcerossiyskaia Politicheskaia Stachka v Oktiabre 1905 goda,* part two, Moscow-Leningrad, 1955, document 691, pp. 203–8. A. Izmailovich, in her brief account of the October 18 event in "Iz Pro-shlogo," *Katorga i Ssylka,* no. 7, 1923, has Police Chief Norov and Governor Kurlov issuing a command to the crowd to disperse. When the people refused to budge, troops were called up and ordered to fire. In Zubkov's account the order to fire is made to seem an accident, with an excited lower officer giving the order and several captains trying in vain to stop the shooting. Zubkov also states witnesses affirmed that no shots were fired by any of the people in the crowd. A footnote added by the Soviet editors of Zubkov's report quotes an order by Governor Kurlov which purports to prove that he was responsible for starting the October 18 massacre.

7

To the Siberian *Katorga:* The Triumphal Journey of *The Six*

In 1906, no longer were long lines of prisoners wearing clanking leg, arm, and, sometimes, neck fetters led through the streets of Moscow, creating the horrible spectacle described in Lev Tolstoy's novel *Resurrection.* Sanya Izmailovich and her fellow prisoners, after completing the three-hundred-mile journey from Minsk to Moscow were taken from their prison cars at the Smolensk Station, loaded into horsedrawn Black Marias, that the Russians called *sobachniki*—dog carriers—and taken in broad daylight through the streets of Moscow to the grim Butyrki Prison. The high red brick walls and turret towers of Butyrki, built in 1879, covered two square blocks.

Did Sanya and her 1906 comrades know that this spot, near the Butyrki gate of ancient walled Moscow, had long been a place of bloody torture and execution of rebels? Here Peter the Great had left a dozen Streltzi traitors hanging from gibbets as a warning to all who entered the city of the price of disloyalty to the Tsar. Here Katerina the Great had the Don Cossack insurrectionist Pugachev put in a cage, so small he could only stand upright, and displayed to the taunting public before he was beheaded and his body quartered. As a remembrance, the most fortified part of Butyrki Prison was called the Pugachev Tower.

Aleksandr Solzhenitsyn wrote that in the Stalin era the hearts of Muscovites shivered when they saw the steel maw of the Butyrki gates open, but Sanya Izmailovich described Butyrki in 1906 as a hotel housing comrades. When the gates of Butyrki opened, the prisoners from Minsk crossed a small courtyard. The heavily carved wooden doors swung back and they entered a dim, high-vaulted entrance hall. Deafening noise and disorder prevailed. Masses of prisoners stood expectantly in little frightened groups, trying but not succeeding in keeping their fetters from clanking. Prison personnel were running about with stacks of official papers, shouting orders. Piles of rough sacks containing the prisoners' belongings were everywhere.

Then came the order: "Women. Take off your skirts." "Men. Take off your pants." Both men and women looked around in embarrassment. When a soldier with a gun began to hit people in a group near Sanya, the prisoners, making a lot of noise with their chains, their faces red as fire and their teeth clenched in anger, carried out the order. Their bodies were searched, their belongings were laid on a long table for inspection, and they were one by one led to a corner of the room where their hair was cropped. Even the men were horrified to see the long hair of the women sheared off.

Finally the prisoners were divided into groups, taken from the noisy, dark entrance station, led into blue-tiled corridors and up various black, wrought-iron stairways. A tall, heavy-set Finnish prison trusty took Sanya to the criminal women's section. They entered a huge room with an arch ceiling and two large, barred windows looking out on a courtyard. On all sides of the courtyard rose tiers of identical barred windows, while below on a grassy triangular plot stood a small octagonal church. The room was crammed with cots, and Sanya, standing in the middle of it, found herself stared at affectionately by more than twenty women sitting and standing on all sides.

The Finnish trusty ordered another cot brought in and handed Sanya some linen, old but freshly laundered. She brought hot water and told Sanya to wash up, then brought tea. Sanya was grateful for the tea, but felt terribly awkward sitting on her cot drinking it, with rows of eyes trained on her. Most of the criminal women said nothing, but one shyly asked: "Did you kill your husband, little auntie?"

After the first timidity wore off, Sanya found the criminal women were a rowdy bunch. On their exercise walks in the courtyard, their exchanges with the male criminals, looking out their barred windows, were ardent and ribald. Sanya soon learned that the relatively small number of *katorzhniki* in Butyrki at the time she entered, were kept in the solitary cells of the prison towers.

One day the Finnish trusty took Sanya to the political women's recreation room. There she was greeted enthusiastically, and she found several women who, like herself, had assassinated officials or had been involved in assassination attempts. Among them were Mariya Shkolnik who had shot the governor of Chernigov; Lydiya Eserskaya who had taken part in a plot on the life of Pleve in 1904 but had escaped from prison, and in 1905 had shot the governor of Mogilev; and eighteen-year-old Rebecca Fialka, arrested in Odessa for making bombs for an assassination plot.

Mariya Shkolnik told Sanya she did not have to remain with the criminal women. She should demand a transfer to a tower room where the other *katorzhniki* were. Sanya followed her advice and the transfer was soon made. As the weeks passed, the dozen or so men and women political prisoners condemned to exile were augmented every day as *katorzhniki* began arriving by the hundreds, soon overcrowding the prison. Every group came with news of strikes and violence, which was quickly circulated.

> The gendarmes and soldiers were indifferent. The inmates were friendly, even the convicts who were mixed among us. The government seemed to look through its fingers at the revolutionary demonstrations inside the prison walls. In the quiet and peaceful courtyard only the iron fetters of the prisoners made somber sounds.

Sanya received letters full of love from Karl, still awaiting his fate and hoping to meet her in Butyrki. She had a round of visitors. Her sisters came from Minsk, as did Minsk comrades and old Esser friends she had known in student days. Two girl cousins came once a week bringing party news and copies of illegal newspapers.

Outside the window, as she lay at night on her cot, Sanya could hear the "sounds of freedom": wheels on the street, the shriek of a train whistle. It made her sad to think of the ebullient, active life going on outside prison walls. The air was damp and warm, the patch of sky she could see was brightened by stars, and some kind of early spring perfume spoke of the sleeping fields of Russia, of dark woods and clouds over a river.

As Sanya's departure to Siberia approached, her father, just back from the Far Eastern War, came to see her. The prison authorities arranged for General Izmailovich to have an open-ended visit with his daughter in a private room. Sanya wrote, "He was very sad, and was obviously stunned at my happy frame of mind. He talked of Katya. He knew no facts about her attempt on Chukhnin, and her fate, but his suspicions were pretty close to the truth." Sanya had promised her sisters not to tell their father what had happened to Katya because they feared she would only succeed in upsetting him even more with her idea of the "beauty" of Katya's death.

It did not take Sanya and her father long to run out of things to say to each other and she brought the short visit to a close. General Izmailovich was a somber, grief-stricken man as he walked out of Butyrki Prison. Aside from the disgrace his daughters' revolutionary activities had brought on the family name, he realized Sanya was lost to him. He would probably never see her again. Sanya was confident of the righteousness of her and Katya's cause, and of the necessity for their acts; but of her father she made a rare statement of compassion for one who was not a comrade, a person who disagreed with everything she stood for. She wrote, "Our father came back from the war, and behind his back an internal war had taken away from him two of his own—one killed and the other a prisoner for life." Not long after his return to Minsk, General Izmailovich committed suicide.

In April two women who were famous all over Russia came to Butyrki. One was Maria Spiridonova, the murderer of General Luzhenovsky; the other was Anastasia (Nastya) Bitzenko, the killer of General Sakharov. Sakharov, like Luzhenovsky, had headed a punitive expedition with orders to repress agrarian disorders in the Volga region. His base was the city of Saratov, where he soon earned the reputation of a ruthless killer and destroyer.

Nastya Bitzenko, at thirty-one, older than most of the *katorzhniki,* was by 1906 a seasoned revolutionary. With her prim pale face, pursed lips, pince-nez, enormous plain felt hat over thin mousy hair, white shirtwaist, long grey skirt and black, high-buttoned shoes, she looked like the school-teacher she started out to be. Unlike most of the Russian terrorists, Nastya was born a peasant. Her family had moved as farm settlers to Siberia in the 1870s and Nastya was born there in 1875. Benefiting from the educational reforms of Tsar Aleksandr II, she acquired enough schooling to qualify as a teacher. Her first revolutionary work was in Kazan where she organized dining rooms for the hungry in 1899. When the Esser party was formed the next year, she joined, and dropped her family name Kameristkaya. She took the name Bitzenko, an adaptation of the Russian word meaning to hit, or to strike a blow. Nastya struck her first blow in Moscow. Using the cover of attending teacher-training classes, she spent most of her time working as an Esser propagandist, organizing revolutionary groups of laborers. In 1901 she was picked up by the police and banished from Moscow; her teacher's license was taken away.

Nastya Bitzenko then became a full-time propagandist and organizer for revolution. She worked in various Russian cities and in 1904 was in St. Petersburg. She joined a group of terrorists led by a woman who had come from the south with a company of women for the express purpose of assassinating the Minister of the Interior, Pleve. Betrayed by an informer, they were all arrested and condemned to exile. Nastya was sent to an area near the Arctic Circle but soon escaped, fled abroad, and settled for a short time in Geneva. She returned to Moscow in the turbulent summer of 1905 where she propagandized railroad workers. In October she led the big railroad strike, one of the events which finally forced Tsar Nikolai II to sign the famous October 17 Manifesto of Freedom. In November 1905, Nastya became a member of the Esser Battle Organization. When it passed a death sentence on General Sakharov, she volunteered to go to his headquarters in Saratov to carry it out. She arrived in Saratov, reconnoitered the situation, and shot him November 22. He died instantly. Sakharov was so widely known and hated that his killer received immediate and widespread attention, becoming overnight a terrorist heroine. At a court-martial trial, Nastya Bitzenko was sentenced to death by hanging, but the sentence was later commuted to life imprisonment in the *katorga.*

When Nastya was brought to Butyrki she was placed in a solitary cell in a tower off the prison courtyard. It was not so isolated as to remove her from conversation with fellow inmates, but she chose to remain aloof— hostile in fact. She regarded the prisoners' interest in her as ridiculous curiosity. Sanya Izmailovich had met Bitzenko several times when they were both in St. Petersburg a few years earlier. Presuming on that acquaintanceship, Sanya succeeded in talking to her through the bars while she was in the courtyard on exercise walks. She learned that Nastya abhorred personal adulation, regarding it as an unbearable nuisance. She could not understand the psychology of these "big children." She even gave one insistent group of comrades, who gathered outside her window during their exercise period, a sharp tongue lashing. She was contemptuous of what she saw as a tendency of party members to advance personality ahead of duty to the revolutionary cause.

Maria Spiridonova was brought to Butyrki secretly at night. She was put in a solitary cell in the Pugachev Tower. The criminal prisoners, avid for news about Maria, learned of her arrival. They also found that she was so ill she could not stand or walk. But, Sanya reported, several of the women prisoners began to receive notes from Maria written on torn scraps of paper. "She didn't know us, but she indicated she already loved us as fellow members of the Esser party. She did not mention her illness. She wrote about party matters, but by inserting subtle endearments she made the general tone of her messages one of tenderness."

Every day, groups of prisoners were brought out of their cells and lined up in the courtyard for deportation to the prisons of Siberia. In June, Sanya began to get hints from the prison personnel that she and three of her companions—Mariya Shkolnik, Lydiya Ezerskaya, and Rebecca Fialka—would soon depart. The order finally came late in the evening on June 21. The women were told they were leaving in a half hour. They packed in wild confusion.

In a pouring rain accompanied by wild claps of thunder, the four women were led into the dark courtyard. From her solitary cell Nastya Bitzenko was brought out. At every window prisoners stood with lamps, singing and shouting out goodbyes, good wishes, and party slogans. Their shouts were almost drowned out by a deafening roll of thunder and a clap of lightning.

Iron doors rumbled and from the gloom emerged a tiny female figure in white. Spiridonova! She was wearing a white prison hospital coat with a white shawl over her head. New shouts of greeting and farewell came from the prison windows as *The Six*, thrown together by the vicissitudes of their lives as terrorists, met for the first time. This meeting marked the beginning of a decade of life together as prisoners in exile, biding time, completely cut off from the revolutionary activity which up to that point had been at the very center of their existence.

At this coming together on that stormy June night in 1906 in the Butyrki

Prison yard, there began to be displayed the differences in personality, attitude, and fundamental belief that were to characterize the association of what one of them later referred to as the "unfriendly six." Three of them rushed to greet Spiridonova, though only Lydiya Ezerskaya displayed the extreme adulation reminiscent of that of the general public of the time. Sanya and Nastya held back and did not even take her hand.

Trying to analyze her initial revulsion to Maria Spiridonova, Sanya later said she recoiled from the faraway look in her big bright eyes with deep black circles under them, her pale face made grim by her clenched teeth and her lips held in a thin line.

Sanya's lack of compassion is demonstrated in this description of her instinctive reaction to Maria. At the moment of their meeting it was only by the exertion of almost superhuman will that Maria could move her shattered body at all. Sanya either did not know or chose to ignore this. But there was a more serious cause for her coolness to Maria. Sanya and Nastya disapproved of Maria's letter describing her mistreatment at the hands of the officers who arrested her, and its publication in the journal *Rus*. The publicity that followed, they felt, had resulted in popularizing Maria Spiridonova—not the cause. After all, was the treatment of Maria so much worse than that received by many other terrorists at the hands of the police? Sanya said this difference created a wall between Marusya (as Maria was popularly called), Nastya, and herself.

The drama of The Six began to unfold slowly. They were taken in a closed black *sobachnik* van, surrounded by mounted dragoons, through the dark, rain-drenched streets of Moscow. They were marched in a convoy of soldiers through the Nikolaev railroad station onto the platform and into a barred prison car of a regularly scheduled Trans-Siberian train. The six female prisoners attracted the attention of the milling crowds. Then as now, Russian railroad terminals were jammed twenty-four hours a day with people disembarking from trains or setting off on journeys. In those pre-revolutionary days, people encountering prison convoys were almost always curious and friendly. So as The Six passed, many stopped to look, to wave, to call out friendly greetings. This attention was just a hint of what lay ahead along the four-thousand-mile journey to Siberia.

For the first few days when their train stopped at stations, The Six encountered small delegations of Esser party workers who made it a practice to meet the trains, since almost all going east at that time were carrying political prisoners to Siberia. The regular passengers soon learned that Maria Spiridonova and Nastya Bitzenko were in the prison car. When they reached their destinations and got off the train, many would telegraph ahead to inform friends and relatives living along the train's route that these women, whom almost everyone in Russia seemed to want to see and greet, would soon be passing through. "Check the train schedules," they advised. And people did. The result was the appearance of crowds at every stop all across Russia and Siberia.

To some of the women, especially Nastya Bitzenko, the presence of adulatory crowds was distasteful. There they were, hundreds, and at some stops, thousands—waiting for a glimpse of Maria or Nastya and the others. The young women prisoners were greeted as beloved heroines. Excited men and women thrust into their hands through the barred windows bouquets of flowers, boxes of sweets, and coins.

To Nastya, this adulation was a travesty of everything she believed. To her, what mattered was the cause. It was the cause these people should be honoring, not an individual. This doctrinal purist would have preferred to turn her back and not utter a word, or to tell the crowds to go away—as she had done when her prison comrades in Butyrki had gathered outside her prison cell.

In contrast to Nastya's rigid stance, Maria Spiridonova dealt with the crowd phenomenon as a political pragmatist. The crowds were there. She did not torture herself with questions of why they were there. She instinctively seized the opportunity to propagandize. So Maria proceeded to make political speeches. What matter that she could not stand up without gripping a train seat or the iron bars of her window? What matter that she collapsed after every speech? She always managed to recover by the time the train reached the next stop. As Sanya observed, "Like a morning storm disappears at the touch of the sun's first rays, so the faces of the crowd had a healing effect on Marusya."

The first sizeable crowd was at Sizran where a trainload of soldiers, returning from the Russo-Japanese War, stood waiting on the station platform when the train of The Six came in. The soldiers crowded around the prison car, soon found out who the prisoners were, and sent up a rousing chorus of "Hurrahs!" "For Spiridonova!" "For Bitzenko!" "For you others, too!" "To your health!" When the cheering finally died down, and after a failed attempt by their officers to force the soldiers to leave the prison car, Maria began to speak. Her voice was light and clear, her tone musical. Her well-phrased flow of words held the men in rapt attention. She explained to them the Esser party principles and its program of action. She sketched the blueprint of the glorious future.

> Go home and tell the people about the inequality and oppression you saw in the armed forces. Open the eyes of your fellow countrymen, and go hand in hand with us, the fighters for land and freedom for all the people. And Comrade Soldiers—don't shoot down your brothers, the peasants!

Burning with fever, holding her shawl over the unhealed side of her face, she ended her talk and began answering the soldiers' endless questions. Smiling, she spoke sometimes in a voice hot with passion, sometimes with quiet tenderness.

Sanya was amazed at this performance. She said that such strength could be felt in the soldiers' answering cries of approval that the hearts of all the women beat with happiness. "At the end of Marusya's talk we could visualize the men going back, all over Mother Russia, sowing in the many deaf corners of the land the seed of hatred of despotism and strengthening the belief in the bright future of socialism."

Sanya may have been impressed by the incident at Sizran, but as the train moved on to ever-larger crowds, the differences among The Six boiled up. At the first sound of people outside the barred windows, day or night, Maria was there, ready to talk. Her comrades did not understand nor approve. They looked on her action simply as vanity, a personal response to admirers who endlessly called out her name. As she spoke, the listeners often shed silent tears of rapture just to be looking at her and hearing her voice. Sanya wrote:

> We did not understand her. We did not understand why she became so angry when we did not want to go to the windows, or want her to go to speak to the people who appeared whenever the train stopped. We forbade her to get up in the night (an order she refused to obey). We did not understand why she did not spare herself, or why she expected us to give of ourselves as she did of herself.

Sanya noted that not everyone was friendly in the crowds Maria addressed, but she did not try to shield herself. She did not ignore rude questions or the taunts by critics of her deed and her beliefs. She countered in cogent, well-expressed phrases her revolutionary ideas, her belief in the necessity for terrorist acts in Russia, and her conviction that a bright future lay ahead for all mankind.

Maria was more than capable of handling the opposition of a few dissidents in the generally adulatory crowds, but the hostility of her comrades in the prison car was painful. Sanya wrote:

> In the drama that unfolded we were the executioners, out to destroy Marusya's faith in man. We were cruel, pitiless executioners, spitting on everything that was for her pure and holy. . . . It was frightful for her because in her childlike simplicity and tender graciousness she had expected to find in us allies, kinfolk, the closest of comrades.

Instead she was faced by Nastya's condemnation, not of the crowds, but of the reason they were there: to see and hear a famous individual, or individuals—a motivation that reduced the socialist cause, in her eyes, to something akin to a Christian cult of saints and martyrs. Sentimentality was reducing the hard reason of socialism to an emotional response. Sanya, while not as flinty in her condemnation as Nastya, admitted her initial difficulty in accepting what she described as "Marusya's loving approach to people."

In the atmosphere of hostility that prevailed in the prison car, the others in varying degrees also lined up against Maria. Between stops, as the train rolled eastward, the animated conversation of the five was full of hateful remarks which Maria, flat on her back at her window, could not help overhearing. Her only response was once to send them a folded piece of paper on which she had written, "Please talk more quietly. I hear everything you say."

In the personal and ideological struggle between those who favored a passive stance toward the crowds and Maria's passionate responsiveness, the latter approach soon won out for several reasons. There was, first of all, the increase in the size of the crowds. It proved impossible to ignore them. Before long the oppositionists, caught up in the excitement, proceeded to follow Maria's example. They too began to propagandize. They also began to talk to Maria between stops, and attitudes toward her slowly changed. Sanya became convinced that, far from elevating personality above duty to the cause, Maria, as a dedicated revolutionary, had ruthlessly wrenched out of herself everything personal.

> She would have called it a betrayal of her duty if her personality had been placed above the common interest. What had driven her into revolutionary action was her passionate concern for the thwarted, humiliated peasants, for all the profaned, lowly people, and those in all walks of life deprived of freedom.

The changes in Maria Spiridonova's life that began with her shooting of General Luzhenovsky, far from diminishing her zeal for revolutionary action, pushed her into more persistent use of whatever means came to hand. She felt it her obligation to go out to meet the crowds, to give the last ounce of her strength to bring them a rousing message, to move them to revolutionary action. She hoped to electrify them by her own example, knowing well the tendency of the Russian people to revere the person they see as sacrificing himself or herself to a cause they could identify as their own.

Inevitably, finding themselves in a sea of friendly faces at each stop, The Six began to think of escape. At Kirgan an enthusiastic crowd of over two thousand met them. Whispered messages informed them to be ready for rescue at Omsk, where great preparations for them were being made. Unrealistic as escape seemed to the women cooped up in their securely barred car, several of them had run away from prisons before and did not rule out the possibility of doing it again.

As they rode eastward toward Omsk, excitement began to build in what The Six were now calling their "Royal Car." Tsarist authorities also had word of the planned escape. Seeking to foil not only the escape of any of The Six, but also to put a stop to their meetings with the crowds that were really rallies for revolution, orders were sent from St. Petersburg to uncouple the prison car from the train five miles outside of Omsk and to leave it there

**The Six on the steps of their railway car in Omsk, 1906.
The women are, clockwise from bottom left,
Spiridonova, Fialka, Shkolnik, Bitzenko, Izmailovich, Ezerskaya**

while the rest of the train came into the station. The car would be picked up later and carried through Omsk without stopping.

On the sunny July day The Six were scheduled to arrive in Omsk, a crowd of some five thousand people waited at the station. They were bearing banners and red flags, and singing revolutionary songs. When the train steamed in without the prison car, the crowd was angry, but it was only momentarily thwarted. Railroad workers took an engine out, hooked up the car, and enveloped in clouds of steam brought The Six into the station. Loud cries immediately went up from the crowd demanding that the women be permitted to come out onto the platform of their car to speak. The small convoy in the prison car looked at the mob and decided to give in. The barred door was opened and the women came out, one after the other, and stood on the car steps. Only one lieutenant, armed with a rifle, was there to guard them, but as they came through the door he warned them in a grim tone, "If you go into that crowd I will shoot every one of you on the spot." They were convinced he would do it. He did not, however, prevent them from answering the greetings of the crowd or from giving their names, specifying their terrorist acts, and proclaiming themselves Essers.

As The Six stood on the prison car platform in Omsk, someone clicked a camera. The resulting snapshot of the woman was put on a postcard and sold illegally by the thousands. The time came for the train's departure, but the people would not leave. It seemed everyone wanted to talk to the terrorist women. In despair, the lieutenant holding the rifle turned to the women and said, "Tell them to go." They did, but no one went away. In fact, it seemed that more and more people came.

The women eventually filed back into the car. People still thronged the platform. Young men climbed on the roof of their car and leaning down stuck their hands through the barred windows with dirty pieces of paper and called "Sisters, dear sisters. Sign, please this piece of paper for me." After hours of this, the women, worn out, asked their admirers again and again to let their car be hooked to the train so it could proceed. Finally the train slowly pulled out of the station, with people running alongside the car. One tall, bearded old fellow in a peasant shirt and high boots, his long, white hair whipping in the wind, ran clutching the hand of a child with a fistful of flowers. He called out "take my darlings this little bunch of flowers from my grandchild so that all her life she can remember whom she gave them to." Soon the train gathered enough speed to leave even the fastest runners behind.

The revolutionary speeches of The Six in their trek across Russia and Siberia propagandized thousands of people. Even in fulfilling the constant requests for their autographs, the women spread Esser socialist ideas, for on the pieces of paper thrust up to them from the crowds they wrote not only their names but short party slogans.

Sanya continued to be amazed at the emotion the Russian people expressed at seeing them, and especially Maria Spiridonova.

> I cannot describe the ecstasy with which the thousands of people along the way to Siberia greeted Maria. At every stop they crowded around her window, expressing such joy at seeing her that their eyes filled with tears. Often they broke down and sobbed. Not knowing any other way to express their burning love for her, they showered her with flowers. Ragged working-men put their hands, trembling with excitement, through the windows to give her copper coins.

> The women who sold milk at the stations would come up to the guards and say, "Kind sir, take these cans of milk to the ladies." Women in the crowds took off their rings and handed them through the bars; one man even took out his watch and gave it. I remember a wounded sailor on crutches, on his way home from the war, standing outside the window. "Please do me the honor of taking some cigarettes and a few copper coins." I remember a nun who brought us a beautiful bouquet of wild flowers with the touching note, "To the beloved martyrs from the nuns of N____ Convent."

Their train pushed farther into Siberia, into the silence of forests, along deep, clear rivers, into the thinly inhabited Trans-Baikal region. There were only small "half-stations" along the railroad tracks with no scheduled stops for their fast-moving train. But from time to time, in what seemed to be the middle of nowhere, the train would give a sudden lurch and grind to a screeching halt.

> Before our windows, as if rising from under the ground, would stand a group of excited, happy workers. On one occasion it was: "Greetings, Maria Aleksandrovna!" "Greetings, other comrades!" A spokesman said, "We were sent by the workers of the Zima Station. We are one hundred people. We seized the train. We greet you in the name of the revolutionary workers of Zima."

Maria answered them in a strong speech. She laid out in simple, clear language the Esser Party program and spoke with fervor about "socialization of the land." They listened with hungry attention. When she stopped speaking, the spokesman thanked her and told them that until that moment the workers of Zima had heard nothing of the Esser program. "We have heard only separate voices and no coordinated plan of action."

At approximately the same time the train carrying The Six was nearing its destination, the armed trains of tsarist generals Rennenkampf and Müller-Zakomelsky's punitive expeditions were cutting across Siberia like scythes. Their "pacification squads" were mowing down demonstrators, striking workers, peasants, and even telegraph girls. Dozens of people had been shot and hanged and hundreds were being rounded up and sent off to prison. In the areas through which The Six were going, the depredations of the "punitive expeditions" had put the people in a rebellious mood. The crowds gathering around their car were small in this part of Siberia but they were receptive as they listened to Maria's inflammatory speeches. They held up their fists and shouted: "We are ready to fight! We will rise in rebellion very soon." The rebelliousness of the crowds was interpreted by The Six as evidence of a rapidly spreading revolutionary spirit in the land.

Sanya made an effort to analyze Maria Spiridonova's hold over the crowds. She said the people who saw and listened to Maria were attracted to her as a woman who had declared war on tyranny and had suffered for it. Torture by tsarist authorities was understood by everyone in the Russian Empire, and when torture was carried out on the small, weak body of a woman like Maria, the people's sympathy for the sacrifice she had made knew no bounds. "They saw her as the proud avenger of the suffering of the people and were convinced that only the possessor of great spiritual strength, of great beauty of soul, would undertake the heavy task of devoting her life to the people. They adored her for it." They elevated her to the ranks of Russia's revered martyrs.

> Under the shade of her canopy every person boiling with discontent could come. They came from all ranks, from all parties. She belonged to them all. They carried her in their souls. She became the symbol, the banner of all their protests.

One of the small triumphs of The Six on their way to Siberia was their success in propagandizing their convoys of soldiers. The young women read Esser brochures to them; for hours on end, as their train raced on, they conversed with their young military guards about socialism, democracy, and constitutional government. The enthusiastic response of the men, either to the women's ideas or to their spirited companionship, led the authorities to change the convoy personnel twice. But each new convoy simply meant additional recruits to the revolutionary cause. As proof, Sanya pointed out that near the end of their journey the news came that a sailor named Akimov had shot and killed Admiral Chukhnin on June 26. Chukhnin was the man Sanya's sister Katya had shot, but not fatally, in January. "We were all delighted with this news and we and the convoys sang songs and made speeches of triumph."

Beyond Lake Baikal the railroad ran along the Ingoda and Shilka rivers between spectacular, lofty mountains. Here the last group of convoys let the women leave their barred prison car whenever the train stopped. All of them except the incapacitated Marusya ran and walked in the fresh green grass and in the woods, enjoying a symbolic last taste of freedom.

Three hundred miles east of Chita, the capital city of the Trans-Baikal region, the Trans-Siberian railroad abruptly ended at Sretensk. The "Royal Train" stopped. The triumphant journey of The Six was over. For several days the women were temporarily incarcerated in Sretensk. Until the coming of the Trans-Siberian railroad this had been a small Cossack settlement surrounding a convict prison, but in 1906 it was a booming railhead of some ten thousand people.

For several days the women waited, wondering where in the strange land beyond they would be sent. One day they were loaded into two *tarantas,* the old-fashioned horse-drawn traveling carriages of Russia. Surrounded by a troop of armed soldiers they set off eastward to their destination: the Akatue Prison. Their carriages rolled through the main, unpaved street of Sretensk, dusty in the July heat. Almost all the town's inhabitants had come out to line up, on both sides of the street, and stood loudly cheering them. Men, women, and children thrust into their hands flowers, tins of canned fruit, candy, and money.

After their carriages had gone a short distance beyond the town, their convoy of soldiers left. With two guards, they traveled slowly, day after day, through an almost uninhabited, often spectacularly beautiful plateau. Sometimes The Six were sobered by grim thoughts of their future, living the dread life of the *katorzhniki.* Sometimes they were uplifted because they knew at Akatue they would meet again many comrades with whom they had worked "in freedom" or whom they had met before in the prisons of Russia.

Finally, after passing through the barren village of Akatue, The Six reached the gates of the low wall surrounding a large stone building. It was Akatue Prison, set in the middle of green fields, surrounded by high, snow-topped mountains. Behind the gates waiting to greet them were hundreds of men, women, and children. Big banners had been unfurled, one of them emblazoned with the words: "Welcome Dear Comrades." Another carried the Esser Party slogan: "In Combat We Will Achieve Our Rights." One spelled out the names of The Six and above them the words "Praise to the Fallen Ones."

As they got out of the *tarantas* and walked through the gates into the prison yard, The Six were greeted with the "Marseillaise" thundering through the quiet air. Then the lusty chorus swung into "Terror, Terror, Terror Against the Tyrants." When the song ended, old friends rushed to greet The Six. They were showered with kisses and flowers. Even the head of the prison appeared, shook their hands, and wished them well. After they were shown their cells they came back to the courtyard where they were served a festive tea, picnic style, and posed for photographs.

Sanya Izmailovich's account of her experience in the Minsk and Butyrki prisons and of the trip of The Six to Siberia ends with their arrival at Akatue. For information on their experience in the Siberian *katorga* it is necessary to turn to the fragments of published reminiscences of her fellow *katorzhnitsy:*[1] Nastya Bitzenko, Maria Spiridonova, and Irina Kakhovskaya.

---

[1]*Katorzhnitsa* is the feminine form of *Katorzhnik. Katorzhnitsy* is the plural form.

From all accounts, in the summer and fall of 1906 the rules of prison life were so loosely enforced at Akatue that the comrades, among whom were well-educated professional people—teachers, doctors, musicians, lawyers—transformed the prison into a veritable university. They conducted courses, gave lectures and concerts, and carried on literacy campaigns among the soldiers, sailors, workers, and peasants who were being brought into the prison in increasing numbers as a result of the tsarist regime's punitive expeditions.

Once a week the mail came, bringing letters, books, and newspapers. The prisoners would assemble while one of the comrades read the newspapers aloud. Journalistic reports of exciting revolutionary activity all over Russia were taken as proof of the near collapse of the Old Regime.

Days and weeks flew by in churning activity at Akatue. Important work was being done in an atmosphere of stimulating companionship. It was a rare moment in time which brought together in the katorga many of the most famous men and women in Russia's revolutionary movement. Convinced the revolution would come momentarily, they were feverishly preparing themselves to play leading roles in building the bright future of Russia and the world.

This euphoria was fated not to last.

In the Nerchinsk prison complex, stretching over hundreds of miles of mountainous terrain north of the Mongolian border, were seven prisons and four mines in 1906. The mild regime at Akatue and all the male prisons of Nerchinsk ended when the prison administration changed in December 1906. Testimony to the harsh treatment of the men is available in accounts by some who survived, and in contemporary reports of hunger strikes, daring escapes, and suicides. These accounts indicate that the men in the katorga retained their zeal, becoming if anything more fanatical as they fought back against a harsh prison regime; but what they gained in combative techniques they lost in the political skills that would be needed when revolution finally came. The women, who were ordered to leave Akatue in February 1907 and proceed to the Mal'tsev Women's Prison one hundred miles away, had a different experience.

Huddled in their heavy grey prison coats, with mittened fingers and wool shawls pulled over their heads and faces, the women could hear the creaking of snow under the sledge runners as the frost-whitened horses, icicles hanging from their nostrils, made their way over treacherous mountain roads. Before they reached their destination, a February blizzard descended on their line of sledges, making the trip even more hazardous.

Near the end of the journey the women looked down to see in a hollow below, a snow-covered square surrounded by a high brick wall. Inside the square they could make out a long, grey, one-story wooden house that one of them said resembled a lizard, and several outbuildings. Outside the wall, to one side, there was a collection of what looked like peasant huts.

This was Mal'tsev Women's Prison. "God! Oh, God! Where have they taken us? Our eyes looked down like into a grave." Inside the lizard-like building the women found six large rooms. Three rooms at one end were assigned to the politicals, and the three at the other end to the criminals. Everything was in disrepair: walls crumbling, windows drafty, doorways falling to pieces. It was like an abandoned barracks.

> We didn't have enough clothes to keep us warm. We froze at night, we froze during the day. We tried to warm ourselves by drinking tea, which was usually cold by the time it got from the samovar to the table, and by running around the courtyard during the exercise period in a temperature of 40° below freezing. . . . In the evening, well-wrapped-up figures, some sharing a blanket, sat around tables, reading and studying in the light of petrol lamps. In moments of dead silence, when you tore yourself away from what you were reading, you had an extraordinary sense of how that room was cut off from the world of life. You felt with penetrating keenness the dead silence of the frost-bound mountain tops, the steppes, the taigas, the dreadful isolation of our microscopic world.

The women who wrote about it gave a kaleidoscopic view of prison life and their reaction to the prison experience. Despite rough handling by local police at the time of their arrests, the ominous symbolism of iron gates clanging shut behind them as they entered local jails in Russia, their detention in the deportation centers in Moscow and initially even in the Siberian *katorga*, their mood at first was jubilant and the prison regime was light. High spirits prevailed in the prisons of Russia, filled with young radicals, in 1906–1908. There was joy, defiance, hope, love for fellow worker and fellow man. Feisty leaders staged hunger strikes, incited demonstrations inside and outside prison walls, circulated broadsides, stretched out their arms through barred windows to wave flags and to cheer incoming and outgoing prisoners, and sang revolutionary songs.

A major difference between the Russian revolutionaries' prison life and their lives outside prison walls was that the men and women were for the first time separated. Several women wrote of an initial prison experience of pleasant shock at being greeted with the special tender sympathy of women comrades locked in cells on either side of the long corridors of the women's quarters they walked through. But comforting as it may have been to have the female presence in the grim confines of prison, these women were not feminists. Their goal was not women's rights. They had no thought of organizing their female comrades. They saw themselves as fighters for freedom and human rights for all. They had joined local illegal Esser or anarchist groups in which they made up around one-third of the membership and served alongside men, often in leadership positions. The Nerchinsk prison world was a world of men's prison areas and women's prison areas. All communication was illegal (although letters were exchanged by stealth and bribery). Losing touch over the years, the horizons of both the men and the women were narrowed by their separation. The spirit of the revolutionary movement itself suffered from it.

Living in Mal'tsev behind high stone walls beyond which sentries marched night and day, surrounded by endless mountain peaks, vistas of emptiness seemed to stretch to infinity. Irina Kakhovskaya said:

> At first one's mind was flooded with pictures of friends and of nature, the dreams of escape. One wrote long letters to friends which had to be immediately torn up, or sat endlessly doing algebraic or geometric problems—all to avoid thinking, to kill time, and to prepare oneself for the night's sleep that one hoped would be filled with wonderful dreams.

The only link with freedom for the women in the *katorga* was the correspondence with their families they were permitted to carry on under strict prison censorship. No political subjects were to be mentioned. They were also permitted, subject to prison regulations, to receive parcels containing items they requested from friends and relatives, such as paints, paper, photographic equipment, musical instruments, and books (until after several years, books were banned and those in their library burned).

Katorga means "hard labor imprisonment" but in the 1906–1911 era there was no hard labor for politicals in the women's prisons of Siberia. At Mal'tsev there was no work at all. "Locked up in our half of the prison, we did whatever we wanted to. The administrator saw us only at the perfunctory roll call," one of the prisoners said. The result was unbelievable monotony—not the bloody drama of the male prisons.

Gradually it became apparent that if the time ever came when they could go back to a free life, there was a real danger they would emerge from the prison experience as spiritual cripples. The escape for many of them was through discussion and disputation in their small community of comrades and in the world of books. "In the course of our many years in prison," wrote Irina Kakhovskaya, "this double world was an unexhaustible spring of life, happiness and anxiety."

Behind bars in the most remote part of the Russian Empire, these women, who had been recruited by their battle organizations to kill, began mercilessly to question their own and each other's motives and political beliefs. Why had they become terrorists? Most of them said it was simply by following their natural instincts of horror over the conditions of life suffered by the people, especially the peasants, of Russia. They were moved to fiery anger, and it was this anger that fueled their will to commit terrorist acts. They acted spontaneously 'from the heart," with a burning desire to avenge injustice by an attack on an official they saw as a symbol of tsarist tyranny. They were inspired by the heroism of the martyrs of freedom in Russia's past and by the "fighting terrorists" of their own day.

The Essers, heirs of the Narodnaya Volya who had gloried in their killing of Tsar Aleksandr II, were the most belligerent of all Russia's political parties. In the ranks of the Esser party the women had found fulfillment. The comradeship of like-minded youth gave their lives meaning. Instead of leading what they saw as the useless lives of their mothers and sisters in the social milieu of their middle- or upper-class families, the Esser activists were engaged in a continuous round of daring acts; quick, risky strikes against hated authorities; breathtaking escapes; and, if they were caught, harrowing experiences at the hands of their captors. As Sanya Izmailovich put it in one of her letters from Mal'tsev:

> How clearly are those days engraved on my soul. . . . They live before my eyes so vividly that even the brightest dream pales in comparison.

Nastya Bitzenko said she was compelled to write about the Mal'tsev women to combat what appeared to be the prevailing view that Russian terrorists were the heartless, soulless beings portrayed by the ex-terrorist Boris Savinkov.[2] In his novel *Kon' Blednyi* (Pale Horse), Savinkov indicated there was little difference between a terrorist killing a man and a hunter killing a rabbit.

Not so, said Nastya. The women's discussions at Mal'tsev showed that it was the sensitive ones who had embraced terrorism, the ones who in their extreme youth "in freedom" had felt sharply the sins of man. They had eagerly grasped revolution as the solution, accepted the necessity of terrorism; in volunteering to kill, they sacrificed the ultimate human value—life itself. They came into the *katorga* morally naked. Their acts came back to overwhelm them with moral anguish.

In a continuous dialogue of merciless questioning the women subjected their motives as revolutionaries to severe scrutiny. They agreed that Russia must be changed. But change of what? Society? Or man? And why must it be accomplished by the sword? Does one person have "the right" to kill another? Can a person really kill "for the love of the people" when, in fact, the heart of the killer is far from loving "the people"? When a person kills for revolution and for socialism, is he or she killing for "all the people, far and near"? Or only for comrades in the party? Or for the somewhat wider circle of those who sympathize with the party's aims and struggles? All values underwent re-evaluation at Mal'tsev, and each woman was faced with the stark question: How do I justify my life? Is there any cause that is pure and undefiled? What is the true path to save the world? Who has proved it is socialism? What is the role of personality? Of conscience? Who says we act in behalf of the masses—to whom actually we do not and cannot relate?

---

[2]Boris Savinkov left Russia and the Esser party after masterminding the assassinations of Pleve in 1904 and the Grand Duke Sergei in 1905. Disillusioned with terror, he turned to novel writing. Writing under the pseudonym V. Ropshin, Savinkov's *Kon' Blednyi* was published in Nice, France, in 1913.

"Who said?" "Who proved?" These questions were voiced over and over again. No one emerged, Nastya said, without suffering a weakening of faith in socialism, in revolution, and in the tactics of terrorism, propaganda, and class warfare.

In her discussion of Mal'tsev, Nastya Bitzenko made no effort to disguise her own lack of love for "the people." Maria Spiridonova, on the other hand, saw the laboring masses of Russia as the first people in the world to move out wholeheartedly into revolutionary action. She saw them selflessly rushing into the revolutionary battle, strong, ready for death, giving themselves freely.

> Their souls burned with the fortunes of the struggle and with their faith in the golden future. No one could be holier, greater, more excellent than the Russian revolutionary masses.

Maria was aware, she said, that when thousands of peasants and laboring people went out, full of revolutionary enthusiasm, in demonstrations and strikes against the 1906–1908 tsarist "pacification drives," were arrested and crowded into prisons, were separated from their work which gave their lives meaning, these men and women became debauched. Drunkenness, gambling, and fighting occurred. In the narrow confines of prison life, behavior which outside, "in freedom," would have been dissipated in society at large, caused consternation and contributed to the questioning by some of the terrorist women of the power of revolutionary faith to change and uplift human behavior.

Sanya Izmailovich said of Maria that her soul shuddered in terror at the animal in man, but still she uttered hymns of bright love for "the people," a love which conquered all torments she and others suffered. To her the love of mankind was one of the basic tenets of socialism.

There seemed to be a possibility for direct contact with "the people" at Mal'tsev, since more than half the prisoners were convict women, mostly peasants or of peasant origin, yet such contact was almost nonexistent. Irina Kakhovskaya maintained that if there had not been strict prison regulations designed to prevent mingling "we would have gone to them with books and had a cultural exchange that would have enriched their lives and ours." As it was, living side by side in the remote vastness of their prison existence, the two types of prisoners could not help developing an awareness of each other.

The politicals, after much effort, succeeded in getting permission for their comrade, Sarra Dantzig, a *feldsher* or medical assistant, to minister to the often serious medical needs of the criminal women, for the prison doctor seldom came to Mal'tsev. The political prisoners also got permission to provide paper and stamps and to write down at the dictation of the illiterate criminal women their pathetic, ungrammatical messages to their families in their home villages. Also, until it was stopped by the authorities, Sanya Izmailovich ran a school for the children of Mal'tsev (there were usually about one hundred of them), most of whose mothers were criminals.

The criminal woman looked upon the terrorist women with adoration. When Irina Kakhovskaya and the criminal prisoner, Danilushkina, who came with her in the same convoy, arrived at Mal'tsev they were met by the famous terrorist inmates: Spiridonova, Bitzenko, Izmailovich, and others. Irina and her companion pronounced their names with reverence and Danilushkina broke down and cried for joy.

The politicals were themselves constantly aware of the shame of their prisoner status, but to the criminal women they were *baryni*, ladies. They responded to the "ladies" with village deference and humble gratitude. It seemed never to occur to the peasant women that the distance between them and the "ladies" could ever be bridged. Nor did the "ladies" know how to bridge the gap. So the two categories of women prisoners never got beyond a "mistress-servant" relationship. Irina Kakhovskaya thought a serious study should be made of the criminal women in the *katorga*, many of whom regarded prison life as heaven compared with that they lived "in freedom."

In Mal'tsev, Nastya Bitzenko said, the political prisoners were desperate for justification, for belief in something to preserve their sanity. Esser party slogans were still mouthed, but they had become empty phrases. Some women sought fulfillment in a kind of Christian humility, in love and forgiveness. Some looked for it in books, in art, in work. Nonetheless, many found themselves utterly without hope and became internally dead. Many made clear their disinclination ever again to assume an active political role. They did not, therefore, come back in 1917 from the prisons of Siberia a solid phalanx of women committed to work together for a common goal.

To Maria Spiridonova the effect of prison life was to reduce everything to a bare minimum—a minimum of comradeship, a minimum of moral principles, a minimum of human dignity. To the sensitive soul this was torment, and she asked: Can anyone under torment be normal and healthy? In prison, she said, no one is healthy. Being in prison for a long time results in an illness she defined as "a horrible emptiness."

Maria dismissed the constant questioning of values and ideals that Nastya made so much of as the quibbling of undisciplined, bourgeois minds. The prison debates of the women, Maria said, reflected their own inadequacies, intensified in the confining conditions of prison life, not the inadequacies of the philosophy of socialism or the revolutionary tactics of Russia's political groups.

Maria saw the very success of the revolutionary movement in the 1905–1906 period as a major reason for its weakening hold on many who had rushed into it. The soaring revolutionary spirit took off so spectacularly that hordes of euphoric people poured into comradely collectives where they sang revolutionary songs and became involved in exciting activities. Revolution was a kind of holiday that took them out of their drab, everyday pursuits. It was those who had joined the revolution for excitement who were the most tormented by having to sit indefinitely in prison. Spiridonova saw the young educated women of bourgeois background as having a smattering of knowledge and a nodding acquaintance with revolutionary ideology but lacking the discipline of serious mental endeavor. So in the *katorga* they spent their days in endless get-togethers, characterized by fractious discord, quarrels over the meaning of words and terminology, and even petty meanness.

Maria attributed the initial instability of the terrorist women to the fact that they had not gone into Siberian exile in an entirely normal state of mind. They had been involved in assassinations or assassination plots. They had been sentenced to death and held in prison for weeks or months expecting to be hanged. Their prison experience in Russia—unlike, that of the Siberian *katorga*—was a time of excitement. Ties with the illegal movements were maintained. Sitting in jail under the immediate threat of death was to the girl revolutionary a time of unearthly radiance. It was a segment of her life when time was not, when plunges into deep loneliness were followed by feelings of loving oneness with every human being in the world. Yet existing between life and death, even if it was only a few weeks, was a terrible strain. In some cases, when a woman had plotted or carried out an assassination with a male comrade, she had experienced the shock of his execution and felt guilty and unworthy that she still lived.

News of executions, assassinations, and brutal reprisals of tsarist authorities filled the corridors of Russia's prisons. Death was the ever-present specter that each terrorist woman was, by turns, rushing to embrace or seeking in a wild frenzy to escape. Then, suddenly, each had her death sentence commuted to life imprisonment in the *katorga*. The return to life was a letdown—a shock to the whole nervous system. To Maria, the shattering experiences of the women as terrorists was explanation enough for the disillusionment that came to so many of them in Siberia.

Maria did not condemn the disgruntled ones, though she disagreed with and pitied them. She said it was only the dedicated revolutionary who in prison could and did find ways to expand his or her knowledge and revolutionary skills. The dedicated engaged in constant work: teaching, writing, reading. They carried on illegal correspondence with other party members in the *katorga*. Maria said she hoped some day her large correspondence with Yegor Sazonov[3] would be found and published. It would throw much

[3]The popular veneration of Yegor Sazonov, the assassin of Pleve, matched that of Spiridonova.

light on the deepening conviction of the dedicated revolutionaries and on significant events, especially the suffering of the men in the Nerchinsk prisons during the harsh years after 1906. These letters would also reveal the efforts of Spiridonova, and the few at Mal'tsev who shared her dedication, to persuade their comrades to engage in hunger strikes and other means of protest over prison cruelties suffered by the male politicals. The ideological disarray at Mal'tsev was such that Maria's efforts failed.

One of The Six, Mariya Shkolnik, became obsessed with one thought—escape. She succeeded in being transferred to the prison hospital in Irkutsk in 1911 for an operation. Once there, she appealed to Esser comrades in Irkutsk to help her escape. She vowed she would die rather than go back to prison. Her prison break is the story of one amazing episode after another. She got out of Siberia and, via China and Europe, eventually arrived in the United States where she settled and wrote of her revolutionary and prison experience. This account was translated and published in 1914 as a book, *The Life Story of a Russian Exile*. She said that only the friendly feeling they had for one another sustained the women of Mal'tsev through their bitter hours.

Irina Kakhovskaya wrote that as the years passed, the women of Mal'tsev worked out a mutual adaptation. Life became more harmonious. Those who had as young girls been drawn into terrorism by an instinctive response to the excitement of the moment, with only a jumble of theories in their heads, realized their unpreparedness for life as revolutionaries. Their study, which included the works of Nietzsche, Darwin, Romain Rolland, the Bible, Indian philosophy, Dostoevsky, Tolstoy, Solov'ev, and Merezhkovsky, their discussions, and the general intellectual atmosphere of Mal'tsev—even the disputes—matured them.

Several of the Mal'tsev women including Maria Spiridonova, were due to be reclassified as disfranchised exiles in 1911. Disfranchised exiles were confined to the prison areas of Siberia but were permitted to live outside prison walls in remote communities. Life for the banished exile was somewhat freer than it was in prison.

On November 28, 1910, Yegor Sazonov committed suicide in the men's prison of Gorni Serentui to protest the cruel prison regime in the men's prisons of Nerchinsk. When his suicide became known, mass demonstrations took place in every city of Russia. Thirty thousand students marched in Moscow to protest the cruel Siberian prison conditions. The pronouncements of tsarist officials and the editorials in the reactionary press linked the names of Sazanov and Spiridonova as the regime's worst criminals. All prospects for a lightened prison regime for the women terrorist *katorzhnitsy* quickly faded, and an unwelcome order soon came to Mal'tsev. As a punitive measure, all Mal'tsev political prisoners must move at once to Akatue.

Maria Spiridonova attempted an escape during the transfer of the women, but it was foiled, largely because she was at the time seriously ill. At Akatue the women were oppressed by a prison regime that had become more severe after Sazanov's suicide. The harsh regime continued until the outbreak of World War I in August 1914, when the chief torturers were called back to Russia where they soon departed for army service on the Austro-German front. The prisoners of Nerchinsk were assigned war work, largely sewing uniforms and making shoes for Russia's armed forces. But life at Akatue for the women bore no resemblance to what one of them nostalgically called "our blessed existence at Mal'tsev."

The days, the months, the years passed in dreary monotony. The once-bright fire of hope of the revolutionaries was almost extinguished.

Statistical Information on 1907–1911 Mal'tsev Inmates

Of the 72 political prisoners who were inmates of Mal'tsev Women's Prison between 1907 and 1911, statistical information gathered on 67 of them appeared as "unpublished documents" in *Na Zhenskoi Katorge*, edited by Vera Figner in 1930.

Age at the Time of Arrest

Under 21	18
21–30	37
30–40	7
Over 40	5

Social Background

Peasants	12
Petty Bourgeois	26
Merchant	5
Clergy	2
Gentry	14
Daughter of a political prisoner	1
Unclassified	7

Nationality

Russians	37
Jews	23
Poles	7
Georgians	3
Latvians	2
No information	5

Reason for Imprisonment

Participant in a battle organization	14
Possession of explosives	13
Terrorist acts	7
Armed resistance	2
Work on an illegal printing press	13
Participating in a party conference	1
Occupying a conspiratorial apartment	1
Running away from forced settlement	3
Possession of a gun	1
Acts of expropriation (armed robbery to obtain money for a political party)	4
Conspiring against Tsar Nikolai II	2
Possession of prohibited literature	2
[4]Mozyrskiiu respubliku	1
No information	3

Sentences

Death (commuted to various terms of imprisonment)	9
Life imprisonment	1
15 years	5
13 years, 6 months	1
12 years	1
10 years	2
9 years	1
8 years	7
6 years	13
5 years	3
4 years	23
3 years	1

Occupation before Arrest

Factory Workers	10
Dressmakers	6
Teachers	5

Fate of the Prisoners

Escaped	1
Forced settlement in Siberia	18

[4]This designation may mean that the woman supported a group favoring a republic in the town of Mozyr (near Minsk).

Occupation before Arrest

Doctor's assistants, dentists, midwives, nurses .	9
Draftswomen	1
Students	10
Professional revolutionaries	20
No regular occupation	4
No information on occupation	2

Fate of the Prisoners

Freed in 1917
   from prison 10
   from settlement 36
By 1930, of the total number of
prisoners, 72, 9 had died; 2 of
these had died before 1917.

Education at time of Arrest

Literate but little education	14
Completed lower school	10
Completed middle school	26
Incomplete higher education	17

Political Affiliation at Time of Arrest

Essers	36
Esser Maximalists	2
Social Democrats (Bolshevik)	5
Social Democrats (Menshevik)	2
Social Democrats (Poles and Latvians)	3
Bund	2
Anarchists	13
P.P.C.	1
No Party affiliation	3

1930 Political Affiliation

Bolsheviks	6
No party affiliation	45
Bund (abroad)	1
No information	7

Year Arrested

1905	1
1906	23
1907	21
1908	13
1909	5
1910	3
1911	1

1930 Occupations[5]

Office jobs	20
Physical labor	10
Socially dependent[6]	16
Student	1
House manager	5
Without occupation	1
Unknown	5

[5]Several of the women, including Maria Spiridonova, Irina Kakhovskaya, Sanya Izmailovich and others had been under house arrest for several years before 1930. Fanny Kaplan had been shot. They are not accurately recorded in these statistics.

[6]Unable to work.

ANNOTATED REFERENCES

Four of The Six wrote and published accounts of their *katorga* experience. One of their associates, a later arrival, Irina Kakhovskaya, also wrote about hers. Vera Figner edited a book, *Na Zhenskoy Katorge* (Moscow, 1930), a collection of articles written by eleven other fellow prisoners based on their recollections. It is from these accounts the information in this chapter has been taken.

Anastasia Bitsenko, "V Mal'tsevskoy Zhenskoy Katorzhnoy Tiur'me 1907–1910 k Kharakteris-tiki Nastroenii" (In the Mal'tsev Woman's Hard Labor Prison 1907–1910 with Reference to Morale), *Katorga i Ssylka*, no. 7, 1923. A fairly detailed account of Bitsenko's early career as a revolutionary appears in the first edition of the *Bol'shaia Sovetskaia Entsiklopediia*, vol. 6 (1927), but not in later editions. After 1917 Bitsenko's main claim to fame was her appointment as an Esser representative to the negotiating team that went to Brest-Litovsk to make peace with Germany in 1918. The Essers, however, opposed the Brest-Litovsk treaty, and Bitsenko soon joined the Communist party. She held minor posts in the party hierarchy.

Aleksandra Izmailovich, "Iz Proshlogo," *Katorga i Ssylka*, no. 8, 1924, describes entering Bu-tyrki, the train ride across Russia and Siberia, and the arrival and welcome of The Six at Akatue.

Irina Kakhovskaya, "Iz Vospominaniy o Zhenskoy Katorge," *Katorga i Ssylka*, no. 1 (22), 1926, gives information on her own arrest and her trip to Siberia. She describes going through awe-some mountain passes to get to Mal'tsev and has details on the prison interior and the daily routine of life there for political and criminal women prisoners. Further details on these matters are given by F. N. Rabzilovska and L. P. Orestova in their article in Figner, *Na Zhenskoy Katorge*. Irina Kakhovskaya's article cited here is also reprinted in Figner's book.

Marie Sukloff (Mariya Shkol'nik), *The Life Story of a Russian Exile*, New York, 1914, written "for the American public" when she settled in the United States after a spectacular escape from the Siberian *katorga* in 1911. In 1918 she returned to Russia, but not until 1927 was a Russian version of her book brought out in Moscow titled *Zhizn' Byvshei Terroristki* (The Life of a Former Terrorist Woman). In the Russian edition, heavily edited to reflect the Bolshevik line, Shkol'nik announced she had recently joined the Communist Party and apologized for having, at an early age, "accidentally" become an Esser. She wrote one of the articles in Figner's *Na Zhenskoy Katorge*, "Moi Pobeg" (My Escape). The best account of her escape is "Pobeg Marii Shkol'nik" (The Escape of Mariya Shkol'nik), *Katorga i Ssylka*, no. 2, 1921. Shkol'nik served as a minor functionary in the Soviet bureaucracy until her death in 1955.

Maria Spiridonova, *Iz Vospominaniy o Nerchinskoy Katorge* (From My Recollections of the Nerchinsk Prison Area), written in 1920, published in Moscow, 1926. An article she wrote for *Pravda* (published December 20, 1918), "Prosh Prosh'ian," at the time of his death, contains information on him as a fellow *katorzhnik* and political associate, as well as a few things about her own prison experience. The *Pravda* article was republished in *Katorga i Ssylka*, no. 9, 1924.

Entsiklopedicheskiy Slovar', 41 volumes, published at the end of the nineteenth century and the beginning of the twentieth in St. Petersburg, has excellent descriptions of towns and cities, many accompanied by maps, including Chita and other Siberian cities. There is a map of the Nerchinsk Prison area in Figner, *Na Zhenskoy Katorge*.

A book containing many excerpts taken from prisoner recollections of former inmates of the Nerchinsk prison area is G. N. Chemodanov, *Nerchinskaia Katorga*, Moscow, 1924.

M. N. Gernet, *Istoriia Tsarskoy Tiur'my* (A History of the Tsarist Prison), Moscow, 1948, in vol. 3, says the Prison Administration in 1900 had 895 prisons, with a prison population of 686,690, and tens of thousands being brought in each year. More is known about Mal'tsev than other prisons because so many of its "politicals" wrote about it.

8

The 1917 Revolution and the Betrayal of the Women Fighters for Freedom

By February 1917, more than five million Russian soldiers lay dead on the battlefields of World War I. A succession of military defeats, added to repeated attacks by revolutionaries in the years before the war, had seriously weakened the tsarist regime. Still, Tsar Nikolai II was ordering military contingents into battle; still, there were masses of soldiers, Cossacks, and gendarmes patrolling the streets of Russia's cities ready to shoot down disturbers of the peace.

There was a severe food shortage. As more husbands, fathers, and sons were drafted into the armed forces, increasing numbers of women worked in factories, often thirteen hours a day for miserable pay. Then they had to stand in long lines on icy streets at bakeries, waiting to buy the mainstay of their sustenance—bread. Often all they got was a "Sold Out" sign and the doors of the bakery slammed shut. When a woman actually did get a loaf of precious bread, she would make a sign of the cross and burst into tears. Anger and resentment were piling up in the hearts of Russia's working women.

Women's Day had been celebrated in Russia on February 23 for four years.[1] Small in comparison to the Women's Day rallies and street demon-

---

[1] It was March 8 in Western Europe. In 1910, at the urging of Clara Zetkin, a member of the Women's Division of the German Social Democratic party, the Second International Conference of Women Socialists meeting in Copenhagen named March 8 (February 23 in Russia) International Women's Day. Beginning in 1911, Women's Day has been celebrated in many countries. The first celebration in Russia was in 1913.

strations in Western European countries such as Sweden, Denmark, Germany, and Switzerland, the day was important to Russia's working women and they were preparing to go into the streets on that day in February 1917.

Meantime, the Bolshevik Party Central Committee had been trying to organize and direct the activities of the working women of the Vyborg District of Petrograd[2] where there were many factories. They had decided that organization and the maintenance of discipline were more important than wasting energy on Women's Day, which they determined was an insignificant event. The Bolshevik leader sent to manage a meeting of women called on the eve of Women's Day explained that although February 23 was a special day, they would not be observing it. He emphasized they must follow the decisions of their true leaders, the Bolsheviks.

The Vyborg women replied not with words but with action. On the morning of February 23, meetings called by the Bolsheviks in several factories to reinforce their instructions to the women not to demonstrate but to go back to their jobs turned into stormy confrontations.

The women did not go back to work. They defiantly went into the streets where they marched from factory to factory shouting "Bread! Bread!" When factory workers heard the chorus of women's voices, they left their machines, looked out windows, and listened to the women's words: "Stop work!" "Come out and join us!" "March for bread!" By twos, threes, then hundreds, factory workers—women and men—stopped their machines, threw on their overcoats, and rushed out to join the march. Before the day was over some 130,000 workers had left their jobs.

To the cries of "Bread" the marchers added "Down with autocracy. Down with the war." Women who were not laborers, waiting in line in front of bakeries, joined the march, as did passers-by and those who came out of their homes to see what was going on.

By the next day the number of strikers was even larger. Bolshevik and other party leaders were no more successful in controlling the crowds in the streets than were the Petrograd police. The police failed to hold back the surge of people approaching a bridge leading to the Nevsky Prospekt, the main street of Petrograd, because this was February. The river was frozen over and the marchers crossed on the ice. They got to Nevsky Prospekt, to the square in front of the Kazan Cathedral, and on to the street where the Duma, or parliament, was meeting.

Cossacks were called in. The marchers were prepared for bloodshed as the mounted Cossacks with unsheathed sabers charged into the crowd. But the Cossacks did not strike! Holding their sabers high, they smiled! One of them even winked! Ordered again to charge, the Cossacks repeated the charade. Again. Then again. Women began to talk to the Cossacks, and

---

[2]During the War, the name of St. Petersburg was Russianized to Petrograd.

when their officers attempted to stop this fraternizing with the crowd, the men did not obey.

For five days the strike continued and grew in size and intensity. On the Tsar's command, troops were sent in to suppress the disorder. The soldiers mutinied. "Enough blood has been shed," said their spokesmen. "It is time to die for freedom." And the soldiers turned not on the masses in the streets, but on their officers.

The revolutionary enthusiasm set off by the women of Petrograd soon spread to all parts of the Russian Empire. The Tsar's ministers, some in disguise, fled their posts in disarray. Tsarist authority collapsed. The Tsar abdicated. This was *The Revolution!* Long-awaited! Long-heralded! The news crackled along miles of telegraph lines, reaching, finally, the prisons of the Nerchinsk *katorga*. Revolution meant freedom! Stunned at first, the prisoners began going through unlocked gates. Their jailors fled. They walked to the stations of the Trans-Siberian railway where, midst flowers and ovations, they got on crowded trains rushing them back to European Russia.

One who did not rush back was Maria Spiridonova. To carry out her vow not to return until she had proof that every political prisoner in the Trans-Baikal was free, she moved only one hundred fifty miles—from Akatue Prison to Chita.

Chita. The Paris of Siberia, some called it. The capital of the Trans-Baikal, long a city of prisons and prisoners, the main transfer point for *katorzhniki* and the place where prison records were filed. The motley population of this city of forty-four thousand in 1917 included Trans-Baikal Cossacks, Buryats and other native people, as well as former Russian prisoners who had settled there after their prison terms were completed. The best-remembered prison settlers were the Decembrists who arrived there in 1828, soon joined by their wives who followed them into exile.

In Chita, too, the tsarist government collapsed in February 1917. Remembering Maria Spiridonova as a beloved heroine, the people of Chita followed her lead when she came from Akatue and immediately set things humming. She helped them create revolutionary self-government, established orderly procedures for getting prisoners on trains, and find temporary employment and aid for stranded prisoners. A representative assembly and city officers were elected. Maria Spiridonova was elected mayor.

In the French Revolution a Parisian mob destroyed the hated Bastille, symbol of *Ancien Régime* oppression. In Russia the order to detonate the Chita Prison, for decades a grim symbol of the tsarist penal system, was given by a small, determined woman, Maria Spiridonova. She hated prisons with a furious fervor. She hated the death penalty. She hated tyranny. To destroy its symbols was to clear the way to build a new world in which such edifices would no longer be needed.[3] As the walls and barred windows shuddered, disintegrated, and fell in a smoking heap, Maria Spiridonova and the people of Chita rejoiced. Satisfied that no political prisoners remained behind bars in the Trans-Baikal area and the revolutionary government in Chita was working, Maria Spiridonova left in May 1917.

As Maria traveled toward European Russia with several of her Mal'tsev comrades who had stayed to work with her in Chita, she must have wondered: How would the women be received by the Esser party? The women sent to Siberia in such large numbers before World War I had carried on illegal Esser party activities as equals of their male comrades. Many had served as leaders and decision makers. Now that the revolution had come, would they resume their former positions in the Esser party organization? Since women had played a larger role in the Esser party than in any other Russian political party, what happened to them after 1917 was crucial to the future of women's political equality in revolutionary Russia.

Of the *Narodniki* women, only two in 1917 got themselves into positions significant enough to give them the potential—momentarily—to affect the course of events: Maria Spiridonova and Katerina Breshkovskaya. Their positions in 1917 rested squarely on their terrorist past! Neither the Mensheviks nor the Bolsheviks—nor any other political party during the revolution—had a woman member whose leadership role compared to that of Maria Spiridonova.[4] Spiridonova and Breshkovskaya soon found that they were remembered and revered by the Russian people, who cheered them whenever they appeared in public, but largely ignored by the male leaders of the Esser party, some of whom had become ministers in the Provisional Government, the temporary government that came into existence when the tsarist regime collapsed.

Katerina Breshkovskaya's return in March was a triumphal journey. She rode in a special car[5] on the Trans-Siberian Railroad train that seven years before had transported her to Siberia handcuffed, surrounded by gendarmes in a prison car with barred windows. Great crowds gathered to greet her at every station. In Petrograd she walked into a huge reception for her in the imperial waiting room of the Nikolaevsky Station, while vast crowds thronged the streets waving red flags and singing the "Marseillaise" as they

---

[3]I. Z. Steinberg (*In the Workshop of the Revolution,* Toronto, 1953, p. 66) stated that on her return to Petrograd in 1917, Spiridonova came to him after his appointment as minister of Justice in the new Soviet government, to demand that he give an order to blow up the Peter Paul Fortress. He regretted that this could not be done because it had become a depository for huge quantities of dynamite.

[4]For a general discussion of women leaders of various parties in the early part of the revolution see Richard Stites, *The Women's Liberation Movement in Russia: Feminism, Nihilism, and Bolshevism 1860–1930,* Princeton, 1978, chapter IX.

[5]Alexander Kerensky, appointed minister of Justice in the first days of the revolution, after proclaiming a general amnesty for all political prisoners, issued a special order that the seventy-three-year-old Babushka be escorted at once to the capital.

waited for a glimpse of her. She was moved into the rooms of the deposed Tsaritsa in the Winter Palace where she received a multitude of guests and held innumerable receptions.

There were headlines galore. News photos of Babushka with a white shawl over her head show her riding in an open touring car with Kerensky, the minister of Justice, and other dignitaries, waving to excited crowds. A photo of Babushka before the delegates of the Petrograd Soviet of Workers' and Soldiers' Deputies illustrates a news story describing the applause that rocked the walls as she appealed to the delegates with a fiery call for unity and dedicated work for the people. She attended the Third Congress[6] of the Esser party in Moscow and was by acclamation made an "honorary" member of the Executive Committee, but she was given no office in the party or in the provisional government.

Two months later, Maria Spiridonova journeyed from Chita to Moscow, cheered at every railroad station, and arrived in time to attend the Third Esser Party Congress. At the May 31 session, the chairman made it the first order of business to greet five returning heroines who had just taken their seats among the delegates: M. A. Spiridonova, A. A. Bitsenko, N. S. Terentieva, I. K. Kakhovskaya, and L. P. Porestova. His praise was high and the applause was prolonged and noisy. But when Maria Spiridonova was nominated for membership on the Executive Committee, she was not elected.

Most of the male Esser, Bolshevik, and Menshevik leaders in 1917 had returned from European, not Siberian, exile. Early in his career Lenin had served a term of banishment to Siberia, but in 1900 he left Russia for Europe and did not return until April 1917. In the interim he helped organize the illegal Russian Social Democratic party and in 1903 became the leader of the Bolshevik faction of that party; members of the other faction were called Mensheviks. Victor Chernov, the head of the Essers, had been under police surveillance for his illegal political activity from the time he entered the university in the 1890s. Later, as an organizer of the illegal Esser (Socialist Revolutionary) party and an active terrorist, he shuttled back and forth from Russia to Europe. Arrested in Russia in 1905, he escaped abroad and remained in Geneva until 1917.

In the decade before 1917, Lenin and Chernov had engaged in political maneuvering in their own party ranks and had closely observed the all-male socialist parties of Western Europe, while their female counterparts in the Siberian *katorga* had been completely cut off from political activity. Maria Spiridonova's contacts, for example, had been through correspondence with other Siberian prisoners, and most of those among them who had been outstanding Esser leaders in the 1903–1908 period had died, escaped, or for other reasons were by 1917 no longer on the political scene. The prison

---

[6]Although it was called the "Third Congress," it was actually the Essers' first legal congress.

Bitzenko, Spiridonova, Terentieva, and Kakhovskaya after release, 1917

experience had, in fact, alienated vast numbers of *katorzhniki* from politics, both men and women. As one observer said, "When the prison gates opened, thousands streamed out devastated souls. They disappeared without a trace. They simply melted into society and ended up involuntary observers of great events."

Women who came back from the *katorga* prepared to take up where they left off a decade earlier soon found they had returned to a different Russia. The political unit was no longer the pre-revolutionary, small, clandestine local organization where the requirement for leadership was reckless daring and total commitment to sacrifice self, family, everything to the revolutionary cause. In sharp contrast, in 1917, people with a wide variety of backgrounds and political interests were flooding into the now-legal political parties. Soldiers, peasants, workers—almost entirely male—were the new political constituency. Each group, and, it often seemed, each individual was making strident demands, with no notion of self-sacrifice. The local political groups were the soviets, or councils, with their constantly changing membership due to frequent elections. Only a gifted orator or an experienced organizer could emerge as a leader in the soviets. Gone were the days when ignorant peasants and workers in the backwater of tsarist society would look up with reverence to the educated girl of gentry origin as their teacher and savior.

Revolutionary politics were in a maelstrom. Old institutions were being swept away. The people were on the move, burning with passions bottled up for generations, driven by loves and hates, and yearning to build a new destiny for themselves and Russia—now. In the midst of this turbulence, leaders and would-be leaders had to act and to control. If they did not, the surging masses would soon leave them behind. The revolution, for all the opportunities to change the world it opened up, turned out to be more like a nightmare than like the dream of Russia's revolutionary women.

In the first exciting days of the revolution, the Provisional Government in a flurry of reforming activity announced the end of the death penalty and the removal of Russia's traditional censorship and repression of civil rights. After that, the new government appeared to be stymied by power struggles and a curious lack of will to push through the major reforms Russian revolutionaries had been advocating for years.

Progress toward enactment of a revolutionary program was hampered because when the tsarist government fell, it was not replaced by a single authority but by two centers of power which sometimes cooperated and sometimes vied for control:

> *The Petrograd Soviet,*[7] a revolutionary council of workers' and soldiers' deputies, whose Executive Committee began to function from the first days of the February Revolution. As a popularly elected body, the Petrograd Soviet often had more power than the Provisional Government, and it had links to the local soviets that were soon elected in almost every town and village of Russia.

> *The Provisional Government,* essentially a cabinet of ministers chosen by remnants of the Fourth Duma (the Russian parliament which disbanded in February 1917), who declared they would serve as the executive head of the Russian state until an assembly to draw up a constitution could be elected. However, they repeatedly postponed the elections, and every few weeks ministers resigned and new ones were appointed. By April 1917 six of the ministers were Essers.

In addition to the confusion in the revolutionary government bodies, Russia's new leaders were overwhelmed by the war issue: Should Russia continue to fight, despite the disintegration of her military forces, despite economic exhaustion and revolution, despite the masses' hatred of the war? With German armies occupying Russia's western borders, threatening to march into her flat heartland, the members of the Provisional Government emerged as Russian nationalists. Even the Essers among them, who as socialists were theoretically anti-war internationalists dedicated to ideas of world peace and brotherhood, had convinced themselves the only way to peace was military victory over the German-Austrian Alliance. This meant cooperation with Russia's allies from tsarist times, Britain and France. The Provisional Government leaders believed Russia's new revolutionary spirit could be rallied for the necessary last big push to victory, which would give Russia Constantinople (Istanbul) and other territories promised her in the "Secret Treaties" tsarist Russia had made with Britain and France.

The Provisional Government's approach to peace was challenged by the Petrograd Soviet. One of its first proclamations, on March 14, 1917, was a demand for immediate negotiations for a just peace—a demand that re-

---

[7]The Russian word *sovet* (or *soviet*) means council.

flected the dominant mood of the war-weary Russian masses. The Petrograd Peace Proclamation "To the Peoples of the World" called on proletarians to rise in revolution, to refuse to serve as slaves of conquest for kings, landowners, and bankers. "Join our drive for a just peace with no annexations, no indemnities, and self-determination for all peoples."

The stirring Petrograd Peace Proclamation led to no socialist uprising for peace in Western Europe, but its terms were often repeated in revolutionary Russia in resolutions by the Petrograd and other soviets. These resolutions contradicted the war-to-victory policy being pursued by the Provisional Government and made revolutionary Russia's stand on war and peace ambiguous. The Esser party, with its huge peasant following, was the largest political party in Russia, but its leaders were unable, or unwilling, to put into effect the land reforms their peasant constituency expected; nor would they bring the pressure of their peasant constituency, with its loathing of the war, to bear on the Provisional Government to achieve the long-proclaimed socialist goal of peace.

Babushka, with no voice in the revolutionary governing bodies, but in her capacity as "honorary" member, attended the Executive Committee meetings of the Esser party and participated in the bitter debates taking place in the spring and early summer of 1917. The sparse reports available of the speeches she made show her impatience with the disunity among the leaders of her party. She sharply attacked them, pointing out that the hopes that so long had revolved around "The Revolution" were threatened with destruction by their inaction.

Oliver K. Radkey, making use of what documentation is available, is critical of Breshkovskaya's furious attacks on the leaders of her party.[8] Certainly there was reason for those attacks, but Babushka, who by 1917 had become a symbol of the party's heroic past, had lost her clout. Her impotence led to an observation she never voiced earlier in her career: despite her experience and knowledge and the fact her "head was in good order," she did not expect statesmen to pay great attention to her words "as is always the case between men and women".[9]

Breshkovskaya's stand on the war complicated her commitment to the revolution. Her conviction that Germany must be defeated was partly ideological and partly a reflection of her Russian patriotism. She identified Germany with Marxism which she had been denouncing for twenty years. She

---

[8]Oliver K. Radkey, The Agrarian Foes of Bolshevism, New York, 1957, pp. 291–92. Copyright © 1957 Columbia University Press. Reprinted by permission.

[9]She wrote this in a letter dated May 12, 1921, to Dr. E. H. Egbert, telling of her expectation that statesmen in the United States would not heed her dire warnings about the Bolsheviks, but she was led to this assumption by her 1917 experience in Russia. The letter is in the Archive Collection of the Hoover Institution on War, Revolution, and Peace, Stanford University, the Egbert Collection, Box 1, Folder A.

was sure the Bolshevik leaders, Lenin in particular, were in the pay of the capitalist German government and that it had in April 1917 brought Lenin back to Russia from his exile in Switzerland for its own purposes. Therefore, Lenin, with his talk of peace, was simply out to betray Russia to his German masters.

Ironically, pursuit of the war, which Babushka insisted on, with its heavy demands on production and manpower, guaranteed the failure of the non-Marxist socialist majority in the Provisional Government to carry out the social reforms that had so long been at the heart of their revolutionary programs. It pushed Babushka herself into the right wing of the Esser party and led her to use the large sums of money her American friends were showering on her to establish a newspaper and a press to propagate the cause. In the chaos of revolutionary politics, Babushka was going in one direction, the revolution in another.

Maria Spiridonova's approach to peace was straightforward. She called on the revolutionary leaders to clarify the issue by declaring an immediate armistice, then moving on with major revolutionary reforms. In calling for this policy she was fighting a losing battle in the ranks of her own party. At the Third Esser Party Congress in May 1917, a peace resolution was voted down 100 to 33. This vote revealed the first serious rift in the Esser party. The rift deepened as Victor Chernov and the Esser leaders sought to force a vote in favor of the Provisional Government's preparation for a spring military offensive. They also sought backing for the Provisional Government's decision to reimpose the death penalty against those who shirked their duty as soldiers to risk their lives for "home, land, and liberty," in an attempt to stop the high rate of desertion in Russia's armed forces.

Maria Spiridonova was as opposed to the death penalty as she was to a renewed war effort, but her spirited opposition did not prevent the majority vote for it. Party regulars also tossed aside Maria's warning that in neglecting land reform and reforms for the working classes the Esser party was betraying the people. She therefore made a decisive move. She joined and was soon elected leader of an opposition faction calling itself the Left Essers. Maria Spiridonova had become the head of what was soon to become a major Russian political party!

Ignored by Esser party leaders at the party congress in Moscow, Maria Spiridonova went in June to Petrograd (still the capital of Russia) where she was soon elected a member of the Petrograd Soviet. Shortly afterward she was elected president of the First Congress of Peasants' Soviets. Also elected to this body were Vera Figner and Katerina Breshkovskaya, neither of whom took an active role in it. Spiridonova joined the editorial board of the Esser newspaper *Znamia Truda* (The Banner of Labor) and edited a short-lived paper, *Nash Put'* (Our Way), which she used as a vehicle for her Cassandra-like calls for revolutionary action. The literary sections of both publications welcomed the enthusiastic outpourings of Russia's futurist writers, including Aleksandr Blok,[10] Andrei Bely, Sergei Esenin, and Alexis Remizov.

As president of the First Peasants' Congress of Soviets, Spiridonova energetically pushed forward what she thought was the most important task of the revolution: a comprehensive law to "socialize the land." This was the oldest reform advocated by Essers and by the Narodniki before them. It meant apportioning Russia's soil among the peasants who tilled it. Maria was convinced that when this task was accomplished, not only would it right an ancient wrong done the peasants when their land was appropriated by the nobility, but it would also bring to an immediate halt the increasing peasant turbulence and would solve the major economic, social, and political problems of twentieth-century Russia.

The question was whether any law worked out by the Peasants' Congress would be put into effect by the Provisional Government. By the summer of 1917, a socialist, Aleksandr Kerensky,[11] was premier, Victor Chernov had been minister of Agriculture since April, and six other socialists held ministerial posts—yet all that had been done about the land problem was turgid debate over the seemingly endless details of classifying landed property and defining existing forms of land tenure. As week followed week, action was postponed.

The Esser Party Congress met in August 1917. Maria Spiridonova, now the leader of the growing Left Esser faction, came with a program of action: first, for the Provisional Government to declare an immediate armistice on all fronts; and second, for the passage of legislation to give land to the peasants and control of production to the workers. Chernov shunted aside these issues and concentrated on wheedling out of the Congress a majority vote in favor of a proposal to back the Provisional Government in still another military effort, despite the disaster of the spring offensive.

The Left Essers failed at the Esser Party Congress so they took their program to the people. They made speeches, wrote articles, and rallied popular support, especially among the soldiers returning to the cities and villages.[12]

In the meantime revolutionary initiative was being seized by another out-of-power political party, the Bolsheviks. Lenin came back to Russia in April 1917. He had no official position in the Provisional Government and

---

[10]Blok's famous poems Skify (The Scythians) and Dvenadtsat' (The Twelve) were first published in Znamia Truda, February 20, 1918 and March 3, 1918.

[11]Kerensky was a Trudovik (from trudovoy-labor). He was a lawyer, not a laborer, and the Trudoviki were moderate socialists, so small in number they could hardly be called a party. He was, for all practical purposes, an Esser.

[12]The Esser party was by no means an exclusively peasant party. Large numbers of urban workers were Essers, as were professional people, especially school teachers and students. In The Workshop of the Revolution, Steinberg puts the number of workers who were Left Essers in Petrograd in November 1917 at 45,000.

wanted none, but he controlled the smallest and best disciplined socialist party in Russia. Immediately on his return, Lenin loosed an avalanche of criticism of the Provisional Government and launched a campaign to get Bolsheviks into the soviets. He expected to use the soviets as a power base for a takeover of the revolutionary government at the earliest possible moment.

The largest Social Democratic party in Russia in 1917 were the Mensheviks. In the early days of the revolution Menshevik leaders, along with the Essers, had played the leading role in the Petrograd Soviet and cooperated with the Provisional Government. They opposed Bolshevik leadership, policies, and tactics, but like the Esser leaders, they lost popular support because of their record of failure to push for peace and revolutionary reform.

Bolshevik speeches and banners boldly proclaimed:

> Down with the War!
> All Land to the People!
> All Power to the Soviets!
> Peace! Bread! Land!

"Socialization of the land" and "Immediate peace—at any price" cried the Bolsheviks. "We have smashed the Gordian knot of the land problem with a hammer." Lenin's fiery statements were the words of an activist and they struck a responsive chord in the heart of Maria Spiridonova. She, like Lenin, saw the necessity to act— to strike while the iron was hot, to grab responsibility and use it. And she did.

As a leader Maria Spiridonova had deficiencies. Her political education, acquired during eleven years of imprisonment in Siberia, had never taught her to use, or even to recognize until it was too late the strategy of lining up political allies to achieve a tactical gain, then brazenly casting them aside as traitors when their usefulness was over. Lenin had used and perfected this strategy in his years of political maneuvering in his Western European base of exile. After embracing Maria Spiridonova and the left Essers as allies in the Bolshevik takeover of power, Lenin's party began to deviate from their stated goals and resort to cruel and extra-legal methods. They found they had in Maria Spiridonova an ally who would not sacrifice her ideals. When they sought to silence her, she did not shut up and bow out of the revolutionary maelstrom.

By September 1917, the February Revolution had gone from euphoria to chaos. The Provisional Government put down a Bolshevik-inspired, bloody garrison mutiny—with its cries of "All Power to the Soviets"—in the first days of July. A few weeks later it suffered the failure of still another military offensive on the war front. In August it barely survived an attempted rightist coup by the ambitious General Kornilov. While the government, now headed by Kerensky, busied itself with paperwork and passing resolutions that never got carried out, a German land and sea breakthrough occurred in the north. The country was plagued by postal, transport, and telecommunication strikes and work stoppages, factory closings, food and fuel shortages, and disorder in the countryside as peasants were dividing up the land and torching manor houses.

Activist soldier and sailor units, factory workers, and other organized groups were swinging to the support of out-of-power leftist leaders and to the belief that the popularly elected soviets were the true revolutionary governing bodies. The Provisional Government, with its repeated promises of revolutionary reforms and its coalitions of parties that did not represent the masses and fell apart in the face of each new crisis, was rapidly losing favor. What the activists were anticipating was not the Provisional Government's long-promised Constituent Assembly; they were looking forward to the Second All-Russian Congress of Soviets scheduled to open October 25. There, it was expected, the delegates would pressure party leaders to challenge the ineffective Provisional Government and push for an immediate peace and revolutionary change through a soviet government.

This was the beginning of the new phase of the revolution which saw the emergence of Maria Spiridonova as a political leader, and her downfall.

In mid-October the Bolsheviks, having gained control of the Petrograd Soviet, spearheaded the establishment of a Military Revolutionary Committee which included Left Essers and a few representatives of other parties. Ostensibly the committee was formed to defend the Congress of Soviets from possible Provisional Government military action against it; but after several days of reconnoitering, on the night of October 24, the military units the Committee commanded were dispatched into the streets of Petrograd. On direct orders from Lenin they took over the transportation and communication centers. With virtually no opposition, they entered one government office after another, presented the officials they could find with ultimatums to surrender in the name of the Military Revolutionary Committee of the Petrograd Soviet, and took them into custody. In this swift maneuver, Bolshevik leaders ousted the unpopular, weak Provisional Government. This was the October Revolution! By the morning of October 25, only the Provisional Government headquarters, the Winter Palace, had not been taken (and Kerensky, among other officials, had fled).

The Bolsheviks expected to "legitimize" their coup d'état by obtaining a vote of confidence in the second All-Russian Congress of Soviets when it opened later that same day. The catch was, the Bolsheviks did not have a majority of delegates in the congress, despite their intensive campaign to infiltrate and control the local and regional soviets that elected them, and there were parties, leaders, and groups who opposed Bolshevik methods even if they approved their goals. Among them was Maria Spiridonova.

Of 670 delegates, 300 were Bolsheviks, 193 were Essers (over half of them Left Essers), 82 were Mensheviks, and the rest were representatives of smaller parties or delegates with no party affiliation. Actually, the Second Congress was made up largely of representatives from workers' and soldiers' soviets. Rural soviets sent delegates to their own congress: The Congress of Peasants' Soviets, of which Maria Spiridonova was president.

By late afternoon on October 25, hundreds of delegates to the Second Congress of Soviets were streaming into the brilliantly lighted assembly hall of the Smolny Institute (until February 1917 a school for daughters of the nobility). They walked through the halls, past doors where the neat, enameled signs of the girls' school were still intact: "Ladies' Classroom Number 4," "Teachers' Room," "Study Room." Above them were tacked up pieces of paper giving evidence of the new order: "Petrograd Soviet," "Union of Socialist Soldiers," "Esser Party," etc.

The delegates, most of them burly, bearded soldiers—some in full battle gear—and workers wearing black caps and smocks, along with a few long-haired peasants, came into the ballroom setting of the assembly hall. They sat on the spindly chairs, and when the chairs ran out settled themselves on the ornate stairways and perched on the balustrades of balconies. The bright light of the chandeliers was dimmed by a blue haze of tobacco smoke. Told by those on the platform not to smoke, they repeated to each other "Don't smoke," and went right on smoking. Voices of delegates rose and fell in a hum of excitement as they waited for the anticipated great events to begin. Also waiting, impatiently, on the platform, were the members of the Presidium (the executive body), holdovers from the First Congress of Soviets, who had a record of cooperating with the now ousted Provisional Government and its unpopular policies.

Against the backdrop of the occasional thud of a cannon's charge, fast-paced events were simultaneously occurring in the streets and the control centers of Petrograd and in the tension-filled back rooms of Smolny where political wheeling and dealing was going on at a furious pace. Lenin was impatiently awaiting news of the seizure of the Winter Palace where the last remnants of the Provincial Government were holding out and frantically working to get together a cabinet that he called the "Council of People's Commissars," commonly known as Sovnarkom. The fact that he asked Maria Spiridonova to serve on it was an indication that through her own efforts she had risen to the status of an important political leader. She requested time to consider.

The offer of cabinet posts to Maria Spiridonova and several other Essers pointed up a crucial question, not only for the Left Essers but for all revolutionary leaders: Would they accept the Bolshevik takeover and join a coalition soviet government? Or would they combine, in a bloc, to engineer a vote of "no confidence," stay in the Congress, and become an embattled opposition? Or would they "take a walk"—leave the Congress in the hope of setting up a rival government and try to carry on from where the Provisional Government had left off?

Typical of the Esser and Menshevik leaders, they went onto the Congress floor with no firm decision on these crucial questions, aside from their appeals to the delegates to see the Provisional Government as the only hope for the establishment of a representative government, their denunciations of the Bolshevik illegal seizure of power, and their threats to walk out. One by one they were angrily shouted down by the rough, brawny working men and the soldiers and sailors who showed scant regard for representative government and wanted action—not promises.

The new Left Esser party was the only one, other than the Bolsheviks, that emerged from the smoke-filled backrooms with a plan of action. Recognizing this as a decisive moment in the revolution, they decided, as Maria Spiridonova put it, "to stay with the Revolution." This meant playing an energetic role in creating a new government. It meant cooperating with the Bolsheviks, not as the lesser partners, but because the Esser constituency— the peasants of Russia—were 80 to 90 percent of the population, the dominant partner. An Esser-Bolshevik coalition would at last put a peasant stamp on the Russian revolution.

In the councils of the Esser party, Maria Spiridonova argued the necessity of cooperating with the Bolsheviks because the "masses are with them." The Bolsheviks, with their emphasis on action—even ruthless action—and their ceaseless sloganizing of socialist aims in simple, often bombastic phrases, were understood by the masses as pushing the stalled revolution forward. Maria Spiridonova and her Left Esser colleagues reasoned that only a strong, non-Bolshevik coalition, functioning on the floor of the Second Congress of Soviets and behind the scenes, could control that push which they saw as heading straight toward Bolshevik domination. Before the opening session of the Congress they tried to persuade the leaders of the Right Essers and those of other parties to join them, but these attempts came to nothing. Only much later did some of them admit their short-sightedness and underestimation of the Bolsheviks. The Menshevik N. N. Sukhanov (Nikolai Nikolayevich Hmmer) wrote:

> By quitting the Congress and leaving the Bolsheviks with only the Left SR [Esser] youngsters . . . we gave the Bolsheviks with our own hands a monopoly of the soviet, of the masses, and of the revolution. . . . I personally committed not a few blunders and errors in the revolution, but I consider my greatest and most indelible crime the fact that I . . . did not stay on at the Congress. To this day I have not ceased regretting this October 25th crime of mine.[13]

---

[13]*Zapiski o Revoliutsii*, Berlin, 1922–23, tom 7, pp. 66–68 (abridged Harper *Torchbook* English edition, *The Russian Revolution*, vol. 2, p. 646). See also Radkey, *The Agrarian Foes*, pp. 466–467, for other examples.

The Left Esser decision "to stay with the revolution" led them into the thick of the fray. As Maria's colleague and biographer, I. Z. Steinberg, put it "the weight of the battle lay on the shoulders of Maria Spiridonova." She was, he said, the party's leader, its inspiration, and its indefatigable worker.[14]

The first dramatic moment of the all-night session of the Second Congress was the changing of the guard. The old Presidium, after declaring the Congress open, picked up their papers and marched out. Quickly elected were twenty-one members of the new Presidium, including Maria Spiridonova and six Left Essers, who took their places accompanied by cheers and foot-stamping. The other fourteen members of the new Presidium were Bolsheviks. Among them was Aleksandra Kollontai[15] who had recently changed her party allegiance from Menshevik to Bolshevik and had just come out of jail, put there by the Provisional Government as an accused accomplice in the Bolshevik-inspired garrison insurrection in July. This occasion was Maria Spiridonova's public debut as the leader of the Left Essers. It symbolized the rise in popular support of the new party and the decline of the Esser parent which began to be called the Right Esser party.

If more tangible evidence of the split in the Essers was needed, it was not long in coming. In an episode of parliamentary wrangling the Right Essers, followed by the Mensheviks, walked out of the congress accompanied by boos and catcalls and general pandemonium. From the platform Trotsky called out his parting shot: "Let them go! They are just so much refuse to be swept into the garbage heap of history!"

Before the walkout the Bolsheviks were far from having a majority in the Congress. Now they had it! Before the night was over a new government had been almost unanimously approved: not a democracy along Western European lines, but a *soviet government*, its central power the Military Revolutionary Committee of the Petrograd Soviet, and its local authority proclaimed to be in the hands of locally elected soviets.

John Reed, in his famous book, *Ten Days That Shook the World*, told how after this tense, bombastic, and wearying opening session of the Congress, he climbed onto a truck in the early morning hours of October 26 to

---

[14] I. Z. Steinberg *Spiridonova, Revolutionary Terrorist*, London, 1935, pp. 176–177.

[15] In contrast to the *Narodniki* and Essers with their large female membership and leadership, the Social Democratic party was overwhelmingly male. An exception was Aleksandra Kollontai, daughter of a general, who became a Marxist in the 1890s. She was a beautiful woman with all the self-esteem of a Russian aristocrat. She wrote an important sociological study, *Society and Motherhood* (1912), as well as novels and critical essays, several of which were translated into English. Appointed commissar of Public Welfare in Lenin's first cabinet, she served long enough to set up *Zhenotdel*, a central Women's Department with branches all over Russia.

drive through Petrograd. He joined in throwing into the streets thousands of copies of the printed proclamation:

TO THE CITIZENS OF RUSSIA:
The Provisional Government is deposed. State power has passed into the hands of the Military Revolutionary Committee of the Petrograd Soviet of Workers' and Soldiers' Deputies.
LONG LIVE THE WORKERS' SOLDIERS' AND PEASANTS' REVOLUTION!

Later that same day the second session of the Congress opened. After some preliminaries, Lenin strode to the podium to the accompaniment of a long, rolling ovation. Holding up his hand for silence he said simply, "We shall now proceed to construct the Socialist Order." In two hours the congress acted on measures the provisional government had bandied about for nearly nine months.

First came the call for a vote on a proclamation "for immediate negotiation of a just and democratic peace" to be addressed to the belligerents of World War I. This was the long-awaited action to take Russia out of the war. The vote was unanimous. Thunderous applause! Caps flung into the air! Lusty shouts of "Hurrah!" and "The War is ended" were deafening. Spontaneously, the delegates' voices broke into a triumphal rendering of the "Internationale." Members of the Presidium stood up and with shining eyes and high-spirited enthusiasm joined in the singing. Then, in a quick mood shift, they began to chant the melancholy revolutionary "Funeral March," so often sung at the graves of those who heroically sacrificed their lives to the cause of freedom:

You fell in the fatal fight
For the liberty of the people . . .
You gave up your lives and everything dear to you,
You suffered in horrible prisons
You went into exile in chains . . .
Because you believed that justice is stronger than the sword
. . . when tyranny falls the people will rise, great and free!

Again Lenin was on his feet, this time to read the Decree on Land: All private ownership of land is abolished, without compensation! A few details of the "equalization of land" formula were read, and irony of ironies, they were identical to those of the Esser land reform program written a decade before by Victor Chernov and recently augmented by the Peasants' Soviet under the chairmanship of Maria Spiridonova. There was heated debate, with Bolshevik delegates from the floor charging that this was an Esser program, not a Bolshevik one. Lenin's dictim was "Origins do not count; results do." At 2 A.M. the Land Decree was passed with only one negative vote.

As the delegates walked out of Smolny in the cold grey dawn of October

27, the Bolsheviks had won an important skirmish in their struggle for control of the government of revolutionary Russia. But victory was not yet theirs. Hard knots of opposition existed on all sides, but they were as nothing compared to the fact they did not yet have the backing of the Peasants' Soviet or any significant number of the peasants of Russia. The Russian historian, Roy A. Medvedev, gives the total number of rural Bolshevik party cells in 1917 as 203 with a total of 4,122 members,[16] in a country of around 150 million people, 80 to 90 percent of them living in peasant villages. If the Bolsheviks were to rule Russia, peasant support was crucial. The question for the Bolsheviks was how to get it. The question for the Esser parties, Left and Right, was how to hold on to their traditional leadership of Russia's peasantry.

The arrogant assumption of the Right Essers was that they controlled the peasants, a control they thought they had strengthened when, after the night of October 25, they read the Left Essers out of the party. With Maria Spiridonova and the Left Essers out, the Right had uncontested control of the party apparatus. They reasoned that, in one way or another, they could successfully challenge the narrow worker- and city-based Bolsheviks. As Chernov put it: "The villages will save us in the end."

To Maria Spiridonova this was sheer madness. She saw Russia's revolutionary masses going over to the Bolsheviks in droves because the Bolsheviks were leading them. The Bolsheviks had stepped into the power vacuum left by the failure of Russia's other socialists to act. At this point, in November 1917, Maria and the Left Essers had come to grips with what was to become a major dilemma of the twentieth century: how to live with the Bolsheviks without being taken over by them?[17] Her solution was a coalition government with the Bolsheviks representing the workers, the Essers the peasants. This solution necessitated activating the Peasants' Soviets, to make them as politically responsive to Esser leadership as the increasingly Bolshevik-controlled worker and soldier soviets were to Bolshevik leaders.

Right Essers had postponed calling a Congress of Peasants' Soviets because they feared repudiation for their failure to end the war and to deal with the pressing problems of the peasantry. Maria Spiridonova broke the impasse by going over the heads of the Right Esser leaders and calling a Congress of Peasants' Soviets to meet November 10. Caught by surprise, the Right Esser leaders tried to stop it, block it, boycott it. But at the appointed time, peasant delegations began to appear in Petrograd. Having failed to prevent the meeting, the Right Esser leaders also rushed to Petrograd and saw to it that the Right Esser-dominated Executive Committee pre-

---

[16]R. A. Medvedev, The October Revolution, New York, 1979, p. 161.
[17]This point was made by Radkey, The Sickle Under the Hammer, p. 142.

sided at the opening session. The committee immediately declared that the meeting was not a congress but merely an "Extraordinary Conference." Then the Right Esser leaders announced: The "official" Second Congress of Peasants' Soviets will meet December 1. Angry cries of disapproval greeted this announcement and the peasant delegates immediately repudiated the traditional leadership by electing Maria Spiridonova president of the assembly. At this point the Right Esser Executive Committee walked out.

The sessions of the "Extraordinary Conference" of Peasants' Soviets were filled with stormy debate. Peasant deputies voiced dissatisfaction not only with Right Esser leaders but with the Bolsheviks and their policies. They bitterly criticized the October 26 Land Decree, which they said provided no guidelines and was creating chaos in the countryside. There were times when it looked as if the conference would break up. The Bolsheviks with a bare 10 percent of the delegates saw their speakers, including Lenin, shouted down.

The Bolsheviks realized they had to make concessions because approval of the Peasants' Soviets was imperative if their shaky government was to survive. Behind the scenes, hard political bargaining was going on. Maria Spiridonova and the Left Essers demanded from the Bolsheviks as the price for their cooperation a basic change in the structure of the soviet government. The highest organ of the government, they said, should be a People's Council, to which worker and peasant soviets, as well as urban and rural governmental bodies would send democratically elected delegates. To make this demand effective the Left Essers needed, but did not get, the cooperation of the Right Essers who stubbornly held that the "Extraordinary Conference" and its decisions were illegal. "Wait for the 'Official' Peasants' Congress," said the Right Essers, and they moved the opening date to November 23. Finally, the Right Essers walked out, fed up with the disapproval they were meeting on every side, leaving the Left Essers to bargain alone with the Bolsheviks.

Despite the loss of support of the Right Essers, the Left Essers convinced the Bolsheviks to accept a coalition government in which the Left Esser-dominated Peasants' Soviets had representation equal to the Bolshevik-dominated Worker Soviets in the Central Executive Committee of the soviet government. There were to be 108 peasant representatives and 108 worker representatives; unfortunately for the future of this equal balance, provision was made for additional representatives from various trade unions which were actually under Bolshevik domination.

It took nearly a week of haggling before the apportionment of cabinet posts was decided, with the Left Essers finally getting seven cabinet ministers, or People's Commissars. Maria Spiridonova decided not to take a commissar position in order to devote herself to party and editorial obligations and to her work on land legislation in the Congress of Peasants' Soviets, but her *katorzhnitsa* colleague, Aleksandra Izmailovich, assumed one of the cabinet posts.

Thus was a "new unity" achieved. The Left Esser spokesmen and women for the peasant masses had agreed to work as co-equal partners with the Bolsheviks! On the evening of November 16, in the assembly hall of the Smolny Institute before a thousand spectators, onto the platform walked the members of the Presidium of the Peasants' Soviets. The Presidium of the Workers' and Soldiers' Soviets rose to embrace them. John Reed, the American reporter, described this event as one of the great moments of history.[18] The two banners of the Peasants' and the Workers' Presidiums

> . . . were intertwined against the white wall, over the empty frame from which the Tsar's picture had been torn. . . . Then opened the 'triumphal session.' After a few words of welcome from Sverdlov, Maria Spiridonova, slight, pale, with spectacles and hair drawn flatly down, in the air of a New England school teacher, took the tribune—the most loved and the most powerful woman in all Russia.

To tumultuous applause she began to speak:

> Before the workers of Russia now open horizons which history has never known. . . . All workers' movements in the past have been defeated. But the present movement is international and . . . invincible. There is no force in the world which can put out the fire of the Revolution! The old world crumbles, the new world begins!

In the first round of the struggle for control that had been fought in the "Extraordinary Conference" of the Peasants' Soviets, the Left Essers had won important, if precarious victories. Would they be able to hold their own in the coalition they had entered with the Bolsheviks?

On November 19 at their first congress, the Left Essers formally affirmed their existence as a separate party. Maria Spiridonova's opening speech articulated the problems faced by the party and the ideals which she insisted must guide it. Theirs was not a new party, she emphasized, because they were the heirs of the great tradition dating back to the 1870s, of those who so courageously sacrificed themselves to the dream of freedom. Quite different was the Bolshevik heritage, founded on hatred, egoism, power, success. These qualities, she conceded, are understandable in times of bitter struggle, but they cannot be the foundations on which to build a new life for the people after the struggle is over. For the present, the Left Essers must remain in the revolution and work in a coalition with the Bolsheviks. Spiridonova's co-worker, I. Z. Steinberg, says in his biography of her that the fundamental resolutions of the First Left Esser Congress were all put into final form under her guidance and inspiration.

---

[18]John Reed, *Ten Days That Shook the World*, New York, 1919, pp. 310–311. Copyright © 1934, 1967, International Publishers, New York.

The "Official" Second Congress of Peasants' Soviets opened on November 25. The Right Esser leaders came with the assumption that the overwhelming majority of delegates would support them. Then all they had to do was wait until the Constituent Assembly met in January 1918 when they would, they thought, have the bulk of Russia's peasants behind them and be in a position to end the Left Esser-Bolshevik Coalition and the Soviet state. They would draw up a constitution for a revolutionary government along the lines of a Western democracy.

Maria Spiridonova was more in touch with reality. She knew events were moving fast and was convinced the character of the revolutionary government would be established before January. Her objective was to stamp the October Revolution with the character of a peasant regime while there was still time. Far from wanting to leave the Right Essers in "the garbage heap of history," she hoped to use the Second Congress of Peasants' Soviets to reunify Esser leadership.

Louise Bryant, like John Reed an American journalist on the scene, observed Maria Spiridonova at this time and said, "Everybody in Russia pours into her office at 6 Fontanka Street to ask advice." She reported that this amazing woman, hardly five feet tall, weighing probably less than a hundred pounds, worked a sixteen-hour day and "is worshipped by the masses." Bryant concluded: "I have not met her equal in any country." Her Left Esser colleague, I. Z. Steinberg, described her day as beginning in the newsroom of the party daily, *Znamia Truda,* where she functioned as an editor. She would go from there to take part in one or more Soviet and Central Committee meetings. In the evening she often addressed a mass meeting.

Maria Spiridonova was trying to persuade Esser leaders, Left and Right, to concentrate all their efforts on a push for peace and reform. That would demonstrate Esser revolutionary leadership to the Russian people and assure the maintenance of a balance of power between the Bolsheviks and Russia's other socialists. Despite the overwhelming size of Russia's peasantry, a permanent split in the leadership of what had always been one peasant party would fatally weaken its political effectiveness. Furthermore, unity was a necessity for facing Russia's foreign foes. Peace negotiations had just begun in the ancient, war-torn Polish city of Brest-Litovsk. There, revolutionary Russia was facing the only belligerents to accept the Bolshevik invitation to negotiate—Imperial Germany and her allies, anxious to get Russia out of the war so German troops could be moved to the Western Front.

Maria shrewdly reasoned that the only bargaining point war-weary Russia had was its revolutionary spirit. She saw revolutionary Russia's defiance of traditional diplomacy in declaring an armistice and calling for direct peace negotiations with all belligerents, as "propaganda of the deed." It was an appeal to action aimed at the war-weary peoples of Europe, over the heads of their governments, just as the individual terrorists in tsarist Russia, by boldly assassinating a tsarist official, inspired people to defy tsarist tyranny.

The prospects for forging a new unity at the "official" Second Congress of Peasants' Soviets were not good. The newspaper, *Delo Naroda* (The People's Cause), reported on November 30 that when Victor Chernov was nominated for the chairmanship of the congress, there were loud shouts of *"doloy"*(down with him) by the delegates. Maria Spiridonova's nomination called forth applause and whistles, as well as scattered calls of *"doloy."* When the votes were counted Maria was elected chairman by a clear majority.

> Presiding over the deliberations of the Second All-Russian Peasants' Congress was like presiding over the eruptions of a geyser, and Maria Spiridonova was not the person to lessen the subsurface tensions. Her inaugural address, instead of pouring oil on troubled waters, poured it on an open fire. She began in a lofty vein, speaking of how the peasantry was essentially one and of how its Congress must also be one despite the partisan strife that threatened to tear it asunder, and then suddenly she began to lash the [Right] Socialist Revolutionaries who responded with shouts of indignation. What had begun as an impartial plea for cooperation ended in a trumpet blast to battle. Spiridonova's speech demonstrated at once the need for class unity and the hopelessness of achieving it.[19]

Surely it was difficult to maintain a spirit of conciliation if it was true, as Maria complained, the Right Essers—in their attempt to immobilize her—cut off the electricity and even stole the bell she used to call the assembly to order!

For six days Maria somehow held the delegates together through stormy proceedings and hotly contested votes on issues that ranged from validating credentials through motions of censure against the Bolsheviks in the Council of People's Commissars and against the Esser Central Executive Committee (still controlled by Right Essers). Finally on December 4, the feared but expected breakdown came. Maria Spiridonova had resigned as chairman (in order to be eligible for the permanent chairmanship), and the man in the chair was unable to restore order during a contested vote on procedure. The Right Esser leaders and about a third of the delegates walked out of the hall, singing the "Marseillaise." They attempted to carry on in a hastily called "Congress" of their own, but day by day attendance dwindled daily. Finally they gave up. At this point they were generals without an army.

On December 5, Maria Spiridonova again went before the congress to plead for unity. Unity, she said, was absolutely essential for the government's peace efforts. She reported that her comrade from *katorga* days, An-

---

[19]Oliver H. Radkey, *The Sickle Under the Hammer,* New York, 1963, pp. 229–230. Copyright © 1963 Columbia University Press. Used by permission.

astasia Bitzenko, a member of the Russian delegation at the peace negotiations in Brest-Litovsk, had sent her by direct wire an urgent appeal for the Peasants' Congress to go on record expressing its approval of the negotiations. She said, "When the Germans learned a serious schism had developed in Russia on the question of peace, they began to voice entirely different terms."[20]

The plea for unity went unheeded. The Right Esser leaders were committed to continuation of the war. In fact, Maria said, the peace issue caused their walkout. "The Right Essers in the old Central Executive Committee cannot bear the thought of the Left Essers and the Bolsheviks negotiating peace. When they break up the party for this, they weaken us, leaving us with no strong front with which to confront the imperialists."[21] And —she might have added—the Bolsheviks!

Maria Spiridonova could be adamant too. The Right Essers, after seeing their rump Peasants' "Congress" dwindle away, sent a delegation to her with a proposal for a truce until a new Peasants' Congress could be called and new officers elected. She refused to see them. She sent a written reply stating that the officers elected at the "official" Second Congress represented the will of the peasants' representatives. The implication was that the Left Essers had won control of the Esser Party and the peasant masses. But in fact the schism had produced two sets of Esser leaders, Left and Right, each claiming to speak for the peasants.

As for the peasants themselves, there was confusion in their ranks. The long narodnik tradition—in which peasant grievances fueled revolutionary fires that could be manipulated by Russia's Esser leaders, almost all of whom were gentry—had ended. The Esser failure to achieve peace and land reform in the provisional government days, and the split in Esser leadership left the peasants open to the message of Bolshevism that was being carried into the villages of Russia by the peasants' future leaders—the returning peasant soldiers who were being thoroughly indoctrinated by the Bolshevik activists in the Soldiers' Soviets.

In July 1917 the Provisional Government had finally announced dates for the election of delegates to the Constituent Assembly, first set for September, then changed to November 12–14. Then the Assembly was rescheduled to meet January 5, 1918. All adults who had reached their twentieth birthday by the date of the election were eligible to vote. Thus were Russia's men and women enfranchised. Revolutionary Russia became the first major nation in the world to give women the vote.

Frustrated by political life in the capital, Babushka had again "gone to

---

[20]Delo Naroda (newspaper), December 6, 1917.

[21]Delo Naroda, December 6, 1917.

the people." Saying she felt her place was among the lowly, in the summer of 1917 she got a railroad car assigned to her and traveled all over European Russia.[22] Her fame was such that an announcement she would appear drew crowds; then her team of young people would come out to explain to the mostly illiterate peasant men and women what the revolutionary government would soon do, and advising them to be patient until the election of a Constituent Assembly.

Babushka was convinced the reason the peasants were not actively opposing the Bolsheviks was because they were ignorant; for this "criminal" ignorance she blamed the tsarist regime. The Bolsheviks, aware of this ignorance, she said, were taking advantage of it. The people believed the inflammatory Bolshevik slogans and promises of immediate peace and land to the peasants *now*. Babushka's efforts to "educate" were submerged in the swirling current of events in the summer and fall of 1917. She was no more successful in her counsel of patience to the people than she had been in achieving unity among the revolutionary leaders of her own Esser party.

The scheduled three days of polling for the delegates to the Constituent Assembly stretched out into weeks. There was confusion in this—the first and only free election in Russia's history. Results came in slowly because lines of communication had been disrupted and the Bolsheviks' attack on the press had closed down many newspapers. The returns that were published, however, showed that in the countryside Bolshevik votes numbered in the thousands, while the Essers' numbered in the millions. Bolshevik candidates were winning only in garrison towns and among workers in industrial cities. Some Bolshevik leaders urged Lenin to call off the elections and cancel the Constituent Assembly, but he decided to let them proceed.

Women participated in the Constituent Assembly election and in the campaigning which consisted largely in getting out the vote. The Bolsheviks had two women candidates on their Petrograd list, and the Constitutional Democrats one. Slates or lists of candidates were drawn up by each political party for each electoral district. Voters then simply designated their preferred list. The Left Esser list in Petrograd included Maria Spiridonova, Sanya Izmailovich, and Anastasia Bitzenko, and throughout the country women candidates were on both the Right and Left Esser lists. In Tambov province Anastasia Sletlova, the wife of Victor Chernov, was elected. A women's organization, The League for Women's Equality, ran a list of ten candidates, all women, but they were not elected. Examples were cited of women being pressured to vote.[23] Soldiers' wives in garrison towns were told to get out

---

[22]Her account of that summer, "1917yi God," was published in *Novyi Zhurnal*, New York, vol. 38, 1954.

[23]Oliver H. Radkey, *The Election of the Russian Constituent Assembly of 1917*, Cambridge 1950, ch. 4.

and vote Bolshevik, for if they did not their husbands would "beat hell out of them." A priest reported women coming to him for advice on how to vote, while looking over their shoulders in fear of Bolshevik soldiers in the vicinity who had threatened to burn down peasant huts or destroy livestock if they did not vote Bolshevik. Aleksandra Kollontai made speeches and wrote a pamphlet urging the wives of workers to vote Bolshevik. Esser and Left Esser women worked to get out the vote, especially in the towns and villages of rural Russia.

When the votes were in and counted, the Essers had received almost two-fifths of the total compared to less than one-fourth received by the Bolsheviks. Of the approximately 700 delegates elected to the Constituent Assembly, there were 380 Right Essers, 40 Left Essers, and 168 Bolsheviks. The remainder belonged to a dozen small parties.

The Left Essers have long claimed that the huge majority vote for Right Esser delegates did not accurately reflect the will of the people at the time of the election. They point out that the electoral lists were drawn up in September before the Left Essers had become a separate party; therefore in relatively few places were Left Esser lists available. Several historians, including Roy A. Medvedev *(The October Revolution)* agree that by November 1918 the Left Essers had the largest following of any political party in Russia, due in no small part to the efforts of Maria Spiridonova. The Bolsheviks also claim the election results did not reflect the rapid expansion of Bolshevik influence that occurred in the fall of 1917. Oliver H. Radkey, the American student of this election, concluded:

> All we can say with certainty is that had there been no confusion and had the vote of the Russian peasantry accorded precisely with its mood, there would have been many more Left SR's [Essers] in the Constituent Assembly and many fewer Right SR's, but also fewer Bolsheviks.[24]

Ominous threats hung in the air as the opening of the Constituent Assembly approached. Chernov and the Right Esser leaders were threatening military force to oust the Left Esser-Bolshevik coalition. The Bolsheviks, who had never indicated any admiration for parliamentary institutions and were well aware of their minority position in the assembly, demonstrated their readiness to use guns and not just threats.

The Tauride Palace, with a light dusting of snow on its roof, lay gleaming in the cold winter sun on the morning of January 5, 1918. With its new coat of light yellow paint it seemed to have a festive air about it, entirely out of keeping with the heavily armed guard the Bolsheviks had placed around it. This beautiful eighteenth-century palace, bestowed by Katerina the Great

---

[24]Radkey, *The Sickle Under the Hammer,* p. 306. Copyright © 1963 Columbia University Press. Used by permission.

on her favorite, Grigory Potemkin, was ready to open its doors to the first session of the Constituent Assembly.

Right Esser demonstrators, carrying banners proclaiming "All Power to the Constituent Assembly" and shouting provocative slogans, made their appearance. Scuffling occurred. Shots were fired into the crowd, presumably at the order of Bolshevik leaders. Several people were killed and nearly one hundred were injured.

In this fevered atmosphere the Constituent Assembly opened at four o'clock in the afternoon in the spacious, semicircular hall of the palace. Again Victor Chernov and Maria Spiridonova were pitted against each other, vying for the presidency of the assembly. This time Chernov won. Maria Spiridonova, with the backing of the Left Essers and the Bolsheviks got 153 votes to Chernov's 244. More striking than the size of his majority was the fact that nearly half the elected delegates either did not vote or had not yet arrived when the poll was taken. It was characteristic of revolutionary assemblies that the attendance was greater on subsequent days than on the first day.

Spokesmen for the People's Commissars of the Soviet government introduced a Declaration of the Rights of the Toiling and Exploited Peoples, which, if adopted, would have recognized the existence of the Soviet government. It was voted down by an overwhelming majority. This action meant the Right Essers who dominated the assembly intended to proceed as if the October Revolution had never occurred. The negative vote was greeted by hissing and shouting from the balconies packed with Bolshevik sympathizers. The Bolshevik delegation noisily stamped out of the hall. The Left Essers remained in their seats while Maria Spiridonova presented the peace proposal of the Soviet government and pleaded for the assembly's approval. It too was voted down, and the Left Essers walked out.

After the initial excitement, the session droned on and on. Then, long after midnight came an order from the Central Committee of the Soviet government to clear the meeting hall. The delegates went out into the pre-dawn darkness through a cordon of armed soldiers and sailors. Aleksandr Blok, as these few lines from his famous poem *Dvenadtsat'* (The Twelve) show, caught their mood of confused despair, faced as they were by the relentless energy of those marching in revolutionary step:

> Black night,
> White snow,
> Wind, wind . . .
> Merrily the wind
> Wicked and gay
> Whirls skirts,
> Mows down passers-by,
> Tears, crumples and carries away
>   A big placard

"All Power to the Constituent Assembly . . ."
And the words are communicated:
. . . And we had an assembly.
. . . There, in that building.
   They judged—
   They decided . . .
The wind romps, the snow flutters,
Twelve men are marching.
Black rifle straps . . .
Keep in revolutionary step!
The relentless foe never sleeps!
Comrade! Aim your rifle, don't be a coward!
Fire some bullets into Holy Russia—

The following day the delegates returned to the Tauride Palace for the next session. The armed guard, still in place, proceeded to carry out the orders of the Soviet government to prevent the delegates from entering. The first day of Chernov's presidency was his last.

Maria Spiridonova had no regrets over the demise of the Constituent Assembly. On January 10, the Third Congress of Soviets met in the Tauride Palace. Fifteen hundred workers, soldiers, and peasant delegates—many of them in colorful regional costumes—from all over Russia were in attendance. After Lenin spoke, Maria came to the podium accompanied by thunderous applause. In a clear voice that reached all parts of the assembly hall, she began to speak. She accused the Menshevik and Right Esser leaders "from Kaladin and Rodzianko to Dan, Tsereteli, and Chernov" of counterrevolution and of a plot to take power from the working classes and return it to the bourgeoisie. In theory, parliamentary government appears good, she said, but the Constituent Assembly proved it is an illusion. Fortunately for Russia, she continued,

there is another way to carry out the people's will, a way which emphasizes all the characteristics of our people. You know this way. Already in 1905 the people became used to the new form of representation. That is the Soviets of Workers', Soldiers', and Peasants' deputies. . . . Now we have this great congress, the heart and soul of the Russian working people. We believe it will solve in the best possible way all the historic problems which will be set before it.[25]

In January 1918 the soviets, with their freely elected delegates, were representative of the Russian people. They were chosen by all existing political parties and social groups, but Maria Spiridonova did not understand the potential for control of the soviets by a disciplined minority. Lenin launched the slogan "All Power to the Soviets," and before the year 1918 had advanced very far, the Bolsheviks were dominating the soviets on all levels.

---

[25]Translated from the speech as reprinted in M. A. Spiridonova, *Dve Stat'i i Rech' k Zacedaniiu Tret'iago C'ezda Sovetov ot 13go ianvaria 1918 goda*, Vologda, 1918.

The Left Esser-Bolshevik coalition was from the beginning an uneasy compromise. The Left Essers were non-Marxian socialist idealists. The Bolsheviks under Lenin were pragmatists with a strong tendency to ruthlessness. The first Left Esser-Bolshevik disagreement came over the Bolshevik imprisonment of the members of the Provisional Government without warrants or any kind of legal procedure. The Bolsheviks defended themselves by saying that in November 1917, when they took over the government, they found hundreds of Bolsheviks in prisons all over Russia, put there on orders from the Provisional Government. When the Left Essers protested, the Bolsheviks announced they had merely put the ex-ministers "under house arrest" and they would soon be freed. Other disagreements arose and the honeymoon stage of the coalition was nearing its end, but Maria Spiridonova remained loyal to the Bolshevik leaders because, with Lenin himself taking a hand in the proceedings, a comprehensive land law was being pushed through. This law contained most of the provisions of the legislation worked out by the Executive Committee of the Peasants' Soviets under her leadership

The Socialization of the Land legislation was crucial to Maria Spiridonova, but peace for Russia was imperative. Her idea of peace continued to be the March 14 Petrograd Peace Proclamation with its demand of no indemnities and no annexations, even though she was aware of its failure to inspire the working classes of Europe to lay down their arms. At the Second Congress of Peasants' Soviets she went so far as to proclaim that Russia's making a separate peace with Germany would not be dishonorable because "we continue to appeal to all belligerent lands to join our peace effort." However, as details of the negotiations at Brest-Litovsk got back to Russia, it became clear that the price for peace demanded by Germany and her allies was high: huge indemnities, vast territories, populations, and resources.

In their campaign to lead the Russian revolutionary government, the Bolsheviks' most popular slogan was "Peace, without annexations or indemnities." They had condemned secret diplomacy. They had exposed the secret agreements of the Allied Powers they found in the Tsarist Archives with their "to the victor belongs the spoils" provisions and proclaimed "Revolutionary Diplomacy"—open agreements openly arrived at. The Soviet government's surrender to the German Empire under the terms of the Treaty of Brest-Litovsk was a repudiation of revolutionary diplomacy. It was a surrender that imposed on the Russian people the heavy burden of paying huge indemnities, and in effect made Russia the ally of Imperial Germany. The Soviet government also agreed to turn over the territories of Finland, White Russia, Latvia, and the Ukraine to German occupation. This meant the surrender of about a third of the population of Russia and an enormous percentage of her economic resources, including coal mines, oil fields, railroads, and grain lands.

At the Third Congress of Soviets in January 1918, Maria Spiridonova and several Left Esser leaders asked Lenin in a private conversation how the Soviet government could carry out Germany's demands without halting "our internal process of socialist reforms?" Lenin cynically replied that anyone who believed "we would permit Russia to fulfill any agreement directed against Soviet power or against the revolution" was a fool.[26] The Soviet government would only give the outward appearance of compliance. The purpose of the treaty was to gain "a breathing space" for the revolution. This was, indeed, a troubling answer.

The Brest-Litovsk Treaty was signed March 3, 1918.[27] It was opposed by most Bolsheviks[28] as well as Left Essers. Lenin's method of getting it accepted and ratified was ruthless and of questionable legality. A Fourth Congress of Soviets was called. This was done so hastily the Left Essers did not have time to line up enough peasant delegates to counter what Maria Spiridonova, as spokesman for the Left Essers, called the "illegally chosen Bolshevik delegates." Speaking on the podium of the Fourth Congress, Maria Spiridonova and other Left Essers charged that the treaty made socialist Russia the tool of German-Austrian imperialism. To ratify this robber treaty would be a betrayal of socialists and revolutionaries everywhere, and a betrayal of the toilers and workers of those parts of Russia being handed over to the Germans.

> We are told we must have a "breathing spell." By the time we get our breath the revolutionary proletariat will be dead.

> We spurn the terms of the treaty. To ratify them is to deliver a death blow to the Russian and international revolution.

When the count was taken on March 15, the delegates to the Fourth Congress of Soviets had voted 784 for the treaty to 376 against or abstaining.

---

[26]Spiridonova reported on this encounter in a speech she made at the Third Congress of Left Essers at the end of June 1918.

[27]By March 3 the Soviet Government had officially shifted to the Gregorian calendar. The day after January 31 was February 14. Thus did 13 days vanish from the calendar.

[28]Included was Aleksandra Kollontai. Because she was a Bolshevik, Kollontai was not so easily moved off the political stage as Maria Spiridonova and the Esser women. But, like them, she believed she had the right to disagree, a belief which insured her early downfall. She voted against the Brest Treaty and was immediately removed from the Central Committee. She continued as head of *Zhenotdel* which entitled her to attend its sessions for a time. In 1921 she joined the struggle for the democratization of the party and the government by supporting the Worker's Opposition. For this action, expulsion from the party was considered, but instead she was "exiled," not to Siberia, but to a non-policy-making diplomatic post.

The next day the Left Essers issued a statement repudiating the ratification of the treaty. They further announced that the Left Esser party would not be bound by its terms and—most important—every Left Esser in the Council of People's Commissars "is resigning to protest Bolshevik treason." This withdrawal ended the Left Esser-Bolshevik coalition government.

In 1917, on the altar of war, the leaders of Russia's largest revolutionary party, the Essers, sacrificed the unity of that party and the reforms generations of Russian revolutionaries had worked and died for. Now, in March 1918, the political forces of revolutionary Russia were split again—this time over the issue of peace.

Since the Left Essers also were convinced peace was imperative, why did they refuse to accept the Brest-Litovsk settlement? Maria Spiridonova explained at length the Left Esser opposition to the treaty. It was a shameful betrayal of the people of Russia as well as the people of Germany and all socialists everywhere. What was the alternative? The Bolsheviks said the only alternative would have been to pit Russia's war-weary, ill-fed and virtually non-existent armies against Germany's mighty military force with the inevitable result of uncountable casualties, Russia's defeat, and the end of the revolution.

Maria Spiridonova and the Left Essers admitted Russia had no disciplined army to meet the Germans, but the country had something infinitely more effective—a revolutionary people. Let the Germans advance; they would confront one hundred million rebels.[29]

In 1921, Maria Spiridonova reminded Emma Goldman that the Russian people had throughout history defeated the invaders of their country. She said it was in fact the Russian people who checked all the counter-revolutionary military attempts of the White Armies and their European allies in 1918 and 1919, and not the Red Armies as Lenin and Trotsky claimed. But, said Maria, the Bolsheviks have no faith in the masses. They proclaim themselves a party of workers, but they refuse to trust the proletariat or the peasants. Instead, they make Russian peasants and workers slaves to the Kaiser and impose a system of bondage on Russia worse than that of the tsars. And Maria Spiridonova was an internationalist. She saw that in strengthening German imperialism against Germany's socialist workers, the Bolsheviks guaranteed the defeat of socialism and revolution in Germany and in other nations around the world.

Maria Spiridonova had worked for a broad coalition of non-Bolshevik socialists which she had seen from the beginning as necessary to control the Bolshevik tendency to lawlessness, but she had failed in the face of Right Esser and Menshevik reluctance to act. From October 1917 to March 1918

---

[29]I.Z. Steinberg described their stand in a pamphlet, *Pochemu My Protiv' Brestkago Mira* (Why We Are Against the Brest Peace), Moscow, 1918.

the Left Essers alone had been a restraining force within the Soviet government against the Bolshevik push toward tyrannical rule. Acutely aware of
that restraint, Spiridonova had opposed the break with Bolsheviks over the
Brest-Litovsk Treaty and pressed for a revision of the decision. A Congress
of Left Essers called to consider the issue opened April 17. Addressing it,
Spiridonova said:

> I do not believe the Bolsheviks have become counter-revolutionaries. They
> have brought humiliation on themselves and on the people. If they do betray
> the Revolution, no more concessions and compromises. But if they are not
> traitors, we can honorably cooperate and work with them.[30]

Debate over the issue lasted several days and there were times when the
party almost split. The sessions ended without approving Spiridonova's call
for rejoining the coalition.

Scarcely a week passed before Lenin, in a speech before the Soviet Executive Committee (April 29), introduced a resolution to institute a dictatorship, saying that there "is no inconsistency between social democracy and
the assumption of dictatorial power by an individual person." Maria Spiridonova listened to this speech, and saw the ghost of autocracy rising from
the grave in the form of a Soviet master. Her attitude toward the Bolsheviks
changed. Now she could see them clearly as the betrayers of the revolution
and the dream of freedom.

ANNOTATED REFERENCES

The description of the "February Days" in Petrograd on pages 299–301 of this chapter relies
on Burdzhalov, pp. 104–106, Hasegawa, chapter 12, and Kaiurov, pp. 159–160.

It is significant that Leon Trotsky in his *History of the Russian Revolution,* anxious to prove the
February Revolution was not "a petticoat rebellion" but a revolution led by "conscious and
tempered workers, educated . . . by the party of Lenin," wrote "workers" not working men
and *women* and completely disregarded the fact that the women acted in defiance of the party
of Lenin! (pp. 131 and 147 in the one-volume 1952 Anchor Book edition). Although by the
time Trotsky wrote his history he had been exiled by Stalin, Soviet historians follow a similar
interpretation, namely, that Bolshevik leaders inspired, organized, and led the February uprising.

In 1967, E. N. Burdzhalov's *Vtoraia Russkaia Revoliutsiia. Vosstanie v Petrograde* (The Second
Russian Revolution [the first was the 1905 Revolution]. The Uprising in Petrograd) was published in Moscow and created a furor among Soviet historians. He dared to take a fresh look
at the archival material, and in his analysis show the disarray of Bolshevik leadership and
policies before and during the "February Days." Once the angry women, crying "bread" and
"down with the war" went pell-mell out of the factories and into the streets, it took the combined efforts of Essers, Mensheviks and Bolsheviks to channel the uprising onto a path that

---

[30]Steinberg, *Spiridonova,* p. 204.

would lead to the overthrow of the tsarist government. He notes that the first revolutionary body, the Petrograd Soviet of Workers' Deputies, was multiparty, with the Bolsheviks a distinct minority. The English translation of Burdzhalov's book by Donald J. Raleigh, *Russia's Second Revolution: The February Uprising in Petrograd*, was published by the Indiana University Press in 1987.

Another author, whose interpretation of the "February Days" is similar to Burdzhalov's is Tsuyoshi Hasegawa, *The February Revolution, Petrograd 1917*, Seattle and London, 1981. Hasegawa drew on a broad range of primary and secondary sources for factual evidence and colorful details.

V. Kaiurov, a worker in the Erekson factory, was a participant in the "February Days." It was he who reported the Cossacks did not use their sabers when they charged, that they smiled, and one even winked. His article "Shest' Dnei Fevral'skoy Revoliutsii" (Six Days of the February Revolution) was published in *Proletarskaia Revoliutsiia*, pp. 157–170, vol. 13, no. 1, 1923.

A. Ia. Pirogova's article in Vera Figner's *Na Zhenskoy Katorge* describes the arrival of the news of the overthrow of the tsarist government in the women's prison in Akatue. The Foreword to the second issue of *Katorga i Ssylka*, no. 2, 1921, describes the thousands of *katorzhniki* and political exiles streaming out of prison gates, scattering all over Russia, and the turning away of most of them from political life, disappearing without a trace.

Books by Radkey, Vladimirova, and Steinberg give Maria Spiridonova more than the usual passing reference. Oliver Henry Radkey, *The Sickle Under the Hammer* (New York, 1963), is the most objective. Vera Vladimirova, in her detailed history of the course of the revolution in 1918, *God Sluzhby "Sotsialistov" Kapitalistam. Ocherki po Istorii Kontr-revoliutsii v 1918 godu* (The Year of the "Socialists' " Subservience to Capitalism. Essays on the History of the Counter-revolution of 1918), Moscow-Leningrad, 1927, makes Spiridonova, as the leader of the Left Essers, the evil genius of the revolution. She is the betrayer of socialism, communism, the Russian people, and her own constituency, the peasants, with what Vladimirova calls her lying slander. I. Z. Steinberg, Spiridonova's biographer and political colleague, wrote of her in the spirit of hero worship in two books: *Spiridonova, Revolutionary Terrorist*, London, 1935, and *In the Workshop of the Revolution*, New York and Toronto, 1953. All of these books rely on texts of official pronouncements and records of proceedings of party and soviet congresses and conferences to the extent they are available. Steinberg was a participant in these events.

John Reed's *Ten Days That Shook the World*, New York, 1919, is full of the kind of details that only a perceptive, articulate eyewitness could provide. It is the best of many eyewitness accounts by journalists published in the early days of the Russian revolution. The "ten" days were approximately October 25–November 16, 1917, according to the Russian calendar (November 7–30 by the Western calendar). Reed is inconsistent in his references to dates.

Roy A. Medvedev, *The October Revolution*, translated by George Saunders, New York, 1979. Medvedev is a Soviet emigré historian whose assessments of Bolshevik policies in 1918 are in full accord with those of Spiridonova.

Louise Bryant, *Six Red Months in Russia*, New York, 1918 (reprinted by the Arno Press, 1970), reported she conversed with Spiridonova in English, a language Spiridonova said she had learned to read and speak during her years in Siberia.

Emma Goldman, *My Disillusionment in Russia*, New York, 1923, devotes chapter XVI to Maria Spiridonova.

Of the several recent biographies of Aleksandra Kollontai, Beatrice Farnsworth's *Aleksandra Kollontai* (Stanford, 1980) contains the best analysis of Kollontai's thwarted efforts at leadership during the period discussed in this chapter.

Newspapers consulted for this chapter are *Delo Naroda, Znamia Truda,* and *Nash Put'*.

9

The Tyranny of the *Cheka*

In tsarist days terror was the political reality of the activist revolutionary women. It was in sharp contrast to their dream: The Revolution. The revolution would bring a world of freedom and well-being for all. The revolution would eliminate forever the need for violence and terror.

The first Left Esser Party Congress in mid-November 1917 renounced terror in ringing words:

> In the Russian Republic no need exists for a system of Terror. The Party rejects Terror as a threat to the sovereign power of the Revolutionary Democracy.

Scarcely three months later, Left Esser leaders were calling Bolshevik policies and methods tyranny and there were rumblings about the "role of terror" *in* the revolution.

On February 19, 1918, the Left Esser newspaper *Znamia Truda* (Banner of Labor) carried on the front page an account of celebrations all over Petrograd in honor of Ivan Kaliaev who on that day thirteen years earlier assassinated the Grand Duke Sergei Aleksandrovich, was hanged for it, and became one of the great revolutionary martyrs. The same issue reported that Maria Spiridonova, as chairman, opened a meeting of the Left Esser Central Committee with a brief sketch of the historical importance of terrorists in the development of the revolutionary movement in Russia. She believed that terrorism still had a significant role to play in the revolution.

It was inevitable that the fires of revolution would bring to the fore the fundamental differences between the Marxian Bolsheviks and the non-Marxian Esser socialists on the role of violence, terror, and freedom. The Bolsheviks operated on the Marxist principle that all government is organized violence, that all social change is the result of class struggle. Violence is the bludgeon the dominant class must use to impose its will on other classes. Therefore, the major task of the dictatorship of the revolutionary workers and toilers of Russia was to suppress and exterminate the class enemy—the bourgeoisie. Other Russian socialists, including the Left Essers, did not "shrink from taking repressive measures against the enemies of Russia's Revolutionary Republic," but not in Marxian terms of mass violence and oppression, and not at the expense of suppressing basic freedoms.

A problem was that the machinery for legal identification and punishment of crimes against the revolution was lacking. The old judiciary and the police disappeared with the fall of the Imperial Regime. The Provisional Government had not set up a police and court system but had tried to maintain order through local militia units. People's Courts and other self-appointed bodies had appeared locally and operated in an uncoordinated way.

To fill the law-enforcement vacuum the Bolsheviks did not propose setting up a judicial system. They wanted an extra-legal body: the Extraordinary Commission to Fight Counter-Revolution, Sabotage, and Speculation, later known as the *Cheka* (the ancestor of the later GPU and KGB). The *Cheka* was to be primarily an investigative body empowered to bring individuals and organizations accused of activities harmful to the revolution before revolutionary tribunals which were to judge each case and to impose punishment on the guilty. Punishment was limited to confiscation of property, confinement, deprivation of ration cards, and publication of names of the guilty with the list of their crimes. The *Cheka* was voted into existence in December 1917 by the Soviet of People's Commissars. The Left Esser Commissars voted for it, persuaded it was a necessary, but temporary, revolutionary expedient whose powers would be used sparingly. Maria Spiridonova as leader of the Left Essers, well aware of the Bolsheviks' tendency to use violent means, insisted—against Lenin's opposition—and succeeded in having Left Essers serve as members of the *Cheka,* in order to exercise some control. A few Essers in the *Cheka* did not prevent the Bolshevik-dominated central *Cheka* and its regional agencies from exceeding their powers.

The *Cheka*, as Lenin and the Bolsheviks saw it, was an instrument to crush the bourgeoisie. As enemies of the revolution they could be allowed no freedom, no liberty of the press, speech, or assembly. It soon became apparent that any opponent of Bolshevik policies was defined either as a bourgeois or as an ally of the class enemy and therefore subject to "merciless suppression." By broadening the definition of "enemies of the Revolution," socialists, including Essers, Mensheviks, and even Left Essers, or anyone who dared to question were suspect and subject to harrassment, arrest, imprisonment, and—as the *Cheka* became increasingly lawless—execution. The prisons of Russia, emptied by the February revolution, began to fill up.

On February 23, 1918, *Pravda* announced that the central *Cheka* had ordered local soviets all over Russia to proceed at once to seek out, arrest, and shoot immediately all counter-revolutionaries, enemy agents, and speculators. In vain the Left Essers tried to control the *Cheka* expansion of Bolshevik mass terror that was akin to tsarist punitive measures but more ruthlessly applied because it was infused with revolutionary zeal. When the Left Essers resigned in protest from the Soviet of People's Commissars in March 1918, Lenin called their action an insurrection of the intelligentsia against the masses. With Left Esser restraint on the *Cheka* gone, its operations expanded.

In the spring of 1918 terror was in the air. Maxim Gorky's newspaper, *Novaia Zhizn'* (New Life) reported on April 19:

Executions continue. Not a day, not a night passes without several people being executed.

Worker delegates representing twenty-five important industries drew up a protest published in *Novaia Zhizn'*, March 20, 1918:

Four months have passed and we find ourselves without faith and without hope. This government which calls itself a Soviet of Workers and Peasants has done everything to oppose the will of the workers. It has blocked every attempt to hold new elections to the soviets, it has threatened to use machine guns against workers, and it has broken up meetings and demonstrations.

We were promised an immediate peace, a democratic peace . . . but we were given a shameful capitulation to German Imperialism. We were promised bread and were given hunger, civil war . . . and economic disorganization. We were promised freedom . . . but where is freedom of speech, assembly, unions, and press? People are executed without trial by men who act as informers, provocateurs, witnesses, prosecuting attorneys, and judges all in one.

In this atmosphere of discouragement and despair, with the Bolshevik rulers of Russia virtually at war with the revolutionary masses, growing opposition ranged all the way from armed attacks by former tsarist, White Russian generals to the Right Esser attempt to revive the provisional government beyond the Urals. The Left Esser Executive Committee in Moscow and its local counterparts in every city in Russia were engaged in debate on how to save the revolution from destruction by Bolshevik tyranny. The Left Essers found themselves in the anomalous position of having rising popular support but no power base to use it.[1] With the Bolsheviks forcibly taking control

---

[1] Roy Medvedev, *The October Revolution*, in a chapter entitled "The Masses Turn Away," uses local soviet election statistics to show the decline in popular support for the Bolsheviks and the rise in support for the Left Essers. By the July 1918 convening of the Fifth All-Russian Congress of Soviets, the number of Bolshevik delegates had declined by 40, and the Left Essers had gained 115. This trend helps explain the increasing use of force to coerce local soviets.

of the soviets, local and national, legitimate political opposition was each day becoming more difficult. Armed opposition was impossible because the Bolsheviks, since January 1918, had been rapidly building the Red Army, while the Left Essers had virtually no military forces at their disposal.

Ratification of the Treaty of Brest-Litovsk, a humiliating surrender to Germany, further complicated the fate of the revolution. Representatives of Imperial Germany became highly visible in Russia. The Kaiser's ambassador, Count von Mirbach, took over as his headquarters a palatial mansion in Moscow, which, following a Bolshevik order on March 12, 1918, became the capital city of Soviet Russia.[2] German military commanders marched in with armies to become the real governors of the provinces detached from Russia according to the terms of the treaty.

The Germans in the Ukraine proceeded to wipe clean the slate of revolutionary achievement and the German General Eichhorn upheld with German troops a puppet governor, the Cossack Hetman Skoropadski. Russian soldiers and prisoners of war were savagely treated. As a final humiliation they were forced to join German military units in their attacks on non-cooperating Russian and Ukrainian peasants and workers as forced requisitions of grain were loaded on freight cars for transportation to the German fatherland. Their poorly coordinated efforts at resistance were brutally put down. In one engagement alone over eighty-five hundred peasants were killed. The Germans were covering the once prosperous land with gibbets and unburied bodies.

In Kiev, the capital of the Ukraine, revolutionaries were jailed and shot. Pogroms against Kiev's large Jewish population became the order of the day. Into the Ukraine, crowding the trains and roads, streamed middle- and upper-class Russians fleeing the northern cities as refugees from the revolution. In the territories left under Russian jurisdiction by the Treaty of Brest-Litovsk there was increasing unrest. In the spring of 1918, there was a breakdown of the food distribution system brought on by loss of Ukrainian grain and strikes by railroad workers called in opposition to Bolshevik policies. This disruption caused near starvation to both the cities and the countryside. The Socialization of the Land Law became meaningless when the Bolsheviks, in response to the food crisis, began to requisition grain from the peasants by force. The administrative machinery was quickly set up, and as resistance appeared, the peasants became fair game for plundering. Bolshevik requisition squads were sent into the countryside to expropriate grain, allegedly being hidden by small landholders and cultivators who were labeled

---

[2]Petrograd, the capital city of the Russian Empire for two centuries, was renamed Leningrad in 1924, soon after Lenin's death.

"petty bourgeois food hoarders."[3] "Class struggle" was induced by creating special Committees of the Poor (landless peasants under Bolshevik direction), empowered to redistribute land and requisition horses and farm tools. These policies resulted in such large-scale rural violence that armed forces, including a detachment under the command of the young Tukhachevsky, had to be sent "to pacify" already devastated areas.[4]

Shades of General Luzhenovsky! Was it for this that generations of revolutionaries had sacrificed their lives and those of their victims? As a young woman Maria Spiridonova had chosen to follow the path of terror because she believed that under tsarist autocracy there was no other way to awaken the populace to act against injustice. Now a "revolutionary government" was beginning to be as autocratic as, and even more ruthless and hypocritical than the tsars. What means remained to oppose it effectively, other than the lethal weapon so often used in tsarist times?

In the deliberations of the Left Esser Executive Committee, Maria Spiridonova and her women associates (pre-revolutionary terrorists some called the "Mal'tsev extremists") argued that the time had come to use dramatic terrorist acts to break the tyrannical Bolshevik stranglehold.[5] The Left Esser leaders who chose to follow this tactic assumed the Russian people, restive from war, violence, food, and fuel shortages, would greet a daring terrorist strike with the enthusiasm they had shown in tsarist days. That enthusiasm could then be channeled into popular pressure on the Bolsheviks to curb their ruthless policies and to link themselves again with more moderate parties in general, and with the Left Essers in particular. Each execution of a carefully targeted official would be carried out by a dedicated revolutionary, selflessly sacrificing himself or herself. The terrorist act would be accompanied by rousing proclamations, distribution of broadsides and posters emblazoned with slogans, fiery speeches in the soviets, and, if need be, a show of force.

It was decided the first official to be "executed" should not be a Bolshevik. Left Esser reasoning continued to be that although Bolshevik leaders had steered the revolution off the track of freedom and onto the path of tyranny, they were still revolutionaries. It was the German imperialists,

---

[3]Roy Medvedev in The October Revolution says the Bolshevik success in the "October Revolution" was due to Lenin's willingness to coopt the Esser land program; their failure in the spring and summer of 1918 was Lenin's inability to understand the peasants' needs, and in the face of their opposition, to turn to violence. Medvedev traces all the Soviet Union's political and economic crises for the next fifty years to this failure.

[4]A general in the Red Army during the Civil War, Tukachevsky won fame in the 1920 Soviet attack on Poland. He was one of many high army officers executed in the Stalinist purges in 1937.

[5]There was one exception: Anastasia (Nastya) Bitzenko, who resigned from the Left Esser party in protest, joined a Communist group and within a year became a Bolshevik.

those generals, troops, and diplomatic representatives whose "invasion" had been legalized by the terms of the Brest Treaty who were upholding Bolshevik tyranny and "suffocating our revolution." The Germans were the hated "hangmen" of the Russian people. Therefore, the first terrorist acts must target German officials.

On June 24, 1918, the Left Esser Central Committee passed and made public a proclamation calling for a series of terrorist acts against "representatives of German imperialism on Russian soil":

> We regard our action as an attack on the present policy of the Soviet government, not as an attack on the Bolsheviks themselves.

The proclamation went on, however, to threaten terrorist acts "against all imperialists and enemies of the revolution" whoever or wherever they might be. It was signed M. Spiridonova.

The Fifth All-Russian Congress of Soviets was scheduled to open July 4 in Moscow. All political parties except the Left Essers had been virtually outlawed and in the election of delegates the Left Essers had been outmaneuvered. The Bolsheviks had seen to it that the bulk of the "peasant" representatives were from their own "Committees of the Poor." If there had been genuine elections, as Maria Spiridonova pointed out, Left Esser peasant delegates would have had a clear majority. As it was, the Left Essers were in a desperate position and in a fighting mood.

The Fifth Congress met in Moscow in the Bolshoi Theater. Brilliantly lighted, its stalls and balconies were packed with more than fourteen hundred delegates, almost nine hundred of them Bolsheviks. Sitting in the boxes was an imposing array of visitors. The German ambassador, Count von Mirbach, sat surrounded by German officers in dress uniform. The unofficial diplomatic representatives of the United States and Great Britain were there, as were American and European journalists. On the stage were all the leading personalities of the revolution. Lenin's bald head glistened in the light; Trotsky's bushy black hair framed his face and his flashing dark eyes; Boris Kamkov, the jovial-looking Left Esser leader, was conferring with Maria Spiridonova as she sat shuffling through a pile of papers.

The session opened and Kamkov quickly stepped to the center of the stage. He demanded that the delegation from the Ukraine, "where the heel of German imperialism is crushing the hopes of workers and peasants," be admitted to the congress with the right to vote. At that point a Ukrainian peasant, dressed in a colorful embroidered shirt, got to his feet saying he had come with news of guerilla warfare in the Ukraine. He said "the peasants rise spontaneously against the German occupation—and they are succeeding!" He pleaded for help, and shouted, "We shall drive the Germans out of Kiev all the sooner if you will drive the German ambassador out of Moscow!"

Trotsky rose to issue dire threats to any who might try to provoke a Russo-German war by attacking Germany's representatives on Russian soil. He called upon the congress to pass a resolution directing the arrest and trial before the Moscow Revolutionary Tribunal of all such agitators. Bolshevik spokesmen asked how Left Esser encouragement to the Ukrainians to attack the German occupation could be anything but a challenge to Soviet authority. Maria Spiridonova came forward to speak for the Left Essers. If it is a challenge, she said, we accept it.

> We accept it before the International,[6] before our oppressed Ukrainian and Finnish brothers, before all the toilers of the world who expect us to go on with the fight and not bow to German imperialism.

To thunderous applause she cried out: "Comrade Bolsheviks, we pick up the gauntlet!"

The July 5 agenda of the congress was reserved for reports by spokesmen of Soviet institutions. Maria Spiridonova spoke as chairman of the Peasants' Section of the Central Executive Committee. In a two-hour speech, followed by a debate with Lenin, she recited the woes of the peasants under Bolshevik policies. She said to the delegates:

> Comrade Trotsky urges you to condemn those who call for a struggle to help our Ukrainian brothers (and there is not a peasant there whose back is not scarred by German whips). If you are to vote that those who sound such a battle cry are to be brought before the revolutionary tribunal to be shot, then it is clear that Comrade Trotsky is trying to trick you into voting a resolution condemning the whole party of the Left Essers to death.

> If this is a challenge to battle, let us fight fairly. . . . Let us have time for a full discussion of the situation and take no final vote until the Committee on Elections has verified the credentials of all delegates entitled to vote.

She cited the accomplishments of the Peasant Section of the Central Executive Committee under her chairmanship and protested the Bolshevik decision to ask the Fifth Congress to vote the elimination of the Peasant Section—the only agency in the Soviet government concerned with improving the lives of the peasants who made up the overwhelming majority of the people of Russia.

> Our party works in the interest of the proletariat *and* the peasantry . . . seeking to unite them into one family of toilers. . . . But when there were brought into play the Bolshevik . . . politics of the dictatorship of abstract theories, the dictatorship of individuals in love with their theories, we came to a parting of the ways.

---

[6]This is a reference to the Socialist International founded in Paris in 1889. To its congresses before World War I came representatives of all the socialist and working class political parties of Europe.

She accused the Bolsheviks of waging war on the peasants, and working herself up to a fervor, she pounded the rostrum with a little silver revolver her friends had given her and declared:

> You Bolsheviks have betrayed the cause of the peasants, and when the peasants are humiliated, oppressed, crushed . . . in my hand you will still find the same pistol, the same weapon which forced me to defend . . .

The end of her sentence was drowned out in a wild torrent of applause as brawny peasants stood up in their seats and shook their fists at the Bolshevik leaders on the stage and the German ambassador in his box.

Maria concluded by saying that the Left Essers would not capitulate but would fight for the revolutionary cause until socialism, equality, fraternity, and justice were realized.

After Maria sat down the Bolshevik leaders, Sverdlov and Trotsky, tried to speak but were shouted down. The delegates were calmed only when Lenin came to the podium and finally was allowed to talk. Lenin admitted the Bolsheviks had made mistakes. One of them, he said to Maria Spiridonova, was the acceptance of her Socialization of the Land Law on October 26, 1917, and he admitted he had yielded only because otherwise she and the Left Essers with their peasant following would not have entered the new Soviet government. The Brest-Litovsk Treaty, however, was not a mistake because the three months of peace it had brought had enabled the Soviet government to introduce beneficial socialist measures.

The Bolsheviks quickly introduced a resolution declaring that all power of decision on matters of war and peace belonged to the All-Russian Congress of Soviets and its organs, and ended with the statement: "The safety of the Soviet republic is the supreme law. Those who oppose this law should be wiped off the face of the earth." When Left Esser objections to an immediate vote were disregarded they announced their decision to leave the meeting. As they marched out, singing the "Internationale," the resolution was passed unanimously with a raising of hands, and the session adjourned.

Maria Spiridonova's speech before the July 5 session of the Congress of Soviets was a brief triumph. The lead article in *Pravda* on July 6 was a long vilification of her:

> The monstrous demagoguery of Maria Spiridonova forces us straight out to condemn what she said as lies, disgraceful lies, even though it is difficult to write in such a way about her because her glorious past cannot be forgotten.

Pravda did print a resume of her speech, the last time this Bolshevik newspaper published a statement of opposition to the Bolsheviks in its news columns.

On that same day, July 6, two Left Essers, one of whom had worked for the *Cheka* and had secured a document that granted him and his companion access to Count von Mirbach's office, went there and requested an audience with the German ambassador to "discuss a matter of direct concern to him." The two supposed *Cheka* agents were admitted, and after some discussion with his aides were permitted to talk to Mirbach. A brief conversation ensued, then one of the men pulled out a pistol and fired. Mirbach was hit and staggered through a door to another room. His two assailants followed him and one of them hurled a bomb which exploded with great force, killing Mirbach. The assassins, Jacob Blumkin and Nikolai Andreev, saved themselves from the bomb explosion by jumping out a window, climbing into a waiting automobile, and speeding away.

The Left Essers seized the Moscow Postal and Telegraph Office and sent out this message "To All Working People and Red Army Members":

> The hangman of the laboring Russian people, the friend and protege of Emperor Wilhelm, Count Mirbach, has been killed by the guarding hand of a revolutionary carrying out the decision of the Central Committee of the Left Socialist-Revolutionary Party International.

Saying that she organized the killing of Mirbach from beginning to end, Maria Spiridonova,[7] as spokesman for the Left Essers, issued a proclamation that accused the German ambassador of using his privileged position in Russia to arm German war prisoners and White Russians with the aim of overthrowing the revolution. The proclamation further stated that the Bolshevik-controlled Soviet government had become little more than an agency carrying out the orders of the German hangmen. The Left Esser Central Committee was therefore compelled to remove Mirbach as a counter-revolutionary agent of international imperialism who was all the more dangerous because he enjoyed diplomatic immunity.

The confusion and lack of immediate popular response to the assassination of Mirbach[8] put the Left Esser leadership in a vulnerable position which the Bolsheviks were quick to exploit. In the afternoon of July 6, the delegates to the Fifth Congress of Soviets were assembling for the next session in the Bolshoi Theater. Newspaper reporters came drifting in, but nothing happened. Two hours passed. People were getting impatient. Then Maria Spiridonova walked in and sat alone on the stage. Her calm gave the Left Esser delegates courage, as she patiently waited for the session to open. She expected to deliver a speech she had prepared explaining to the Congress the

---

[7]Although Maria Spiridonova was arrested the next day and tried in November 1918, Blumkin and Andreev escaped and were never prosecuted by the Soviets, despite vehement protests by the German government. Blumkin was officially pardoned in 1919 and joined the Communist party. He was executed a decade later as a supporter of Trotsky, by then out of power and exiled.

[8]Publicly, official Bolshevik reaction was condemnation, but Bruce Lockhart, the author of *British Agent,* reported that the Commissar for Foreign Affairs, Georgi Chicherin, and Leo Karakhan, one of his assistants, registered great joy upon hearing of Mirbach's assassination.

necessity for the dread act of Mirbach's assassination and to issue a call to the Russian people to save the revolution from the imminent danger of take-over by Imperial Germany. With the speech she hoped to gain the backing of the congress, a move that would force the Bolsheviks to change their policies and repudiate the Brest-Litovsk Treaty. But her statement was never delivered to the assembled delegates. The Bolsheviks threw an armed guard around the building while officials came in and gave orders that no one was to leave. Around midnight the few Bolshevik delegates who were there, the journalists, and all visitors were allowed to go. Maria Spiridonova and the more than four hundred sixty Left Esser delegates were placed under arrest and taken away to various places of detention. The Fifth Congress resumed its sessions on July 8 and passed a resolution calling for the expulsion of the Left Essers from all the soviets and from the Central Executive Committee.

The Left Essers still had hope for the fruition of their plans as news went out of the arrest of the peasants' champion, Maria Spiridonova, and the delegates of the peasants' party. Surely this would trigger a popular uprising! It did not. The Left Esser leadership failed to recognize that in the ongoing violence of the revolution, the individual terrorist act no longer had the impact it had commanded in tsarist times. Symbolic gestures of resistance, far from evoking mass action, simply got lost in the confusion and disarray of fast-moving events. The individual terrorist act as a summons for political action was no match for the fear-instilled repression and mass terror of *Cheka* raids and shootings in the night.

The Bolshevik way of confronting the Left Essers, who still had the largest following in Russia, was to keep their most prominent leaders behind bars. At the same time they held out the promise that all Left Essers who categori-cally renounced their party's leadership and the Mirbach assassination would be permitted to function in the Soviet government. Many did, but as time went on the promise became meaningless; the Bolsheviks began to hound the "renouncers" out of the positions to which they had been elected or appointed. These tactics not only removed the Left Esser leadership from the political scene but discredited it in the eyes of the rank and file.

The Bolsheviks dealt with the Left Esser leaders they arrested in the Bol-shoi Theatre in various ways. According to an article in the newspaper *Iz-vestia* on July 14, thirteen, whose names were listed, were shot immediately. Eighty had renounced the Esser leadership for the Mirbach assassination and were freed. Remaining were over three hundred fifty who were being held in various places of detention. Maria Spiridonova and twenty-four others were in the Kremlin Barracks where she was held until November 1918 when she was brought before the Moscow Revolutionary Tribunal.

The charge against Maria Spiridonova was "Counter-revolution against Soviet power and against the revolution." She refused to recognize the juris-diction of the tribunal or the legality of the indictment. She was given permission to make a brief statement in court, but refused. Instead she detailed her case against the Bolsheviks in an open letter to the members of the Central Executive Committee of the Bolshevik party, accusing them of betraying the working classes and destroying the revolution.

> In the name of the proletariat, in the name of the peasantry, you have wiped out all the moral achievements of the revolution. We know the enormity of the injustice committed by the *Cheka* on the souls and bodies of men and women: torture, deception, all-devouring trickery, naked plunder, and murder. Murder with no accounting, with no inquiry, done at the drop of a word, a denunciation, a slander, with no kind of investigation, no proof.

> What kind of terror is this?

> Terror. The whole course of Russian revolutionary history is intertwined with this word. Terror that was done not for such petty things as revenge, intimidation, not even just to remove physically a butcher of the people. The primary and distinguishing feature of that terror was protest. Protest against oppression and coercion. The next feature of that terror was that it served as a means to exert psychological pressure to awaken honor and dignity in the souls of the downtrodden working people, and to awaken the consciences of those who looked upon the oppression of the working people and remained silent. Each [of our revolutionary acts of terror] . . . was a visual demonstration to the masses of how proudly and without fear of consequences, without flinching, we could strike at their oppressors. And another almost inseparable feature of that terror was the terrorist's sacrifice of his own life, his own freedom, everything. . . . For only by that sacrifice could the terrorist act be justified.

> Where are these noble features in the deeds of the *Cheka?* The utterances of the members of the *Cheka* printed in the newspapers are testimony to the unbelievable mediocrity of their intelligence and their morality.

Maria ended her catalog of accusation by saying that no Bolshevik threat could force her to recognize any shadow of legitimacy in their acts:

> Against me even the *Cheka* is powerless. Too long have I been on the very bottom rungs of life's ladder, too strongly have I with all my thoughts, all my heart, loved the revolution that I should fear any kind of experience, including death. . . . So take aim . . . for only by murdering me can you separate me from my attachment to the revolution and from agitating for it.

In November 1918 Maria's spirit was still what it was in 1906, but in 1906 a trial could be used by a revolutionary as a tribune. In 1906 the press carried Maria's words to a broad public. Her 1918 "open letter" was not published in any newspaper in the Soviet Union. It was illegally printed, on cheap paper, as a sixteen-page brochure in 1919 in Khar'kov, and was seen by very few people.

The Moscow Revolutionary Tribunal found Maria Spiridonova guilty of counter-revolution, yet the Bolsheviks were reluctant to deal harshly with the still enormously popular revolutionary heroine who had for months been an active participant at the highest level of the revolutionary government. She was given the light sentence of one year's imprisonment, then was immediately released.

As she promised she would, Maria Spiridonova continued to work and to speak out against Bolshevik policies. She traveled about the country, often in peasant dress, under an assumed name, with false papers. She addressed peasant conferences, workers in factories, soldiers in their barracks. She was especially active among the peasants of her native province of Tambov. From time to time she returned to Moscow where from her hiding places she wrote articles for the illegal press and countless letters to underground groups all over Russia to encourage those who wavered. She also tried to keep up a correspondence with comrades who had escaped abroad, to keep them informed of Bolshevik betrayal of the revolution.

On the night of February 9, 1919, a mass meeting was held in a large steel plant just outside Moscow. Up to the podium stepped Maria Spiridonova. She spoke softly and resolutely, without her usual flamboyance, but with a moral fervor that brought home to the workers the cause of their rapid material impoverishment and the miasma of fear in which they were living. She said Bolshevik mass terror, now being intensified by the growing power of the Red Army, was being ruthlessly used to insure Bolshevik mastery over the people, a mastery that meant enslavement. A Bolshevik speaker rose and interrupted her with a rebuke for maligning "our glorious army which is winning so many glorious victories." She turned on him with indignation and said, "Have you lost all shame? The old army talked just like you, in the same bloated patriotic terms."

Maria was arrested that very night. Again she was imprisoned in the Kremlin Barracks. Bruce Lockhart, the British agent who occupied a cell across a corridor from her, described her as being poorly dressed and looking ill and nervous, with great, dark circles under her eyes.

In the small book, *Kreml' za Reshetkoy* (The Kremlin Behind Bars), published in Berlin in 1922, appeared some of the letters of Sanya Izmailovich who was also imprisoned in the Kremlin Barracks. She wrote:

An eternity, it seemed, separated us from the many years we spent in tsarist prisons, leaving them far behind . . . but again we are behind bars, and it is as if this eternity of our sixteen months of freedom had never been.

There was the autocracy of the monarchy. Then came the Soviet Federation of "Socialist" Republics. But the jails are the same—only dirtier.

Despite the almost unendurable condition of prison life under the Bolsheviks as Sanya described it, despite her torturous worry the Bolsheviks were going to shoot Maria, the weeks passed and she had not lost hope.

The Kremlin jail stinks . . . but through the open window wafts the smell of the flowering linden trees from the Kremlin garden . . . in the quiet river the

stars are reflected. . . . Where is peace? Is there some place where there are
no lies and sordid, filthy slander calling itself governmental politics? Where
there are no bars, where there is no shooting each other? Where a people can
stand face to face freely, and look out naturally, breathing in fully the exciting
smell of the fields . . . and no violent coercion, no bloodshed and no moans
and no apprehension of scandal and meanness?

Sanya goes on to answer her own questions: "It will be! It will be! . . . by
suffering, the new regime of the future will arise. By blood and tears!"

After two months in the Kremlin Barracks, Maria Spiridonova made a
daring escape. The young soldier guarding her cell, supposedly one of the
Cheka's most trusted men, endangered his own life by leading her out from
behind the Kremlin walls to safety. She went at once into the underground
and for over a year and a half engaged in political activity as the leading
member of the Executive Committee of the Left Esser party.

One of Maria's visitors at this time was Emma Goldman, the Russian-
born American anarchist who was deported from the United States to the
Soviet Union in 1919. Zigzagging through the streets of Moscow to foil the
Cheka, Emma walked into the poor yard of an old tenement house, up five
flights of stairs, and entered a room she said was about the size of the cell
she had occupied in the Missouri Penitentiary.[9]

A frail little woman got up from a table piled high with papers to greet
Emma Goldman with a tender embrace. It was Maria Spiridonova. Though
only thirty-three years old, she was shriveled in body, her face was flushed,
her fiery blue eyes feverishly brilliant, her revolutionary enthusiasm undi-
minished. As Emma talked with this woman whom Zorin and Jack Reed
had told her had experienced a breakdown and suffered from hysteria and
neurasthenia, she concluded that Zorin was a liar and Jack Reed had been
misled by his unfamiliarity with the Russian language and by Bolshevik du-
plicity.

Emma saw Maria as calm, sincere, well-poised and fully in command of
the enormous body of information she had collected about the true condition of the country. On one occasion, when Maria detected doubt on Emma's face, she remarked, "I fear you do not quite believe me. Well, here is
what the peasants write me." And she pulled out letter after letter, reading
passages that were heart-rending in their misery and their bitterness against
Bolshevik exactions. Some wrote to ask if she too had gone over to the
Bolsheviks. "If you also forsake us *Matushka* (little mother), we will have
no one to turn to." The peasants reported the inefficiency of the Bolshevik

---

[9]Emma Goldman's account of her meetings with Spiridonova appears in chapter 16, entitled
"Maria Spiridonova," of her book *My Disillusionment with Russia,* New York, 1924. An almost
identical account, with a few additional details, appears in Goldman's autobiography *Living
My Life,* vol. 2, pp. 802–805, New York, 1931.

regime, telling how their produce lay piled up around the railroad stations until it rotted, or passed into the possession of speculators. They reported the punitive expeditions that were leaving death and ruin in their wake.[10]

After three days of conversation with Maria Spiridonova, Emma concluded that she was the most sincere, capable, and convincing person she had met in Russia. In her account of one of her meetings, when Maria's long-time Left Esser comrade Boris Kamkov (Katz) was present, Emma got the impression that Kamkov was more to Maria than a party comrade, that they were lovers.[11] Emma supplied no evidence beyond her observation of Maria's solicitousness at her parting with Boris who was leaving on a dangerous mission. Emma witnessed just one example of the tenderness observers often saw Maria demonstrate, but all evidence points to the conclusion that she had only one love: the revolution. In an article Maria wrote about a male comrade of her *katorga* days, she reported that he advised her to marry and have children and leave the treacherous political arena—advice many an activist woman has received from male associates; there is no indication she ever thought seriously of following it.

Broken into Left and Right by dissension and the chaos of physical and spiritual life as primitive passions raged in Russia, the Esser revolutionaries were victimized as the revolution turned on itself. The Bolsheviks were fast filling the prisons of Russia with—*revolutionaries!*

As Maria Spiridonova lay ill with typhus in October 1920, she was arrested and taken to Butyrki Prison in Moscow. There the typhus infection abated, but her health steadily deteriorated. In a letter dated February 23, 1921, she wrote that she was convinced the Bolsheviks were trying to figure out how to do her in.

> To kill me outright would be awkward for them. To send me to penal servitude would be shameful, or to leave me in an infected barracks like this one would just be another way to kill me, and would clearly demonstrate for everybody to see, the bared teeth, the ugly mug of a self-proclaimed Socialist government. . . . So, they may do something entirely Jesuitical such as announce that I am mad and set me down in a psychiatric institution . . . or they may strike a moral note and invent something that is entirely unbelievable, such as an "accidental shooting," or, if I die in the company of a friend, force him, or her, to sign a document saying he, or she killed me.[12]

Maria was moved to the Kremlin Hospital in March 1921, and her physical condition became worse. Completely neglected medically, surrounded by

---

[10]Texts of several of these pathetic letters appear in Steinberg's *Spiridonova, Revolutionary Terrorist,* pp. 224–225.

[11]Not long after this, Kamkov was arrested and sentenced to three years of imprisonment. A defendant in Stalin's 1938 Purge Trial, he was sentenced to death and executed.

[12]A. A. Izmailovich, *Krem' za Reshetkoy,* Berlin, 1922. pp. 17–19.

guards who observed her every move, lying on a blood-soaked mattress, her head pounding with pain, there kept ringing in her brain the phrase, "I will not surrender"; "I will not surrender." As she did fifteen years earlier in the Tambov prison, Maria survived ill treatment in the Kremlin Barracks on sheer will power.

Meanwhile, in the old hotels of Moscow—refurbished for the occasion and decorated with huge banners bearing red-lettered revolutionary slogans—delegates to the Third Congress of the Third International,[13] and the First Congress of Red Trade Unions International, were being wined and dined. The leading Bolsheviks delivered orations on their great revolutionary accomplishments, elaborating on the wonderful future awaiting the workers of the world as soon as they began to follow in the footsteps of revolutionary Russia. Emma Goldman reported that since the foreign delegates had access to Bolshevik leaders, some of Maria Spiridonova's friends who feared for her life in the terrible conditions of her imprisonment, prevailed upon a woman delegate who was scheduled to interview Trotsky to deliver to him a request for Maria's release. The woman did so, and reported that Trotsky refused. He said Spiridonova was "too dangerous to be liberated."[14]

Finally the Moscow Revolutionary Tribunal again passed sentence on Maria Spiridonova: one year in a sanitarium "to engage in healthy physical and intellectual labor" and then "permanent isolation from political and social life." Her friends did not think the weak, sick Maria would survive the railroad trip to the sanitarium at Malakhovka. The old driver of a horse-drawn carriage who took her to the railroad station helped her onto the train then took off his cap, crossed himself and muttered, "Save her, O God! Save her."

The revolutionary career of Maria Spiridonova was over. For the second time in her life she faced incarceration and exile. But this time she faced something worse: extinction. Not death and martyrdom, not exile with the bright hope that the revolution would come to deliver her and the people of Russia from misery and injustice. In her "open letter" to the Bolshevik Central Executive Committee she had warned that the time would surely come when the Bolsheviks' "stifling of the living soul of the revolution" would provoke opposition in their own ranks; but by the time she got on the train for Malakhovka these words had acquired a hollow ring.

In the early phase of the Russian Revolution, when turbulent events were far outdistancing the ability of the Provisional Government to control them, the old-line Esser leaders ignored Maria Spiridonova, even though she was more often right than they were in her assessment of the issues that needed

---

[13]The Third, or Communist International (Comintern) was created by Lenin in 1919.
[14]Emma Goldman, *My Further Disillusionment in Russia*, New York, 1923, pp. 107–109.

swift, decisive action. Shunted aside by the traditional leaders of her own party, she turned to the Bolsheviks. And they betrayed her. The outside observer, far removed in time and space, finds it easy to lay the blame for her mistakes on her political inexperience (a flaw characteristic of most of Russia's revolutionary leaders) but there is evidence that she linked the Russian revolution's failures to the paucity of women in the ranks of revolutionary leaders once the revolution actually came. In reply to a question asked her by the American journalist, Louise Bryant, as to why so few women held public office in revolutionary Russia, Maria Spiridonova said:

> Before the revolution as many women as men went to Siberia; some years there were even more women. . . . Now that was all a very different matter from holding public office. It needs temperament and not training to be a martyr. Politicians are usually not very fine; they accept political positions when they are elected to them—not because they are especially fitted for them. I think women are more conscientious. Men are used to overlooking their consciences; women are not[15]

Maria Spiridonova, like the Russian girl on the threshhold in Turgenev's poem, decided early in life to sacrifice herself to the cause of freedom, to commit a crime for it. She had come to know that she had been mistaken in placing her trust in those she thought were true revolutionaries. Was she a fool? Or a saint?

ANNOTATED REFERENCES

In addition to newspaper accounts, including those in *Znamia Truda, Novaia Zhizn', Pravda,* and *Izvestiia,* the course of events in party and soviet councils in 1918 in which Maria Spiridonova participated are covered in considerable detail and with diametrically opposite interpretations in I. Z. Steinberg, *Spiridonova, Revolutionary Terrorist,* London, 1935, and Vera Vladimirova, *God Sluzhby "Sotsialistov" Kapitalistam. Ocherki po Istorii Kontr-revoliutsii v 1918 godu* (The Year of the "Socialists" Subservience to Capitalism. Essays on the History of the Counter-Revolution of 1918), Moscow-Leningrad, 1927. Beginning on page 265, Vladimirova gives the Soviet version of Left Esser and Right Esser terrorist policies in the summer of 1918, and devotes considerable space to recounting the "criminal" acts, contemplated acts, and even the dreams of Maria Spiridonova. Oliver Henry Radkey, *The Sickle Under the Hammer,* New York, 1963, also has many references to Spiridonova's role during this period.

Bruce Lockhart, *British Agent,* London and New York, 1932, described Spiridonova's July 4 speech and the audience reaction to it, p. 298, and her appearance as a prisoner in the Kremlin Barracks, p. 332.

Spiridonova's colleague who advised her to marry and give up politics was Prosh Prosh'ian. Her article "Prosh Prosh'ian" appeared in *Katorga i Ssylka,* no. 9, 1924.

---

[15]Louise Bryant, *Six Red Months in Russia,* New York, 1918, p. 169.

A. A. Izmailovich, *Kreml' za Reshetkoy. Pis'ma iz Kremlevskoy Tiur'my M.A. Spiridonovoy i*

A. A. Izmailovskoy (Behind Kremlin Bars. Letters from the Kremlin Prison by M. S. Spiridonova and A. A. Izmailovich), Podpol'naia Rossiia (Underground Russia), printed by "Skiffy," Berlin, 1922. Aleksandra Izmailovich was arrested July 6 along with Maria Spiridonova and imprisoned in the Kremlin Barracks but was not held long. In January 1919 she was arrested in her home town, Minsk, and soon released. In October 1919 she was sent to the Butyrki Prison and held until September 1921. After that, for the rest of her life, she, with Maria Spiridonova and several other of the Mal'tsev women, was kept under house arrest—"free confinement," the Bolsheviks called it! The old *izvozchik's* prayer for Maria as he put her on the train in 1921, appears on p. 48.

Pis'mo M. Spiridnovoy Tsentral'nomu Komitetu Partii Bol'shevikov, Noiabria, 1918. (The letter of M. Spiridonova to the Central Committee of the Bolshevik party, November 1918). On the title page: Moscow, 1919, but on the last page: Khar'kov, Tipografiia Partiy Levykh Sotsialistov-Revoliutsionov. A translation of much of this letter appears in I. Z. Steinberg, *In the Workshop of the Revolution*, New York and Toronto, 1953.

10

Revolutionary Women Versus
the Bolsheviks

In May 1918, more than a month before the Left Essers made public their decision to execute selected German Imperial officials on Russian soil (the "hangmen of the Russian revolution"), their oblique way of combating Bolshevik tyranny, they sent a combat group to Kiev to investigate the possibility of making General Eichhorn their first target. Eichhorn, who led the German military occupation of the Ukraine, carried out in fulfillment of the terms of the Brest-Litovsk Treaty, was the real ruler of the Ukraine.

Irina Kakhovskaya was chosen to head the combat group. A pretty, fair-skinned woman with blue eyes and brown hair, she looked much younger than her twenty-nine years. She had returned in the spring of 1917 from the Siberian *katorga* after serving half of the twenty-year sentence passed on her in 1907 by a tsarist court-martial. Her crime was organizing Esser revolutionary cells of workers in St. Petersburg.

In taking the path of revolutionary radicalism, Irina resumed a family tradition started by Peter Kakhovsky, one of the five young aristocrats hanged for their roles in the 1825 Decembrist insurrection against Tsar Nikolai I. Young Peter, convinced that regicide was a necessary moral weapon against tyranny, volunteered to signal the start of the planned uprising by shooting the new Tsar when he appeared on Senate Square in St. Petersburg on December 14 to accept the oath of allegiance from his army officers. The Tsar, learning of the plot, did not appear as scheduled, so Peter was deprived of the honor of shooting him. Instead he shot and killed two officers who came to issue the Tsar's order to the assembled officers to disperse. In prison, just before he was hanged, Peter wrote:

A person carried away by a pure idea sacrifices himself, not in order to receive glory or a line in history, but to perform good for the sake of good, without reward.

Irina, like Peter, was carried away by the "pure idea" and in the end sacrificed herself for it.

Born on her family's estate near the village of Tarashcha, not far from Kiev, Irina Kakhovskaya spent her childhood and her university days in St. Petersburg where her father was a land surveyor and her mother a teacher. She became politically active at age seventeen during the Revolution of 1905 when she joined the newly formed Bolshevik faction of the illegal Social Democratic Party. She was secretary of the St. Petersburg district organization of the Bolshevik party for over a year; then she found the radical program of the Socialist Revolutionary Maximalists more to her liking and joined them in 1906.[1] In this decision she was strongly influenced by her admiration of the Esser women activists. In the articles she wrote describing her prison experience after her arrest in 1907, she portrayed vividly and movingly how she and her high-spirited young women companions coped with prison life.

Upon her return from Siberia in the spring of 1917, Irina plunged into Esser party work. When the party split she joined the Left Essers, led by Maria Spiridonova, her long-admired heroine and *katorga* comrade. Soon recognized for her remarkable organizing ability, Irina became a member of the Left Esser Executive Committee and was appointed Director of Propaganda.

For the Eichhorn expedition, the Left Essers assigned to Irina's combat group the old revolutionary, Comrade Smolyanski, and a young sailor, Boris Donskoi. The Left Essers, always conscious of the international character of socialism, wanted to test public reaction abroad before making final their decision to target German officers in Russia for assassination. Smolyanski's first task, therefore, was to leave Russia and make a survey of the reaction of socialist leaders in other European countries. It was left to Irina and Boris Donskoi to reconnoiter the Ukraine.

They went by train, first to Sevastopol where they gathered information, made contact with local Left Essers, and were instructed in the use of explosives. Then they circled back to Kiev. The train trip gave Irina the opportunity she needed to assess her young associate. She was satisfied with what she identified as a strong will, courage, stamina, and the ability to remain cool under trying circumstances.

A native of Kazan, Donskoi as a boy of fifteen had come to St. Petersburg to work in a factory. He told Irina that it was there, for the first time in his life, he was able to obtain books. From them he educated himself. He was

---

[1]The Maximalists were a small radical faction of the Esser party.

Irina Kakhovskaya

strongly drawn to the ideas of Tolstoy. In the Russian mobilization at the outbreak of World War I he was drafted as a sailor in the Baltic Fleet, headquartered at the great naval base of Kronshtadt. There he came under the influence of socialist propaganda. He organized protest meetings after he observed and experienced the insolence and cruelty of Russian naval officers toward sailors.

On one occasion Donskoi inaugurated a hunger strike. Imprisoned for this, he was transformed into a thoroughgoing revolutionary. On his release he joined the Esser party and energetically served as its spokesman in the Baltic Fleet. When the Esser party split, he went over to the Left Essers. Despite his reputation for militancy, Irina was impressed with the young man's gentleness and his eagerness to learn. He brought books with him to read on the train and was excited to be traveling through a part of Russia unknown to him.

As their train made its way across the Ukraine, Irina and Donskoi saw firsthand the confusion, destruction, and suffering in the small towns and the countryside. The train was often halted or rerouted because of military skirmishes. Therefore, even though she had not made all the contacts she thought necessary to insure the success of a strike against Eichhorn, Irina decided to return to Moscow. If they stayed longer she feared they might find themselves stranded, completely cut off from party headquarters where in this time of fast-moving events momentous decisions were being made.

Irina and Donskoi arrived in Moscow while the Second Congress of the Left Essers was in session. Smolyanski had returned from his mission convinced that the Left Esser "execution" of Eichhorn would be positively received abroad. Irina and Donskoi reported that the suffering people of the Ukraine needed a terrorist strike against Eichhorn who was a cruel tyrant. As proof of Ukrainian readiness, they introduced three members of a Ukrainian combat committee who had come to join forces with the Moscow group in the plot against Eichhorn. Following that, they were ready to strike down Eichhorn's Ukrainian puppet, the Hetman Skoropadski.

The go-ahead for the assassination of Field Marshal Eichhorn was given by the Executive Committee at the end of May. Irina, Donskoi, and the three Ukrainians, armed with explosives, guns, money, and a cache of false passports, left by train for Kiev. Of the Ukrainians, the most important was a young woman called Marusya, described by Irina as an experienced party worker entirely devoted to the revolution. In appearance she was so elegant and so beautiful Irina felt she would never be suspected, even by the cleverest of the secret police, of being a revolutionary. She was their liaison agent. In the chaos and confusion of Kiev, a city unknown to them and in the throes of rapid revolutionary changeovers from one regime to another, the information she was able to relay to Irina more than once saved not only their mission but their lives.

Traveling from Moscow on separate trains, the five revolutionaries quickly melted into crowds of Russians at the railway stations, most of them trying to flee the revolution. They hoped to get through the Red Guards on one side of the frontier, and the array of armed Germans on the other, with their jewels, money, and other precious possessions. The revolutionaries carried all their illicit goods concealed on their persons except a supply of false passports, which was carefully hidden in the lining of a valise.

After several days Irina and Donskoi's train stopped in the middle of the night, in a driving rain, at a point near the frontier. Forced out of the train, they stood in the rain, worrying about keeping their explosives dry until permitted by the border guards to pass. Dawn finally came and the Ukrainian comrades were nowhere to be seen. Hundreds of horse-drawn vehicles of every conceivable description were lined up alongside the train waiting to take the passengers cleared by Russian border guards across the frontier. Donskoi and Irina rented a wagon at an exorbitant price and were slowly driven the short distance to the border where German guards stopped them, brusquely searched them, and inspected their baggage. The revolutionaries saw people arrested, brutally treated, and turned back, but they got through. They were taken to a little railroad station, and when the train steamed in, were crowded into a car by the German officials in charge. They soon arrived in Kiev and hired a carriage to take them to an address previously given them by Marusya.

Kiev was beautiful. The rain had stopped, and in brilliant sunshine they saw flowers everywhere, green grass, and the rainbow spray of fountains. The people crowding the streets were well-dressed, the women in light spring frocks. The shop windows were alluring, the cafes overflowing with people. Elegantly dressed German officers walked the streets, along with Ukrainian officers of the Hetman's guard. Everywhere soldiers were singing German military songs and Ukrainian melodies accompanied by the roll of drums. There were orchestras in the gardens; the air was filled with music and the perfumed scent of flowering trees. What a striking contrast to Moscow—famished and icy! As Irina saw it, here, under the protection of German bayonets, people were frantically amusing themselves, playing, singing, living an artificial life, trying to forget the doom in the offing.

The plotters were soon joined by Smolyanski. Although housing accommodations in overcrowded Kiev were almost unattainable, Marusya and her co-workers succeeded in finding each of the three Moscow comrades a room in the heart of the city—each with a landlady who was dealing in some illegal commodity, such as saccharine or alcohol. They used false passports, went under assumed names, and posed as temporary lodgers. Irina passed as a visiting relative of a Kiev family, Smolyanski as a businessman, and Donskoi as a tourist. They also rented a small villa in the suburbs where they could meet together, and if necessary, spend a night or hide out in nearby woods. They bought a fiacre and a horse, and rented a shanty where these could be left when not in use. There they stored their dynamite and guns and set up a primitive laboratory, where—when the right moment arrived—they would put together the necessary bombs.

According to information supplied by Marusya, Field Marshal Eichhorn was living in the Lipki quarter of Kiev. The Moscow plotters immediately headed for Lipki, one of the city's most beautiful residential districts which they found had been transformed into a veritable military camp. Every home was occupied by a member of the German high command and every avenue was patrolled by a guard corps. All shops and boutiques had been vacated. There was not a house nor a room for rent. The streets were so deserted and under such heavy surveillance by the secret police and posted guards that for a person to walk along them was to subject him or herself to suspicion. Irina had to admit that the procedures used by the Esser Battle Organizations in tsarist times were inadequate for this assignment.

Irina had been told Eichhorn walked every day the short distance from his residence on Katerina Street to the nearby General Headquarters, surrounded by a heavy guard. She decided they should plan their attack at that point of the Field Marshal's daily routine. To be seen on any street in the Lipki district more than once was to invite being picked up for interrogation. Therefore, the problem was how to conduct the continuous observation necessary to acquire minute knowledge of the streets Eichhorn traversed, the exact time of his emergence from his residence, the path he followed to General Headquarters, the length of time he usually stayed there, and the number and location of his guard.

The plotters used the ruse of having one of their number walk alone, casually enter the Lipki district and proceed along a designated street, making mental notes of every detail, then just as casually turn and saunter back. By means of costume changes and disguises—wigs, false beards, moustaches, paste, paint and powder—they managed to frequent the Lipki district every day without detection.

All this observation was time consuming. The month of June went by and the Left Esser plotters in Kiev still had not assassinated Field Marshal Eichhorn. Meanwhile the Left Essers in Moscow had made public their decision to rouse public opinion against Bolshevik tyranny by assassinating on Russian soil carefully targeted German officials. In accordance with that decision, the German Ambassador, Count von Mirbach, had been assassinated in Moscow on July 6. The next day the Bolshevik Government ordered the jailing of the four hundred fifty Esser delegates to the Fifth Congress of Soviets, including the members of the Esser's Executive Committee.

Growing opposition to Bolshevik policies and the Bolsheviks' bloody reprisals were rapidly pushing revolutionary Russia into civil war. On July 18, a startling news item was flashed from Moscow by radio to the world:

> The ex-Tsar, Nikolai the Bloody, was shot July 16, 1918, in the Siberian mining town of Katerinburg [present day Sverdlovsk] by order of the Ural Regional Soviet.

The Bolshevik commissar who announced the execution said Nikolai was shot as a "stern warning to counter-revolutionaries who are trying to drown the workers' and peasants' revolution in blood." It would prevent counter-revolutionary armies, which, he said, were closing in on the Ural region, from releasing the Tsar and restoring him to the throne. "They never shall, because we have shot him!" The killing of the Tsar was accompanied by the shooting of hundreds of others in Katerinburg as Bolshevik mass terror gained momentum.

The carefully laid plans to effect restoration of Left Esser revolutionary leadership through a few terrorist acts were swept into disarray by these fast-running tides of violence. In Kiev, Irina Kakhovskaya and her small combat group were left in limbo. Cut off as they were from Moscow and left without further instructions, they proceeded nonetheless with their plans against Eichhorn.

Their first stroke of luck occurred one day as Irina was doing her daily turn of observation on a street in the Lipki district. She suddenly found herself "nose to nose" with Eichhorn, and learned from her encounter that he left his dwelling punctually at one o'clock, cane in hand, accompanied by his aide-de-camp. He nonchalantly responded to the salute of a row of soldiers who made up his guard, seemingly convinced the forest of bayonets guarding the district assured his absolute security. Exactly three minutes after he left his residence, he disappeared inside General Headquarters. Except for a row of soldiers the street was so deserted that the silhouette of Eichhorn and his aide could be clearly seen for a considerable distance. Most important of all, Irina saw that when the general and his aide crossed the street, they were almost without escort. After one hour in the General Headquarters building, Eichhorn repeated the three-minute trip back to his residence.

How could they take advantage of Irina's discovery? A plotter could not simply wait in the street. With pistol and well-secreted bomb, he or she would have to be walking casually along the street in the three-minute space of time it took Eichhorn to get to or from his residence and Army Headquarters.

While working out the way to accomplish this juxtaposition during the daylight hours, Irina was spending her nights staking out the movements of the Hetman Skoropadsky. She hid behind the thick trunks of linden trees lining the driveway to his palace, taking note of the elegant automobiles entering and leaving the palace gates all night long. In colorful Ukrainian costumes and glittering evening dress the courtesans of the Hetman ascended the brilliantly lighted front stairway of the palace. A successful attempt on the Hetman seemed easy because of his careless ways and his expansive evenings of entertainment during which he frequently came out to greet or say farewell to his guests. However, Eichhorn had to be dispatched first. Execution of the Hetman would put the Germans on their guard.

Just as Irina's group was ready to strike at Eichhorn, he suddenly departed for the Crimea. There were days of idleness. Then the date of his return to Kiev was published, along with information about a reception planned for him. The plotters shifted the locus of attack to the railroad station on the assumption that there he would be a more conspicuous target than on the street in the Lipki district.

On the scheduled day Irina and two co-plotters were at the railroad station, each armed with a bomb. The designated train pulled into the station, but to their chagrin Eichhorn did not appear. They soon found that he had returned to Kiev the day before. Irina then shifted back to the original plan. She later wrote:

> Then began the terrible period. In a state of extreme excitement, hollow-eyed, nerves as tight as coiled springs, on the edge of desperation but with your heart in your mouth, you determine each day to hold your spirit ready for the sacrifice of your life.

Since the purpose of assassinating Eichhorn was to produce the maximum political agitation, it was necessary that the terrorist who carried out the deed be caught and tried before a court of law. The perpetrator must divulge his or her name and explain the significance of the act for all the world to hear, while expressing the wish to die for the cause of restoring justice and the sanctity of the revolutionary idea of freedom.

Boris Donskoi succeeded in convincing Irina that he must be the first to make the attempt on Eichhorn's life. Irina said his eyes shone with joy at the prospect of being able to sacrifice his young life to the promise of the future. The necessity of having to kill a man was to him tragic. It was a crime, and only by his own death could he redeem himself and his cause. He rejected all plans for escape, and wrote a letter to his mother for delivery after his death. He simply asked for her blessing—not her pity—telling her of his supreme joy at having the privilege of sacrificing himself for the cause he held sacred.

For several days, each time in a different costume, makeup and wig, and armed with a bomb, Donskoi walked into the Lipki district. At a discreet distance the other plotters, on the *qui vive,* strolled casually, listening intently for the explosion. On four different occasions Donskoi walked out of the Lipki district, furious—with his bomb intact. He was checked once by a fiacre crossing the street at the crucial moment, another time by a group of children passing close to the general. Once Eichhorn did not appear at all. On another occasion Donskoi was positioned exactly right, reached for the bomb, the cover came off and he dropped it almost at the general's feet. Donskoi bent over, picked it up, and walked off without anyone paying any attention to him!

Irina was worried. Donskoi was visibly tired, but he was obstinate. With a constant flame in his eye, each day he returned to the task to which he had dedicated his life.

On July 30, following the usual routine, Donskoi walked up and back the length of Katerina Street without encountering Eichhorn. Crestfallen and near desperation, he joined his strolling co-plotters outside the Lipki district. As they turned to go, each on a separate street, a man approached and insistently demanded that someone tell him the way to General Eichhorn's residence. As the man went off down the street toward Lipki, Donskoi suddenly whirled around and walked behind him. Five minutes later the plotters heard a violent explosion.

They ran toward the Lipki district and found people gathering. Soldiers were blocking the way. They heard voices saying, "The general is dead." "The general is lightly wounded." "The aide-de-camp is dead." Hurrying away, Irina and two plotters got into a hired fiacre and ordered the driver to take them to a place near their suburban villa. Along the way they picked up an evening newspaper with a headline announcing that Field Marshal Eichhorn was near death. According to the lead story the general's aide-de-camp was dead and the assassin was alive. From the newspapers the next morning the plotters learned Eichhorn was dead. His assassin was identified as a sailor of the Baltic Fleet and a Left Esser.

After that news—nothing. Rumors floated wildly. The Germans were preparing to bombard the city in reprisal. Mass arrests were taking place. Kiev would be razed by the Germans. But none of these things happened.

Writing later about the event, Irina reported that in the villages and towns of the Ukraine there was joy. Everyone was saying, "Now it's the Hetman's turn." In great haste the plotters proceeded with plans for the Hetman's assassination. They were also putting the finishing touches on their proclamation to the world on the purpose and meaning of their assassinations.

The occasion chosen for the attack on the Hetman was Eichhorn's funeral, scheduled for August 1 in the Lutheran Church of Kiev. The Hetman would assist at the service. The plan was to assassinate him when he came out of the church. The plotters worked feverishly. Irina was hampered because she did not dare return to her room in the city. Some of the Ukrainian comrades had been arrested, but one who was thought to be still free was scheduled to deliver two bombs at an assigned meeting place. He did not appear. She went to his residence. The landlady said German officers had come in an automobile during the night and taken him away. Irina rushed off and with a comrade prepared another bomb, but she arrived at the funeral too late. The Hetman had already departed.

Badly needing rest, Irina and two comrades decided to spend the night at their suburban villa. After the long drive, they got out of the fiacre at a corner some distance away and approached the villa on foot. As they reached the garden, even though everything outside appeared normal, Irina noticed in the lighted living room a shadow falling across the tea table. "Someone is there," she whispered. Then came the deafening crack of a dozen rifles being fired into the air.

Suddenly Irina found herself standing alone, blinded by the light of a lantern dangling in front of her face. Her companions had gotten away, but she was pinned against the wall of the verandah with ten armed German soldiers in front of her. On all sides stood the Cossacks who had directed the ambush.

During the night she was interrogated, and the next morning an automobile arrived to take her to a German prison. The two German officers "of repugnant grossness and vulgarity" who conducted her, appeared to delight in recounting in detail the tortures being inflicted on Donskoi.

Irina was indicted for the murder of Field Marshal Eichhorn and was put in irons in solitary confinement in a cell, empty except for dirty straw on the floor. Donskoi was in the same prison, but no one would give her any word of him.

After about a week, still in irons, Irina was moved. One day a prisoner, whose crime was an insignificant misdemeanor, was put into her cell. Seeing her in irons, he said, "You must be here for the same reason as the sailor they hanged on Sunday morning." He told her Donskoi's body was left for two hours hanging from a telephone pole with a placard—"Assassin of General Eichhorn"—hanging round his neck. This was how Irina learned of the death of Boris Donskoi on August 10, 1918.

The prisoner told Irina, and she too had observed, that most of the prisoners were peasants and working men. They were being very badly treated, he said. They were aware of Donskoi's deed and the tortures he was subjected to and they felt he had suffered and died for them. They honored him for his bravery and his sacrifice. She also learned from the prisoner that during three days of the most horrible torture, Donskoi had not revealed the names of any of his comrades. Irina knew that she herself faced the same fate as Donskoi and tried to resign herself to it.

With the successful strike against Field Marshall Eichhorn, another Left Esser strategic objective had been accomplished. But again, the expected rising tide of public support for the terrorists and their party and the anticipated surge of opposition to Bolshevik tyranny did not appear.

In the summer of 1918 violence prevailed in revolutionary Russia. Bolshevik party chiefs, by heavy-handed suppression of opposing political parties accompanied by threats, jailings, and executions, had succeeded in intimidating but by no means eliminating their opponents. As long as the very numerous Left Esser activists functioned underground and continued their dedication to political assassination, there was always the possibility the next target might be a Bolshevik leader. Plots by Right Essers, anarchists and other disaffected groups were festering under the surface. There was reason to fear that one of the myriad of foreign agents swarming over Moscow might be commissioned as an assassin. Outside the capital, too, anti-Bolshevik insurrections were taking place, and troops of the West European Allies and Japan had landed in Archangel and Siberia.

Apprehensive over the danger to the lives of their leaders, the Bolsheviks made more and more stringent efforts to protect them and keep their movements and whereabouts secret. Yet it was essential that these leaders—especially Lenin—appear constantly before the public to whip up enthusiasm with promises, threats, and demagogic appeals.

The usual procedure was to call an evening meeting at a factory, a school, or an office. Rumors would at once begin: "Lenin is going to speak tonight," or Trotsky, or some other luminary. Considerably later than the announced hour the speaker would suddenly arrive, usually by motor car, deliver a rousing speech, then depart as quickly as he had come, to be speeded away to another meeting.

On the rainy evening of August 30, 1918, at the Mikhelson Factory, across the Moscow River from the Kremlin, the Factory Committee announced a meeting for that evening. After a hard day's work, tired people filed into the factory block where the meeting was to be held. When asked who the speaker would be, the chairman of the Factory Committee replied, "Comrade Lenin." Two women had been standing, chain-smoking, in the rear of the hall at a table where revolutionary pamphlets were on sale. They pricked up their ears on hearing the name "Lenin."

About seven o'clock Lenin walked rapidly into the hall and spoke on the subject of "Bourgeois Dictatorship and Proletarian Dictatorship." In lurid detail he threatened the assembled workers with the perils of bourgeois dictatorship if they did not give their full support to the Bolshevik dictatorship, the only power that could save the revolution and its glorious promise for the future.

After his speech, which lasted about an hour, Lenin—still talking and gesticulating—strode out of the factory, surrounded by a crowd of workers as he raced down a short flight of stairs and across a small open space to his waiting automobile. When he was about three steps away from the car, the voice of a young woman called out, "You are taking away the people's bread." Then she, or someone near her, raised a bare arm, aimed a Browning pistol, and fired three shots in quick succession. Two of the bullets found their target, penetrating Lenin's neck and shoulder. He plummeted to the ground.

The sound of the shots, like the dry popping of the motor cars of that day, attracted no attention. Then it was noticed that Lenin lay prone and seemingly dead. Confusion and mounting panic spread as people ran in all directions and shouted for vengeance on the murderer of Lenin. Meanwhile, the woman who fired the shots had dropped her pistol and melted into the crowd.

Lenin was lifted into his car and driven back to his apartment in the Kremlin. According to newspaper accounts in the following days, Lenin, though wounded, was recuperating rapidly. Within a week it was enthusiastically announced he had fully recovered. These over-optimistic reports were designed to obscure the seriousness of the Bolshevik leader's wounds, since one bullet broke his shoulder and the other passed through his lungs and lodged in his neck. There are indications he never fully recovered.

The person who later claimed he caught Lenin's would-be assassin said that he saw a woman nervously standing aside from the turbulent crowd, holding a briefcase and an umbrella. She had the fightened look of a person contemplating escape. He walked up to her and roughly asked, "Did you shoot Lenin?" She said, "Why do I have to tell you that?" Again he asked her.

When it became apparent to the milling crowd that this woman was being accused of the crime, it quickly became a lynch mob. Only fast action by the militia and Red Army men who moved in to encircle the accused woman made it possible to escort her unharmed to the War Commissariat of the Moscow District where she immediately underwent interrogation by several *Cheka* agents.

During the two days in 1918 when she figured in the headlines, the woman accused of shooting Lenin was referred to in the foreign press as Dora Kaplan, which may have been one of the aliases she used as a revolutionary. In her testimony before the *Cheka* agents on the night of August 30, 1918, she said her name was Fanya Efimovna Roidman, but that from the year 1906 she had gone by the name Fanny Kaplan.[2] This information was not made public until extracts were published in the Soviet historical journal *Proletarskaia Revoliutsiia* (Numbers 6–7, 1923), following the 1922 trial of Essers. She said she was twenty-eight years old, born in Volynski Province (which was in the Pale of Jewish settlement), and educated at home. Her father, a Jewish teacher, had taken his family to America in 1911. She had remained in Russia and had found a job in Kiev training workers for participation in local government assemblies, the *zemstva*. Secretly she had joined an anarchist group and in 1906 was apprehended in what she called "a bombing incident in Kiev." From other sources it is known that she participated in an assassination attempt on the life of the governor-general of Kiev. The bomb she was carrying exploded, injuring her, causing her arrest and trial in a military court where she was sentenced to death. The sentence was later changed to life imprisonment in Siberia, where she resided in one prison after another (several years in Mal'tsev) until the general amnesty following the February Revolution in 1917. She testified to the *Cheka* that in Siberia she was converted from anarchism to socialism by her fellow prisoners, some of whom she named, including Maria Spiridonova and Anastasia Bitzenko.

Coming out of prison into revolutionary Russia in 1917, she said she had

---

[2]Several of the women whose recollections were published in *Na Zhenoskoi Katorge*, edited by Vera Figner, mention her as a fellow prisoner, give her name as Fanny Roitblat, and list it in the roster of the names of inmates as Roitblat-Kaplan.

become active in the Esser party and had gone on missions in various parts of the country. She said she had also become increasingly disturbed by Bolshevik policies and decided, on her own, to shoot Lenin because she considered him a traitor to the cause of socialism. "I decided that the longer Lenin lived, the longer he would betray the ideas of socialism."

Most historians outside Russia give credence to Fanny Kaplan's claim that she was a loner. They regard as untrustworthy the testimony given in the 1922 Trial of the Essers which linked her and several other Esser women to plots on the lives of Lenin, Trotsky, and other Bolshevik leaders, including Mikhail Uritsky, head of the Petrograd *Cheka*. A young officer, a member of a dissident group called the Union of Regeneration, got to Uritsky before the Essers did and shot him on August 30, the same day as the attempt on Lenin's life.

Traditionally, Esser terrorist targets were carefully chosen by the party's central organization, but revolutionary upheaval had disrupted the chain of command and there was great leeway for action by individuals or small detached groups. One such individual, Elizabeta Pilenko, an Esser leader in the Black Sea area, and Mayor of the town of Anapa, got caught up in the excitement of the revival of terrorism when she came to Moscow as a delegate to the Congress of Soviets and decided to shoot Trotsky. She said she was revolted by his political chicanery. Lacking experience as a revolutionary plotter, she told several friends of her plan and they succeeded in tricking her out of it.[3]

Fanny Kaplan was shot without a trial two days after her alleged attempt on Lenin's life. In his notebook, published in the journal *Moskva* in 1958, Pavel Malkov, commandant of the Kremlin, wrote that he was ordered to bring Kaplan from her cell on Lubyanka Square to the Kremlin where she was put in a basement room.

While Fanny Kaplan was still at Lubyanka she was seen by Bruce Lockhart, the British agent who was picked up at 3:30 A. M. the night Lenin was shot and questioned as to whether he knew Kaplan. According to *Pravda* headlines, Lenin's would-be assassin was the lackey of an Anglo-French imperialist clique. When Lockhart refused to answer any questions, claiming diplomatic immunity, an attempt to trick him into giving some sign of recognition was made when at six o'clock in the morning a woman was brought into his cell. He had never seen her before, but in his book *British Agent* he identified her as Kaplan and wrote this description of her:

---

[3]Lisa Pilenko is better known as a Russian emigré in Paris under the name "Mother Maria." She was a benefactor of the victims of the Nazi occupation of France, and finally a victim herself, dying in a Nazi concentration camp during World War II. See T. Stratton Smith, *The Rebel Nun*, London, 1965.

She was dressed in black. Her hair was black and her eyes, set in a fixed stare, had great black rings under them. Her face was colorless. Her features, strongly Jewish, were unattractive. She might have been any age between 20 and 35. Her composure was unnatural. She went to the window, and, leaning her chin upon her hand, looked out into the daylight, and there she remained, motionless, speechless, apparently resigned to her fate, until presently the sentries came and took her away. She was shot before she knew whether her attempt to alter history failed or succeeded.

Far more revealing than this unattractive sketch of a woman, who, when Lockhart saw her, had just emerged from a seven-hour grilling by *Cheka* agents, are the character traits that somehow come through the excerpted statements of her interrogation. Among other things she said that the decision to shoot Lenin had been maturing in her mind for some time, but like Boris Donskoi in Kiev, she refused to reveal any accomplices. Confronted with the names of a number of women who had committed terrorist acts in tsarist times and had returned, as she had, in 1917 from the *katorga*, she said she had known them only in various prisons in Siberia. Some of them she had recently seen on the street, or had accidentally met on streetcars, but the only subject of conversation was the questions ex-prisoners always ask each other about former prisonmates: Who was alive? Who was dead?

Repeatedly asked about links to other known terrorists, Fanny either denied such links, or said "I do not wish to speak about this." She said she had recently returned from the Crimea and that the present rule there and in the Ukraine—the German occupation—was hated by the people. Asked where she got the revolver she used to shoot Lenin, she refused to answer.

Fanny Kaplan's interrogators went through her purse and questioned her about its contents. They found a professional union card. She denied being a member of any union and insisted she simply found the card, put it in her purse, and forgot about it. Asked how she acquired a Tomilino-Moscow railway ticket, she said she did not remember. They found pieces of paper in one of her shoes. She said when she was in the Commissariat she asked for something to put in her shoe because there was a nail sticking up through the sole. "They gave me these pieces of paper, they or the soldiers. I don't remember."

After their interrogation, the *Cheka* officers ordered Malkov to shoot Fanny immediately. When he asked where he should bury her, his superior said, "We shall not bury Kaplan. Destroy her remains so no trace is left." Malkov's published notes record that he removed several trucks from the Kremlin garage into the courtyard and started the motors. Then he led Fanny out of the prison and ordered her to walk toward a car. At her first step he shot her from behind. Fanny Kaplan was the first woman to be executed by the revolutionary government.

The assassination of Mirbach had given Bolshevik mass terror a sharp impetus, but the attempt on the life of Lenin opened the floodgates. The *Red Terror* was justified in decrees, banners, headlines, speeches. On September 4, *Pravda* announced:

> We have declared mass terror against our enemies and after the murder of Comrade Uritzky and the wounding of Comrade Lenin, we have decided to make this mass terror not a paper thing but a reality. Mass shootings of hostages are taking place in many cities. This is good. . . . Without the least wavering nor the least indecision in the application of mass terror we will rid ourselves of all vile plotters.

In a few days in Petrograd alone, five hundred "counter-revolutionaries" were shot. Reports of *Cheka* officials in various parts of Russia in the 1918–1920 period put the figures of killings in the Red Terror at approximately fifty thousand. In the course of this bloodbath the leadership of the Esser party, Right and Left, was systematically destroyed. Individuals and groups who did not succeed in escaping Russia were shot and exiled. As one observer said, "Lenin's massive state terror brings to an end the terror of the individual assassin."

Fanny Kaplan was dead. All over Russia the Red Terror was raging, and in a Kiev prison Irina Kakhovskaya, in irons, lying on dirty straw on the floor of her prison cell, awaited her fate as the accused accomplice in the murder of Field Marshall Eichhorn.

There came a night when the corridor to Irina's cell was bolted. Several German officers came in and subjected her to an all-night session of interrogation mixed with violence as they attempted to force her to reveal the names of her comrades. In the morning, with bruised arms and legs, she lay stretched out, half-conscious, when the German commandant of the prison came in. He got down on one knee, gave her a lecture on the uselessness of terrorism, and left with her a copy of the Bible. That night the guards took the irons off her arms and legs and gave her a fresh straw pallet.

The next day they began the interrogation in preparation for her court-martial trial. Every morning the German officer from the legal department who had been appointed prosecutor came in with a chair, a table, and a secretary. He questioned Irina until evening with a short stop for lunch. She later wrote that she spoke freely to him about the motives of the terrorist campaign of the Left Essers and about the ideology and psychology of terrorism, and the secretary took it all down. She had no idea whether this *proces verbeaux* was kept in the German Army files after the trial.

The evening before the trial, her interrogator, a well-educated, seemingly not unkind man who made it clear that terrorism was repugnant to him, asked Irina whether she regretted her role in the assassination of Eichhorn. "Does what you said correspond exactly to your political and moral convictions? If Donskoi had failed, would you yourself have made the attempt on the life of General Eichhorn?" The secretary took down her affirmative responses. The officer rose, put the paper into the dossier, said "Now we have all we need," and walked out.

The trial took place in the prison office. The prosecutor asked for the death penalty. The officially appointed German defender mumbled something about the idealism of people like Irina Kakhovskaya and Boris Donskoi who cannot be compared to vile murderers. Irina said she saw brutishness and indifference on the faces of the German officers serving as judges. She was asked if she had aided in the murder, if she had participated in it in every way, and from her testimony they concluded that she had. Their verdict: death by hanging. But, as the prosecutor explained when announcing the sentence, Germans are not Russians; therefore, it was "not so easy to hang a woman under German law." The sentence and trial records had to be sent to Germany for the Kaiser himself to approve them.

Weeks passed. October came and went. Life in prison became tolerable for Irina. She corresponded with her friends "in freedom," and talked with several fellow prisoners and her German jailors. German soldiers came to the door of her cell to stare at "the condemned Russian lady." One day

> a young officer, trembling from his violation of discipline, came to my cell to talk to me. He said, "How are you, mademoiselle?" And without waiting for an answer went on to say, "I am not able to help you. I am only an insignificant person, but I cordially shake your hand. Remain faithful to your idea. It is the true path to happiness." Then he disappeared.

The jail trusty who brought her food and had fed her when she was bound in irons, often came with special treats and quantities of newspapers and journals in German and Russian.

The Western Allies had been given new strength and fighting spirit during 1918 with the arrival of American soldiers and supplies. By November the German government was near collapse. Several German cities were in a state of insurrection and the Allies were demanding the Kaiser's abdication as a precondition for negotiating an armistice. The Kaiser had not yet acted on the case of Irina Kakhovskaya when, on November 10, he fled Germany and soon abdicated. Germany signed the Armistice November 11, and the German officers and troops in Russia began preparing to leave. The Hetman Skoropadsky, losing his German support, was faced with a peasant-led armed uprising. There was the threat of a Bolshevik invasion from the north, and from the east—preparing to march into the Ukraine—were the armies of the anti-revolutionary White Russian generals.

Before leaving the Ukraine at the end of December, the German high command turned over to the Hetman the political prisoners they had been holding. The prisoners' lot under the Hetman became a mad scene of torture and executions without trial. In the city of Kiev there was wild confusion against a backdrop of continuous explosion of hand grenades, and cannon and machine-gun fire. The Hetman's government collapsed almost at once, and a soldier of fortune, Petliura, leading bands of revolutionary peasants, took over the city.

With the Hetman's downfall Irina expected to be freed. Instead, she was transferred to Lukanovsky Prison where the inmates included partisans of the Hetman, German-speaking Russians who had been employed by the German army of occupation, White Russians, Bolsheviks, tsarist agents, and Right and Left Essers. Petliura's partisans butchered them indiscriminately. By the end of January 1919, the Petliura government was tottering, threatened by a small Bolshevik force that was about to take Kiev.

In the confusion Irina escaped and went into hiding, but not before going into the prison cemetery to search out the grave of Donskoi. She found it, covered with debris, in the area designated "for mendicants." She cleaned it up and placed on the grave a wooden cross. Irina remained in hiding in Kiev for a few weeks, then managed to get on a troop train bound for Moscow.

The attempt to use traditional Esser terrorism was one way *narodniki* women sought to oppose the Bolsheviks, whom they saw as destroyers of their dream of revolution which they equated with freedom. Other of their old colleagues and mentors used other ways, including the two very different types of effort carried on by Babushka (Katerina Breshkovskaya) and Vera Figner.

The Bolshevik takeover of the revolutionary government in October 1917 was to Katerina Breshkovskaya a betrayal of the revolution. "Where there is no freedom there is no revolution," she said. Elected to the Constituent Assembly, on which she had placed such great hopes, she had to witness the Bolsheviks' dismissal of the delegates by force at the end of the first, and only, day of its existence. Immediately she began secret work again. She joined the Esser Party underground. She traveled the roads of Russia, calling on people to rise against the Bolshevik subverters of freedom. She covered much of Russia and Siberia. Finally, toward the end of 1918, despite the hopelessness of her cause, she made her way to America. Her aim was to inform the American people of the nature of Bolshevism. Once informed, she expected American intervention in Russia to bring about the defeat of the Bolsheviks.

Landing in Seattle, Babushka was soon on the lecture platform, speaking in English with a marked accent but with a vocabulary that one friendly observer said, for "directness, simplicity, and dignity was faultless." Crowds gathered in churches, theaters, and halls, eager for firsthand information from a participant in the Russian Revolution. She deplored the Bolshevik victory and said she was speaking in behalf of Russia's children, five million of whom had been orphaned during the war and the revolution. The schools of Russia were empty, she said, because the Bolsheviks had thrown out the teachers and destroyed the books. She reported that Russia's teachers had asked her "to come to America and to pray, and pray very deeply, to bring millions of books back, for our children have none." In raising money for the education of Russia's children she appeared to believe the Bolshevik nightmare would soon be over, then the "real revolution" could get underway.

Again Babushka visited Wellesley College and spoke in Houghton Memorial Chapel—crammed to the doors with eager listeners. She appeared before a Senate Committee in Washington answering questions on the nature of Bolshevism and giving her estimate of how much American military aid would be needed to overthrow the Bolsheviks. Her campaign against Bolshevism in the United States prompted Leon Trotsky to dub her the self-appointed "God-Mother of the Counterrevolution." It was a campaign which failed. Many Americans, repelled by what they heard and read about Bolshevism, were sympathetic to Babushka's cause; there were many, even among her most ardent admirers, who were listening to other voices. Some who had long supported the Russian revolutionary cause were impressed by favorable reports of Lenin and the Bolshevik experiment. As Lillian Wald tried to explain to Babushka in a letter she wrote on February 27, 1919, Americans know that revolutions do not bring tranquil transitions from one regime to another, and when there is more than one side to an issue they want to hear both sides. Miss Wald and many other Americans even accepted invitations by the Bolshevik government to visit the Soviet Union and returned full of enthusiasm about much of what they saw of health, education, and other facilities.

It had become evident that Babushka would have no role to play in educating Russia's children in the Soviet Union. In the meantime she discovered the Russian children of Karpatorossiia, that small pocket of land in the Carpathian Mountains inhabited by Russians who for centuries had been under Hungarian rule. The Hungarians, disregarding their Russian nationality, had called them Ruthenians. When the Austro-Hungarian Empire was broken up after World War I, Karpatorossiia was attached to the eastern end of newly created Czechoslovakia. Babushka went to settle among the Russians there.

The mails were soon flooded with Babushka's correspondence with Americans, seeking funds for "her children." The Catherine Breshkovsky Russian Relief Fund was set up in New York City in 1919.[4] By the end of the year it had sent her more than $60,000 which she used to build an orphanage for two thousand children. When the Relief Fund went out of existence, Babushka continued to make personal appeals to her American

---

[4]Katerina Breshkovskaya was always known as Catherine Breshkovsky in the United States.

friends and labeled herself a "professional beggar." With the money do-
nated by Americans she built orphanages and schools. These provided an
education for many of the tens of thousands of children of the Russian families of the south Carpathian Mountain region who had suffered the horrors
of war, semi-starvation, and cultural deprivation.

Katerina Breshkovskaya died in Prague in 1934, in her ninetieth year,
active and hopeful to the end, still communicating with her American
friends when she could no longer write and had to dictate her letters. These
letters indicate she never lost faith in the Russian people and their eventual
triumph over tyranny.

One of Breshkovskaya's hopes was fulfilled—though she did not live to
see it: The return of Karpatorossiia to the Russian motherland. After World
War II the re-drawing of the western borders of the U.S.S.R. put Karpatorossiia inside the borders of Soviet Russia.

Katerina Breshkovskaya, a pariah in her own land where the Bolsheviks
labeled her an enemy of revolution, has all but been forgotten. In America,
where in 1917 she was hailed as "a heroine to be ranked with Joan of Arc,
Florence Nightingale, and Abraham Lincoln," she soon sank into obscurity,
suffering the fate of many who momentarily achieve fame. Nevertheless, as
Alexander Kerensky said in an unpublished tribute to her, one thing stands
out as a monument to Babushka's work and to the movement she led—the
future of Russia has passed into the hands of the laboring classes. The people who rule Russia are no longer the scions of Russia's nobility; they are
the sons and grandsons of peasants and workers. The Russian millions have
never heard of her, but it was Babushka and her fellow agrarian socialists
who sounded the tocsin call that aroused them from their centuries-old leth-
argy.

Old revolutionaries outside the orbit of politics had the brief but heady
experience in 1917 of functioning as citizens in a free society. One of them
was Vera Figner, who in 1916 had received permission to live in St. Petersburg. She was there to observe the "February Days" of 1917 and the top-
pling of the tsarist government. She immediately swung into action on several fronts. Concerned about the thousands of amnestied political prisoners
flooding back from Siberia to take up the broken threads of their lives, she
organized the Liberated Political Prisoners Support Society, made countless
public appearances to raise money, recruit staff, and see to it that aid got
to the returning revolutionary veterans.[5] She lobbied for the establishment of
the Memorial Museum of the Revolution. Aware of the ignorance of Russia's

---

[5]According to Figner, this Society raised over 2 million rubles and aided some 4,000 returning
katorga veterans. "Avtobiografiia Very Figner" (Autobiography of Vera Figner), *Entsiklopedicheskiy Slovar'*, (Granat), vol. 40, Moscow, 1926.

peasantry, she spearheaded a book drive to collect and distribute books to peasant villages. In April 1918 she helped found the Culture and Liberty Society,[6] with its speeches at every meeting (while it lasted) reminding people that there could be no rebirth of Russian culture without liberty.

Vera Figner had no political party affiliation and avoided public office, but was elected by the new revolutionary government's All-Russian Congress of Peasants' Deputies to its Executive Committee in the summer of 1917. Holding this post automatically made her a member of the Preparliament, called by Alexander Kerensky, head of the Provisional Government, to prepare the way for the Constituent Assembly scheduled to meet in January 1918. As a member of the Preparliament, Vera Figner suffered her first humiliation at the hands of a revolutionary government. The Preparliament was still in session when the Bolshevik takeover, the "October Revolution," occurred. The Bolsheviks immediately sent a contingent of armed soldiers and sailors to clear the Mariinsky Palace where the deputies were sitting. The Preparliament was brought to a dismal end with the deputies, including Vera Figner, turned out into the street.

The Bolshevik dismissal of the Preparliament was but a dress rehearsal for their dissolution of the Constituent Assembly in January 1918 at the end of its first and only day in session. Figner called this action an insult to the cherished dream of freedom of several generations of Russian revolutionaries.[7]

Another brush with Bolshevik lawlessness came on August 27, 1921, when Figner was bodily escorted by *Cheka* officers out of a meeting of the All-Russian Famine Sufferer's Relief Committee formed by Figner and several intellectuals in 1921 to aid the millions of famine victims in the Volga River Valley.[8] To the Bolsheviks the Committee's existence was an admission that there was a famine. Lenin, therefore, had it banned. He ordered the arrest of the some one hundred members attending the meeting and exiled them to places in the far north where there were no railroads.[9]

---

[6]Formation of this Society was a slap at the Bolsheviks on two counts: (1) it commemorated the February Revolution of 1917, not the October (Bolshevik); (2) its leaders expressed bitter disapproval of the Brest Treaty.

[7]"Avtobiografiia . . .," *Entsiklopedicheskiy Slovar'* (Granat), vol. 40.

[8]Estimates of deaths from starvation in the 1921–23 famine range from 1.3 to 25 million. The high death rate resulted from the long delay of the Bolshevik government to admit there was a famine, to do anything about it, or to take the outside aid offered by many "bourgeois" countries. To date, no serious study of this famine and no eyewitness accounts have been published in the Soviet Union.

[9]IU. N. Maksimov, "Komitet Pomoshchi Golodaiushchim," *Pamiat'*, Moscow, 1979, Paris 1981. (*Pamiat'*, a *samizdat* [typescript] journal started in Moscow in 1976. In 1978, Khronika Press began printing each Moscow issue of *Pamiat'* in Paris.) The story of the Famine Relief Committee is also told in Wada Haruki, "Vera Figner in the Early Post-Revolutionary Period, 1917–23," *Annals of the Institute of Social Science*, University of Tokyo, no. 25 (1983–84), p. 58.

Why did the revolution bring, not freedom, but civil strife, arrests, mass terrorization, and executions? Vera Figner and some of her intellectual associates, including Maxim Gorky, saw the ignorance of the Russian people as the answer. Tsarism had kept the people in mud and poverty so long their souls had become crooked. They did not understand freedom nor the struggle for freedom, but someday they would. And when that day came they would need to know their past. They would need to know the story of Russia's revolutionaries, their struggle against tyranny and the humanistic goals they fought for. Vera Figner was convinced that only the freely told recollections of the veteran revolutionaries of the 1870s, 1880s, and later, could convey this story. Therefore a task of first importance was to convince the veterans to write and to get their words into print, in books, pamphlets, and journals before it was too late. N. A. Morozov said in his memoirs he once asked Vera Figner what she wanted from him as a New Year's gift. Her reply was, "Write something about your life. That is all I want."[10]

With each passing day a precious detail risked obliteration as the political climate in Soviet Russia was becoming less hospitable to the old revolutionaries, as censorship was distorting or eliminating evidence.[11] In 1922 Vera Figner wrote in the Preface of the second volume of *Zapechatlennyi Trud* (titled *Kogda Chasy Zhizni Ostanovilis'*—When the Clock of Life Stopped):

> For new times there are new songs; my book is a song about the past, about things that are over and will never return. But even if my book tells only about the past and brings nothing to the practical life of the present revolutionary moment, there will come a time when it will be needed. The dead are never resurrected, but books are.[12]

As the new tyranny closed in, those revolutionaries still clinging to their dream of freedom were either going into opposition or emigrating. Vera Figner did neither. In response to an invitation by the widow of Sergei Kravchinski (Stepniak) to leave the Soviet Union and come to live with her in London, Figner replied she would not go abroad; she chose to stay and to live through everything the Russian people were living through.[13] Her words

---

[10]N. A. Mozorov, *Povesti Moyey Zhizni*, Moscow, 1932.

[11]In her haste to get the story of the past into print, Figner herself wrote biographies, edited collections of letters, and provided introductions and forewords to works by or about her former comrades. Issue after issue of half a dozen journals devoted to recording the past (until they were taken over by the Bolsheviks or forced to stop publication) carried hundreds of memoirs, recollections, documents, photographs, and letters of the revolutionaries. That there exists today a remarkably full printed record of Russia's revolutionary past in the words of its participants, is due in no small measure to the tireless efforts of Vera Figner.

[12]The independent publisher, Zadruga Press, which brought out Figner's books was soon forced to cease and its 160 employees were exiled. The journal it published, *Golos Minuvshego*, also went out of existence.

[13]R. I. Pimenov, "Vospominaniia," *Pamiat'*, Moscow, 1977, Paris, 1979, vypusk 2, pp. 252–253.

are similar to those in the opening lines of Anna Akhmatova's famous poem
Rekviem (Requiem):

> No, not under foreign skies
> Not under the shelter of strangers' wings—
> I was with my people then,
> There, where my people were, in their misfortune.

In 1883, when she could have left Russia and avoided arrest, trial, a death
sentence, and twenty years in solitary confinement, she remained because
she felt she had a moral obligation to suffer the consequences of her revolutionary acts. Again after 1917 she stayed because she saw her generation
of revolutionaries as the source of what was happening. They bore responsibility for it.

By not emigrating, by not going into opposition, by not speaking out
against the Soviet regime, Vera Figner established an uneasy relationship
with the Soviet authorities. Unsatisfactory as it was, it left her inside Russia
and not in prison or exile.[14] The Bolsheviks for their part had much to gain
by having one of the most famous of the old revolutionaries in the Soviet
Union and not in open opposition. To the world at large the Soviets made
Vera Figner an icon of their revolution—not a martyr—with the result that
she was considered a Communist by the people of the Soviet Union. She
was addressed by countless communist youth groups as "Our Dear Old
Bolshevik, Vera Nikolaevna Figner." Soviet sources of information on her
present Figner as an ardent supporter of the Communist party and the Soviet
system.[15]

As Vera Figner lost touch with the outside world, those who had known
her asked how could a woman who had spent her politically active years
fighting tsarist tyranny accept Soviet tyranny with its betrayal of the revolutionary goals of freedom that were the core of the 1870s *narodniki* credo.
How could Vera Figner accept the imprisonment, exiling, and execution of
old revolutionaries under Lenin and Stalin—some of them once her close
associates? In the words of the author of an essay on Vera Figner in the New
York *Novyi Zhurnal* at the time of her death in 1942, "In the last quarter
century the aureole radiating around her name for four decades has been
somewhat dimmed."[16]

---

[14]Figner was 70 in 1922, and far from robust health. This may have influenced her choice.
Also she had ties with many close relatives and friends, some of them ill and dying. Wada
Haruki's article provides some details on these personal relations based on her letters. Also
Lidiia Dan (*Iz Vstrech s Veroy Nikolaevnoy Figner* (Of My Meetings With Vera Figner), typescript interview, 13 pages, University Project on the History of the Menshevik Movement,
1961) throws light on Figner's personal problems.
[15]All editions of the *Bolshaia Sovetskaia Entsiklopediia;* her obituary in *Pravda,* June 16, 1942;
I. E. Matveeva's 1962 biographical pamphet, *Vera Figner.*
[16]*Novyi Zhurnal,* 1942, vol. 3, pp. 348–356.

Beginning in the mid-1960s, shreds of evidence began to appear which make it possible to put Vera Figner's seeming betrayal of her ideals in a different light. E. Pavliuchenko, in the introduction to the 1964 edition of Figner's *Zapechatlennyi Trud*, wrote:

> It was a great shock for Vera Nikolaevna to see the unlawful repression of many honorable people, some of them very close to her. She bravely protested against unwarranted and unjust arrests, and often wrote protests to the Central Executive Committee and to Stalin personally—using all her influence—pleading, in vain, to save the lives of people who had become victims of tyranny.[17]

Several other bits and pieces from archival sources that show Figner as an internal opponent of the Soviet system made their way into print in the 1970s and 1980s. Examples include quotations from her private correspondence, delineation of organizations independent of the Soviet state and the Communist party she set up or cooperated in (only to see them ended or taken over by the Soviets), her speeches at memorials and commemorations in which her criticism of Bolshevik methods and policies was clearly though not blatantly stated, and her refusal to attend Bolshevik-sponsored celebrations.[18] The content of her 1932 letter refusing to join the Society of Former Political Prisoners and Exiles was apparently well known. The Bolsheviks organized this Society in 1921 to replace Figner's Society for Liberated Political Prisoners that she founded in 1917. Not only she but nearly 40 percent of the other old revolutionaries refused to join it. In an article in *Pamiat'*, N. Garelin said he was told about it by an old Esser comrade in 1942 when they were both prisoners in a Stalinist Siberian labor camp. The old revolutionist remembered very accurately her list of the horrors of Soviet rule she said the Society not only endorsed but practiced on its own membership, including torture, purges, and rule by a party faction which oppressed the majority.[19] In 1988, the *Moscow News* (an English-language Soviet publication), in its November 6 issue, printed the entire text of Figner's letter.

James E. Albee, an American news photographer, reported that he saw Vera Figner in 1932, along with several other famous revolutionaries, in a

---

[17]In this section of the introduction, Pavliuchenko's references are numbered sources in the Central State Archives of Literature and Art. The quotation is on p. 36.

[18]Two sources for these examples are The *samizdat* journal *Pamiat'* and Wada Haruki's article, "Vera Figner in the Early Post-Revolutionary Period, 1917–23," *Annals of the Institute of Social Science*, no. 25 (1983–1984), University of Tokyo, pp. 43–73. Wada Haruki obtained access to the Vera Figner file in the Central State Archives of Literature and Art.

[19]N. Garelin, "V. N. Figner i Obshchestvo Politkatorshan i Ssyl'noposelentsev (V. N. Figner and the Society of Political Prisoners and Exiles), *Pamiat'*, No. 3, Moscow, 1978, Paris, 1980, pp. 392–396. The *Moscow News* article also printed the Society presidium's reply to Figner, denouncing her at great length for being soft on the enemies of the proletarian revolution. This denunciation, forwarded to the Central Executive Committee of the Communist Party, would have sent anyone but Figner to a Stalinist death camp.

retirement home run by the Society of Former Political Prisoners and Exiles. She lived there, even though she refused to join the Society! Although she was over eighty, he said her delicate face and figure were still beautiful. To Albee's surprise, she approached and began to speak to him in English:

> The conversation veered to the present Soviet system. As Vera Figner discussed the government she had devoted her life to establishing, her comment came softly and her eyes were dull with tragedy. Her words caused me to glance sharply over my shoulder for fear she might be overheard. "This is not what we fought for," she murmured.[20]

Late in 1941 German armies were driving deep into the Russian heartland. Moscow was threatened with capture and women and children were being evacuated. Vera Figner, old and feeble, refused to leave. "Concern yourselves with the living," she told the authorities. The Germans were less than one hundred miles from Moscow when, on June 15, 1942, Vera Figner died there, only a few days short of her ninetieth birthday. She was buried with honors in the Novodevich'e Cemetery.

ANNOTATED REFERENCES

Personal information on Kakhovskaya by the editors and translators of her book appears in Irène Kachowskaja, *Souvenirs d'une Révolutionnaire*, translated from the Russian by Marcel Livane and Joe Newman, 3d ed., Paris, 1926. Kakhovskaya herself wrote an "Avtobiografiia" to accompany her article "Zapiski i Zaiavleniia" (Notes and Revelations) which appeared in the Russian emigré journal, *Politicheskiy Dnevnik* (Political Diary), Amsterdam, April 1970, pp. 740–742.

Kakhovskaya's *Souvenirs* is the source of the account in this chapter of Eichhorn's assassination and the events surrounding it.

P. S. Shchegolev, "Petr' Grigorevich Kakhovskiy" *Byloye*, January and February, 1906, an article in two parts on Irina's ancestor, Peter. The quotation appears in the January issue of *Byloye* which discusses Peter as a writer and a poet. He was hanged July 13, 1826.

Izvestiia, August 31, 1918, published a full description of the crowd scene in its account of the shooting of Lenin.

I. Volkovicher, "K Istorii Pokusheniia na Lenina" (For the History of the Attempt on Lenin), *Proletarskaia Revoliutsiia*, Numbers 6–7 (18, 19), 1923, pp. 275–285. A collection of abstracts of the deputations taken from eyewitnesses of the shooting, including that of Lenin's chauffeur, the infantryman who picked Kaplan out of the crowd and held her, and the five interrogations of Kaplan immediately after the shooting. Unsatisfactory as this information is, all accounts of the shooting of Lenin and the fate of Fanny Kaplan are dependent on these documents and on Pavel Malkov's account of how he shot her, "Zapiski Komendanta Kremlia" (Notes of a Kremlin Warden), *Moskva*, no. 11, November, 1958.

---

[20]James E. Albee, *I Photograph Russia*, New York, 1934.

R. H. Bruce Lockhart, *British Agent,* London and New York, 1932 provided the description of Kaplan, p. 317.

Pravda, July 16, 20 and 21, 1922, reported the Trial of the Right Essers. Among other crimes, Fanny Kaplan's attempt on Lenin's life was reviewed and additional Essers were implicated. In the 1937–1938 Purge Trial the circle of accusations widened. N. I. Bukharin, designated a "Left Communist," was named the instigator of Fanny Kaplan's crime (*The Great Purge Trial,* edited and with notes by Robert C. Tucker and Stephen F. Cohen, New York, 1965, pp. 32, 387, 544).

A brief biographical entry on Fanny Kaplan, with excellent references to Russian and English sources of information on her, by Richard Johnson appears in *The Modern Encyclopedia of Russian and Soviet History,* edited by Joseph L. Wieczynski, Volume 5.

Breshkovskaya's testimony before the United States Senate on February 14, 1919, appears in Senate Judiciary Subcommittee, *Hearings on the Brewing and Liquor Interests and German Propaganda,* 65 and 66th Congress, vol. 3, Washington, 1919.

Leon Trotsky's statement on Breshkovskaya as the "Godmother of the Counterrevolution" appears in his *History of the Russian Revolution* (Max Eastman translation), New York, 1932, vol. 1, p. 230.

Lillian Wald on Babushka and the Russian Revolution, in *Windows on Henry Street,* Boston, 1934.

11

Irina Kakhovskaya and the Faustian Bargain

To be a Left Esser leader in any area controlled by the Bolsheviks in the early months of 1919 was to be in a precarious position. Many, including Maria Spiridonova, the head of the party and Irina Kakhovskaya's friend from *katorga* days, were in prison. Yet the Left Essers, working underground, continued their struggle against Bolshevik tyranny.

In the meantime, however, other enemies of the revolution had assumed threatening proportions. The German surrender to the Western Allied powers in November ended the Great War of 1914–1918, releasing revolutionary Russia from subservience to Imperial Germany, but French, British, and American "imperialists" had decided to aid the efforts of anti-revolutionary former tsarist military officers, Czechoslovak prisoners of war stranded in Russia, and various other groups. All were attempting to overthrow either the Bolsheviks or the revolution, or both.

Scattered groups of monarchist officers and ex-tsarist functionaries had from the beginning opposed the revolution. Until 1919 they had posed no real threat, but were being transformed by the material, technical, and financial aid supplied by Western governments.

Grouped around Admiral Kolchak, who had been proclaimed the Admiral General of Russia, were all the forces of reaction of Russia and Europe. As his military units successfully marched from their Siberian headquarters across the Ural mountains, and as Western powers made incursions through Russia's European borders, it seemed that an armed circle was closing in on socialist, revolutionary Russia. The success of the White Russian, General Kolchak, who would take over as dictator and crush the revolution, became each day more probable.

The Left Esser leaders, out of power, menaced on all sides by Bolshevik ruthlessness, still felt the majority of the Russian people were with them and remained convinced they had a major role to play in the revolution. They decided the White generals were a greater threat to the revolution than the Bolsheviks, and prepared to launch an attack with their old weapon—political assassination.

In view of her success in organizing the assassination of Field Marshal Eichhorn, Irina Kakhovskaya was put in charge of a combat group of six people whose assignment was to kill Kolchak. The underground Left Esser Executive Committee turned over to her the money and the explosives she and her group would need for their foray into enemy territory.

Early in May 1919, as the members of the combat group were in Moscow preparing their departure on the mission to assassinate Kolchak, agents of the *Cheka* swooped down on the conspirators' hiding place. Irina and two of her comrades were arrested. Their arms, money, and documents were seized. Their passports bore false names, but when Romanowski, the examining magistrate, saw Irina, he recognized her.

"Who is the dynamite meant for?" he demanded. Irina refused to answer, but checking the seized documents the officials soon discovered the nature of her mission. In the custody of *Cheka* guards, Irina and her comrades were taken to the old, red-brick tsarist Butyrki Prison. It was from Butyrki, twelve years before, that Irina had departed for the Siberian *katorga*.

After a few days, Irina was again taken before Romanowski. He had a proposition to put to her. Would she proceed with her mission if the Bolsheviks freed her and made provision for her and her group to be transported to a place where they could continue into enemy territory and launch their attack? Completely taken aback by this proposal, Irina did not reply and was returned to Butyrki to think it over. To carry out her mission under the aegis of the Bolsheviks was repugnant to her. Would she not become an instrument of Bolshevik tyranny? She finally concluded that of the two dangers confronting the Russian revolution—Bolshevik tyranny or capitalist-imperialist suppression of the revolution—the latter was the greater threat.

Irina decided to accept the Bolshevik offer. She and one of her two jailed companions were set free and negotiations began with the authorities. After a stint of tortuous bargaining the Bolshevik officials agreed to take Irina and her group into territory where they could proceed with their assassination plot. The target, however, was changed from Kolchak to Denikin: in the summer of 1919 General Denikin was marching through the Ukraine and was expected to take Kiev. It was assumed he would set up his headquarters in Kiev and become an easy target. The Bolsheviks assumed that if Denikin were killed, his forces would soon disintegrate and the whole area from Rostov to the western borders of the Ukraine could be taken and held by the Red Army.

At this point in the negotiations, Magistrate Romanowski made a proposal that was the crux of the bargain. After the execution of Denikin, if Irina escaped with her life, would she agree to come back to Moscow, give herself up, and return to prison? With a gasp she comprehended the awful truth: the Bolsheviks were not above using a dedicated Left Esser terrorist against their mutual enemy, the White General Denikin, but would not tolerate her as a free citizen in the Soviet Union! She gave Romanowski a contemptuous look, laughed, and agreed to this Faustian bargain. That she had survived one assassination assignment was a miracle. She did not expect to survive another.

Irina cleared the Bolshevik proposal with the Left Esser Central Committee. A new combat group was recruited. Plans completed, supplies and money in place, Irina and her group left Moscow early in August 1919 for Kiev. Kiev was temporarily in the hands of the Bolsheviks who were not strong enough to hold the city and the surrounding countryside as the armies of Denikin cut through the Ukraine. It was important for the plotters to get to Kiev before Denikin's forces so they could make the contacts they needed. They arrived on August 10, the first anniversary of the execution of Boris Donskoi, their comrade who had killed Eichhorn. The Bolsheviks were evacuating the city. Long lines of vehicles loaded with Communist functionaries and sympathizers were heading north to Moscow. In the distance could be heard the thunder of cannons, the signal of Denikin's approach.

In the summer of 1919 Kiev was a city in turmoil. The Soviets and those with Soviet sympathies suspected everyone of being a White partisan. Those who hated the Bolsheviks, including Ukrainian nationalists, White sympathizers and a large variety of anti-Bolshevik socialists, suspected everyone of being a Bolshevik. As long as Soviet authorities ruled Kiev, in order to get a lodging permit a person had to be able to prove he or she was a Soviet worker or a Bolshevik party member. Landlords with rooms to rent were almost all anti-Bolshevik but they had to rent to whoever presented a permit even though they considered such persons enemies. People were using all kinds of stratagem to disguise their real political views and attachments because as each new conqueror entered the city, the 'in'' and "out" beliefs shifted. And Kiev changed hands at least a dozen times during the Civil War. The best procedure, said Irina, was to affect an indifference to politics and declare oneself a disciple of Tolstoy.

In addition to the pitfalls involved in the necessity of a declared political preference to obtain housing and ration cards, Irina was jittery about the cohesion of the group she had assembled. The Muscovites did not know the Ukrainians, or whether they could be trusted. The Ukrainians were suspicious of the Muscovites. Somehow Irina's group found temporary residences in the outskirts of Kiev. By painting her face, wearing wigs, and frequently changing her mode of dress, Irina sought to make herself unrecognizable on the chance she might meet someone who would remember her from the Eichhorn plot.

After the departure of the Bolsheviks, Kiev was taken over for three days by the peasant leader Petliura. It was a time of wild confusion during which the troops and populace turned on known Bolsheviks and Jews, murdering them indiscriminately. The brief interlude of Petliura was followed by the takeover of the city by Denikin's troops who continued the murderous attacks on known or suspected Bolsheviks, and the cruelty to the Jews was intensified.

Denikin himself was expected momentarily. The plans of the plotters were in place. Each person had been assigned his or her task, each with the proper costume, wig, beard, or moustache; false passports and railroad tickets for a quick getaway had been assigned. At that point the group became involved in a struggle over a moral issue which troubled most of them, especially the Muscovites. In the volatile atmosphere of Kiev in the summer of 1919, the plotters asked themselves: Did they have the right to commit an act—the assassination of Denikin—which they knew would unleash a pogrom of unprecedented dimensions against the Jews of Kiev? Could they rightfully take on the responsibility for the sure death and suffering of hundreds, probably thousands, of human beings?

The Kiev comrades, some of them Jews who had experienced dozens of pogroms, dismissed the question categorically. The pogrom they said is an ongoing phenomenon. "Nothing we do will start it. It started centuries ago. Our task is to end it, to eliminate Denikin, the leader of the forces dedicated to continue the pogrom. The disorganization of his forces following his assassination will have the effect in the end of saving the lives of Jews as well as making possible a just life for all." This argument convinced the plotters and they speeded up their preparations.

A robbery in which the thief took some of their false passports forced the plotters to find new lodgings and hiding places for their explosives. Then the most unstable member of the group through carelessness was arrested. Only by exerting great effort and using most of their funds for bribes was Irina able to get him released before he underwent interrogation.

Beset by perpetual tension, by fear at every instant of being caught because of some insignificant negligence, Irina and the combat group waited with impatience for the arrival of Denikin. But Denikin's headquarters remained in Rostov. As his arrival in Kiev was delayed, the plotters considered making the long trip to Rostov. They were advised by Left Essers there not to come because rail travel was unpredictable and the security situation in Rostov was tight.

Finally the newspapers announced the day and hour of the arrival of Denikin in Kiev. The inhabitants of the city were instructed to deck the street and houses with flags. Denikin was scheduled to arrive on Sunday. On Friday night Irina approached the house where she lodged and saw an unknown man strolling in the courtyardd. She quickly turned and walked in the opposite direction, intending to spend the night in the rooms of another comrade. He was not at home. A neighbor told her he had gone out earlier in the evening and had not come back.

It was 3 A.M. Suddenly the silence of the sleeping city was broken by the thunder of cannon. The detonations continued, quite close by. What was going on? The newspapers had said nothing about impending combat. At dawn, after a harrowing night, Irina walked toward the center of Kiev hoping to find out what was happening. She learned that the city was under a surprise attack by the Red Army. Bolshevik troops were marching into the streets. The officials of the Denikin government hastily began to move out, along with long lines of fleeing people. It was rumored that in the prisons the Denikin secret police were executing as many people as they could before they had to retreat.

Electricity was cut off. Running water stopped. Lines of women, in spite of the danger of gunfire, queued up with buckets at the municipal fountains. There were explosions, street fighting, robberies. After three days, the Bolsheviks were forced out. Denikin's troops marched back in, and little by little some semblance of order was reestablished, accompanied by ferocious attacks on the Jews which went on day and night.

It was obvious to Irina's combat group that Denikin would not be coming to Kiev in the near future. Irina decided that, whatever the cost, they must go to Rostov. The journey proved to be a terrible experience, and they arrived in Rostov in harsh December weather to find the city overflowing with refugees and beset with a raging typhus epidemic.

On the very evening of their arrival Irina met with her comrades and several Rostov Essers to work out a plan of action. The Rostov comrades informed her that Denikin came in from his headquarters outside the city once a week to attend meetings of his Supreme Council. He went in disguise, by automobile, from the railway station to a house, the location of which they knew. To confuse any observer who might want to attack the general, a line of identical closed cars came to the station to meet his train. He entered one of them. Then all the cars drove off, one after the other, in the same direction. The plotters decided to establish four posts, each manned by a person with a bomb. If the first bomb thrown merely wrecked the general's car, or wrecked the wrong car, a second bomb would be thrown, and possibly a third and a fourth.

The only lodging Irina could find in crowded Rostov was a half-room, divided by a curtain. It was there the bombs would have to be manufactured. Her main accomplice's lodging was a bathroom in a house not far away, where he slept in the tub. The handicaps to successful achievement of an assassination were overwhelming, but on the Tuesday before Christmas 1919, the attack was scheduled to take place.

Suddenly two comrades, Vera and Lena, came down with typhus. A new deadline was set. On Friday, Chukov, Irina's sole remaining comrade appeared even though he was ill. He tried to carry on but collapsed and Irina had to take him to a hospital. There she found the sick on the floor, without care or medication, the dead and the living lying side by side. She began a week-long search for a place where Chukov could get adequate medical care. At the same time she made the necessary bombs and recruited two other comrades to go with her to the street where the Supreme Council met so they could see and be able to recognize Denikin when the time came for their strike at the railway station. They found that the Supreme Council had begun to meet every day, each time in a different place. The cause of the intensified effort of the Whites in Rostov was the threat of a major offensive by the Red Army.

The three conspirators ran all over Rostov all day long. Then one of them collapsed from cold and exhaustion. The expenses for medical care were depleting Irina's funds and she began selling their personal belongings in the old clothes market. The odds against the plotters had become too great for a strike against Denikin to succeed, but Irina was loath to give up. Fast-moving events, however, caught up with her. Shortly after Christmas Rostov fell to the Red Army. Irina decided to keep the explosives against the possibility the Whites might retake the city, but when the Red infantry entered Rostov she proceeded to sift the dynamite into the sewer.

In Denikin-controlled Rostov, in order to get lodgings, Irina and her comrades had passed themselves off as White partisans. In Red-ruled Rostov, Irina's immediate problem was how to keep herself and her group from being killed as White sympathizers. They were saved by one of their fellow conspirators who had been caught and jailed by Denikin's police. When the Reds entered the city he was able to establish his credentials as a revolutionary and was, in fact, appointed a local commissar. Thus, he was in a position to vouch for Irina and her group as true revolutionaries.

With the retreat of Denikin and the severe weakening of the White forces everywhere, as they suffered the effect of faltering aid from the Western Allies and the growing strength of the Red Army, Irina's mission became meaningless. Six months earlier, in the summer of 1919, her goal had significance: kill the man heading the White forces considered the greatest threat to the revolution. In the early months of 1920, with the White armies in retreat before the increasingly successful strikes of the Red Army, everything had changed.

Rostov, which had for two years been under German and White Russian rulers, was ignorant of what had transpired in Moscow. Taking advantage of the moment, in the first two weeks after the Red Army takeover, Irina and her colleagues made contact with local Essers, organized public meetings, and distributed pamphlets and broadsides with the Left Esser program of action. They got a very favorable response from local political groups. Then, suddenly their work was stopped. Word arrived from Moscow ordering the Bolshevik-controlled Soviets to outlaw Essers, Left Essers, and all other political parties and groups.

Irina proceeded to organize illegal meetings, but the local revolutionaries saw the Red Army as their saviors. The Left Esser following that had briefly mushroomed virtually disappeared. Again faced with defeat, Irina decided her only alternative was to return to Moscow.

Conditions of civil war made the journey long and difficult. It was complicated by Irina's becoming ill with typhus, her overwhelming feeling of guilt for having failed to carry out the mission entrusted to her by the Left Essers, and her worry about the bargain she had made with the Bolshevik magistrate, Romanowski. He had granted her a reprieve from imprisonment as a Left Esser enemy of the Bolsheviks so she could eliminate a White general, their common foe—but only if she agreed to return to prison if she lived. Now her reprieve was over. What could she expect but to spend the rest of her life as a prisoner?

From the time she departed for Kiev in July 1919, Irina's comrades in Moscow had no word from her. The Left Essers were leading an increasingly beleagured existence, hiding in attics and basements, illegally printing and circulating party communiques, sneaking out in disguises to work among peasants and laborers as they tried to guide the waning opposition to the Bolsheviks to their political purpose of "saving the revolution." But the tentacles of the *Cheka* were long and tireless as they hunted down outlawed foes. Some of her comrades had given Irina and her associates up for dead; in view of the fighting and disorder reigning in the south, this was a plausible assumption. But she had escaped before, and a friend reported later that her old mother, ill and crippled, never gave up hope. Looking for some sign that her daughter was still alive, she bought a bouquet of hortensias on Irina's birthday. She looked after the flowers lovingly and said, "So long as these flowers do not fade, my daughter is alive." The hortensias did not fade.

On the night of February 28, 1920, in the room of one of the few Left Essers still living legally in Moscow, the telephone rang. The strange voice of a man, speaking insistently and identifying himself only as a comrade, asked to come immediately on a matter of great urgency. Given permission, he lost no time, and soon arrived at the Moscow comrade's door. He introduced himself as Chukov, a member of Irina's battle group, then reported he and Irina had just completed the long and difficult journey from Rostov. She was, he reported, at that very moment lying on the platform of a Moscow railroad station along with many others, ill with typhus. Chukov said he feared she might be recognized at any moment by *Cheka* agents who would take her off to prison where she would surely die. What she needed was medical care in a hospital. Responding to this appeal, the Moscow comrade succeeded in finding a doctor who agreed to treat an ill woman, identified to him only as a revolutionary in danger of arrest by the Bolsheviks. He took her into his small nursing facility.

Dangerously ill, Irina was delirious. In her raving she spoke of only one thing—her guilt for not carrying out her task. "Forgive me, comrades. Forgive me," she said over and over again. Her convalescence was long, and she remained troubled by her feeling of guilt. She desperately wanted to see Maria Spiridonova, and in the spring of 1920, after Spiridonova escaped from prison and was living in hiding, she came to see Irina. They talked for several hours and Maria's reassurances helped restore Irina's mental peace.

The day came when the *Cheka*, which had known for some time of Irina's whereabouts, came to enforce Magistrate Romanowski's bargain. She was again put behind bars in the Butyrki Prison.

Outside the prison walls civil war raged. Widespread but uncoordinated revolt flared in many parts of Russia. The most virulent peasant outbreak was in Maria Spiridonova's home province of Tambov. From time to time, she succeeded in returning to Tambov in disguise, with the aim of organizing the opposition. But peasant action remained chaotic and achieved little more than terrorist attacks which killed many Bolsheviks serving in food requisition squads.

On March 1, 1921, the Tenth Congress of Soviets, its membership all Bolshevik, opened in Moscow. On the same day in Kronshtadt, the great Gulf of Finland naval base, fifteen thousand sailors and workers held a mass meeting in Anchor Square. Their spokesmen demanded that their Bolshevik rulers restore free elections to the soviets. They demanded restoration of freedom of speech and the press for workers, peasants, anarchists, and Left Essers, and the end of punitive expeditions against the peasants and repression of workers and their unions.

Receiving no positive response from the Bolshevik leaders, the Kronshtadt sailors and workers proceeded to arrest all Bolshevik officers on the island base and appealed to the rank and file of Bolshevik functionaries to join them. Many did. Leon Trotsky, as head of the Red Army, marshaled his troops, as well as *Cheka* and other special forces, including members of the Tenth Congress, in an all-out military attack on Kronshtadt. After nearly a week of intense fighting, with heavy loss of life by the Red forces, the Kronshtadt fortress was taken. Virtually every insurgent was mercilessly butchered.

Sitting in Butyrki Prison, Irina Kakhovskaya was apprehended and found guilty of complicity in plotting Kronshtadt revolt. She was sentenced to exile in Kaluga.

In prison Irina contracted tuberculosis. News of her illness had reached Russian emigrés in France where a rescue committee was set up. The committee appealed in vain to the Bolshevik government to permit her to convalesce in a French sanitarium. Instead she was sent to Samarkand in Turkestan. There she found many former *katorga* comrades, including Maria Spiridonova and Aleksandra Izmailovich.

In Samarkand the women were assigned menial jobs. Irina worked in a home for homeless children. In the 1920s when occasional letters from Maria Spiridonova still reached the outside world, she wrote that Irina worked eighteen to twenty hours a day, then at night watched over her sick mother. Maria feared Irina was working herself to death. "It is a tragedy to see this energetic, talented, noble human being breaking up."

In Samarkand, living as though "under a heavy screw press," one by one the Esser women were dismissed from their pitiful jobs. Life was increasingly desolate. At the end of 1928, some of them, including Spiridonova, Kakhovskaya, and Izmailovich, were transferred to Tashkent, where, under constant surveillance, they were kept rigorously separated from the population of the town. About a year later Spiridonova contracted typhoid fever. Through underground sources, news of her serious illness spread beyond the women's place of "enforced freedom." The Soviet government decided to bring Spiridonova to Moscow for treatment. Physicians there decided to send her and Sanya Izmailovich to a sanitarium in Yalta, but made no provision for paying for their lodgings, medication, or treatment. Spiridonova's friend and biographer, I. Z. Steinberg, wrote that despite the great difficulty of transferring funds to the U.S.S.R., friends abroad raised the necessary money. This dependence greatly embarrassed the two women, and Izmailovich soon went back to Tashkent. Spiridonova stayed on and her health improved until August 1930 when Soviet politics began to close in on her. She was removed to Moscow and put in prison.

After this time, the fate of Maria Spiridonova and the Esser women was only a subject for speculation as revolutionary Russia passed from the Lenininist to the Stalinist era.

ANNOTATED REFERENCES

Irène Kachowskaja, *Souvenirs d'une Révolutionnaire*, troisième édition, Paris, 1926. Edited and translated from the Russian by Marcel Livane and Joe Newman.

I. Z. Steinberg, *Spiridonova, Revolutionary Terrorist*, London 1935. In part 4, chapter 5, Steinberg's telling of the Eichhorn expedition was taken directly from Kakhovskaya's *Souvenirs*. On pages 263–264 he adds information on what happened when she got back to Moscow. In part 4, chapter 6, pp. 288–289, he gives the text of Spiridonova's 1926 letter from Samarkand, and tells of her and her friends' transfer to Tashkent, Spiridonova's illness and new imprisonment in 1930.

12

Political Heroines in the Gulag

Bolshevik ambivalence on the role of terror in the long history of the Russian revolutionary struggle was evident from the beginning of the party's existence. On the one hand, the 1870 *narodniki*, and their immediate heirs the *narodovol'tsi*, who invented and used political terror against the tsarist regime, were revered by the Bolsheviks. Lenin never forgot that his older brother, Aleksandr, was hanged as a terrorist for his role in an unsuccessful assassination plot on the life of Tsar Aleksandr III. Yet those of Russia's revolutionaries who accepted Marxism and the idea that the proletariat was the driving force in modern history, proclaimed their rejection of the revolutionary tactic of the individual terrorist act—not on humanitarian but on practical and theoretical grounds. Political assassination, they said, was an ineffective revolutionary strategy. Furthermore, its aim, the arousing of Russia's peasantry to revolution, was an exercise in futility. In strongest terms the Marxist Social Democrats condemned the Socialist Revolutionaries (the Essers) for continuing the *narodovol'tsi* tradition of terrorism and their use of it in the 1903–1906 period.

In truth, Esser use of political assassination proved to be a more effective revolutionary tactic against the tsarist government than any pursued in the early twentieth century by the Marxian Social Democrats. Esser terrorism was regarded by many as a major cause of the Revolution of 1905. Its effectiveness was not lost on Lenin who had in 1903 formed the Bolshevik faction which split the Social Democratic party into Bolsheviks and Mensheviks. The role of Esser terrorism in the 1903–1905 turbulence was an eye-opener. In strong language, Lenin began to authorize terrorist acts by individuals and armed bands:

> Let revolutionary detachments arm themselves however they can with guns, revolvers, bombs, knives, brass knuckles, clubs, rags soaked in kerosene [for arson], rope or a rope ladder, a shovel for building barricades, barbed wire, nails. . . . They must be ready to kill spies, policemen, gendarmes, to blow up police stations and free the prisoners, rob banks and the government treasury . . .

The wild, unbridled violence and terror Lenin enthusiastically demanded of his followers was quite different from the carefully targeted terrorist tactics of the Essers. His conversion to terrorism may have helped initiate working men in Russia's cities into terrorist activity, but it came too late to affect the outcome of the Revolution of 1905, and earned Lenin the condemnation of "purist Social Democrats," including Vera Zasulich, who visualized the coming revolution as a mass proletariat uprising, the inevitable consequence of slow-moving economic change.

After 1905 Bolshevik terrorism largely shifted to daring robberies of banks and government payrolls. The loot provided most of the funds for Bolshevik party work inside and outside Russia. The Georgian Bolshevik Djugashvili, later known as Stalin, first attracted Lenin's attention through his terrorist deeds in the Caucasus.

Covert support and use of individual terrorist acts by the Bolsheviks, and their willingness to accept, even to honor, Esser terrorist blows against tsarism, were part of the Bolshevik tradition up to the 1917 October Revolution. The revival of Esser terrorism, that turned against Bolshevik tyranny in 1918, brought to an end Bolshevik acceptance of the individual terrorist act. In spite of this decision, as late as 1926, on the occasion of the forty-fifth anniversary of the assassination of Tsar Aleksandr II, the aged survivors of that terrorist plot were honored by the Soviet government with a large celebration. The eight women and one man so honored were also granted pensions amounting to $112 a month. Meanwhile the surviving twentieth-century terrorist women were kept under heavy surveillance. To foreign delegations who approached them with requests to release one or more of them, Bolshevik officials invariably replied: "Never. They are too dangerous."

A new kind of terror was born in the fires of the Russian Revolution—the Red Terror—mass killing and torture by the *Cheka*. Mass terror became the means used under Lenin's leadership to impose the will of the Bolsheviks, a minority party, on the Russian people. As Trotsky explained in his essay *Terrorism and Communism*, "Dictatorship without the willingness to apply terror is a knife without a blade." The problem of revolution, as of war, he said, consists of breaking the will of the foe, forcing him to capitulate and accept the conditions of the conqueror. The motivating force of revolution, said Trotsky, is intimidation. Mass terror kills individuals and intimidates thousands.

After the Bolshevik victory in the Civil War, after the shaky restoration of the economy following Lenin's decision to initiate the limited capitalism of the New Economic Policy, Lenin died and Stalin won control of the dictatorship. The assumption of many Bolshevik leaders was that the revolution had been won and communism's long-range goals would be achieved gradually by a process of education and persuasion of the masses. Stalin, however, chose the path of fast, spectacular development of heavy industry (with mammoth engineering projects financed by ignoring consumer needs and impoverishing the working class), and collectivization of agriculture (accomplished against universal peasant opposition). The cost in suffering is incalculable, the cost in human life is conservatively estimated at five million. Collectivization brought famine and the permanent dislocation of Russian agricultural production. The concentration on heavy industry at the expense of consumer production pushed Russia's living standard far below that of any industrialized country.

Under Lenin, mass terror could be justified as a necessity to save the revolution from its internal and external enemies. Under Stalin, mass terror became a method of government and social control. However terrible Stalin's mass-terror methods were, by the mid-1930s he had achieved the communist goals as he defined them. He appeared to be at the pinnacle of his power. But even though communist officials of the Soviet Union from top to bottom publicly proclaimed Stalin and his methods, Stalin, ever suspicious, was apprehensive over what appeared to him to be pockets of nonagreement among certain Old Bolsheviks, and the discussion among a new generation of communist leaders of a "New Course." One of them was Sergei Kirov, the popular Leningrad leader who was elected in 1934 to the powerful post of secretary of the Central Committee of the Communist party. Kirov was clever enough not to dispute Stalin's methods or his goals, but was reputed to believe a period of stabilization without mass terror was necessary for the well-being of the Russian people and the future of the Soviet regime.

The "New Course" which many hoped for, and some worked to bring about, did not come. A new wave of terror began in 1935.

The enigmatic Stalin, always outwardly calm, seemed to accept the "New Course." Then on December 1, 1934, came the news that Kirov had been shot and killed in Leningrad by the bullet of a young Communist, Leonid Nikolaev. In the published record of his trial Nikolaev was presented as a member of the Leningrad terrorist "Center," a group of young Communists who were inspired by reading about the terrorists of tsarist times to commit terrorist acts. During his interrogation Nikolaev is supposed to have said that some day his name would be coupled with those of Zhelyabov and Balmashev.

Twenty-two years later many of the facts of the Kirov murder were revealed by Nikita Khrushchev in his famous speech before the secret session of the Twentieth Congress of the Communist party. The organizers of Kirov's murder, he said, were not the "Leningrad terrorists," nor Nikolaev, who was a stooge, nor the hundreds of people rounded up after the shooting by Stalin's secret police and systematically annihilated. In the intervening years, as more evidence of Kirov's murder has come to light, it appears that the real plotters were Stalin's henchmen acting on Stalin's orders.

Stalin saw Kirov's "New Course" as challenging his mass-terror method of achieving party goals, and, if put into effect, as ending his own control of the party. He launched charges of "terrorist plots" and "terrorist centers" to gather into an ever-widening net of annihilation thousands and eventually millions of Soviet citizens. Pursuit of the plotters turned up accusations against "enemies" everywhere who had to be destroyed to prevent them from wrecking the Soviet system.

Caught up in Stalin's net were the Esser former terrorist women. The attack on them made sense only in a completely Kafkaesque way. If "centers" of young Communist terrorists had existed, and if those young Communists, as published reports at the time indicated, were inspired by *narodovol'tsi* and Esser terrorists (who had targeted tsarist officials for assassination) to engage in plotting against the life of Stalin, there was a linkage. But Roy Medvedev's evidence in his study of the Kirov murder proves there was no Leningrad "Center," no Moscow "Center," just two lists of names written out in Stalin's own handwriting that he had copied from lists of known "oppositionists" that were in the secret police files![1]

The linkage in Stalin's mind between the non-existent terrorist "centers" and the deeds, and the stories of the deeds, of the revolutionary opponents of tsarim led to his ordering the disbanding of all societies of former tsarist political prisoners and exiles. All their publications were stopped. A projected five-volume *Biographical Dictionary of Eminent Persons in the Revolutionary Movement of Russia* was left unfinished. The volume on the Essers was not even begun.

What happened to the former terrorist Left Esser women was not revealed until after Khrushchev's Twentieth Congress speech. In 1961, the seventy-two-year-old Irina Kakhovskaya sent what she called "Zapiski i Zaiavleniia"

---

[1] *Let History Judge,* New York, 1972, p. 164. Medvedev also tells of the bizarre case of the 1934 attempt on V. M. Molotov's life—which never occurred. The attempt was staged in order to blame and kill another Communist leader (p. 180).

(Notes and Explanations) to the Central Committee of the Communist party, to the Council of Ministers, and to the Office of the Public Prosecutor. Like many other "official documents," Irina's "Notes and Explanations" saw the light of day in the pages of the underground journal *Politicheskyi Dnevnik* (Political Diary), published in the Soviet Union between 1964 and 1971 by the historian Roy Medvedev and his twin brother, the scientist Zhores Medvedev. Irina's "Notes and Explanations" appeared in the April 1970 issue.

In 1961, when Irina addressed her "Notes and Explanations" to Soviet officials, tens of thousands of people were doing the same thing, seeking personal rehabilitation for the wrongs done them in Stalin's time. Irina's motive, she said, was not rehabilitation for herself, for she was old and ill and had nothing to gain by it. She simply wanted to put on the official record what only she could as the last survivor of a whole generation of dedicated revolutionaries who had been unjustly calumnied, tortured, imprisoned and killed by the Soviet government.

In her "Notes and Explanations" Irina told the story of how after the Civil War the women Left Essers were taken from Moscow prisons and sent into exile in provincial cities: Stavropol, Samarkand, and Tashkent. Finally, in 1930 she, Sanya Izmailovich, and Maria Spiridonova were taken to Ufa where there were many political exiles. She emphasized that from the beginning of their exile the Left Esser leaders, under house arrest and the constant surveillance of official and unofficial spies and police, deprived of all political rights, had neither the means nor the desire to play any political role whatsoever. Her and her companions' rooms were frequently entered and searched. One or another of them would be picked up by the police, interrogated, and packed off to some remote town for weeks or months. When this happened to Maria Spiridonova, her physical condition seriously deteriorated, but she joked about her "iron constitution" and said that in view of what she had been through she could survive any punishment her jailors could devise.

By the 1930s, some of them, including Sanya Izmailovich, had turned away from politics in disgust. Irina said Sanya scarcely ever looked at a newspaper. Furthermore, her health had deteriorated to the point she could not do the office job assigned her, so she took over housekeeping duties for her comrades. She devoted as much of her day as possible to writing, and by 1937 had managed to produce a book-length manuscript on literature and art.

In her "Notes and Explanations," Irina's main concern was to prove her Left Esser comrades were not and never had been counter-revolutionaries, nor were they the enemies of the socialist order their accusers portrayed them to be. Their lives, deeds, and beliefs were their revolutionary credentials.

Not only had the Left Essers sprung from the same fires of revolution as the Bolsheviks, but their daring acts against tsarism had weakened it and hastened the revolution. And although they were soon pushed off center stage of the revolutionary drama after 1917, the Left Essers had suffered for the cause of socialism on all fronts. During the Civil War they had died for socialism just as the Bolsheviks had.

> They worked in underground organizations and accomplished unknown heroic deeds in partisan detachments in the Ukraine, in the Don region, in Siberia, the Trans-Baikal. In that time when the Bolsheviks were filling up Butyrki, Tagatiski, and other Soviet prisons with Left Essers, other Essers were rotting in German, Petliura, and Semenovski torture chambers. Essers and Left Essers were shot and hanged by Whites of all denominations. Whenever there was a possibility for fighting for the cause, the Left Essers, like the Bolsheviks, gave up their strength and their lives in the struggle. . . . Even if the Left Essers found themselves objectively opposed to certain Bolshevik policies they regarded as tactical mistakes, never at any time did they have anything in common with the counter-revolutionaries.

And finally, Irina said, the Left Esser women even accepted the Bolshevik regime. They recognized that the only leading strength of the revolution had become the Bolshevik party and their opposition stopped. She said that Maria Spiridonova succeeded in convincing herself the Bolsheviks, after their early lawlessness and deviations from socialist principles, had begun to carry out the socialist revolution, an ideal to which the Esser women had devoted their lives.

Irina portrayed the Left Esser women as working hard and conscientiously at the dull, laborious, clerical jobs assigned them, feeling they were making their small contribution to building socialism. Maria Spiridonova, with her usual concentration and enthusiasm, would work all day in an office analyzing district financial plans and reports, then, her work table heaped high with documents, she would labor far into the night. She astonished her friends with her capacity for work.

By 1937 the women had already served nearly twenty years in prison and exile, seven in Ufa, and were, they thought, near the end of their term. In February 1937, a group of particularly obnoxious officials descended on the Left Esser women and other political exiles in Ufa. This action coincided with the beginning of the 1937–1938 Moscow Trials of "enemies, spies, and wreckers" which crucified most of the Old Bolsheviks and opened the floodgates of mass execution and punitive exile of millions of Soviet citizens.

After ransacking the rooms of the Esser women, the officials put them into isolation prisons, with fourteen to twenty people crammed into each "solitary" cell. There they were kept for eleven months of "interrogation." The women were charged with assassination attempts on Stalinist big wigs, as well as other heinous crimes. Irina was accused of plotting the assassination of Klementi Voroshilov, commissar of Defense and deputy premier of the U.S.S.R. Every means of torture, physical and mental, was used to force Maria Spiridonova to confess that she was the center of a monstrous international plot against the Soviet government and its leaders. She was accused of plotting to kill not just one Soviet official, but all the commissars of the Bashkir political region of the Russian Socialist Federation of the Soviet Republic, of which Ufa is the capital. Her accusers said she was in constant contact with bourgeois governments as she worked to overthrow the Soviet regime.[2]

The interrogation, which went on month after month, was carried on in secret, but for the "enlightenment" of the public as to the true nature of Maria Spiridonova, articles appeared portraying her as a hysterical, virtually demented creature, and a film was made showing her as the embodiment of evil, plotting at night in a cemetery with her henchmen to exterminate the people's soviets.

Irina said there seemed to be a real or imagined fear on the part of the Soviet authorities that a popular cult had grown up around Maria Spiridonova, that a halo, which had to be destroyed, had been placed over her head by the Russian people. So they strove to humiliate, discredit, and disgrace her "bright heroic image."

Under the circumstances of the Esser women's restricted existence, their ill health, and changed views, the charges against them were ludicrous. Nevertheless, after months of tortuous interrogation, on December 25, 1937, in a trial before the Military Collegium of the Supreme Court of the Soviet Union, which lasted seven minutes, Irina Kakhovskaya was pronounced guilty of plotting to assassinate Klementi Voroshilov, of fomenting peasant revolts, and other crimes for which she was sentenced to ten years of imprisonment plus five years of exile and deprivation of civic rights.

Irina wrote that Sanya Izmailovich, despite her weak physical condition, became like iron as she defied the relentless Stalinist "interrogators" and judges. To Sanya, the massive destruction of people who had devoted their lives to the revolution was "a monstrous lie," which had to be exposed. Her bravery was to no avail. She, like the others, was found guilty of crimes against the Soviet state and was sentenced to a long prison term.

Throughout the interrogation, Maria Spiridonova stubbornly defended herself and her comrades against the lies hurled at them and demanded the case be moved to a higher, more competent court in Moscow. When no attention was paid to her demand, she went on a hunger strike. Then she

---

[2] Lest accusations of those in prison, or under rigid surveillance, of crimes they could not possibly have committed be thought of as a purely Stalinist technique, it should be recalled that in 1921, while Irina Kakhovskaya was sitting in Butyrki Prison in Moscow, she was found guilty of complicity in plotting the Kronshtadt Revolt and sentenced to exile in Kaluga.

was actually taken to Moscow, but "Moscow showed her justice," Irina wrote, by sentencing her to twenty-five years in prison.

Maria Spiridonova was shunted from one isolation prison to another. Still, Irina reported, she single-handedly continued to fight against the humiliating demands of Stalin's Gulag. Her jailors constantly flung her into punishment cells, which finally ruined her health. The last glimpse Irina had of her, at a way station as each of them was being shifted to yet another prison, was of a frightfully aged Maria, scarcely able to stand, but with a bright and peaceful look on her face. She was fifty-five years old.

Maria was imprisoned in the Yaroslavl isolation prison, then in Vladimir, and finally in Oryol, where she found, among other former comrades, her old friend Sanya Izmailovich. In the summer of 1941, when German armies were closing in on Oryol, the city was evacuated, but the five thousand inmates of the prison were not. Irina assumed they were all shot, but Anton Antonov-Ovseynako reported that the prisoners were herded into the basement of the Oryol isolation prison which was then flooded. All of them were drowned.[3]

One of the few escapees from the Oryol prison reported to Irina that Sanya Izmailovich's cool and collected behavior and her witty ripostes and ironic comments served to lighten the hearts of her fellow sufferers. By an irony of fate, Sanya, who expected to be hanged in 1906 for her attempt on the life of a tsarist police chief in Minsk, was, instead, killed in 1941 in the old prison of Oryol, a victim of the revolutionary regime she, as a woman terrorist, helped to bring into being.

Irina Kakhovskaya was briefly put in isolation prisons, but was soon declared a person physically able to work. She was sent to Siberia to the N.K.V.D.'s Kraslag labor camp in the Krasnoyarsk District where she worked as a logger and farm laborer for seven years. After completing her sentence she was immediately charged again with the same 1937 accusations, found guilty, and resentenced.

After Stalin's death in 1953, Irina finally got a passport—with restrictions. Two years later she managed to get back to European Russia and settled in Kaluga. There, she said in her 1961 "Notes and Explanations," she began to write her memoirs. If she completed them, and they ever become available, they should provide rare insight into an important and virtually unknown segment of twentieth-century Russian history.

---

[3] A. Antonov-Ovseynako, *The Time of Stalin*, New York, 1980. Apparently in response to the revival of interest in Spiridonova, especially among young people in the Soviet Union, the July 30, 1989 issue of the weekly newspaper *Nedelia* (Week) printed an article "Sud'ba Marii Spiridonova" (The Fate of Maria Spiridonova) by Boris Ileshin. This article, a brief survey of Spiridonova's career, ends with the statement that she was shot just hours before the Germans entered Oryol. There is no mention of the thousands of other prisoners.

Political assassination—feared by tyrants and democrats alike; valued by groups too weak to achieve their goals or attract attention to their cause through regular political channels. From 1878 to the early 1920s, Russia's radical revolutionaries firmly believed in the necessity of political assassination. For two generations individuals eager to sacrifice themselves for revolutionary goals shot and bombed targeted officials. They became the symbols of opposition to tsarist tyranny and were revered by great segments of the Russian public for their idealism and their self-sacrifice.

Did the Russian terrorist women whose careers have been outlined here ever repudiate or abandon their belief in political assassination as a weapon against tyranny? Irina Kakhovskaya might have expressed the conviction that the revolutionary experience of the Esser women had proved political assassination to be a self-defeating tactic. She did not. She defended the whole record of her associates. She maintained they had earned a glorious place in the revolutionary record because of their deeds. Her "Notes and Explanations" makes it obvious the Left Essers in general, and the women in particular, were in no position to plan or carry out terrorist acts in the 1920s and 1930s. Under constant surveillance, they were as politically helpless as they had been in the tsarist *katorga*, but this did not prevent the Communist regime under Stalin from accusing and torturing them.

Vera Figner, while behind bars in Schlisselburg in 1888, got word to a fellow prisoner asking him if he were to be released, to take a message to her mother: to tell her she has no regrets and is still true to her ideals.[4] Neither then nor later did Figner repudiate her terrorist past and the justification she gave of it before the court in the Trial of the Fourteen in 1884. Nevertheless, writing her memoirs years later, in her usual frank style, she was critical of terror and its effect on those who practiced it:

> It aroused ferocity, let loose brutal instincts, stirred up evil impulses and stimulated treachery. Humanity and magnanimity are incompatible with them. And in that sense, when the government and the party engaged in hand-to-hand combat, they competed in corrupting everything around them . . . the party proclaimed that any means was valid in the battle with its opponent, that in this struggle the end justified the means, and it created the cult of dynamite and the revolver, and put a halo around the terrorists. Assassination and the scaffold acquired a magnetic power over the minds of the youth, and the weaker were its nerves, the stronger was the impact of the [revolutionary] environment and the more did revolutionary terror lead to ecstacy.[5]

Long before 1917 Vera Figner had abandoned active politics and all thought of resorting to terror. She did not agree with Bolshevik policies and practices and tried various means to show her opposition—but not terror.

---

[4] Vera Figner, *Polnoye Sobraniye Sochinenie*, vol. 4, p. 270.
[5] Ibid., vol, 1, pp. 265–266.

Lev Deich in the second volume of his book *Za Polveka* (Half a Century Ago), said the shooting of Trepov made an indelible impression on Vera Zasulich and had a great influence on her life. She never repudiated her terrorist act, but she repudiated terror as a revolutionary tactic. Drawing on her own experience, she said the terrorist act takes its toll on the terrorist hero. "Fortunate are the ones who are quickly executed. They escape the pangs of conscience . . . the horrors of imprisonment." And aside from what a terrorist act does to the individual who commits it, she pointed out that it does not stimulate political activity; it rivets hypnotic concentration on terror itself, something like audience appreciation of a theatrical performance. But, having written this repudiation of terror in 1901, within a year she was calling for a hero to fire a well-aimed shot at a provincial governor who went unpunished for having workers whipped when they tried to demonstrate on May 1, 1902.

Maria Spiridonova turned to political assassination in 1918—reluctantly. She had ardently backed the Left Esser measure proclaiming the end of the party's use of terror at its First Congress in November 1917. Scarcely six months later she spearheaded adoption of the tactic of political assassination to oppose Bolshevik policies and methods when, following Lenin's forcing ratification of the Treaty of Brest-Litovsk, the Bolsheviks proceeded rapidly to eliminate the means for legal opposition. The Left Esser terrorist strikes that were carried out, the assassination of Count von Mirbach and General Eichhorn, and several others by Right Essers, neither forced the Bolsheviks to change their policies nor sparked a popular uprising against them. Political assassination in the midst of revolutionary violence did not work. But Spiridonova may have believed to the end what she wrote to the Central Executive Committee of the Bolshevik party in her letter of November 1918: Terror of the individual against the tyrant must exist if the revolution is to survive.

Examining the careers of the women who committed terrorist deeds, survived imprisonment and exile, and, during the 1917 revolutions, had the possibility of articulating their motivation and aims, the image that emerges is not of bloodthirsty irrationality. Their words and deeds are those of intelligent, idealistic people, believing in the attainment of freedom and a new moral climate. They talked and wrote not of hate, but of love, not of destruction but of building. The revolution, said Spiridonova on January 13, 1918, would build a new society based on justice, equality, and brotherhood—a worldwide brotherhood of all people. What was missing in the revolution was the colossal moral power of those of the past generation who sacrificed themselves to the dream of freedom. At the First Congress of the Left Essers in November 1917 she said:

> The time has come for us social revolutionaries to put our great social ideals into effect. . . . Large masses stand behind the Bolsheviks today, but that is

a temporary phenomenon. It is temporary because Bolshevism has no inner
inspiration. Everything in it is founded on hatred and bitterness. These feelings, founded on egoism, are intelligible in times of bitter struggle. But in the
second stage of the struggle, in which organic labor will be necessary, in
which a new life will have to be built up on foundations of love and altruism,
the Bolsheviks will show themselves bankrupt. We, faithful to the legacy be-
queathed to us by our forerunners, must always bear in mind the second stage
of the struggle[6]

Writing in 1922, Vera Figner said, "The dead are never resurrected, but
books are." There would come a time, she said, when her words would be
needed. As the twentieth century nears its end, and as Soviet society is in the
process of soul-searching on the causes for the great Russian Revolution's
degeneration into the monstrosity of the Stalinist system, has that time
come—the time to look not only at Figner's published words, but her unpublished words? Has the time also come to examine the speeches of Maria
Spiridonova and the writing of Vera Zasulich on party matters starting as far
back as 1903?

ANNOTATED REFERENCES

Lenin (Vladimir Ilich Ulianov), "Tasks of the Detachments of the Revolutionary Army," an
essay written in October 1905, is nothing more than a list of terrorist acts that individuals and
groups of revolutionaries must prepare themselves to carry out. V. I. Lenin Sochineniia, Izdanie
Chetvertoe (V. I. Lenin's Collected Works, 4th ed.), Moscow, 1947, vol. 9, pp. 389–393.

The quotation from Leon Trotsky, Terrorism and Communism (written and originally published
in England, 1920), Ann Arbor paperback edition, second printing, 1963, p. 58.

Nikita Sergeevich Khrushchev, The Secret Speech (delivered at the Twentieth Congress of the
C.P.S.U, February 24, 1956) with an Introduction and Explanatory Notes by Zhores A. and Roy
A. Medvedev. The Bertrand Russell Peace Foundation, London, 1976. This speech contained
revelations about Stalin's role in the Kirov murder.

"The Letter of an Old Bolshevik" contained additional details of Kirov's murder, the "New
Course," and the Leningrad terrorists. It is included in Boris I. Nicolaevski, Power and the
Soviet Elite, New York, Washington, and London, 1965.

Roy A. Medvedev, Let History Judge, New York, 1972, chapter 5, "The Assassination of
Kirov."

Robert Conquest, Stalin and the Kirov Murder, New York, 1989.

Irina K. Kakhovskaya, "Zapiski i Zaiavleniia" (Notes and Revelations), Politicheskiy Dnevnik
(Political Diary), Aleksandr Herzen Foundation, Amsterdam, April 1970. The journal Politicheskiy Dnevnik was published in Amsterdam from October 1964 to March 1971 by the historian Roy Medvedev and his twin brother, the scientist Zhores Medvedev. In 1972 nineteen

---

[6] I. Z Steinberg, Spiridonova Revolutionary Terrorist, p. 185.

unabridged articles from the journal, including Kakhovskaya's, were brought out, in Amsterdam, in a two-volume edition. In 1982, *An End to Silence*, edited by Stephen F. Cohen was published by the Princeton University Press. It presented in English articles (abridged) selected from the *Politicheskiy Dnevnik*, including Kakhovskaya's "Zapiski i Zaiavleniia" (retitled "Our Fate").

Afterword

The relatively large number of women leaders in the *narodniki* movement and the political parties it spawned were unique phenomena in Russian and world history.[1] Can anything be learned, from this brief consideration of the careers of a few of them, about the baffling question of women and political leadership?

There was almost universal acceptance of male-female partnership by the youth who made up the clandestine political groupings during the half-century between Vera Zasulich's shooting Trepov and the 1917 Revolution.[2] This acceptance, combined with the receptivity of large segments of the Russian populace to their inflammatory language and daring deeds, including political murder, gave the mostly gentry, and upper bourgeois educated[3] women members of these groups the opportunity not only to play a

---

[1] Exact numbers of percentages of female membership in these movements and parties are impossible to determine. Estimates range from 15% to 30%. Numbers of women leaders are also difficult to determine, but some of the yardsticks include counting the number of women among the accused in the trials of the 1870s and 1880s, the number of women members of the executive committees of the political groups and parties, the number of women sentenced to death or life imprisonment in the first decade of the twentieth century.

[2] Robert H. McNeal, in his article "Women in the Russian Radical Movement," speculates on reasons for male receptivity to women in Russian radical circles beginning in the 1860s. *Journal of Social History*, Winter, 1971–72, vol. 5, no. 2, pp. 143–163.

[3] "Educated" rarely means university or professional education, but, especially in the twentieth century, it means attendance at, or completion of the gymnazium. By the twentieth century, lower class (but rarely peasant) women could attain this level of education, and once they did, many entered the revolutionary movement in one capacity or another.

leading role in the Russian revolutionary movement but for many of them, as individuals, to serve as political leaders alongside their male colleagues.

In this social milieu a terrorist act could put a woman on the path to fame even if her goal was not fame. By sacrificing herself, she could show the Russian people that abuse of power—the cause of their suffering—stemmed from their lack of freedom. The enthusiasm generated by the idea of sacrificing oneself for freedom was as infectuous as panic (as Vera Figner put it) and lured many of the best and the brightest young women into terrorism. When such a woman survived (often after long years of imprisonment), she had the possibility of using her fame to work for freedom—and for the revolution believed necessary to achieve it—in other ways. The famous and unassuming Vera Zasulich became an influential political theorist; Vera Figner, a prolific publicist and political analyst; Katerina Breshkovskaya, a political organizer; and the most spectacular example, Maria Spiridonova, the 1917–1918 political leader. The near-worship Spiridonova won in 1906 survived—or, actually, grew to legendary proportions—during her eleven years in Siberia. This, combined with her own magnetic personality, transformed her into a powerful political figure.

A populace which venerated the political murderer, especially a woman, is difficult to understand today. Even more difficult to comprehend is why—when the revolution the women leaders of the *narodniki* tradition had tirelessly worked to bring about actually came—these women in general and Maria Spiridonova in particular so quickly lost their leadership positions while retaining an enormous, enthusiastic popular following. (Maria Spiridonova's following was so great and so loyal, that the Soviet government for years carried on a campaign of vilification against her in an effort to blot out all memory of her.)

One is forced to conclude that just as the pre-revolutionary Russian social milieu made possible the rise of women political leaders in clandestine, out-of-power political groupings, revolutionary Russia destroyed that milieu and created another. Political leaders unaccustomed to working with politicized women as equals won the fight to impose a new stamp on the Russian Empire. They were a different breed from the leaders of the old clandestine parties with their tradition of male-female partnership. Furthermore, revolutionary Russia was a country that had lost its moorings. Traditional government agencies were destroyed, or simply collapsed, and the population, widely opposed to the Bolsheviks, had no institutions through which to channel its angry, frustrated, often violent opposition. It found no way to put a brake on Bolshevik lawlessness and ruthlessness. Of course, those who commit terrorist acts cannot be thought of as devoid of ruthlessness. The decision of Spiridonova, her women associates, and other Esser leaders to use political murder "to save the revolution" proved that. But the idealism of the *narodniki* women and their dedication to the dream of freedom—

the dream for which in the past they risked their lives and were ready to do so again—left them unprepared effectively to counter betrayal by other revolutionaries: from Vera Figner's betrayal by Degaev, to the double betrayal of Maria Spiridonova in 1917–1918, first by the leaders of her own Esser party, then by the Bolsheviks.

Having suffered these heavy blows, it was sheer bravado and the vain hope of an outburst of popular support that induced Spiridonova and the Left Esser leadership to lay down the challenge to the Bolsheviks in July 1918, a move which spelled their doom. The price paid by the *narodniki* women was loss of the political stronghold their revolutionary daring had won for them before 1917.

An element that was absent in the maelstrom of Russian revolutionary politics was a female constituency, a factor which cannot be left out of any attempt to analyze the end of the woman political leader after 1918. The *narodniki* movement, never more than one percent of the Russian population, was characterized by its highly visible, active, and effective women participants on all levels who made up a constituency upon which the movement's women leaders depended. They also had peripheral support by women outside the movement, including their mothers and sympathetic friends and relatives, many of whom gave generously of their fortunes to the cause. Even feminists, whose method was using influence rather than violence to achieve women's rights, understood why they chose "the path of dynamite" and did not condemn them.[4]

In July 1917, the Provisional Government enfranchised the whole population of the former tsarist empire, changing the political constituency to millions of mostly illiterate, politically inexperienced men and women. There was no way the female part of this enormous new constituency, deeply mired in a patriarchal society, would or could provide the support essential to the continuation or the development of women political leaders.[5]

---

[4] Testimony to the pervasiveness of this support was first documented in a report prepared in 1874 by the Minister of Justice, Count Palen, which not only presented facts and figures of the involvement of increasing numbers of young women and girls in radical organizations, but the backing of their activities by middle-aged women, who instead of rebuking them expressed approval in many ways, including putting their fortunes at the disposal of their revolutionary daughters. The text of this report appears in V. L. Burtsev, *Za Sto Let*, 1897, pp. 113–123. Writing a quarter of a century later, Peter Kropotkin said no chasm existed between the older generation of feminists and their younger sisters, the revolutionists. "The [older] leaders did not mix with them . . . but they never repudiated them." *Memoirs of a Revolutionist*, Boston and New York, 1899, p. 262.

[5] One of the more unfortunate gaps in the *narodniki* women's priorities was their failure to organize or to activate tsarist Russia's huge reservoir of female workers, mostly of peasant background, who toiled as house servants and in factories and fields.

has adopted. A possible source of the Communist party's recognition of women's rights may be the tradition of women's equal partnership with men in Russia's pre-revolutionary political parties, although the source usually cited is the words of Marx and Engels. However, nothing in the actual working of the Soviet government or the Communist party compares with the pre-revolutionary political parties which not only welcomed women but encouraged those who had leadership potential to rise to decision-making positions. For example, the membership of the *Narodnaya Volya* Executive Committee was never less than one-third women. In contrast, the Politburo of the Communist party of the Soviet Union has never had a woman member. In the 1950s a few women began to be appointed to the party's Central Committee, but the number of women members is not permitted to rise above four percent. Furthermore, the four percent is selected from low-status occupations, effectively guaranteeing they will never advance in the party hierarchy.[6]

Soviet women today are in a situation different only in degree from that of women of other countries concerning their absence from positions of political leadership. They have, nevertheless, one great advantage. Thanks to the revolutionary women of Russia's past they have a heritage of women's political leadership unique in modern political history, the full story of which they, and women everywhere, need to know.

---

[6] Genia K. Browning (*Women and Politics in the U.S.S.R.*, Sussex and New York, 1987), while quoting facts and figures on the absence of women in the top echelons of the Communist party, shows that women do hold fairly high positions in the Soviet government. However, due to the universal oversight of all aspects of government by the Communist party, those in government jobs have virtually no influence in policy making.

Bibliography

Nineteenth and early twentieth century books, newspapers and journals in the Russian language which are not readily available in most libraries are the main source of information on the subjects covered in this book. Exact citations to this material appear in the text or in the references at the end of each chapter.

This brief bibliography consists of books and articles in the English language which have a direct bearing on one or more aspects of the subjects covered in the book.

Almedingen, E. J. (1962). *Emperor Alexander II*. London: Bodley Head.

Bergman, Jay. (1974, June). The political thought of Vera Zasulich. *Slavonic Review.*

Bergman, Jay. (1977). "Vera Zasulich and the Politics of Revolutionary Writing." Unpublished doctoral dissertation, Yale University.

Bibesco, Princess Marthe (Lahovary). (1939). *Katia*. New York: Doubleday, Doran and Co.

Breshkovsky, Catherine (Katerina Breshko-Breshkovskaya). (1919). *The little grandmother of the Russian Revolution*. Alice Stone Blackwell, Editor. Boston: Little, Brown and Company.

Breshkovsky, Catherine. (1931). *Hidden springs of the Russian Revolution*. Lincoln Hutchinson, Editor. Stanford and London: Stanford University Press.

Broido, Vera. (1977). *Apostles into terrorists. Women in the revolutionary movement in the Russia of Alexander II*. New York: Viking.

Browning, Genia. (1987). *Women and politics in the USSR*. New York: St. Martin's Press.

Bryant, Louise. (1918). *Six red months in Russia.* New York: G. H. Doran. (Reprinted by the Arno Press 1970, distributed by Ayer Company Publishers, Salem, NH.)

Burdzhalov, E. N. (1987). *Russia's second revolution: The February uprising in Petrograd.* Bloomington and Indianapolis, IN: Indiana University Press. (Translation by Donald J. Raleigh of *Vtoraia Russkaia revoliutsiia, vosstanie v Petrograde.* Moscow, 1967.)

Durland, Kellogg. (1907). *The red reign in Russia.* New York: The Century Company.

Engel, Barbara Alpern & Rosenthal, Clifford N. (Eds. & Trans.) (1975). *Five women against the Tsar.* New York: Alfred A. Knopf.

Farnsworth, Beatrice. (1980). *Aleksandra Kollontai.* Stanford: Stanford University Press.

Figner, Vera Nikolaevna. (1927). *Memoirs of a revolutionist.* New York: International Publishers Co., Inc. (A one volume abridgment in English translation of *Zapechatlennyi Trud,* first published in Moscow by Zadruga Press, 1922.)

Footman, David. (1945). *Red prelude: The life of the Russian terrorist Zhelyabov.* New Haven: Yale University Press.

Goldman, Emma. (1924). *My disillusionment in Russia.* New York: Doubleday, Page and Company.

Goldman, Emma. (1924). *My further disillusionment in Russia.* New York: Doubleday, Page and Company.

Good, Jane E. & Jones, David R. (1989). *Babushka: The life of the Russian revolutionary Katerina Breshko-Breshkovskaya 1844–1934.* Newtonville, MA: Oriental Research Partners.

Hare, J. C. (1885). *Russia.* London: Smith, Elder and Company.

Haruki, Wada. (1984). Vera Figner in the early post-revolutionary period 1917–23. *Annals of the Institute of Social Science,* No. 25, pp. 43–73.

Hasegawa, Tsuyoshi. (1981). *The February revolution: Petrograd 1917.* Seattle and London: University of Washington Press.

Kakhovskaya, Irina. (1982). Our fate. In Stephen Cohen (Ed.) *An End to Silence.* Princeton: Princeton University.

Kelly, Rita Mae Cawley. (n.d.). The role of Vera Ivanovna Zasulich in the development of the Russian revolutionary movement. Unpublished doctoral dissertation, University of Indiana.

Kovalevskaia, Sof'ya Vasilevna. (1895). *Vera Vorontsoff.* Boston: Wolfe and Company. (Translation of *Nigilistka,* Switzerland, 1892).

Kropotkin, Peter Alekseevich. (1899). *Memoirs of a revolutionist.* New York: Houghton, Mifflin and Company.

Krupskaya, Nadezhda. (Circa 1930). *Memories of Lenin.* New York: International Publishers. (Translation by E. Verney of *Vospominaniya,* Moscow, 1924.)

Lenin, V. I. (1965). *V. I. Lenin on the emancipation of women*. Moscow.

Lockhart, R. H. Bruce. (1932). *British Agent*. London and New York: Putnam and Company Ltd.

McNeal, Robert H. (1971–1972, Winter). Women in the Russian radical movement. *Journal of Social History*, 5(2), 143–163.

Medvedev, Roy A. (1979). *The October revolution* (George Saunders, Trans.). New York: Columbia University Press.

Narishkin-Kurakin, Elizabeth. (1931). *Under three Tsars*. René Fülöp-Miller, Editor. New York: E. P. Dutton and Co. (Translated from the German by Julia E. Loesser.)

Paleologue, Georges Maurice. (1927). *The tragic romance of Alexander II of Russia*. London: Hutchinston and Company. (Translation of *Le roman tragique de L'Empereur Alexander II*. Paris: Plon, circa 1923.)

Pollock, Simon O. (1908). *The Russian Bastille*. Chicago: C. H. Kerr and Co.

Radkey, Oliver H. (1958). *The Agrarian foes of Bolshevism*. New York: Columbia University Press.

Radkey, Oliver H. (1963). *The sickle under the hammer*. New York: Columbia University Press.

Reed, John. (1919). *Ten days that shook the world*. New York: Boni and Liveright.

Selivanova, Nina Nikolaevna. (1923). *Russia's women*. New York: Dutton and Co.

Steinberg, I. Z. (1935). *Spiridonova: Revolutionary terrorist*. London: Methuen and Company.

Steinberg, I. Z. (1953). *In the workshop of the Revolution*. New York: Rinehart.

Stepniak (Sergei Kravchinsky). (1889). *The career of a nihilist*. New York: Harper and Brothers.

Stepniak (Sergei Kravchinsky). (1883). *Underground Russia: Revolutionary profiles and sketches from life*. London: Smith, Elder and Company. (Translation of the Italian translation of *Podpol'naia Rossiia*.)

Stites, Richard. (1978). *The women's liberation movement in Russia: Feminism, nihilism and Bolshevism 1860–1930*. Princeton: Princeton University Press.

Sukloff, Marie (Mariya Shkolnik). (1915). *The life story of a Russian exile*. New York: The Century Company.

Tarsaidzé, Alexandre. (1970). *Katia: Wife before God*. New York: Macmillan.

Trotsky, Leon. (1959). *The Russian Revolution*. New York: Anchor Book. (Abridged version of the Max Eastman translation of *Istoriia Russkoi Revoliutsiia*. Berlin, 1931–1935.)

Trotsky, Leon. (1961). *Terrorism and Communism*. Ann Arbor: University of Michigan Press. (Published in Great Britain in 1920 as *The Defense of Terror*.)

Trotsky, Leon. (circa 1971). *Lenin: Notes for a biographer* (Tamara Deutscher, Trans.). New York: G. P. Putnam's Sons.

Valentinov (Volsky), Nikolai. (1968). *Encounters with Lenin.* London and New York: Oxford University Press. (Translation of *Vstrechi s Leninym,* New York, 1953.)

Wald, Lillian. (1934). *Windows on Henry Street.* Boston: Little, Brown and Company.

Wiecsynski, Joseph L. (Ed.) (1976–1987). *The modern encyclopedia of Russian and Soviet history.* Gulf Breeze, FL: Academic and International Press.

Yourievsky, Princess Catherine. (1924). *My book: Some pages from my life.* London: E. Nash and Grayson, Ltd.

Index

About the Author

Margaret Maxwell, after a career as Professor of European History at New York University and Finch College, is now devoting herself to writing, translating and editing in the field of Russian history and literature. Recently she has translated some of Marina Tsvetaeva's poems, as well as those of Tatyana Mamonova, and of the late Russian/Israeli bard, Alexander Alon.

Dr. Maxwell's introduction to Russia came at age 17 in her native Topeka, Kansas, when she worked as an assistant to Bertram Maxwell at Washburn University while he was writing *The Soviet State*. When they were later married, she worked with him on his books and articles on Russia and international relations. She made her first of many trips to Russia in 1962 after receiving a grant from the American Philosophical Society for a study of Nikolai Karlovich Giers, the Foreign Minister under Alexander III. Her article on Giers was published in the English journal, *European Studies Review*.

While at Finch College, Margaret, along with her colleague Dr. Jean Ellis, set up a Women's Studies Program in 1970. While teaching a course in Revolutionary Women, Margaret discovered Russia's "Narodniki Women." This book is the result of many years of careful research in the New York Public Library's Slavonic Division.